Structural Macroeconometrics

Structural Macroeconometrics

David N. DeJong with Chetan Dave

PRINCETON UNIVERSITY PRESS PRINCETON AND OXFORD

Published by Princeton University Press, 41 William Street, Princeton, New Jersey 08540

In the United Kingdom: Princeton University Press, 3 Market Place, Woodstock, Oxfordshire OX20 1SY

ISBN-13: 978-0-691-12648-7
ISBN-10: 0-691-12648-8

Library of Congress Control Number: 2006939729

British Library Cataloging-in-Publication Data is available

This book has been composed in Galliard

Printed on acid-free paper. ∞

press.princeton.edu

Printed in the United States of America

10 9 8 7 6 5 4 3 2 1

For Denise, Andrew, and Alex: thanks for your patience, love, and support. Dedicated to the memory of Peter J. DeJong.

DND

To my wife, thoughts of whom keep me going. Dedicated to the Dave, Pande, and Yagnik families.

CD

Contents

Figures

Tables

Preface

> Let me only say that what econometrics—aided by electronic computers—can do, is only to push forward by leaps and bounds the line of demarcation from where we *have to* rely on our intuition and sense of smell.
>
> —Ragnar Frisch, Nobel Prize Lecture, June 1970.

> It is a capital mistake to theorize before one has data. Insensibly one begins to twist facts to suit theories, instead of theories to suit facts.
>
> —Sir Arthur Conan Doyle

A STEADY STREAM of conceptual and computational advances realized over the past three decades has helped to bridge the gulf that has historically separated theoretical from empirical research in macroeconomics. As a result, measurement is becoming increasingly aligned with theory. The purpose of this text is to provide guidance in bringing theoretical models to the forefront of macroeconometric analyses.

The text is suitable for use as a supplementary resource in introductory graduate courses in macroeconomics and econometrics, and as a primary textbook in advanced graduate courses devoted to the pursuit of applied research in macroeconomics. The lecture notes that ultimately gave rise to the text were designed for this latter purpose. The text's historical perspective, along with its unified presentation of alternative methodologies, should also make it a valuable resource for academic and professional researchers.

Readers of the text are assumed to have familiarity with multivariate calculus, matrix algebra and difference equations, and cursory knowledge of basic econometric techniques. Familiarity with dynamic programming is also useful but not necessary. This is the tool used to map the class of models of interest here into the system of nonlinear expectational difference equations that serve as the point of departure for the empirical methodologies presented in the text. However, familiarity with dynamic programming is not needed to follow the text's presentation of empirical methodologies.

We decided to write this text because through our own teaching and research, we have sought to contribute towards the goal of aligning theory with empirical analysis in macroeconomics; this text is a natural extension of these efforts. We set out to accomplish two objectives in writing it. First, we wished to provide a unified overview of this diverse yet interrelated area of active research. Second, we wanted to equip students with a set of tools that would expedite their own entry into the field.

The content of this text reflects much that we have learned over many years spent pursuing collaborative research with a fabulous group of co-authors: Sheryl Ball, Patty Beeson, Dan Berkowitz, Stefan Dodds, Scott Dressler, Catherine Eckel, Emilio Espino, Steve Husted, Beth Ingram, Roman Leisenfeld, John Nankervis, Jean-François Richard, Marla Ripoll, Gene Savin, Werner Troesken, and Chuck Whiteman. We are deeply indebted to them for their implicit and explicit contributions to this project. We have also benefitted from input provided by Charlie Evans, Jim Feigenbaum, Jesús Fernández-Villaverde, Peter Ireland, Naryana Kocherlakota, Chris Otrok, Barbara Rossi, Juan Rubio-Ramírez, Tom Sargent, Thomas Steinberger, Yi Wen, and Tao Zha on various aspects of the text. Finally, Hariharan Dharmarajan provided valuable research assistance on the empirical application presented in chapter 11.

Part I

Model and Data Preparation

In order to test a theory against facts, or to use it for predictions, either the statistical observations available have to be "corrected," or the theory itself has to be adjusted, so as to make the facts we consider the "true" variables relevant to the theory. . . .
—Trygve Haavelmo, *Econometrica*

Chapter 1

Introduction

Science is facts; just as houses are made of stones, so is science made of facts; but a pile of stones is not a house and a collection of facts is not necessarily science.

—Henri Poincaré

1.1 Background

The seminal contribution of Kydland and Prescott (1982) marked the crest of a sea change in the way macroeconomists conduct empirical research. Under the empirical paradigm that remained predominant at the time, the focus was either on purely statistical (or reduced-form) characterizations of macroeconomic behavior, or on systems-of-equations models that ignored both general-equilibrium considerations and forward-looking behavior on the part of purposeful decision makers. But the powerful criticism of this approach set forth by Lucas (1976), and the methodological contributions of, for example, Sims (1972) and Hansen and Sargent (1980), sparked a transition to a new empirical paradigm. In this transitional stage, the formal imposition of theoretical discipline on reduced-form characterizations became established. The source of this discipline was a class of models that have come to be known as dynamic stochastic general equilibrium (DSGE) models. The imposition of discipline most typically took the form of "cross-equation restrictions," under which the stochastic behavior of a set of exogenous variables, coupled with forward-looking behavior on the part of economic decision makers, yield implications for the endogenous stochastic behavior of variables determined by the decision makers. Nevertheless, the imposition of such restrictions was indirect, and reduced-form specifications continued to serve as the focal point of empirical research.

Kydland and Prescott turned this emphasis on its head. As a legacy of their work, DSGE models no longer serve as indirect sources of theoretical discipline to be imposed upon statistical specifications. Instead, they serve directly as the foundation upon which empirical work may be conducted. The methodologies used to implement DSGE models as foundational empirical models have evolved over time and vary considerably.

The same is true of the statistical formality with which this work is conducted. But despite the characteristic heterogeneity of methods used in pursuing contemporary empirical macroeconomic research, the influence of Kydland and Prescott remains evident today.

This book details the use of DSGE models as foundations upon which empirical work may be conducted. It is intended primarily as an instructional guide for graduate students and practitioners, and so contains a distinct how-to perspective throughout. The methodologies it presents are organized roughly following the chronological evolution of the empirical literature in macroeconomics that has emerged following the work of Kydland and Prescott; thus it also serves as a reference guide. Throughout, the methodologies are demonstrated using applications to three benchmark models: a real-business-cycle model (fashioned after King, Plosser, and Rebelo, 1988); a monetary model featuring monopolistically competitive firms (fashioned after Ireland, 2004a); and an asset-pricing model (fashioned after Lucas, 1978).

The empirical tools outlined in the text share a common foundation: a system of nonlinear expectational difference equations derived as the solution of a DSGE model. The strategies outlined for implementing these models empirically typically involve the derivation of approximations of the systems, and then the establishment of various empirical implications of the systems. The primary focus of this book is on the latter component of these strategies: This text covers a wide range of alternative methodologies that have been used in pursuit of a wide range of empirical applications. Demonstrated applications include: parameter estimation, assessments of fit and model comparison, forecasting, policy analysis, and measurement of unobservable facets of aggregate economic activity (e.g., measurement of productivity shocks).

1.2 Overview

This book is divided into three parts. Part I presents foundational material included to help keep the book self-contained. Following this introduction, chapter 2 outlines two preliminary steps often used in converting a given DSGE model into an empirically implementable system of equations. The first step involves the linear approximation of the model; the second step involves the solution of the resulting linearized system. The solution takes the form of a state-space representation for the observable variables featured in the model.

Chapter 3 presents two important preliminary steps often needed for priming data for empirical analysis: removing trends and isolating cycles. The purpose of these steps is to align what is being measured in the data with what is being modelled by the theory. For example, the separation of trend from cycle is necessary in confronting trending data with models of business cycle activity.

Chapter 4 presents tools used to summarize properties of the data. First, two important reduced-form models are introduced: autoregressive-moving average models for individual time series, and vector autoregressive models for sets of time series. These models provide flexible characterizations of the data that can be used as a means of calculating a wide range of important summary statistics. Next, a collection of popular summary statistics (along with algorithms available for calculating them) are introduced. These statistics often serve as targets for estimating the parameters of structural models, and as benchmarks for judging their empirical performance. Empirical analyses involving collections of summary statistics are broadly categorized as limited-information analyses. Finally, the Kalman filter is presented as a means for pursuing likelihood-based, or full-information, analyses of state-space representations. Part I concludes in chapter 5 with an introduction of the benchmark models that serve as examples in part II.

Part II, composed of chapters 6 through 9, presents the following empirical methodologies: calibration, limited-information estimation, maximum likelihood estimation, and Bayesian estimation. Each chapter contains a general presentation of the methodology, and then presents applications of the methodology to the benchmark models in pursuit of alternative empirical objectives.

Chapter 6 presents the most basic empirical methodology covered in the text: the calibration exercise, as pioneered by Kydland and Prescott (1982). Original applications of this exercise sought to determine whether models designed and parameterized to provide an empirically relevant account of long-term growth were also capable of accounting for the nature of short-term fluctuations that characterize business-cycle fluctuations, summarized using collections of sample statistics measured in the data. More generally, implementation begins with the identification of a set of empirical measurements that serve as constraints on the parameterization of the model under investigation: parameters are chosen to insure that the model can successfully account for these measurements. (It is often the case that certain parameters must also satisfy additional a priori considerations.) Next, implications of the duly parameterized model for an additional set of statistical measurements are compared with their empirical counterparts to judge whether the model is capable of providing a successful account of these additional features of the data. A challenge associated with this methodology arises in judging success, because this second-stage comparison is made in the absence of a formal statistical foundation.

The limited-information estimation methodologies presented in chapter 7 serve as one way to address problems arising from the statistical informality associated with calibration exercises. Motivation for their implementation stems from the fact that there is statistical uncertainty associated with the set of empirical measurements that serve as constraints in the parameterization stage of a calibration exercise. For example, a sample mean has an associated sample standard error. Thus there is also statistical uncertainty associated with model parameterizations derived from mappings onto empirical measurements (referred to generally as statistical moments). Limited-information estimation methodologies account for this uncertainty formally: the parameterizations they yield are interpretable as estimates, featuring classical statistical characteristics. Moreover, if the number of empirical targets used in obtaining parameter estimates exceeds the number of parameters being estimated (i.e., if the model in question is over-identified), the estimation stage also yields objective goodness-of-fit measures that can be used to judge the model's empirical performance. Prominent examples of limited-information methodologies include the generalized and simulated methods of moments (GMM and SMM), and indirect-inference methods.

Limited-information estimation procedures share a common trait: they are based on a subset of information available in the data (the targeted measurements selected in the estimation stage). An attractive feature of these methodologies is that they may be implemented in the absence of explicit assumptions regarding the underlying distributions that govern the stochastic behavior of the variables featured in the model. A drawback is that decisions regarding the moments chosen in the estimation stage are often arbitrary, and results (e.g., regarding fit) can be sensitive to particular choices. Chapters 8 and 9 present full-information counterparts to these methodologies: likelihood-based analyses. Given a distributional assumption regarding sources of stochastic behavior in a given model, chapter 8 details how the full range of empirical implications of the model may be assessed via maximum-likelihood analysis, facilitated by use of the Kalman filter. Parameter estimates and model evaluation are facilitated in a straightforward way using maximum-likelihood techniques. Moreover, given model estimates, the implied behavior of unobservable variables present in the model (e.g., productivity shocks) may be inferred as a by-product of the estimation stage.

A distinct advantage in working directly with structural models is that, unlike their reduced-form counterparts, one often has clear a priori guidance concerning their parameterization. For example, specifications of subjective annual discount rates that exceed 10% may be dismissed out-of-hand as implausible. This motivates the subject of chapter 9, which details the adoption of a Bayesian perspective in bringing full-information procedures to bear in working with structural models. From the Bayesian perspective, a priori views on model parameterization may be incorporated formally in the empirical analysis, in the form of a prior distribution. Coupled with the associated likelihood function via Bayes' Rule, the corresponding posterior distribution may be derived; this conveys information regarding the relative likelihood of alternative parameterizations of the model, conditional on the specified prior and observed data. In turn, conditional statements regarding the empirical performance of the model relative to competing alternatives, the implied behavior of unobservable variables present in the model, and likely future trajectories of model variables may also be derived. A drawback associated with the adoption of a Bayesian perspective in this class of models is that posterior analysis must be accomplished via the use of sophisticated numerical techniques; special attention is devoted to this problem in the chapter.

Part III outlines how nonlinear model approximations can be used in place of linear approximations in pursuing the empirical objectives described throughout the book. Chapter 10 presents three leading alternatives to the linearization approach to model solution presented in chapter 2: projection methods, value-function iterations, and policy-function iterations. Chapter 11 then describes how the empirical methodologies presented in chapters 6–9 may be applied to nonlinear approximations of the underlying model produced by these alternative solution methodologies.

The key step in shifting from linear to nonlinear approximations involves the reliance upon simulations from the underlying model for characterizing its statistical implications. In conducting calibration and limited-information estimation analyses, simulations are used to construct numerical estimates of the statistical targets chosen for analysis, because analytical expressions for these targets are no longer available. And in conducting full-information analyses, simulations are used to construct numerical approximations of the likelihood function corresponding with the underlying model, using a numerical tool known as the particle filter.

The organization we have chosen for the book stems from our view that the coverage of empirical applications involving nonlinear model approximations is better understood once a solid understanding of the use of linear approximations has been gained. Moreover, linear approximations usefully serve as complementary inputs into the implementation of nonlinear approximations. However, if one wished to cover linear and nonlinear applications in concert, then we suggest the following approach. Begin exploring model-solution techniques by covering chapters 2 and 10 simultaneously. Then having worked through chapter 3 and sections 4.1 and 4.2 of chapter 4, cover section 4.3 of chapter 4 (the Kalman filter) along with section 11.2 of chapter 11 (the particle filter). Then proceed through chapters 5–9 as organized, coupling section 7.3.4 of chapter 7 with section 11.1 of chapter 11.

In the spirit of reducing barriers to entry into the field, we have developed a textbook Web site that contains the data sets that serve as examples throughout the text, as well as computer code used to execute the methodologies we present. The code is in the form of procedures written in the GAUSS programming language. Instructions for executing the procedures are provided within the individual files. The Web site address is http://www.pitt.edu/˜dejong/text.htm. References to procedures available at this site are provided throughout this book. In addition, a host of freeware is available throughout the Internet. In searching for code, good starting points include the collection housed by Christian Zimmerman in his Quantitative Macroeconomics Web page, and the collection of programs that comprise DYNARE:

http://dge.repec.org/

http://www.cepremap.cnrs.fr/~michel/dynare/

Much of the code provided at our Web site reflects the modification of code developed by others, and we have attempted to indicate this explicitly whenever possible. Beyond this attempt, we express our gratitude to the many generous programmers who have made their code available for public use.

1.3 Notation

A common set of notation is used throughout the text in presenting models and empirical methodologies. A summary is as follows. Steady state values of levels of variables are denoted with an upper bar. For example, the steady state value of the level of output y_t is denoted as $\overline{y}$. Logged deviations of variables from steady state values are denoted using tildes; e.g.,

$$\widetilde{y}_t = \log\left(\frac{y_t}{\overline{y}}\right).$$

The vector x_t denotes the collection of model variables, written (unless indicated otherwise) in terms of logged deviations from steady state values; e.g.,

$$x_t = [\widetilde{y}_t \quad \widetilde{c}_t \quad \widetilde{n}_t]'.$$

The vector υ_t denotes the collection of structural shocks incorporated in the model, and η_t denotes the collection of expectational errors associated with intertemporal optimality conditions. Finally, the $k \times 1$ vector μ denotes the collection of "deep" parameters associated with the structural model.

Log-linear approximations of structural models are represented as

$$Ax_{t+1} = Bx_t + C\upsilon_{t+1} + D\eta_{t+1}, \tag{1.1}$$

where the elements of the matrices A, B, C, and D are functions of the structural parameters μ. Solutions of (1.1) are expressed as

$$x_{t+1} = F(\mu)x_t + G(\mu)\upsilon_{t+1}. \tag{1.2}$$

In (1.2), certain variables in the vector x_t are unobservable, whereas others (or linear combinations of variables) are observable. Thus filtering methods such as the Kalman filter must be used to evaluate the system empirically. The Kalman filter requires an observer equation linking observables to unobservables. Observable variables are denoted by X_t, where

$$X_t = H(\mu)'x_t + u_t, \tag{1.3}$$

with

$$E(u_t u_t') = \Sigma_u.$$

The presence of u_t in (1.3) reflects the possibility that the observations of X_t are associated with measurement error. Finally, defining

$$e_{t+1} = G(\mu)\upsilon_{t+1},$$

the covariance matrix of e_{t+1} is given by

$$Q(\mu) = E(e_t e_t'). \tag{1.4}$$

Given assumptions regarding the stochastic nature of measurement errors and the structural shocks, (1.2)–(1.4) yield a log-likelihood function $\log L(X|\Lambda)$, where Λ collects the parameters in $F(\mu)$, $H(\mu)$, Σ_u, and $Q(\mu)$. Often, it will be convenient to take as granted mappings from μ to F, H, Σ_u, and Q. In such cases the likelihood function will be written as $L(X|\mu)$.

Nonlinear approximations of structural models are represented using three equations, written with variables expressed in terms of levels. The first characterizes the evolution of the state variables s_t included in the model:

$$s_t = f(s_{t-1}, \upsilon_t), \tag{1.5}$$

where once again υ_t denotes the collection of structural shocks incorporated in the model. The second equation is known as a policy function, which represents the optimal specification of the control variables c_t included in the model as a function of the state variables:

$$c_t = c(s_t). \tag{1.6}$$

The third equation maps the full collection of model variables into the observables:

$$X_t = \widetilde{g}(s_t, c_t, \upsilon_t, u_t) \tag{1.7}$$

$$\equiv g(s_t, u_t), \tag{1.8}$$

where once again u_t denotes measurement error. Parameters associated with $f(s_{t-1}, \upsilon_t)$, $c(s_t)$, and $g(s_t, u_t)$ are again obtained as mappings from μ, thus their associated likelihood function is also written as $L(X|\mu)$.

The next chapter has two objectives. First, it outlines procedures for mapping nonlinear systems into (1.1). Next, it presents various solution methods for deriving (1.2), given (1.1).

Chapter 2

Approximating and Solving DSGE Models

EMPIRICAL INVESTIGATIONS involving DSGE models invariably require the completion of two preparatory stages. One stage involves preparation of the model to be analyzed, which is the focus of this chapter. The other involves preparation of the data, which is the focus of chapter 3.

Regarding the model-preparation stage, DSGE models typically include three components: a characterization of the environment in which decision makers reside, a set of decision rules that dictate their behavior, and a characterization of the uncertainty they face in making decisions. Collectively, these components take the form of a nonlinear system of expectational difference equations. Such systems are not directly amenable to empirical analysis, but can be converted into empirically implementable systems through the completion of the general two-step process outlined in this chapter.

The first step involves the construction of a linear approximation of the model. Just as nonlinear equations may be approximated linearly via the use of Taylor Series expansions, so too may nonlinear systems of expectational difference equations. The second step involves the solution of the resulting linear approximation of the system. The solution is written in terms of variables expressed as deviations from steady state values, and is directly amenable to empirical implementation.

Although this chapter is intended to be self-contained, far more detail is provided in the literature cited below. Here, the goal is to impart an intuitive understanding of the model-preparation stage, and to provide guidance regarding its implementation. But we acknowledge that there are alternatives to the particular approaches to model approximation and solution presented in this chapter. Three such alternatives are provided by projection methods, value-function iterations, and policy-function iterations, which are presented in chapter 10. (For additional textbook discussions, see Judd, 1998; Adda and Cooper, 2003; Ljungqvist and Sargent, 2004; Heer and Maussner, 2005; and Canova, 2006.) These alternatives yield nonlinear approximations of the model under investigation. Details regarding empirical implementations based on nonlinear approximations are provided in chapter 11. In addition, a leading alternative to model approximation is provided by perturbation methods; for a textbook discussion see Judd (1998).

2.1 Linearization

2.1.1 Taylor Series Approximation

Consider the following n-equation system of nonlinear difference equations:

$$\Psi(z_{t+1}, z_t) = 0, \tag{2.1}$$

where the z's and 0 are $n \times 1$ vectors, and the z's represent variables expressed in levels. The parameters of the system are contained in the vector μ. DSGE models are typically represented in terms of such a system, augmented to include sources of stochastic behavior. We abstract from the stochastic component of the model in the linearization stage, because models are typically designed to incorporate stochastic behavior directly into the linearized system (a modest example is provided in section 2.2; detailed examples are provided in chapter 5). Also, whereas expectational terms are typically included among the variables in z (e.g., variables of the form $E_t(z_{t+j})$, where E_t is the conditional expectations operator), these are not singled out at this point, because they receive no special treatment in the linearization stage.

Before proceeding, note that although (2.1) is written as a first-order system, higher-order specifications may be written as first-order systems by augmenting z_t to include variables observed at different points in time. For example, the pth-order equation

$$\omega_{t+1} = \rho_1 \omega_t + \rho_2 \omega_{t-1} + \cdots + \rho_p \omega_{t-p+1}$$

can be written in first-order form as

$$\begin{bmatrix} \omega_{t+1} \\ \omega_t \\ \vdots \\ \omega_{t-p+2} \end{bmatrix} - \begin{bmatrix} \rho_1 & \rho_2 & \cdots & \cdots & \rho_p \\ 1 & 0 & \cdots & \cdots & 0 \\ \vdots & \vdots & \cdots & \cdots & \vdots \\ 0 & 0 & \cdots & 1 & 0 \end{bmatrix} \begin{bmatrix} \omega_t \\ \omega_{t-1} \\ \vdots \\ \omega_{t-p+1} \end{bmatrix} = 0,$$

or more compactly, as

$$z_{t+1} - \Pi z_t = 0, \qquad z_{t+1} = [\omega_{t+1}, \omega_t, \ldots, \omega_{t-p+2}]'.$$

Thus (2.1) is sufficiently general to characterize a system of arbitrary order.

The goal of the linearization step is to convert (2.1) into a linear system, which can then be solved using any of the procedures outlined below. The reason for taking this step is that explicit solutions to (2.1) are typically unavailable, rendering quantitative assessments of the system as problematic. For textbook discussions of the analysis of nonlinear systems, see Azariadis (1993) and Sedaghat (2003).

Anticipating the notation that follows in section 2.2, the form for the system we seek is given by

$$Ax_{t+1} = Bx_t, \tag{2.2}$$

where x_t represents a transformation of z_t. Denoting the steady state of the system as $\Psi(\overline{z}) = 0$, where $\overline{z}$ is understood to be a function of μ, linearization is accomplished via a first-order Taylor Series approximation of (2.1) around its steady state, given by

$$0 \approx \Psi(\overline{z}) + \frac{\partial \Psi}{\partial z_t}(\overline{z}) \times (z_t - \overline{z}) + \frac{\partial \Psi}{\partial z_{t+1}}(\overline{z}) \times (z_{t+1} - \overline{z}), \tag{2.3}$$

where $(z_t - \overline{z})$ is $n \times 1$, and the $n \times n$ matrix $\frac{\partial \Psi}{\partial z_t}(\overline{z})$ denotes the Jacobian of $\Psi(z_{t+1}, z_t)$ with respect to z_t evaluated at $\overline{z}$. That is, the $(i,j)^{\text{th}}$ element of $\frac{\partial \Psi}{\partial z_t}(\overline{z})$ is the derivative of the ith equation in (2.1) with respect to the jth element of z_t. Defining

$$A = \frac{\partial \Psi}{\partial z_{t+1}}(\overline{z}), \qquad B = -\frac{\partial \Psi}{\partial z_t}(\overline{z}), \qquad x_t = (z_t - \overline{z})$$

yields (2.2), where variables are expressed as deviations from steady state values. (It is also possible to work with higher-order approximations of (2.2); e.g., see Schmitt-Grohé and Uribe, 2002.)

2.1.2 Logarithmic Approximations

It is often useful to work with log-linear approximations of (2.1), due to their ease of interpretation. For illustration, we begin with a simple example in which the system is 1×1, and can be written as

$$z_{t+1} = f(z_t).$$

Taking natural logs and noting that $z_t = e^{\log z_t}$, the system becomes

$$\log z_{t+1} = \log\left[f(e^{\log z_t})\right].$$

Then approximating,

$$\log z_{t+1} \approx \log\left[f(\overline{z})\right] + \frac{f'(\overline{z})\overline{z}}{f(\overline{z})}(\log(z_t) - \log(\overline{z})),$$

or because $\log\left[f(\overline{z})\right] = \log \overline{z}$,

$$\log\left(\frac{z_{t+1}}{\overline{z}}\right) \approx \frac{f'(\overline{z})\overline{z}}{f(\overline{z})}\left(\log\left(\frac{z_t}{\overline{z}}\right)\right).$$

Note that $\frac{f'()\overline{z}}{f()}$ is the elasticity of z_{t+1} with respect to z_t. Moreover, writing z_t as $\overline{z} + \varepsilon_t$, where ε_t denotes a small departure from steady state,

$$\log\left(\frac{z_t}{\overline{z}}\right) = \log\left(1 + \frac{\varepsilon_t}{\overline{z}}\right) \approx \frac{\varepsilon_t}{\overline{z}},$$

and thus $\log\left(\frac{z_t}{\overline{z}}\right)$ is seen as expressing z_t in terms of its percentage deviation from steady state.

Returning to the $n \times 1$ case, rewrite (2.1) as

$$\Psi_1(z_{t+1}, z_t) = \Psi_2(z_{t+1}, z_t), \tag{2.4}$$

because it is not possible to take logs of both sides of (2.1). Again using $z_t = e^{\log z_t}$, taking logs of (2.4) and rearranging yields

$$\log \Psi_1(e^{\log z_{t+1}}, e^{\log z_t}) - \log \Psi_2(e^{\log z_{t+1}}, e^{\log z_t}) = 0. \tag{2.5}$$

The first-order Taylor Series approximation of this converted system yields the log-linear approximation we seek. The approximation for the first term is

$$\log \Psi_1(z_{t+1}, z_t) \approx \log\left[\Psi_1(\overline{z})\right] + \frac{\partial \log\left[\Psi_1\right]}{\partial \log\left(z_t\right)}(\overline{z}) \times \left[\log\left(\frac{z_t}{\overline{z}}\right)\right]$$
$$+ \frac{\partial \log\left[\Psi_1\right]}{\partial \log\left(z_{t+1}\right)}(\overline{z}) \times \left[\log\left(\frac{z_{t+1}}{\overline{z}}\right)\right], \tag{2.6}$$

where $\frac{\partial \log[\Psi_1]}{\partial \log(z_t)}(\overline{z})$ and $\frac{\partial \log[\Psi_1]}{\partial \log(z_{t+1})}(\overline{z})$ are $n \times n$ Jacobian matrices, and $\left[\log(\frac{z_t}{\overline{z}})\right]$ and $\left[\log(\frac{z_{t+1}}{\overline{z}})\right]$ are $n \times 1$ vectors. The approximation of the second term in (2.5) is analogous. Then defining

$$A = \left[\frac{\partial \log\left[\Psi_1\right]}{\partial \log\left(z_{t+1}\right)}(\overline{z}) - \frac{\partial \log\left[\Psi_2\right]}{\partial \log\left(z_{t+1}\right)}(\overline{z})\right],$$

$$B = -\left[\frac{\partial \log\left[\Psi_1\right]}{\partial \log\left(z_t\right)}(\overline{z}) - \frac{\partial \log\left[\Psi_2\right]}{\partial \log\left(z_t\right)}(\overline{z})\right],$$

$$x_t = \log\left(\frac{z_t}{\overline{z}}\right),$$

we once again obtain (2.2). The elements of A and B are now elasticities, and the variables of the system are expressed in terms of percentage deviations from steady state.

In part II we will discuss several empirical applications that involve the need to approximate (2.1) or (2.5) repeatedly for alternative values of μ. In such cases, it is useful to automate the linearization stage via the use of a numerical gradient calculation procedure. We introduce this briefly here in the context of approximating (2.1); the approximation of (2.5) is analogous.

Gradient procedures are designed to construct the Jacobian matrices in (2.3) or (2.6) without analytical expressions for the required derivatives. Derivatives are instead calculated numerically, given the provision of three components by the user. The first two components are a specification of μ and a corresponding specification of $\bar{z}$. The third component is a procedure designed to return the $n \times 1$ vector of values ς generated by (2.1) for two cases. In the first case z_{t+1} is treated as variable and z_t is fixed at $\bar{z}$; in the second case z_t is treated as variable and z_{t+1} is fixed at $\bar{z}$. The gradient procedure delivers the Jacobian

$$\frac{\partial \Psi}{\partial z_{t+1}}(\bar{z}) = A$$

in the first case and

$$\frac{\partial \Psi}{\partial z_t}(\bar{z}) = -B$$

in the second case. Examples follow.

2.1.3 Examples

Consider the simple resource constraint

$$y_t = c_t + i_t,$$

indicating that output (y_t) can be either consumed (c_t) or invested (i_t). This equation is already linear. In the notation of (2.1) the equation appears as

$$y_t - c_t - i_t = 0;$$

and in terms of (2.3), with

$$z_t = [y_t \quad c_t \quad i_t]'$$

and the equation representing the ith of the system, the ith row of

$$\frac{\partial \Psi}{\partial z_t}(\bar{z}) = [1 \quad -1 \quad -1].$$

In the notation of (2.5), the equation appears as

$$\log y_t - \log[\exp(\log c_t) - \exp(\log i_t)] = 0,$$

and in terms of (2.2), the ith row of the right-hand-side matrix B is

$$\left[\frac{\partial \log\,[\Psi_1]}{\partial \log(z_t)}(\bar{z}) - \frac{\partial \log\,[\Psi_2]}{\partial \log(z_t)}(\bar{z})\right] = \left[\frac{1}{\bar{y}} \quad \frac{-\bar{c}}{\bar{c}+\bar{i}} \quad \frac{-\bar{i}}{\bar{c}+\bar{i}}\right]. \tag{2.7}$$

Finally, to use a gradient procedure to accomplish log-linear approximation, the ith return of the system-evaluation procedure is

$$\varsigma_i = \log y_t - \log\,[\exp(\log c_t) - \exp(\log i_t)]\,.$$

As an additional example consider the Cobb-Douglas production function

$$y_t = a_t k_t^{\alpha} n_t^{1-\alpha}, \qquad \alpha \in (0,1),$$

where output is produced by the use of capital (k_t) and labor (n_t) and is subject to a technology or productivity shock (a_t). Linear approximation of this equation is left as an exercise. To accomplish log-linear approximation, taking logs of the equation and rearranging maps into the notation of (2.5) as

$$\log y_t - \log a_t - \alpha \log k_t - (1-\alpha)\log n_t = 0.$$

With

$$z_t = \left[\log\frac{y_t}{\bar{y}} \;\; \log\frac{a_t}{\bar{a}} \;\; \log\frac{k_t}{\bar{k}} \;\; \log\frac{n_t}{\bar{n}}\right]',$$

the ith row of the right-hand-side matrix in (2.2) is

$$\left[\frac{\partial \log\,[\Psi_1]}{\partial \log(z_t)}(\bar{z}) - \frac{\partial \log\,[\Psi_2]}{\partial \log(z_t)}(\bar{z})\right] = [1 \;\; -1 \;\; -\alpha \;\; -(1-\alpha)]\,. \tag{2.8}$$

And to use a gradient procedure to accomplish log-linear approximation, the ith return of the system-evaluation procedure is

$$\varsigma_i = \log y_t - \log a_t - \alpha \log k_t - (1-\alpha)\log n_t.$$

2.2 Solution Methods

Having approximated the model as in (2.2), we next seek a solution of the form

$$x_{t+1} = Fx_t + Gv_{t+1}. \tag{2.9}$$

This solution represents the time series behavior of $\{x_t\}$ as a function of $\{v_t\}$, where v_t is a vector of exogenous innovations, or as frequently referenced, structural shocks.

Here we present four popular approaches to the derivation of (2.9) from (2.2). Each approach involves an alternative way of expressing (2.2), and uses specialized notation. Also, each approach makes intensive use of linear algebra: background for this material is available at the undergraduate level, for example, from Lay (2002); and at the graduate level, for example, from Roman (2005).

Before describing these approaches, we introduce an explicit example of (2.2), which we will map into the notation used under each approach to aid with the exposition. The example is a linearized stochastic version of Ramsey's (1928) optimal growth model. (See, e.g., Romer, 2006, for a detailed textbook exposition.) The model is represented as:

$$\widetilde{y}_{t+1} - \widetilde{a}_{t+1} - \alpha\widetilde{k}_{t+1} = 0 \tag{2.10}$$

$$\widetilde{y}_{t+1} - \gamma_c\widetilde{c}_{t+1} - \gamma_i\widetilde{i}_{t+1} = 0 \tag{2.11}$$

$$\theta_{1c}E_t(\widetilde{c}_{t+1}) + \theta_a E_t(\widetilde{a}_{t+1}) + \theta_k E_t(\widetilde{k}_{t+1}) + \theta_{2c}\widetilde{c}_t = 0 \tag{2.12}$$

$$\widetilde{k}_{t+1} - \delta_k\widetilde{k}_t - \delta_i\widetilde{i}_t = 0 \tag{2.13}$$

$$\widetilde{a}_{t+1} - \rho\widetilde{a}_t = \varepsilon_{t+1}. \tag{2.14}$$

The variables $\{\widetilde{y}_t, \widetilde{c}_t, \widetilde{i}_t, \widetilde{k}_t, \widetilde{a}_t\}$ represent output, consumption, investment, physical capital, and a productivity shock, all expressed as logged deviations from steady state values. The variable ε_t is a serially uncorrelated stochastic process. The vector

$$\mu = [\alpha\ \gamma_c\ \gamma_i\ \theta_{1c}\ \theta_a\ \theta_k\ \theta_{2c}\ \delta_k\ \delta_i\ \rho]'$$

contains the "deep" parameters of the model.

Two modifications enable a mapping of the model into a specification resembling (2.2). First, the expectations operator $E_t(\cdot)$ is dropped from (2.12), introducing an expectational error into the modified equation; let this error be denoted as η_{ct+1}. Next, the innovation term ε_{t+1} in (2.14) must be accommodated. The resulting expression is

$$\underbrace{\begin{bmatrix} 1 & 0 & 0 & -\alpha & -1 \\ 1 & -\gamma_c & -\gamma_i & 0 & 0 \\ 0 & \theta_{1c} & 0 & \theta_k & \theta_a \\ 0 & 0 & 0 & 1 & 0 \\ 0 & 0 & 0 & 0 & 1 \end{bmatrix}}_{A} \underbrace{\begin{bmatrix} \widetilde{y}_{t+1} \\ \widetilde{c}_{t+1} \\ \widetilde{i}_{t+1} \\ \widetilde{k}_{t+1} \\ \widetilde{a}_{t+1} \end{bmatrix}}_{x_{t+1}}$$

$$= \underbrace{\begin{bmatrix} 0 & 0 & 0 & 0 & 0 \\ 0 & 0 & 0 & 0 & 0 \\ 0 & -\theta_{2c} & 0 & 0 & 0 \\ 0 & 0 & \delta_i & \delta_k & 0 \\ 0 & 0 & 0 & 0 & \rho \end{bmatrix}}_{B} \underbrace{\begin{bmatrix} \widetilde{y}_t \\ \widetilde{c}_t \\ \widetilde{i}_t \\ \widetilde{k}_t \\ \widetilde{a}_t \end{bmatrix}}_{x_t}$$

$$+ \underbrace{\begin{bmatrix} 0 & 0 & 0 & 0 & 0 \\ 0 & 0 & 0 & 0 & 0 \\ 0 & 0 & 0 & 0 & 0 \\ 0 & 0 & 0 & 0 & 0 \\ 0 & 0 & 0 & 0 & 1 \end{bmatrix}}_{C} \underbrace{\begin{bmatrix} 0 \\ 0 \\ 0 \\ 0 \\ \varepsilon_{t+1} \end{bmatrix}}_{\upsilon_{t+1}}$$

$$+ \underbrace{\begin{bmatrix} 0 & 0 & 0 & 0 & 0 \\ 0 & 0 & 0 & 0 & 0 \\ 0 & 0 & 0 & 1 & 0 \\ 0 & 0 & 0 & 0 & 0 \\ 0 & 0 & 0 & 0 & 0 \end{bmatrix}}_{D} \underbrace{\begin{bmatrix} 0 \\ 0 \\ 0 \\ \eta_{ct+1} \\ 0 \end{bmatrix}}_{\eta_{t+1}}. \tag{2.15}$$

2.2.1 Blanchard and Kahn's Method

The first solution method we present was developed by Blanchard and Kahn (1980), and is applied to models written as

$$\begin{bmatrix} x_{1t+1} \\ E_t(x_{2t+1}) \end{bmatrix} = \widetilde{A} \begin{bmatrix} x_{1t} \\ x_{2t} \end{bmatrix} + Ef_t, \tag{2.16}$$

where the model variables have been divided into an $n_1 \times 1$ vector of endogenous predetermined variables x_{1t} (defined as variables for which

$E_t(x_{1t+1}) = x_{1t+1}$), and an $n_2 \times 1$ vector of endogenous nonpredetermined variables x_{2t} (for which $x_{2t+1} = E_t(x_{2t+1}) + \eta_{t+1}$, with η_{t+1} representing an expectational error). The $k \times 1$ vector f_t contains exogenous forcing variables.

In the event that the linearization of the model under investigation does not automatically lend itself to the form given by (2.16), a preliminary step due to King and Watson (2002) may be implemented. The step is referred to as a system reduction: it involves writing the model in terms of a subset of variables that are uniquely determined. In terms of the example, note that observations on $\widetilde{a}_t$ and $\widetilde{k}_t$ are sufficient for determining $\widetilde{y}_t$ using (2.10), and that given $\widetilde{y}_t$, the observation of either $\widetilde{c}_t$ or $\widetilde{i}_t$ is sufficient for determining both variables using (2.11). Thus we proceed in working directly with $\{\widetilde{c}_t, \widetilde{k}_t, \widetilde{a}_t\}$ using (2.12)–(2.14), and recover $\{\widetilde{y}_t, \widetilde{i}_t\}$ as functions of $\{\widetilde{c}_t, \widetilde{k}_t, \widetilde{a}_t\}$ using (2.10) and (2.11). Among $\{\widetilde{c}_t, \widetilde{k}_t, \widetilde{a}_t\}$, $\widetilde{k}_t$ is predetermined (given $\widetilde{k}_t$ and $\widetilde{i}_t$, $\widetilde{k}_{t+1}$ is determined as in (2.13)); $\widetilde{c}_t$ is endogenous but not predetermined (as indicated in (2.12), its time-$(t+1)$ realization is associated with an expectations error); and $\widetilde{a}_t$ is an exogenous forcing variable. Thus in the notation of (2.16), we seek a specification of the model in the form

$$\begin{bmatrix} \widetilde{k}_{t+1} \\ E_t(\widetilde{c}_{t+1}) \end{bmatrix} = \widetilde{A} \begin{bmatrix} \widetilde{k}_t \\ \widetilde{c}_t \end{bmatrix} + E\,\widetilde{a}_t. \tag{2.17}$$

To obtain this expression, let

$$\xi_t = [\widetilde{y}_t \quad \widetilde{i}_t]', \qquad \zeta_t = [\widetilde{k}_t \quad \widetilde{c}_t]',$$

and note that

$$E_t(\widetilde{a}_{t+1}) = \rho\widetilde{a}_t.$$

In terms of these variables, the model may be written as

$$\underbrace{\begin{bmatrix} 1 & 0 \\ 1 & -\gamma_i \end{bmatrix}}_{\Psi_0} \xi_t = \underbrace{\begin{bmatrix} \alpha & 0 \\ 0 & \gamma_c \end{bmatrix}}_{\Psi_1} \zeta_t + \underbrace{\begin{bmatrix} 1 \\ 0 \end{bmatrix}}_{\Psi_2} \widetilde{a}_t \tag{2.18}$$

$$\underbrace{\begin{bmatrix} \theta_k & \theta_{1c} \\ 1 & 0 \end{bmatrix}}_{\Psi_3} E_t(\zeta_{t+1}) = \underbrace{\begin{bmatrix} 0 & -\theta_{2c} \\ \delta_k & 0 \end{bmatrix}}_{\Psi_4} \zeta_t + \underbrace{\begin{bmatrix} 0 & 0 \\ 0 & \delta_i \end{bmatrix}}_{\Psi_5} \xi_t + \underbrace{\begin{bmatrix} -\theta_a\rho \\ 0 \end{bmatrix}}_{\Psi_6} \widetilde{a}_t. \tag{2.19}$$

Next, substituting (2.18) into (2.19), which requires inversion of Ψ_0, we obtain

$$\Psi_3 E_t(\zeta_{t+1}) = [\Psi_4 + \Psi_5\Psi_0^{-1}\Psi_1]\zeta_t + [\Psi_6 + \Psi_5\Psi_0^{-1}\Psi_2]\widetilde{a}_t. \tag{2.20}$$

Finally, premultiplying (2.20) by Ψ_3^{-1} yields a specification in the form of (2.17); Blanchard and Kahn's solution method can now be implemented. Hereafter, we describe its implementation in terms of the notation used in (2.16).

The method begins with a Jordan decomposition of $\widetilde{A}$, yielding

$$\widetilde{A} = \Lambda^{-1} J \Lambda, \tag{2.21}$$

where the diagonal elements of J, consisting of the eigenvalues of $\widetilde{A}$, are ordered in increasing absolute value in moving from left to right.[1] Thus J can be written as

$$J = \begin{bmatrix} J_1 & 0 \\ 0 & J_2 \end{bmatrix}, \tag{2.22}$$

where the eigenvalues in J_1 lie on or within the unit circle, and those in J_2 lie outside of the unit circle. J_2 is said to be unstable or explosive, because J_2^n diverges as n increases. The matrices Λ and E are partitioned conformably as

$$\Lambda = \begin{bmatrix} \Lambda_{11} & \Lambda_{12} \\ \Lambda_{21} & \Lambda_{22} \end{bmatrix}, \quad E = \begin{bmatrix} E_1 \\ E_2 \end{bmatrix}, \tag{2.23}$$

where Λ_{11} is conformable with J_1, etc. If the number of explosive eigenvalues is equal to the number of nonpredetermined variables, the system is said to be saddle-path stable and a unique solution to the model exists. If the number of explosive eigenvalues exceeds the number of nonpredetermined variables, no solution exists (and the system is said to be a source); and in the opposite case an infinity of solutions exist (and the system is said to be a sink).

Proceeding under the case of saddle-path stability, substitution for $\widetilde{A}$ in (2.16) yields

$$\begin{bmatrix} x_{1t+1} \\ E_t(x_{2t+1}) \end{bmatrix} = \Lambda^{-1} J \Lambda \begin{bmatrix} x_{1t} \\ x_{2t} \end{bmatrix} + \begin{bmatrix} E_1 \\ E_2 \end{bmatrix} f_t. \tag{2.24}$$

[1] Eigenvalues of a matrix Θ are obtained from the solution of equations of the form $\Theta e = \lambda e$, where e is an eigenvector and λ the associated eigenvalue. The GAUSS command `eigv` performs this decomposition.

Next, the system is premultiplied by Λ, yielding

$$\begin{bmatrix} \acute{x}_{1t+1} \\ E_t(\acute{x}_{2t+1}) \end{bmatrix} = \begin{bmatrix} J_1 & 0 \\ 0 & J_2 \end{bmatrix} \begin{bmatrix} \acute{x}_{1t} \\ \acute{x}_{2t} \end{bmatrix} + \begin{bmatrix} D_1 \\ D_2 \end{bmatrix} f_t, \tag{2.25}$$

where

$$\begin{bmatrix} \acute{x}_{1t} \\ \acute{x}_{2t} \end{bmatrix} = \begin{bmatrix} \Lambda_{11} & \Lambda_{12} \\ \Lambda_{21} & \Lambda_{22} \end{bmatrix} \begin{bmatrix} x_{1t} \\ x_{2t} \end{bmatrix} \tag{2.26}$$

$$\begin{bmatrix} D_1 \\ D_2 \end{bmatrix} = \begin{bmatrix} \Lambda_{11} & \Lambda_{12} \\ \Lambda_{21} & \Lambda_{22} \end{bmatrix} \begin{bmatrix} E_1 \\ E_2 \end{bmatrix}. \tag{2.27}$$

This transformation effectively "de-couples" the system, so that the non-predetermined variables depend upon only the unstable eigenvalues of $\widetilde{A}$ contained in J_2, as expressed in the lower part of (2.25).

Having decoupled the system, we derive a solution for the nonpredetermined variables by performing a forward iteration on the lower portion of (2.25). Using f_{2t} to denote the portion of f_t conformable with D_2, this is accomplished as follows. First, re-express the lower portion of (2.25) as

$$\acute{x}_{2t} = J_2^{-1} E_t(\acute{x}_{2t+1}) - J_2^{-1} D_2 f_{2t}. \tag{2.28}$$

This implies an expression for $\acute{x}_{2t+1}$ of the form

$$\acute{x}_{2t+1} = J_2^{-1} E_{t+1}(\acute{x}_{2t+2}) - J_2^{-1} D_2 f_{2t+1}, \tag{2.29}$$

which can be substituted into (2.28) to obtain

$$\acute{x}_{2t} = J_2^{-2} E_t(\acute{x}_{2t+2}) - J_2^{-2} D_2 E_t(f_{2t+1}) - J_2^{-1} D_2 f_{2t}. \tag{2.30}$$

In writing (2.30) we have exploited the Law of Iterated Expectations, which holds that

$$E_t[E_{t+1}(x_t)] = E_t(x_t)$$

for any x_t (e.g., see Ljungqvist and Sargent, 2004). Because J_2 contains explosive eigenvalues, J_2^{-n} disappears as n approaches infinity, thus continuation of the iteration process yields

$$\acute{x}_{2t} = -\sum_{i=0}^{\infty} J_2^{-(i+1)} D_2 E_t(f_{2t+i}). \tag{2.31}$$

Mapping this back into an expression for x_{2t} using (2.26), we obtain

$$x_{2t} = -\Lambda_{22}^{-1}\Lambda_{21}x_{1t} - \Lambda_{22}^{-1}\sum_{i=0}^{\infty} J_2^{-(i+1)} D_2 E_t(f_{2t+i}). \tag{2.32}$$

In the case of the example model presented above,

$$E_t(f_{2t+i}) = \rho^i \widetilde{a}_t,$$

and thus (2.32) becomes

$$x_{2t} = -\Lambda_{22}^{-1}\Lambda_{21}x_{1t} - \Lambda_{22}^{-1}J_2^{-1}(I - \rho J_2^{-1}D_2)^{-1}\widetilde{a}_t. \tag{2.33}$$

Finally, to solve the nonexplosive portion of the system begin by expanding the upper portion of (2.24):

$$x_{1t+1} = \widetilde{A}_{11}x_{1t} + \widetilde{A}_{22}x_{2t} + E_1 f_t, \tag{2.34}$$

where $\widetilde{A}_{11}$ and $\widetilde{A}_{22}$ are partitions of $\Lambda^{-1}J\Lambda$ conformable with x_{1t} and x_{2t}. Then substituting for x_{2t} using (2.32) yields a solution for x_{1t} of the form given by (2.9).

We conclude this subsection by highlighting two requirements of this solution method. First, a model-specific system reduction may be required to obtain an expression of the model that consists of a subset of its variables. The variables in the subset are distinguished as being either predetermined or non-predetermined. Second, invertibility of the lead matrices Ψ_0 and Ψ_3 is required in order to obtain a specification of the model amenable for solution.

Exercise 2.1

Write computer code for mapping the example model expressed in (2.10)–(2.14) into the form of the representation given in (2.16).

2.2.2 *Sims's Method*

Sims (2001) proposes a solution method applied to models expressed as

$$Ax_{t+1} = Bx_t + E + C\upsilon_{t+1} + D\eta_{t+1}, \tag{2.35}$$

where E is a matrix of constants.[2] Relative to the notation we have used above, E is unnecessary because the variables in x_t are expressed in terms of deviations from steady state values. Like Blanchard and Kahn's (1980) method, Sims' method involves a decoupling of the system into explosive and nonexplosive portions. However, rather than expressing variables in terms of expected values, expectations operators have been dropped, giving rise to the expectations errors contained in η_{t+1}. Also, although Blanchard

[2] The programs available on Sims's Web site perform all of the steps of this procedure. The Web address is: http://www.princeton.edu/~sims/. The programs are written in Matlab.

and Kahn's method entails isolation of the forcing variables from x_{t+1}, these are included in x_{t+1} under Sims' method; thus the appearance in the system of the vector of shocks to the variables υ_{t+1}. Third, Sims' method does not require an initial system-reduction step. Finally, it does not entail a distinction between predetermined and nonpredetermined variables.

Note from (2.15) that the example model has already been cast in the form of (2.35); thus we proceed directly to a characterization of the solution method. The first step uses a "*QZ* factorization" to decompose A and B into unitary upper triangular matrices:

$$A = Q'\Lambda Z' \tag{2.36}$$

$$B = Q'\Omega Z', \tag{2.37}$$

where (Q, Z) are unitary, and (Λ, Ω) are upper triangular. (A unitary matrix Θ satisfies $\Theta'\Theta = \Theta\Theta' = I$. If Q and/or Z contain complex values, the transpositions reflect complex conjugation; that is, each complex entry is replaced by its conjugate and then transposed.) Next, (Q, Z, Λ, Ω) are ordered such that, in absolute value, the generalized eigenvalues of A and B are organized in Λ and Ω in increasing order moving from left to right, just as in Blanchard and Kahn's Jordan decomposition procedure. (Generalized eigenvalues of Θ are obtained as the solution to $\Theta e = \lambda \Xi e$, where Ξ is a symmetric matrix.) Having obtained the factorization, the original system is then premultiplied by Q, yielding the transformed system expressed in terms of $z_{t+1} = Z'x_{t+1}$:

$$\Lambda z_t = \Omega z_{t-1} + QE + QC\upsilon_t + QD\eta_t, \tag{2.38}$$

where we have lagged the system by one period in order to match the notation (and code) of Sims.

Next, as with Blanchard and Kahn's (1980) method, (2.38) is partitioned into explosive and nonexplosive blocks:

$$\begin{bmatrix} \Lambda_{11} & \Lambda_{12} \\ 0 & \Lambda_{22} \end{bmatrix} \begin{bmatrix} z_{1t} \\ z_{2t} \end{bmatrix} = \begin{bmatrix} \Omega_{11} & \Omega_{12} \\ 0 & \Omega_{22} \end{bmatrix} \begin{bmatrix} z_{1t-1} \\ z_{2t-1} \end{bmatrix} + \begin{bmatrix} Q_1 \\ Q_2 \end{bmatrix} [E + C\upsilon_t + D\eta_t]. \tag{2.39}$$

The explosive block (the lower equations) is solved as follows. Letting

$$w_t = Q(E + C\upsilon_t + D\eta_t),$$

partitioned conformably as w_{1t} and w_{2t}, the lower block of (2.39) is given by

$$\Lambda_{22} z_{2t} = \Omega_{22} z_{2t-1} + w_{2t}. \tag{2.40}$$

Leading (2.40) by one period and solving for z_{2t} yields

$$z_{2t} = Mz_{2t+1} - \Omega_{22}^{-1} w_{2t+1}, \tag{2.41}$$

where

$$M = \Omega_{22}^{-1} \Lambda_{22}.$$

Then recursive substitution for $z_{2t+1}, z_{2t+2}, \ldots$ yields

$$z_{2t} = -\sum_{i=0}^{\infty} M^i \Omega_{22}^{-1} w_{2t+1+i}, \tag{2.42}$$

since

$$\lim_{t\to\infty} M^t z_{2t} = 0.$$

Recalling that w_t is defined as $w_t = Q(E + C\upsilon_t + D\eta_t)$, note that (2.42) expresses z_{2t} as a function of future values of structural and expectational errors. But z_{2t} is known at time t, and

$$E_t(\eta_{t+s}) = E_t(\upsilon_{t+s}) = 0, \qquad s > 0,$$

thus (2.42) may be written as

$$z_{2t} = -\sum_{i=0}^{\infty} M^i \Omega_{22}^{-1} Q_2 E_2, \tag{2.43}$$

where $Q_2 E_2$ are the lower portions of QE conformable with z_2. (Sims also considers the case in which the structural innovations υ_t are serially correlated, which leads to a generalization of (2.43).) Postmultiplying (2.43) by $(\Omega_{22}^{-1} Q_2 E_2)^{-1}$ and noting that

$$-\sum_{i=0}^{\infty} M^i = -(I - M)^{-1},$$

the solution of z_{2t} is obtained as

$$z_{2t} = (\Lambda_{22} - \Omega_{22})^{-1} Q_2 E. \tag{2.44}$$

Having solved for z_{2t}, the final step is to solve for z_{1t} in (2.39). Note that the solution of z_{1t} requires a solution for the expectations errors that appear in (2.39). As Sims notes, when a unique solution for the model exists, a systematic relationship will exist between the expectations errors associated with z_{1t} and z_{2t}; exploiting this relationship yields a straightforward means of solving for z_{1t}. The necessary and sufficient condition for uniqueness is given by the existence of a $k \times (n-k)$ matrix Φ that satisfies

$$Q_1 D = \Phi Q_2 D, \tag{2.45}$$

which represents the systematic relationship between the expectations errors associated with z_{1t} and z_{2t} noted above. Given uniqueness, and thus the ability to calculate Φ as in (2.45), the solution of z_{1t} proceeds with the pre-multiplication of (2.38) by $[I - \Phi]$, which yields

$$\begin{aligned}[\,\Lambda_{11} \quad \Lambda_{12} - \Phi\Lambda_{22}\,]\begin{bmatrix} z_{1t} \\ z_{2t} \end{bmatrix} \\ = [\,\Omega_{11} \quad \Omega_{12} - \Phi\Omega_{22}\,]\begin{bmatrix} z_{1t-1} \\ z_{2t-1} \end{bmatrix} + [Q_1 - \Phi Q_2][E + Cv_t + D\eta_t].\end{aligned} \tag{2.46}$$

Then due to (2.45), the loading factor for the expectational errors in (2.46) is zero, and thus the system may be written in the form

$$x_t = \Theta_E + \Theta_0 x_{t-1} + \Theta_1 v_t, \tag{2.47}$$

where

$$H = Z\begin{bmatrix} \Lambda_{11}^{-1} & -\Lambda_{11}^{-1}(\Lambda_{12} - \Phi\Lambda_{22}) \\ 0 & I \end{bmatrix} \tag{2.48}$$

$$\Theta_E = H\begin{bmatrix} Q_1 - \Phi Q_2 \\ (\Omega_{22} - \Lambda_{22})^{-1} Q_2 \end{bmatrix} E \tag{2.49}$$

$$\Theta_0 = Z\Lambda_{11}^{-1}[\Omega_{11}(\Omega_{12} - \Phi\Omega_{22})]Z' \tag{2.50}$$

$$\Theta_1 = H\begin{bmatrix} Q_1 - \Phi Q_2 \\ 0 \end{bmatrix} D. \tag{2.51}$$

Exercise 2.2

Using the code cited for this method, compute the solution for (2.10)–(2.14) for given values of μ.

2.2.3 Klein's Method

Klein (2000) proposes a solution method that is a hybrid of those of Blanchard and Kahn (1980) and Sims (2001).[3] The method is applied to systems written as

$$\widetilde{A}E_t(x_{t+1}) = \widetilde{B}x_t + Ef_t, \tag{2.52}$$

[3] GAUSS and Matlab code that implement this solution method are available at http://www.ssc.uwo.ca/economics/faculty/klein/

where the vector f_t (of length n_z) has a zero-mean vector autoregressive (VAR) specification with autocorrelation matrix Φ; additionally $\widetilde{A}$ may be singular. (See chapter 4, section 4.1.2, for a description of VAR models.)

Like Blanchard and Kahn, Klein distinguishes between the predetermined and nonpredetermined variables of the model. The former are contained in x_{1t+1}, the latter in x_{2t+1}:

$$E_t(x_{t+1}) = [x_{1t+1} \quad E_t(x_{2t+1})]'.$$

The solution approach once again involves de-coupling the system into nonexplosive and explosive components, and solving the two components in turn.

Returning to the example model expressed in (2.10)–(2.14), the form of the model amenable to the implementation of Klein's method is given by (2.20), repeated here for convenience:

$$\Psi_3 E_t(\zeta_{t+1}) = [\Psi_4 + \Psi_5 \Psi_0^{-1} \Psi_1]\zeta_t + [\Psi_6 + \Psi_5 \Psi_0^{-1} \Psi_2]\widetilde{a}_t. \qquad (2.53)$$

An advantage of Klein's approach relative to Blanchard and Kahn's is that Ψ_3 may be singular. In addition, it is also faster to implement computationally. To proceed with the description of Klein's approach, we revert to the notation used in (2.52).

Klein's approach overcomes the potential noninvertibility of $\widetilde{A}$ by implementing a complex generalized Schur decomposition to decompose $\widetilde{A}$ and $\widetilde{B}$. This is in place of the QZ decomposition used by Sims. In short, the Schur decomposition is a generalization of the QZ decomposition that allows for complex eigenvalues associated with $\widetilde{A}$ and $\widetilde{B}$. Given the decomposition of $\widetilde{A}$ and $\widetilde{B}$, Klein's method closely follows that of Blanchard and Kahn.

The Schur decompositions of $\widetilde{A}$ and $\widetilde{B}$ are given by

$$Q\widetilde{A}Z = S \qquad (2.54)$$

$$Q\widetilde{B}Z = T, \qquad (2.55)$$

where (Q, Z) are unitary and (S, T) are upper triangular matrices with diagonal elements containing the generalized eigenvalues of $\widetilde{A}$ and $\widetilde{B}$. Once again the eigenvalues are ordered in increasing value in moving from left to right. Partitioning Z as

$$Z = \begin{bmatrix} Z_{11} & Z_{12} \\ Z_{21} & Z_{22} \end{bmatrix}, \qquad (2.56)$$

Z_{11} is $n_1 \times n_1$ and corresponds to the nonexplosive eigenvalues of the system. Given saddle-path stability, this conforms with x_1, which contains the predetermined variables of the model.

Having obtained this decomposition, the next step in solving the system is to triangularize (2.52) as was done in working with the QZ decomposition. Begin by defining

$$z_t = Z^H x_t, \tag{2.57}$$

where Z^H refers to a Hermitian transpose. (Given a matrix Θ, if the lower triangular portion of Θ is the complex conjugate transpose of the upper triangle portion of Θ, then Θ is denoted as Hermitian.) This transformed vector is divided into $n_1 \times 1$ stable (s_t) and $n_2 \times 1$ unstable (u_t) components. Then since

$$\widetilde{A} = Q'SZ^H$$

and

$$\widetilde{B} = Q'TZ^H,$$

(2.52) may be written as

$$\begin{bmatrix} S_{11} & S_{12} \\ 0 & S_{22} \end{bmatrix} E_t \begin{bmatrix} s_{t+1} \\ u_{t+1} \end{bmatrix} = \begin{bmatrix} T_{11} & T_{12} \\ 0 & T_{22} \end{bmatrix} \begin{bmatrix} s_t \\ u_t \end{bmatrix} + \begin{bmatrix} Q_1 \\ Q_2 \end{bmatrix} Ef_t; \tag{2.58}$$

once again, the lower portion of (2.58) contains the unstable components of the system. Solving this component via forward iteration, we obtain

$$u_t = Mf_t \tag{2.59}$$

$$vec(M) = [(\Phi^T \otimes S_{22}) - I_{n_z} \otimes T_{22}]^{-1} vec(Q_2 E). \tag{2.60}$$

The appearance of the vec operator accommodates the VAR specification for f_t. In the context of the example model, Φ^T is replaced by the scalar ρ^T, and (2.60) becomes

$$M = [\rho^T S_{22} - T_{22}]^{-1} Q_2 E.$$

This solution for the unstable component is then used to solve the stable component, yielding

$$s_{t+1} = S_{11}^{-1} T_{11} s_t + S_{11}^{-1} \{T_{12} M - S_{12} M \Phi + Q_1 E\} f_t - Z_{11}^{-1} Z_{12} M \upsilon_{t+1}, \tag{2.61}$$

where υ_{t+1} is a serially uncorrelated stochastic process representing the innovations in the VAR specification for f_{t+1}. In the context of our example model, f_t corresponds to $\widetilde{a}_t$, the innovation to which is ε_t. In terms of the original variables the solution is expressed as

$$x_{2t} = Z_{21}Z_{11}^{-1}x_{1t} + Nf_t \tag{2.62}$$

$$x_{1t+1} = Z_{11}S_{11}^{-1}T_{11}Z_{11}^{-1}x_{2t} + Lf_t \tag{2.63}$$

$$N = (Z_{22} - Z_{21}Z_{11}^{-1}Z_{12})M \tag{2.64}$$

$$\begin{aligned} L = & -Z_{11}S_{11}^{-1}T_{11}Z_{11}^{-1}Z_{12}M + Z_{11}S_{11}^{-1} \\ & \times [T_{12}M - S_{12}M\Phi + Q_1E] + Z_{12}M\Phi. \end{aligned} \tag{2.65}$$

This solution can be cast into the form of (2.9) as

$$\begin{aligned} x_{1t+1} = & [Z_{11}S_{11}^{-1}T_{11}Z_{11}^{-1}Z_{21}Z_{11}^{-1}]x_{1t} \\ & + [Z_{11}S_{11}^{-1}T_{11}Z_{11}^{-1}N + L]f_t. \end{aligned} \tag{2.66}$$

Exercise 2.3

Apply Klein's code to the example model presented in (2.10)–(2.14).

2.2.4 An Undetermined Coefficients Approach

Uhlig (1999) proposes a solution method based on the method of undetermined coefficients.[4] The method is applied to systems written as

$$0 = E_t[Fx_{t+1} + Gx_t + Hx_{t-1} + Lf_{t+1} + Mf_t] \tag{2.67}$$

$$f_{t+1} = Nf_t + \upsilon_{t+1}, \qquad E_t(\upsilon_{t+1}) = 0. \tag{2.68}$$

With respect to the example model in (2.10)–(2.14), let

$$x_t = [\widetilde{y}_t \, \widetilde{c}_t \, \widetilde{i}_t \, \widetilde{k}_t]'.$$

Then lagging the first two equations, which are subject neither to structural shocks nor expectations errors, the matrices in (2.67) and (2.68) are given by

$$F = \begin{bmatrix} 0 & 0 & 0 & 0 \\ 0 & 0 & 0 & 0 \\ 0 & \theta_{1c} & 0 & \theta_k \\ 0 & 0 & 0 & 1 \end{bmatrix}, \quad G = \begin{bmatrix} 1 & 0 & 0 & -\alpha \\ 1 & -\gamma_c & -\gamma_i & 0 \\ 0 & \theta_{2c} & 0 & 0 \\ 0 & 0 & -\delta_i & -\delta_k \end{bmatrix}, \tag{2.69}$$

$H = 0$, $L = [0\,0\,\theta_a\,0]'$, $M = [-1\,0\,0\,0]'$, and $N = \rho$.

[4] Matlab code available for implementing this solution method is available at: http://www.wiwi.hu-berlin.de/wpol/html/toolkit.htm

Solutions to (2.67)–(2.68) take the form

$$x_t = Px_{t-1} + Qf_t. \tag{2.70}$$

In deriving (2.70), we will confront the problem of solving matrix quadratic equations of the form

$$\Psi P^2 - \Gamma P - \Theta = 0 \tag{2.71}$$

for the $m \times m$ matrix P. Thus we first describe the solution of such equations.

To begin, define

$$\underset{2m\times 2m}{\Xi} = \begin{bmatrix} \Gamma & \Theta \\ I_m & 0_{m\times m} \end{bmatrix}, \quad \underset{2m\times 2m}{\Delta} = \begin{bmatrix} \Psi & 0_{m\times m} \\ 0_{m\times m} & I_m \end{bmatrix}. \tag{2.72}$$

Given these matrices, let s and λ denote the generalized eigenvector and eigenvalue of Ξ with respect to Δ, and note that $s' = [\lambda x', x']$ for some $x \in \Re^m$. Then the solution to the matrix quadratic is given by

$$\begin{aligned} P &= \Omega \Lambda \Omega^{-1}, \\ \Omega &= [x_1, \dots, x_m], \\ \Lambda &= diag(\lambda_1, \dots, \lambda_m), \end{aligned} \tag{2.73}$$

so long as the m eigenvalues contained in Λ and $(x_1, \dots, x_m)$ are linearly independent. The solution is stable if the generalized eigenvalues are all less than one in absolute value.

Returning to the solution of the system in (2.67)–(2.68), the first step towards obtaining (2.70) is to combine these three equations into a single equation. This is accomplished in two steps. First, write x_t in (2.67) in terms of its relationship with x_{t-1} given by (2.70), and do the same for x_{t+1}, where the relationship is given by

$$x_{t+1} = P^2 x_{t-1} + PQf_t + Qf_{t+1}. \tag{2.74}$$

Next, write f_{t+1} in terms of its relationship with f_t given by (2.68). Taking expectations of the resulting equation yields

$$0 = [FP^2 + GP + H]x_{t-1} + [(FP + G)Q + M + (FQ + L)N]f_t. \tag{2.75}$$

Note that in order for (2.75) to hold, the coefficients on x_{t-1} and f_t must be zero. The first restriction implies that P must satisfy the matrix quadratic equation

$$0 = FP^2 + GP + H, \tag{2.76}$$

the solution of which is obtained as indicated in (2.72) and (2.73). The second restriction requires the derivation of Q which satisfies

$$(FP + G)Q + M + (FQ + L)N = 0. \tag{2.77}$$

The required Q can be shown to be given by

$$Q = V^{-1}[-vec(LN + M)], \tag{2.78}$$

where V is defined as

$$V = N' \otimes F + I_k \otimes (FP + G). \tag{2.79}$$

The solutions for P and Q will be unique so long as the matrix P has stable eigenvalues.

As noted by Christiano (2002), this solution method is particularly convenient for working with models involving endogenous variables that have differing associated information sets. Such models can be cast in the form of (2.67)–(2.68), with the expectations operator $\mathring{E}_t$ replacing E_t. In terms of calculating the expectation of an $n \times 1$ vector X_t, $\mathring{E}_t$ is defined as

$$\mathring{E}_t(X_t) = \begin{bmatrix} E(X_{1t}|\Xi_{1t}) \\ \vdots \\ E(X_{nt}|\Xi_{nt}) \end{bmatrix}, \tag{2.80}$$

where Ξ_{it} represents the information set available for formulating expectations over the ith element of X_t. Thus systems involving this form of heterogeneity may be accommodated using an expansion of the system (2.67)–(2.68) specified for a representative agent. The solution of the expanded system proceeds as indicated above; for details and extensions, see Christiano (2002).

Exercise 2.4

Apply Uhlig's code to the example model presented in (2.10)–(2.14).

We conclude by repeating our acknowledgement that there are alternatives to the approaches to model approximation and solution presented in this chapter. Those interested in exploring alternatives at this point may wish to jump to chapter 10. There, we present three leading alternatives: projection methods, value-function iterations, and policy-function iterations. Each yields a nonlinear approximation of the model under investigation.

Chapter 3

Removing Trends and Isolating Cycles

JUST AS DSGE MODELS must be primed for empirical analysis, so too must the corresponding data. Broadly speaking, data preparation involves three steps. A guiding principle behind all three involves the symmetric treatment of the actual data and their theoretical counterparts. First, correspondence must be established between what is being characterized by the model and what is being measured in the data. For example, if the focus is on a business cycle model that does not include a government sector, it would not be appropriate to align the model's characterization of output with the measure of aggregate GDP reported in the National Income and Product Accounts. The collection of papers in Cooley (1995) provide a good set of examples for dealing with this issue, and do so for a broad range of models.

The second and third steps involve the removal of trends and the isolation of cycles. Regarding the former, model solutions are typically in terms of stationary versions of variables: the stochastic behavior of the variables is in the form of temporary departures from steady state values. Corresponding data are represented analogously. So again using a business cycle model as an example, if the model is designed to characterize the cyclical behavior of a set of time series, and the time series exhibit both trends and cycles, the trends are eliminated prior to analysis. In such cases, it is often useful to build both trend and cyclical behavior into the model, and eliminate trends from the model and actual data in parallel fashion. Indeed, a typical objective in the business cycle literature is to determine whether models capable of capturing salient features of economic growth can also account for observed patterns of business cycle activity. Under this objective, the specification of the model is subject to the constraint that it must successfully characterize trend behavior. Having satisfied the constraint, trends are eliminated appropriately and the analysis proceeds with an investigation of cyclical behavior. Steady states in this case are interpretable as the relative heights of trend lines.

Regarding the isolation of cycles, this is closely related to the removal of trends. Indeed, for a time series exhibiting cyclical deviations about a trend, the identification of the trend automatically serves to identify the cyclical deviations as well. However, even after the separation of trend from cycle is accomplished, additional steps may be necessary to isolate cycles by the frequency of their recurrence. Return again to the example of a business cycle model. By design, the model is intended to characterize patterns of fluctuations in the data that recur at business cycle frequencies: between approximately 6 and 40 quarters. It is not intended to characterize seasonal fluctuations. Yet unless additional steps are taken, the removal of the trend will leave such fluctuations intact, and their presence can have a detrimental impact on inferences involving business cycle behavior. (For an example of a model designed to jointly characterize both cyclical and seasonal variations in aggregate economic activity, see Wen, 2002.)

The isolation of cycles is also related to the task of aligning models with appropriate data, because the frequency with which data are measured in part determines their cyclical characteristics. For example, empirical analyses of economic growth typically involve measurements of variables averaged over long time spans (e.g., over half-decade intervals). This is because the models in question are not designed to characterize business cycle activity, and time aggregation at the five-year level is typically sufficient to eliminate the influence of cyclical variations while retaining relevant information regarding long-term growth. For related reasons, analyses of aggregate asset-pricing behavior are typically conducted using annual data, which mitigates the need to control, for example, for seasonal fluctuations. Analyses of business cycle behavior are typically conducted using quarterly data. Measurement at this frequency is not ideal, because it introduces the influence of seasonal fluctuations into the analysis; but on the other hand, aggregation to an annual frequency would entail an important loss of information regarding fluctuations observed at business cycle frequencies. Thus an alternative to time aggregation is needed to isolate cycles in this case.

This chapter presents alternative approaches available for eliminating trends and isolating cycles. Supplements to the brief coverage of these topics provided here are available from any number of texts devoted to time series analysis (e.g., Harvey, 1993; Hamilton, 1994). Specific textbook coverage of cycle isolation in the context of macroeconomic applications is provided by Sargent (1987a) and Kaiser and Maravall (2001).

To illustrate the concepts introduced in this chapter, we work with a prototypical data set used to analyze business cycle behavior. It is designed for alignment with the real business cycle model introduced in chapter 5. The data are contained in the text file `rbcdata.txt`, available for downloading at the textbook Web site. A description of the data is contained in an accompanying file. Briefly, the data set consists of four time series: consumption of nondurables and services; gross private domestic investment; output, measured as the sum of consumption and investment; and hours of labor supplied in the nonfarm business sector. Each variable is real, measured in per capita terms, and is seasonally adjusted. The data are quarterly, and span 1948:I through 2004:IV. In addition, we also work with the nonseasonally adjusted counterpart to consumption. Logged time series trajectories of the seasonally adjusted data are illustrated in figure 3.1.

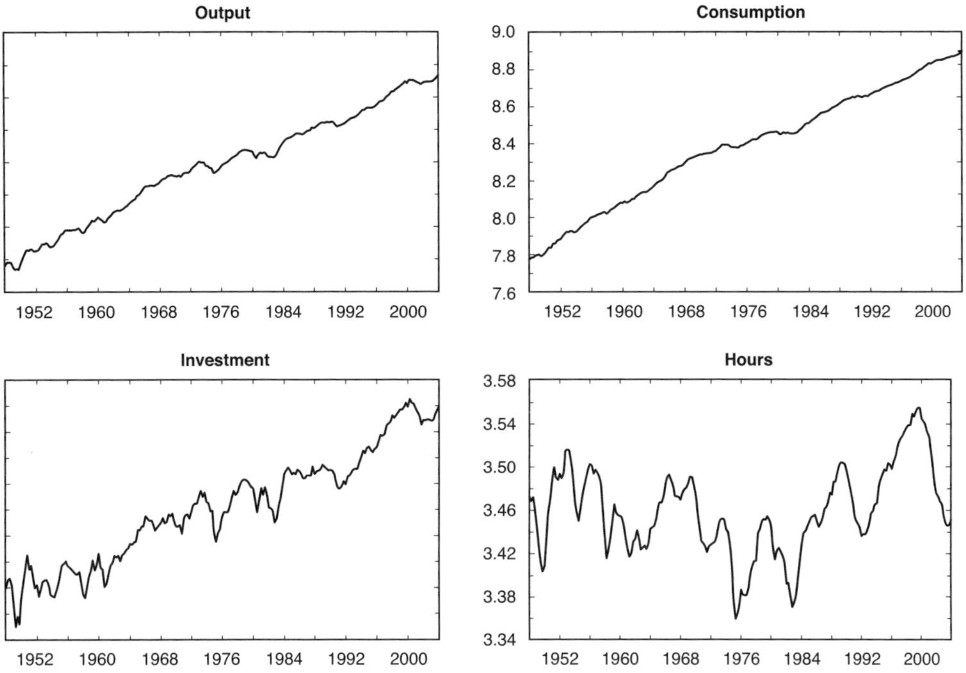

Figure 3.1 Business cycle data.

3.1 Removing Trends

There are three leading approaches to removing trends from macroeconomic time series. The goal under all three is to transform the data into mean-zero covariance stationary stochastic processes (CSSPs). By definition, such processes have time-invariant second moments; therefore, sample averages may be used to estimate population averages of these moments, and functions thereof. Trend removal is not sufficient to induce covariance stationarity, but is of first-order importance.

Before describing the three approaches, we note that it is common to work with logged versions of data represented in levels (e.g., as in figure 3.1). This is because changes in the log of a variable y_t over time represent the growth rate of the variable:

$$\frac{\partial}{\partial t}\log y_t = \frac{\frac{\partial}{\partial t}y_t}{y_t} \equiv \frac{\dot{y}_t}{y_t} \equiv g_{y_t}, \tag{3.1}$$

where $\dot{y}_t = \frac{\partial}{\partial t}y_t$. In addition, when using log-linear approximations to represent the corresponding structural model, working with logged versions of levels of the data provides symmetric treatment of both sets of variables.

The first two approaches to trend removal, detrending and differencing, are conducted under the implicit assumption that the data follow roughly constant growth rates. Detrending proceeds under the assumption that the level of y_t obeys

$$y_t = y_0(1+g_y)^t e^{u_t}, \qquad u_t \sim CSSP. \tag{3.2}$$

Then taking logs,

$$\log y_t = \log y_0 + g_y t + u_t, \tag{3.3}$$

where $\log(1+g_y)$ is approximated as g_y. Trend removal is accomplished by fitting a linear trend to $\log y_t$ using an ordinary least squares (OLS) regression, and subtracting the estimated trend:

$$\widetilde{y}_t = \log y_t - \widehat{\alpha}_0 - \widehat{\alpha}_1 t = \widehat{u}_t, \tag{3.4}$$

where the $\widehat{\alpha}'s$ are coefficient estimates. In this case, $\log y_t$ is said to be trend stationary.

In working with a set of m variables characterized by the corresponding model as sharing a common trend component (i.e., exhibiting balanced growth), symmetry dictates the removal of a common trend from all variables. Defining α_1^j as the trend coefficient associated with variable j, this is accomplished via the imposition of the linear restrictions

$$\alpha_1^1 - \alpha_1^j = 0, \qquad j = 2, \ldots, m,$$

easily imposed in an OLS estimation framework.[1]

Differencing proceeds under the assumption that y_t obeys

$$y_t = y_0 e^{\varepsilon_t}, \tag{3.5}$$

$$\varepsilon_t = \gamma + \varepsilon_{t-1} + u_t, \qquad u_t \sim CSSP. \tag{3.6}$$

Note from (3.6) that iterative substitution for $\varepsilon_{t-1}, \varepsilon_{t-2}, \ldots,$ yields an expression for ε_t of the form

$$\varepsilon_t = \gamma t + \sum_{j=0}^{t-1} u_{t-j} + \varepsilon_0, \tag{3.7}$$

and thus the growth rate of y_t is given by γ. From (3.5),

$$\log y_t = \log y_0 + \varepsilon_t. \tag{3.8}$$

Thus the first difference of $\log y_t$, given by

$$\log y_t - \log y_{t-1} \equiv (1-L)\log y_t,$$

[1] The GAUSS procedure `ct.prc`, available at the textbook Web site, serves this purpose.

where the lag operator L is defined such that $L^p y_t = y_{t-p}$, is stationary:

$$\log y_t - \log y_{t-1} = \varepsilon_t - \varepsilon_{t-1} \qquad (3.9)$$
$$= \gamma + u_t.$$

In this case, $\log y_t$ is said to be difference stationary. Estimating γ using the sample average of $\log y_t - \log y_{t-1}$ yields the desired transformation of y_t:

$$\widetilde{y}_t = \log y_t - \log y_{t-1} - \widehat{\gamma} = \widehat{u}_t. \qquad (3.10)$$

Once again, a common growth rate may be imposed across a set of variables via restricted OLS by estimating $\widehat{\gamma}^j$ subject to the restriction[2]

$$\widehat{\gamma}^1 - \widehat{\gamma}^j = 0, \qquad j = 2, \ldots, m. \qquad (3.11)$$

The choice between detrending versus differencing hinges on assumptions regarding whether (3.3) or (3.9) provides a more appropriate representation for $\log y_t$. Nelson and Plosser (1982) initiated an intense debate regarding this issue, and despite the large literature that has followed, the issue has proven difficult to resolve. (For overviews of this literature, see, e.g., DeJong and Whiteman, 1993; and Stock, 1994.) A remedy for this difficulty is to work with both specifications in turn, and evaluate the sensitivity of results to the chosen specification.

As figure 3.2 illustrates, the choice of either specification is problematic in the present empirical context, because the data do not appear to follow a constant average growth rate throughout the sample period. The figure depicts the logged variables, along with fitted trends estimated for consumption, investment, and output (subject to the common-trend restriction). A trend was not fitted to hours, which as expected, does not exhibit trend behavior.

As figure 3.2 indicates, consumption, investment, and output exhibit a distinct reduction in growth in approximately 1974, coinciding with the reduction in productivity observed during this period (for a recent discussion of this phenomenon, see Nordhaus, 2004). Note in particular the persistent tendency for consumption to lie above its estimated trend line over the first half of the sample period, and below its trend line during the second half of the period. This illustrates that if the series were truly trend stationary, but around a broken trend line, the detrended series will exhibit a spurious degree of persistence, tainting inferences regarding their cyclical behavior (see Perron, 1989 for a discussion of this issue). Likewise, the removal of a constant from first differences of the data will result in series that persistently lie above and below zero, also threatening to taint inferences regarding cyclicality.

[2] The GAUSS procedure `ct.prc` is also available for this purpose.

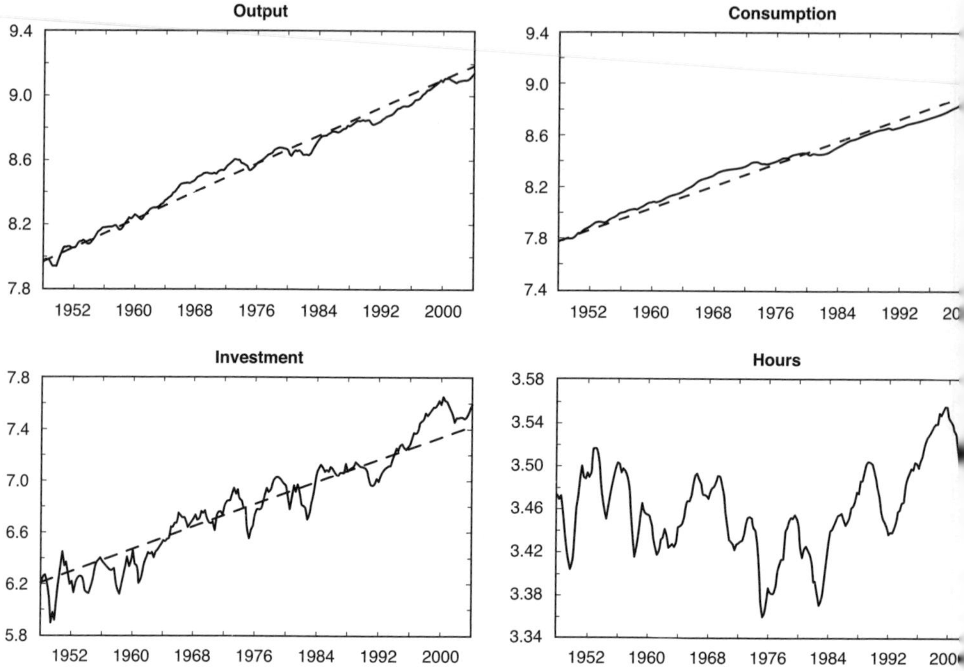

Figure 3.2 Logged trajectories and fitted trends.

The third approach to detrending involves the use of filters designed to separate trend from cycle, but given the admission of a slowly evolving trend. In this section we introduce the Hodrick-Prescott (H-P) filter, which has proven popular in business cycle applications. In section 3.2, we introduce a leading alternative to the H-P filter: the band pass filter.

Decomposing $\log y_t$ as

$$\log y_t = g_t + c_t, \tag{3.12}$$

where g_t denotes the growth component of $\log y_t$ and c_t denotes the cyclical component, the H-P filter estimates g_t and c_t in order to minimize

$$\sum_{t=1}^{T} c_t^2 + \lambda \sum_{t=3}^{T} [(1-L)^2 g_t]^2, \tag{3.13}$$

taking λ as given.[3] Trend removal is accomplished simply as

$$\widetilde{y}_t = \log y_t - \widehat{g}_t = \widehat{c}_t. \tag{3.14}$$

[3] The GAUSS procedure `hpfilter.prc` is available for this purpose.

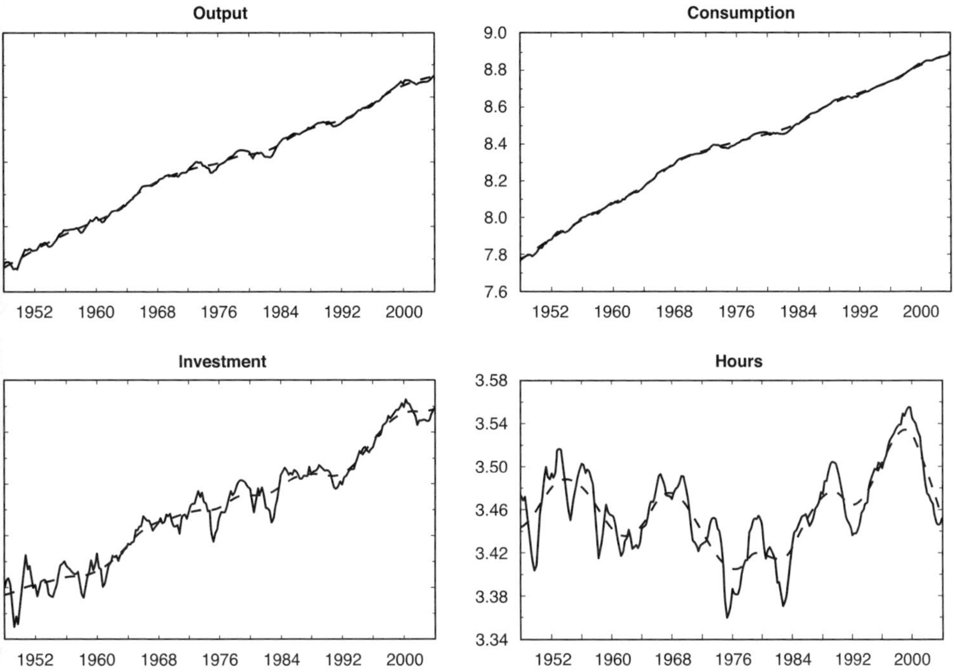

Figure 3.3 Logged trajectories and H-P trends.

The parameter λ in (3.13) determines the importance of having a smoothly evolving growth component: the smoother is g_t, the smaller will be its second difference. With $\lambda = 0$, smoothness receives no value, and all variation in $\log y_t$ will be assigned to the trend component. As $\lambda \to \infty$, the trend is assigned to be maximally smooth, that is, linear.

In general, λ is specified to strike a compromise between these two extremes. In working with business cycle data, the standard choice is $\lambda = 1,600$. To explain the logic behind this choice and what it accomplishes, it is necessary to venture into the frequency domain. Before doing so, we illustrate the trajectories of $\widehat{g_t}$ resulting from this specification for the example data, including hours. (In business cycle applications, it is conventional to apply the H-P filter to all series, absent a common-trend restriction.) These are presented in figure 3.3. The evolution of the estimated $\widehat{g_t}$'s serves to underscore the mid-1970s reduction in the growth rates of consumption, investment, and output discussed above.

The versions of detrended output $\widetilde{y}_t$ generated by these three trend-removal procedures are illustrated in figure 3.4. Most striking is the difference in volatility observed across the three measures: the standard deviation of the linearly detrended series is 0.046, compared with 0.010 for the

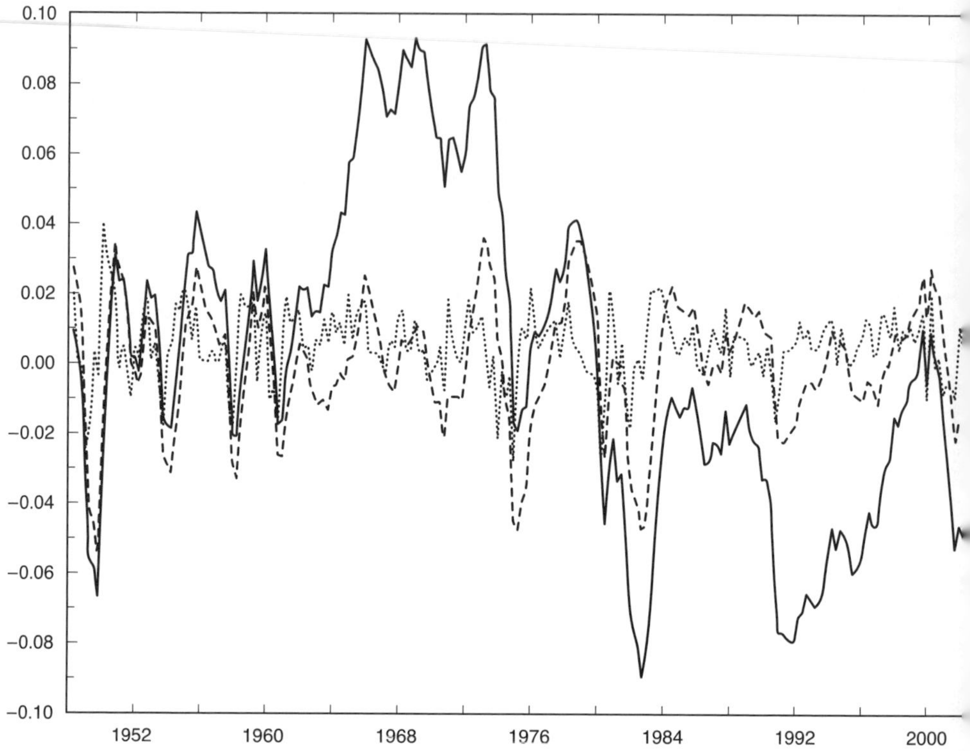

Figure 3.4 Detrended output. (Lin. Det.: solid; Diff'ed: Dots; H-P Filtered: Dashes)

differenced series and 0.018 for the H-P filtered series. The behavior of the linearly detrended series is dominated by the large and extended departure above zero observed during the mid-1960s through the mid-1970s, and the subsequent reversal at the end of the sample. This behavior provides an additional indication of the trend break observed for this series in the mid-1970s. The correlation between the linearly detrended and differenced series is only 0.12; the correlation between the linearly detrended and H-P filtered series is 0.49; and the correlation between the H-P filtered and differenced series is 0.27.

3.2 Isolating Cycles

3.2.1 Mathematical Background

In venturing into the frequency domain, background information on complex variables is useful. Brown and Churchill (2003) and Palka (1991) are good undergraduate and graduate textbook sources of background information. And as noted above, expanded textbook treatments on the isolation of cycles are available from Sargent (1987a), Harvey (1993), Hamilton (1994), and Kaiser and Maravall (2001).

To help keep this section relatively self-contained, here we briefly sketch some key points regarding complex variables. Let i be imaginary, so that

$$\sqrt{i} = -1.$$

A variable z is complex if it can be represented as

$$z = x + iy, \tag{3.15}$$

where x and y are real; x is referenced as the real component of z, and y as the imaginary component. This representation of z is in terms of rectangular coordinates. In a graphical depiction of z, with the real component of z depicted on the horizontal axis and the imaginary component depicted on the vertical axis, the distance of z from the origin is given by

$$\begin{aligned}\sqrt{x^2 + y^2} &= \sqrt{(x + iy)(x - iy)} \\ &\equiv |z|.\end{aligned} \tag{3.16}$$

In (3.16), $(x - iy)$ is known as the complex conjugate of z, and $|z|$ is known as the modulus of z. If $|z| = 1$, z is said to lie on the unit circle. See figure 3.5 for an illustration.

An additional representation of z is in polar coordinates. Let ω denote the radian angle of z in (x, y) space: that is, ω is the distance traveled counterclockwise along a circle starting on the x axis before reaching z (again, see figure 3.5 for an illustration). In terms of polar coordinates, z may be represented as

$$\begin{aligned}z &= |z|(\cos\omega + i\sin\omega) \\ &= |z|e^{i\omega},\end{aligned} \tag{3.17}$$

where the second equality may be derived by taking Taylor Series expansions of $\cos\omega$, $\sin\omega$, and $e^{i\omega}$ about 0 and matching terms. Using (3.17), we obtain DeMoivre's Theorem:

$$\begin{aligned}z^j &= |z|^j e^{i\omega j} \\ &= |z|^j(\cos\omega j + i\sin\omega j).\end{aligned} \tag{3.18}$$

In addition to DeMoivre's Theorem, another important result from complex analysis we shall reference below comes from the Riesz-Fischer

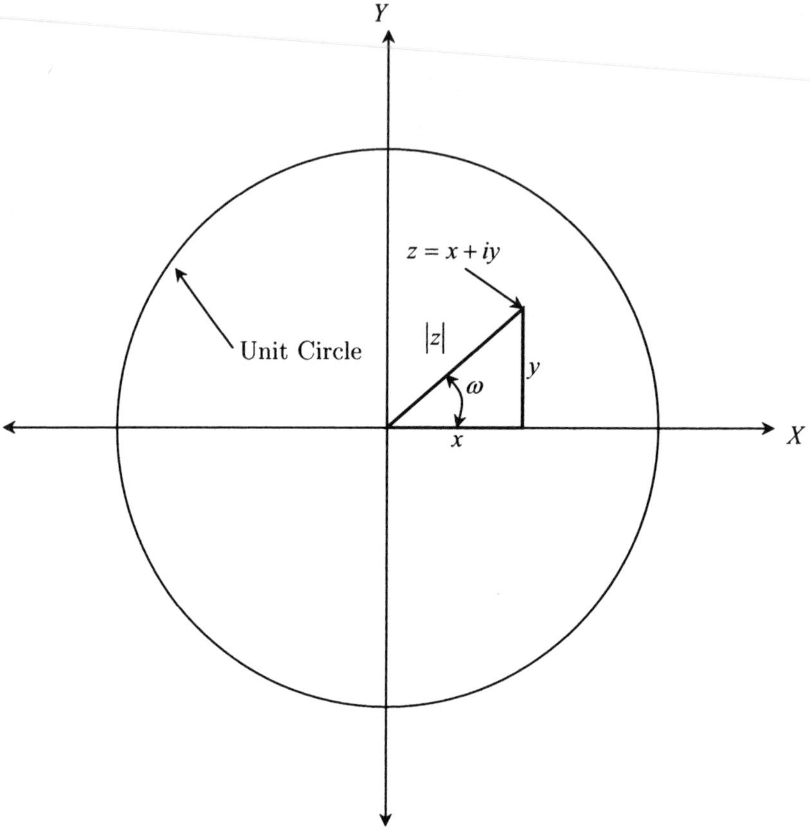

Figure 3.5 The unit circle.

Theorem, which we now sketch. For a sequence of complex numbers $\{a_j\}_{j=-\infty}^{\infty}$ that satisfy

$$\sum_{j=-\infty}^{\infty} |a_j|^2 < \infty, \tag{3.19}$$

known as a square-summability condition, there exists a complex function $f(\omega)$ such that

$$f(\omega) = \sum_{j=-\infty}^{\infty} a_j e^{-i\omega j}, \tag{3.20}$$

where $\omega \in [-\pi, \pi]$. Note from (3.17) that

$$e^{-i\omega} = (\cos\omega - i\sin\omega).$$

The construction of $f(\omega)$ from $\{a_j\}_{j=-\infty}^{\infty}$ is known as the Fourier transform of $\{a_j\}_{j=-\infty}^{\infty}$. Given $f(\omega)$, the elements of $\{a_j\}_{j=-\infty}^{\infty}$ can be recovered using the inversion formula

$$a_j = \frac{1}{2\pi} \int_{-\pi}^{\pi} f(\omega) e^{i\omega j} \, d\omega. \tag{3.21}$$

Finally, note that for any two functions $f(\omega)$ and $g(\omega)$, where

$$f(\omega) = \sum_{j=-\infty}^{\infty} a_j e^{-i\omega j}, \qquad g(\omega) = \sum_{j=-\infty}^{\infty} b_j e^{-i\omega j},$$

we have

$$f(\omega)+g(\omega) = \sum_{j=-\infty}^{\infty} (a_j + b_j) e^{-i\omega j};$$

$$\alpha f(\omega) = \sum_{j=-\infty}^{\infty} \alpha a_j e^{-i\omega j}.$$

This establishes that the Fourier transform of the sum of sequences is the sum of their Fourier transforms, and that the Fourier transform of $\{\alpha a_j\}_{j=-\infty}^{\infty}$ is α times the Fourier transform of $\{a_j\}_{j=-\infty}^{\infty}$.

3.2.2 *Cramér Representations*

Consider the behavior of a time series y_t^{ω} given by

$$y_t^{\omega} = \alpha(\omega)\cos(\omega t) + \beta(\omega)\sin(\omega t), \tag{3.22}$$

where $\alpha(\omega)$ and $\beta(\omega)$ are uncorrelated zero-mean random variables with equal variances. As above, ω is measured in radians; here it determines the frequency with which $\cos(\omega t)$ completes a cycle relative to $\cos(t)$ as t evolves from 0 to 2π, 2π to 4π, and so on (the frequency for $\cos(t)$ being 1). The upper panels of figure 3.6 depict $\cos(\omega t)$ and $\sin(\omega t)$ as t evolves from 0 to 2π for $\omega = 1$ and $\omega = 2$. Accordingly, given realizations for $\alpha(\omega)$ and $\beta(\omega)$, y_t^{ω} follows a deterministic cycle that is completed ω times as t ranges from 0 to 2π, and so on. This is depicted in the lower panels of figure 3.6, using $\alpha(\omega) = \beta(\omega) = 1$, $\omega = 1$ and $\omega = 2$.

Consider now the construction of a time series y_t obtained by combining a continuum of y_t^{ω}'s, differentiated by infinitessimal variations in ω over the interval $[0, \pi]$:

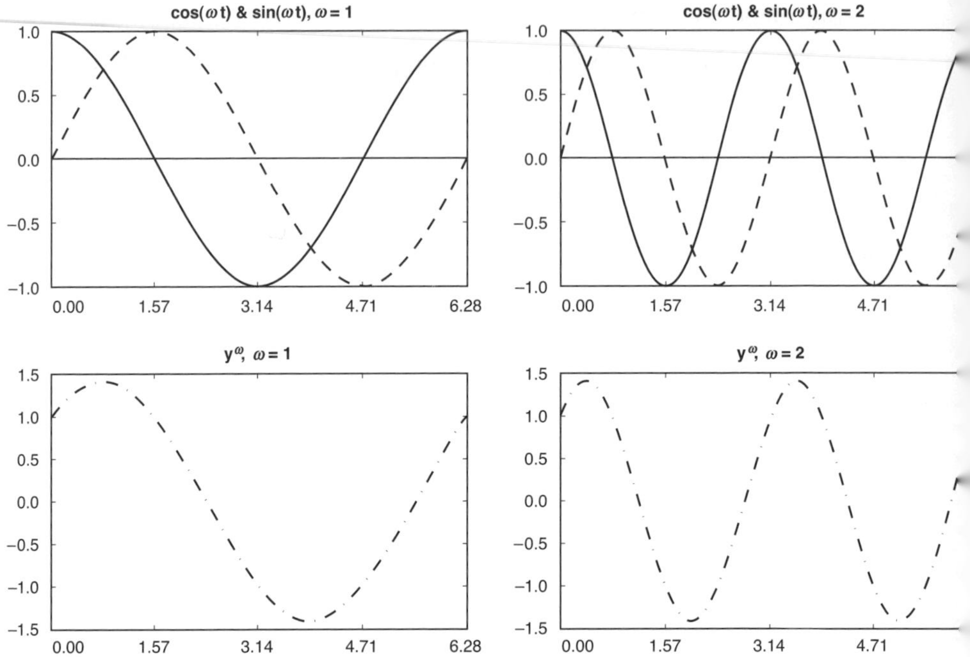

Figure 3.6 Evolution of $\cos(\omega t)$ (solid), $\sin(\omega t)$ (dashes), and y_t^{ω} (bottom panels).

$$y_t = \int_0^{\pi} \alpha(\omega)\cos(\omega t)d\omega + \int_0^{\pi} \beta(\omega)\sin(\omega t)d\omega. \tag{3.23}$$

(The symmetry of $\cos(\omega t)$ and $\sin(\omega t)$ between $t \in [0, \pi]$ and $t \in [\pi, 2\pi]$ renders the latter range as redundant.) Given appropriate specifications for $\alpha(\omega)$ and $\beta(\omega)$, any time series y_t may be represented in this manner. This is referred to as the spectral representation, or Cramér representation, of y_t. It represents y_t as resulting from the combined influence of a continuum of cyclical components differing by the frequency with which they complete their cycles.

3.2.3 Spectra

Closely related to the spectral representation of y_t is its spectrum. This is a tool that measures the contribution to the overall variance of y_t made by the cyclical components y_t^{ω} over the continuum $[0, \pi]$. Specifically, the spectrum is a decomposition of the variance of y_t by frequency.

To explain why, let $\gamma(\tau)$ denote the autocovariance between y_t and $y_{t+\tau}$ (or equivalently, between y_t and $y_{t-\tau}$):

$$\gamma(\tau) = E(y_t - \mu_t)(y_{t+\tau} - \mu_{t+\tau}), \qquad E(y_t) = \mu_t.$$

Note that $\gamma(0)$ denotes the variance of y_t. So long as the sequence $\{\gamma(\tau)\}_{\tau=-\infty}^{\infty}$ is square-summable, by the Riesz-Fischer Theorem, we may calculate its Fourier transform:

$$f_y(\omega) = \sum_{\tau=-\infty}^{\infty} \gamma(\tau) e^{-i\omega\tau}. \tag{3.24}$$

Moreover, by the inversion formula,

$$\gamma(\tau) = \frac{1}{2\pi} \int_{-\pi}^{\pi} f_y(\omega) e^{i\omega\tau} d\omega. \tag{3.25}$$

The power spectrum of y_t (spectrum hereafter) is defined as

$$s_y(\omega) = \frac{1}{2\pi} f_y(\omega). \tag{3.26}$$

From (3.25) and (3.26), note the sense in which the spectrum can be viewed as a decomposition of the variance of y_t by frequency: setting $\tau = 0$, the integral of $s_y(\omega)$ over the range $[-\pi, \pi]$ yields $\gamma(0)$, and comparisons of the height of $s_y(\omega)$ for alternative values of ω indicate the relative importance of fluctuations at the chosen frequencies in influencing variations in y_t.

For an alternative representation of the spectrum, note that DeMoivre's Theorem allows us to rewrite $e^{-i\omega\tau}$ as $(\cos\omega\tau - i\sin\omega\tau)$. Thus combining (3.24) and (3.26), we obtain

$$s_y(\omega) = \frac{1}{2\pi} \sum_{\tau=-\infty}^{\infty} \gamma(\tau)(\cos\omega\tau - i\sin\omega\tau). \tag{3.27}$$

Moreover, since $\gamma(\tau) = \gamma(-\tau)$, $\cos(0) = 1$, $\sin(0) = 0$, $\sin(-\omega) = -\sin\omega$, and $\cos(-\omega) = \cos\omega$, (3.27) simplifies to

$$s_y(\omega) = \left(\frac{1}{2\pi}\right)\left[\gamma(0) + 2\sum_{\tau=1}^{\infty}\gamma(\tau)\cos(\omega\tau)\right]. \tag{3.28}$$

Because $\cos(\omega\tau)$ is symmetric over $[-\pi, 0]$ and $[0, \pi]$, so too is $s(\omega)$; thus it is customary to represent $s_y(\omega)$ over $[0, \pi]$.

To obtain an interpretation for frequency in terms of units of time rather than radians, it is useful to relate ω to its associated period p, defined as the number of units of time necessary for y_t^ω in (3.22) to complete a cycle: $p = 2\pi/\omega$. In turn, $1/p = \omega/2\pi$ indicates the number of cycles completed by y_t^ω per period. For example, with a period representing a quarter, a 10-year or 40-quarter cycle has an associated value of ω of $2\pi/40 = 0.157$. For a 6-quarter cycle, $\omega = 2\pi/6 = 1.047$. Thus values for ω in the range $[0.157, 1.047]$ are of central interest in analyzing business cycle behavior.

3.2.4 Using Filters to Isolate Cycles

Returning to the problem of trend removal, it is useful to think of a slowly evolving trend as a cycle with very low frequency; in the case of a constant trend, the associated frequency is zero. Filters are tools designed to eliminate the influence of cyclical variation at various frequencies. Detrending filters such as the first-difference and H-P filters target low frequencies; seasonal filters target seasonal frequencies; etc.

The general form of a linear filter applied to y_t, producing y_t^f, is given by

$$y_t^f = \sum_{j=-r}^{s} c_j y_{t-j} \equiv C(L) y_t. \tag{3.29}$$

In other words, the filtered series y_t^f is a linear combination of the original series y_t. In the frequency domain, the counterpart to $C(L)$ is obtained by replacing L^j with $e^{-i\omega j}$. The result is the frequency response function: $C(e^{-i\omega})$.

To gain an appreciation for how the filter works to isolate cycles, it is useful to derive the spectrum of y_t^f; here we do so following Sargent (1987a). Suppose $\{y_t\}$ is a mean-zero process with autocovariance sequence $\{\gamma(\tau)\}_{\tau=-\infty}^{\infty}$. The autocovariance between y_t^f and $y_{t-\tau}^f$ is given by

$$\begin{aligned}
E\left(y_t^f y_{t-\tau}^f\right) &= E\left(\sum_{j=-r}^{s} c_j y_{t-j}\right)\left(\sum_{k=-r}^{s} c_k\, y_{t-k-\tau}\right) \\
&= E\sum_{j=-r}^{s}\sum_{k=-r}^{s} c_j c_k y_{t-j} y_{t-k-\tau} \\
&= \sum_{j=-r}^{s}\sum_{k=-r}^{s} c_j\, c_k \gamma(\tau + k - j) \\
&\equiv \gamma_{y^f}(\tau).
\end{aligned} \tag{3.30}$$

Taking the Fourier transform of $\gamma_{yf}(\tau)$, the spectrum of y_t^f is given by

$$\begin{aligned} s_{yf}(\omega) &= \frac{1}{2\pi}\sum_{\tau=-\infty}^{\infty}\gamma_{yf}(\tau)e^{-i\omega\tau} \\ &= \frac{1}{2\pi}\sum_{\tau=-\infty}^{\infty}\sum_{j=-r}^{s}\sum_{k=-r}^{s}c_j c_k \gamma(\tau+k-j)e^{-i\omega\tau}. \end{aligned} \tag{3.31}$$

Let $h = \tau + k - j$, and re-write $e^{-i\omega\tau}$ in (3.31) as

$$\begin{aligned} e^{-i\omega\tau} &= e^{-i\omega(h+j-k)} \\ &= e^{-i\omega h}e^{-i\omega j}e^{i\omega k}. \end{aligned} \tag{3.32}$$

Finally, substituting for $e^{-i\omega\tau}$ in (3.31) using (3.32), we obtain

$$\begin{aligned} s_{yf}(\omega) &= \frac{1}{2\pi}\sum_{j=-r}^{s}c_j e^{-i\omega j}\sum_{k=-r}^{s}c_k e^{i\omega k}\sum_{h=-\infty}^{\infty}\gamma(h)e^{-i\omega h} \\ &= \sum_{j=-r}^{s}c_j e^{-i\omega j}\sum_{k=-r}^{s}c_k e^{i\omega k}s_y(\omega) \\ &= C(e^{-i\omega})C(e^{i\omega})s_y(\omega), \end{aligned} \tag{3.33}$$

where the second equality stems from the definition of $s_y(\omega)$.

Before interpreting this expression, we introduce the gain function:

$$G(\omega) = |C(e^{-i\omega})|, \tag{3.34}$$

where $|C(e^{-i\omega})|$ denotes the modulus of $C(e^{-i\omega})$:

$$|C(e^{-i\omega})| = \sqrt{C(e^{-i\omega})C(e^{i\omega})}. \tag{3.35}$$

For example, for the first-difference filter $(1 - L)$, the gain function is given by

$$\begin{aligned} G(\omega) &= \sqrt{(1-e^{-i\omega})(1-e^{i\omega})} \\ &= \sqrt{2}\sqrt{1-\cos(\omega)}, \end{aligned} \tag{3.36}$$

where the second equality follows from the identity

$$e^{-i\omega} + e^{i\omega} = 2\cos(\omega). \tag{3.37}$$

Given the definition of the gain function, the relationship between $s_{y^f}(\omega)$ and $s_y(\omega)$ in (3.33) can be written as

$$\begin{aligned} s_{y^f}(\omega) &= |C(e^{-i\omega})|^2 s_y(\omega) \\ &\equiv G(\omega)^2 s_y(\omega), \end{aligned} \tag{3.38}$$

where $G(\omega)^2$ is referred to as the squared gain of the filter. This relationship illustrates how filters serve to isolate cycles: they attenuate or amplify the spectrum of the original series on a frequency-by-frequency basis. For example, note from (3.36) that the first-difference filter $(1 - L)$ shuts down cycles of frequency zero.

3.2.5 The Hodrick-Prescott Filter

Regarding the H-P filter, the specification of λ determines the division of the influence of y_t^{ω} on y_t between g_t and c_t in (3.12). Following Kaiser and Maravall (2001), its gain function is given by

$$G(\omega) = \left[1 + \left(\frac{\sin(\omega/2)}{\sin(\omega_0/2)}\right)^4\right]^{-1}, \tag{3.39}$$

where

$$\omega_0 = 2 \arcsin\left(\frac{1}{2\lambda^{1/4}}\right). \tag{3.40}$$

The parameter ω_0, selected through the specification of λ, determines the frequency at which $G(\omega) = 0.5$, or at which 50% of the filter gain has been completed. The specification $\lambda = 1,600$ for quarterly data implies 50% completion at a 40-quarter cycle. The choice of $\lambda = 400$ moves the 50% completion point to a 20-quarter cycle, and $\lambda = 6,400$ to a 56-quarter cycle.

Squared gains $G(\omega)^2$ associated with the first-difference and H-P filter (for the choices of λ highlighted above) are illustrated in figure 3.7. In all cases, the filters shut down zero-frequency fluctuations, and rise monotonically with frequency (reported hereafter in terms of cycles per quarter: $\omega/2\pi$).

Although the first-difference and H-P filters are capable of eliminating trends, they are not designed to eliminate seasonal fluctuations. For quarterly data, seasonal frequencies correspond with 1/4 and 1/2 cycles per quarter, and the squared gains associated with each of these filters are positive at these values. As noted, business cycle models are typically not

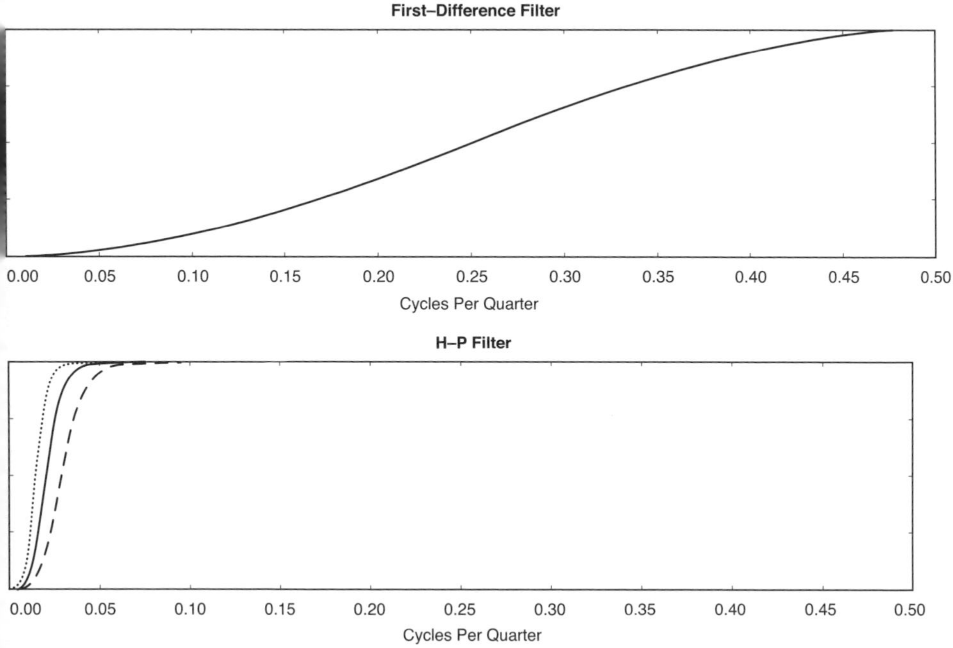

Figure 3.7 Squared gains of the first-difference and H-P filters. (Bottom Panel: $\lambda = 6,400$: Dots; $\lambda = 1,600$: Solid; $\lambda = 400$: Dashes)

designed to explain seasonal variation, thus it is desirable to work with variables that have had seasonal variations eliminated.

3.2.6 Seasonal Adjustment

As with the example analyzed above, it is most often the case that aggregate variables are reported in seasonally adjusted (SA) form. Seasonal adjustment is typically achieved using the so-called X-11 filter (as characterized, e.g., by Bell and Monsell, 1992). So typically, seasonal adjustment is not an issue of concern in the preliminary stages of an empirical analysis. However, it is useful to consider this issue in order to appreciate the importance of the seasonal adjustment step; the issue also serves to motivate the introduction of the band pass filter, which provides an important alternative to the H-P filter.

As an illustration of the importance of seasonal adjustment, figure 3.8 presents the consumption series discussed above, along with its nonseasonally adjusted (NSA) counterpart (including H-P trends for both). Trend behavior dominates both series, but the recurrent seasonal spikes associated

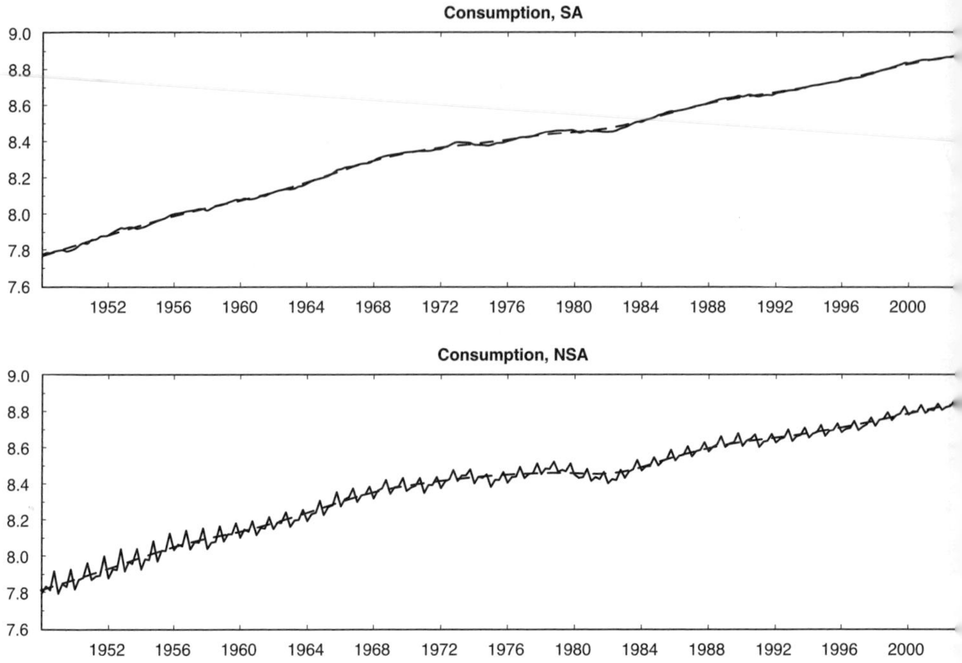

Figure 3.8 Seasonally adjusted and non–seasonally adjusted consumption.

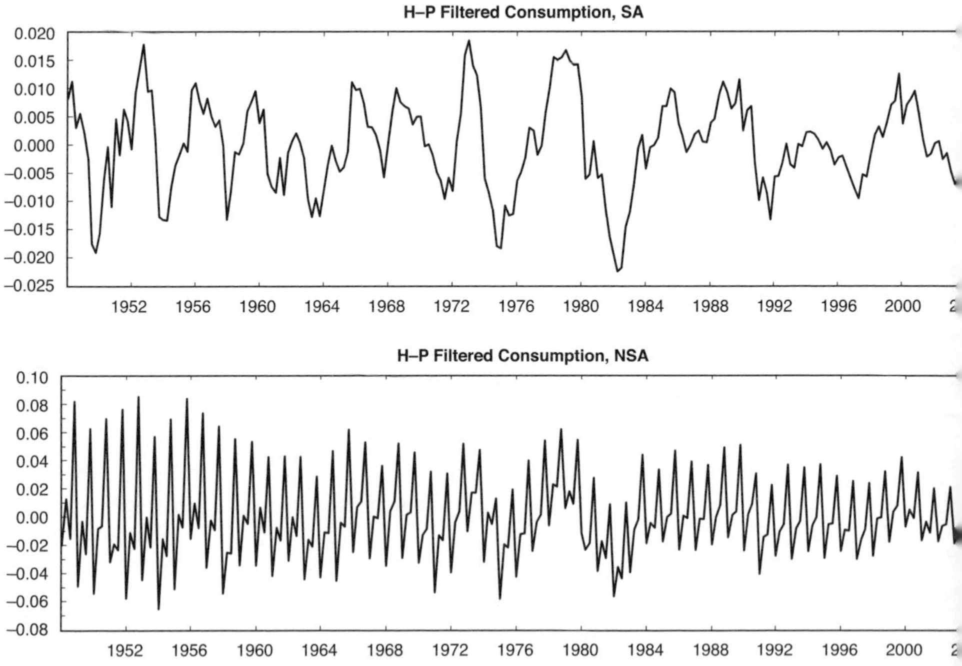

Figure 3.9 H-P filtered consumption.

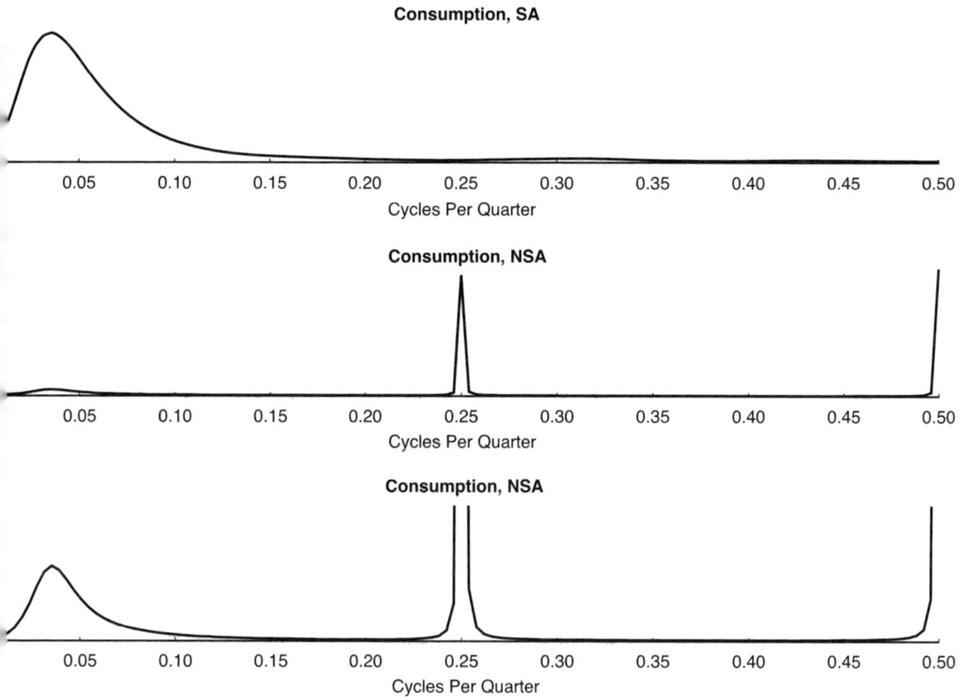

Figure 3.10 Spectra of H-P filtered consumption. (Note: The third panel zooms in on the middle panel.)

with the NSA series are distinctly apparent. The spikes are even more apparent in figure 3.9, which presents the H-P filtered series.

Figure 3.10 presents spectra estimated for both versions of the H-P filtered data (chapter 4, section 4.2 presents methods for estimating spectra). The bottom panel of the figure truncates the seasonal spikes associated with the spectrum of the NSA series to better illustrate the extent to which the seasonal fluctuations dominate the contribution of business cycle fluctuations to the overall variance of the series (recall that business cycle fluctuations lie roughly between 1/40 and 1/6 cycles per quarter).

3.2.7 Band Pass Filters

We turn now to the band pass (B-P) filter. This is a filter designed to shut down all fluctuations outside of a chosen frequency band. Given an interest in cycles with periods between p_l and p_u (again, roughly between 6 and 40 quarters in business cycle applications), the ideal B-P filter has a squared gain that satisfies

$$G(\omega)^2 = \begin{Bmatrix} 1, & \omega \in [2\pi/p_u, 2\pi/p_l] \\ 0, & otherwise. \end{Bmatrix} \tag{3.41}$$

As (3.42) below indicates, it is not feasible to implement the ideal B-P filter, because doing so requires as input an infinite number of observations of the unfiltered series. However, several approaches to estimating approximate B-P filters have been proposed. Here, we present the approach developed by Baxter and King (1999); for alternatives, for example, see Woitek (1998) and Christiano and Fitzgerald (1999).[4]

Let the ideal symmetric B-P filter for a chosen frequency range be given by

$$\alpha(L) = \sum_{j=-\infty}^{\infty} \alpha_j L^j, \tag{3.42}$$

where symmetry implies $\alpha_{-j} = \alpha_j \, \forall j$. This is an important property for filters because it avoids inducing what is known as a phase effect. Under a phase effect, the timing of events between the unfiltered and filtered series, such as the timing of business cycle turning points, will be altered. The Fourier transformation of a symmetric filter has a very simple form. In the present case,

$$\begin{aligned} \alpha(e^{-i\omega}) \equiv \alpha(\omega) &= \sum_{j=-\infty}^{\infty} \alpha_j e^{-i\omega j} \\ &= \alpha_0 + \sum_{j=1}^{\infty} \alpha_j (e^{-i\omega j} + e^{i\omega j}) \\ &= \alpha_0 + 2\sum_{j=1}^{\infty} \alpha_j \cos(\omega), \end{aligned} \tag{3.43}$$

where the second equality follows from symmetry and the last equality results from (3.37).

Baxter and King's approximation to $\alpha(\omega)$ is given by the symmetric, finite-ordered filter

$$A(\omega) = a_0 + 2\sum_{j=1}^{K} a_j \cos(\omega), \tag{3.44}$$

[4] The collection of GAUSS procedures contained in `bp.src` are available for constructing Baxter and King's B-P filter.

where

$$A(0) = \sum_{j=-K}^{K} a_j = 0,$$

insuring that $A(\omega)$ is capable of removing a trend from the unfiltered series (see their Appendix A for details). $A(\omega)$ is chosen to solve

$$\min_{a_j} \int_{-\pi}^{\pi} |\alpha(\omega) - A(\omega)|^2 d\omega \qquad \text{subject to } A(0) = 0; \tag{3.45}$$

that is, $A(\omega)$ minimizes departures from $\alpha(\omega)$ (measured in squared-error sense) accumulated over frequencies. The solution to this objective is given by

$$a_j = \alpha_j + \theta, \qquad j = -K, \ldots, K;$$

$$\alpha_j = \left\{ \begin{array}{ll} \frac{\omega_u - \omega_l}{\pi}, & j = 0 \\ \frac{\sin(\omega_2 j) - \sin(\omega_1 j)}{\pi j} & j = \pm 1, \ldots, K; \end{array} \right\}$$

$$\theta = \frac{-\sum_{j=-K}^{K} \alpha_j}{2K+1}, \tag{3.46}$$

where $\omega_l = 2\pi/p_u$ and $\omega_u = 2\pi/p_l$.

Baxter and King propose the selection of $K = 12$ in working with quarterly data, entailing the loss of 12 filtered observations at the beginning and end of the sample period. Figure 3.11 illustrates the squared gains associated with the ideal and approximated B-P filters constructed over the 1/40 and 1/6 cycles per quarter range.

Application of the B-P filter constructed using $K = 12$ to the SA and NSA consumption data produces the smoothed series illustrated in figure 3.12. The series exhibit close correspondence, with no discernible trends or seasonal variations. The spectra estimated for these series, illustrated in figure 3.13, confirm the absence of both influences on the variations in the series.

3.3 Spuriousness

We conclude this chapter with some words of caution. The common presence of trends in macroeconomic time series requires the completion of a preliminary trend-removal step in most empirical applications. But because it is difficult to convincingly establish the precise nature of the driving process that gives rise to trend behavior, and the separation of trend from cycle

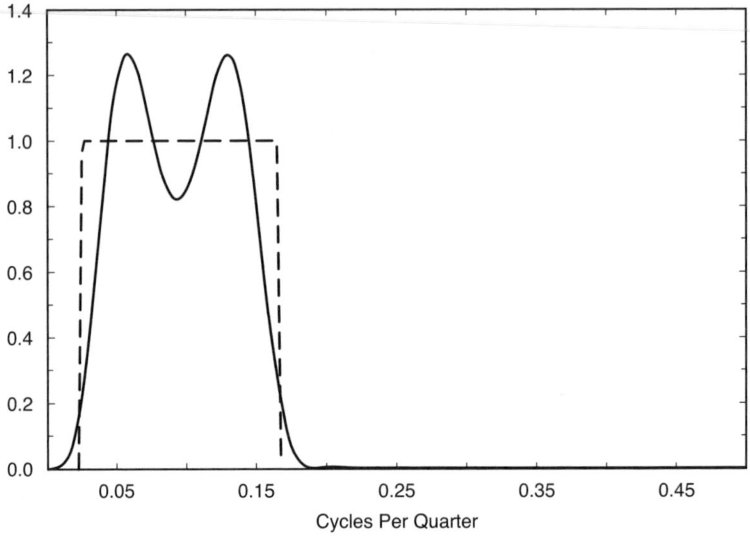

Figure 3.11 Squared gains of band pass filter and optimal filter. (fB-P filter: solid; Optimal filter: Dashes)

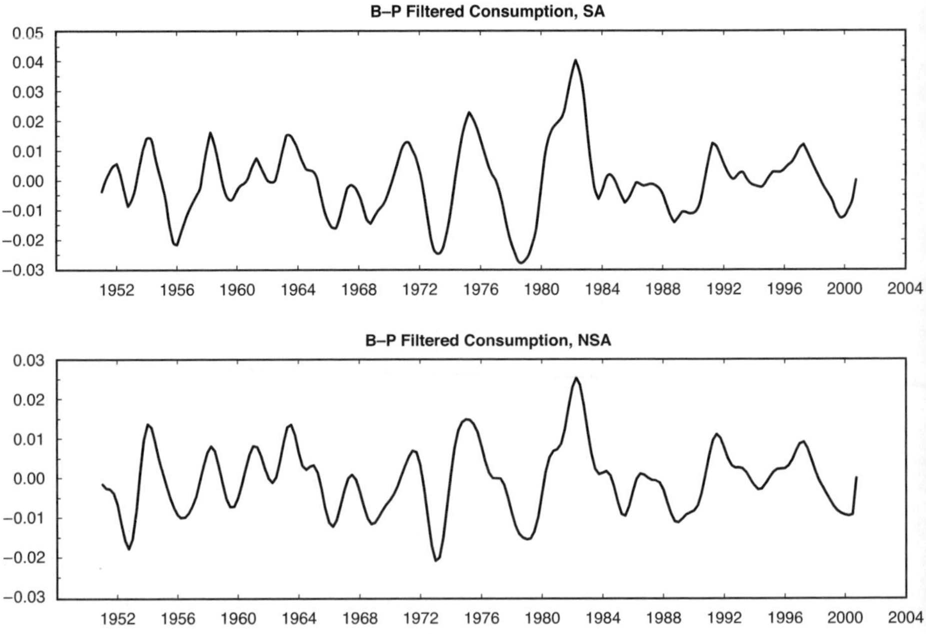

Figure 3.12 B-P filtered consumption.

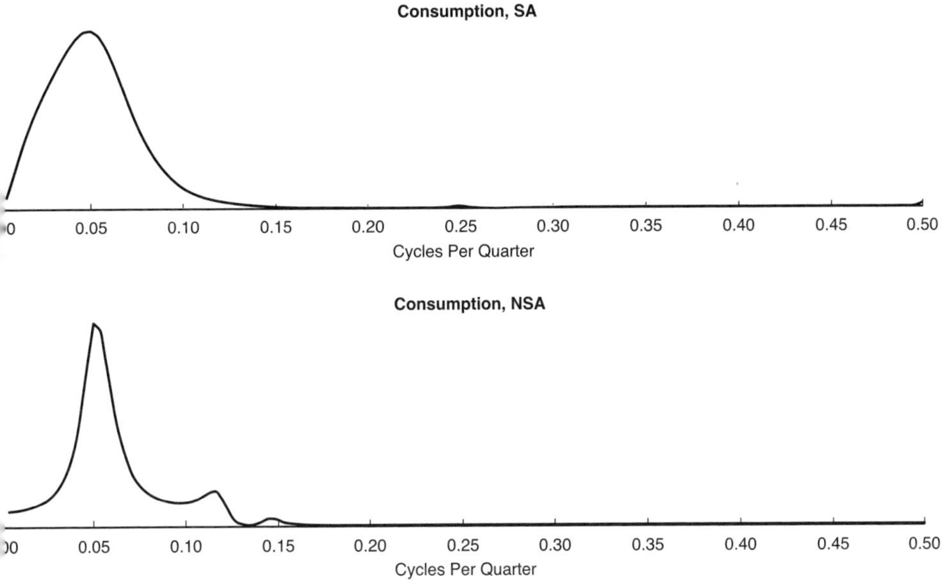

Figure 3.13 Spectra of B-P filtered consumption.

can also pose challenges, it is difficult to insure that appropriate steps have been taken in this preliminary stage. Unfortunately, this is an important issue due to a common problem involving spurious stochastic behavior.

In general, spuriousness is used to characterize situations in which the stochastic behavior of a filtered variable differs systematically from its unfiltered counterpart along the dimension of original interest in the empirical analysis. Of course, the stochastic behavior of the two series will differ in general, but for example, if the removal of a trend induces systematic differences in the business cycle properties of filtered variables, spuriousness is said to have been induced.

Spuriousness can arise both in removing trends and isolating cycles. Regarding the latter, consider the extreme but illustrative case in which an H-P or B-P filter is applied to a collection of zero-mean serially uncorrelated CSSPs. Such CSSPs are referred to as white noise: their spectra are uniform. In this case, spectra of the filtered series will identically assume the shape of the squared gains of the filters, and thus the filtered series will exhibit spurious cyclical behavior. Harvey and Jaeger (1993) provide an analysis of spurious behavior arising from H-P filtered data.

Regarding trend removal, we have seen that the removal of fixed trends from the levels of series that have evidently undergone trend breaks can induce considerable persistence in the detrended series. So even if the underlying data were trend-stationary, the application of a fixed trend specification in this case would induce undue persistence in the detrended series. Moreover, as noted, it is difficult to distinguish between trend- and difference-stationary specifications even given the ideal case of constant average growth over the sample period. And as shown by Chan, Hayya, and Ord (1977) and Nelson and Kang (1981), both the removal of a deterministic trend from a difference-stationary specification and the application of the difference operator $(1 - L)$ to a trend-stationary process induces spurious autocorrelation in the resulting series. Similarly, Cogley and Nason (1995) and Murray (2003) illustrate spuriousness arising from the application of the H-P and B-P filters to nonstationary data.

Having painted this bleak picture, we conclude by noting that steps are available for helping to mitigate these problems. For example, regarding the trend- versus difference-stationarity issue, although it is typically difficult to reject either specification in applications of classical hypothesis tests to macroeconomic time series, it is possible to obtain conditional inferences regarding their relative plausibility using Bayesian methods. Such inferences can be informative in many instances. (See DeJong and Whiteman, 1991a,b, for examples in macroeconomic applications; and Phillips, 1991, for skepticism. Tools for implementing Bayesian methods in general are presented in chapter 9.) And the use of alternative filtering methods in a given application is a useful way to investigate the robustness of inferences to steps taken in this preliminary stage.

Chapter 4

Summarizing Time Series Behavior

The sign of a truly educated man is to be deeply moved by statistics.
—George Bernard Shaw

THIS CHAPTER OPENS WITH the assumption that both the model- and data-preparation stages characterized in chapters 2 and 3 have been completed successfully. Completion of the model-preparation stage implies that the structural model under investigation is written as

$$x_t = F(\mu)x_{t-1} + e_t,$$

$$e_t = G(\mu)\upsilon_t,$$

$$E(e_t e_t') = G(\mu)E(\upsilon_t \upsilon_t')G(\mu)' = Q(\mu).$$

These equations are collectively referred to as the state system, describing the evolution of the $n \times 1$ vector x_t of model variables. Certain variables contained in x_t are unobservable, whereas others (or linear combinations thereof) are observable. Observable variables are contained in the $m \times 1$ vector X_t, and are related to x_t via either

$$X_t = H(\mu)'x_t$$

or

$$X_t = H(\mu)'x_t + u_t, \qquad E(u_t u_t') = \Sigma_u,$$

either of which is known as a measurement equation. Hereafter, the dependence of $[F, G, Q, H]$ upon the structural parameters contained in μ will often be taken as granted for ease of notation.

Completion of the data-preparation stage implies that the variables contained in X_t are mean-zero covariance stationary stochastic processes (CSSPs) exhibiting fluctuations isolated to desired frequencies. The data represent deviations from steady state values.

This chapter has three purposes. First, it presents two important reduced-form models that provide flexible characterizations of the time-series behavior of X_t. The autoregressive-moving average (ARMA) model is presented for representing a single element of X_t, and the vector autoregressive (VAR) model is presented for representing the elements of X_t collectively. Second, the chapter presents a collection of summary statistics that frequently serve as targets for estimating the parameters of structural models, and as benchmarks for judging their empirical performance. Empirical analyses involving collections of summary statistics are broadly categorized as limited-information analyses. The statistics are all calculable as functions of the parameters of either an ARMA or VAR model. The chapter concludes with a presentation of the means by which full-information analyses of structural models are conducted: evaluation of the likelihood functions corresponding with their associated state-space representations.

The chapter uses the following notation. A univariate time series considered in isolation is denoted as y_t. The variable X_{it} denotes the ith element of X_t. The parameters of a given reduced-form model are collected in the vector ϑ, and a generic function of these parameters is denoted as $g(\vartheta)$. The corresponding generic function of the parameters of a given structural model is denoted as $g(\mu)$.

As with chapter 3, supplements to the brief coverage of these topics provided here are available from any number of texts devoted to time series analysis (e.g., Harvey, 1993; Hamilton, 1994). Also, the example business cycle data set introduced in chapter 3 is used to illustrate the material presented in this chapter.

4.1 Two Useful Reduced-Form Models

4.1.1 The ARMA Model

The foundation of the models presented in this section is a mean-zero covariance-stationary stochastic process $\{\varepsilon_t\}$, which is serially uncorrelated at all leads and lags: $E(\varepsilon_t \varepsilon_s) = 0,\ t \neq s$. The variance of ε_t is denoted as σ^2. Recall from chapter 3 that such a process is referred to as white noise, due to the shape of its spectrum. The variable y_t constructed as

$$\begin{aligned} y_t &= \varepsilon_t + \theta \varepsilon_{t-1} \\ &\equiv (1 + \theta L)\varepsilon_t \end{aligned} \tag{4.1}$$

is said to follow a moving average process of order 1, or MA(1) process: it is a moving average of the two most recent observations of ε_t. The variance of y_t, denoted as σ_y^2 or $\gamma(0)$, is given by

$$\begin{aligned} \sigma_y^2 &= E(y_t^2) \\ &= E(\varepsilon_t^2 + 2\theta \varepsilon_t \varepsilon_{t-1} + \theta^2 \varepsilon_{t-1}^2) \\ &= (1 + \theta^2)\sigma^2, \end{aligned} \tag{4.2}$$

and its autocovariance pattern is simply

$$
\begin{aligned}
\gamma(1) &= E(y_t y_{t-1}) \\
&= E(\varepsilon_t + \theta\varepsilon_{t-1})(\varepsilon_{t-1} + \theta\varepsilon_{t-2}) \\
&= \theta\sigma^2; \qquad (4.3) \\
\gamma(s) &= E(y_t y_{t-s}) = 0, \qquad s > 1.
\end{aligned}
$$

Denoting the sth-order autocorrelation of y_t as $\varphi(s) = \gamma(s)/\gamma(0)$, the corresponding autocorrelation pattern is

$$
\begin{aligned}
\varphi(1) &= \frac{\theta}{(1+\theta^2)}; \\
\varphi(s) &= 0, \qquad s > 1. \qquad (4.4)
\end{aligned}
$$

Thus the impact of ε_t on $\{y_t\}$ persists one period beyond its initial realization, imparting first-order serial correlation in $\{y_t\}$.

An MA(q) process specified for y_t generalizes to

$$
\begin{aligned}
y_t &= \varepsilon_t + \theta_1\varepsilon_{t-1} + \cdots + \theta_q\varepsilon_{t-q} \\
&= \sum_{j=0}^{q} \theta_j \varepsilon_{t-j} \\
&= \sum_{j=0}^{q} (\theta_j L^j)\varepsilon_t \\
&\equiv \theta(L)\varepsilon_t, \qquad (4.5)
\end{aligned}
$$

where $\theta_0 = 1$. The variance of y_t in this case is given by

$$
\sigma_y^2 = \sigma^2 \sum_{j=0}^{q} \theta_j^2, \qquad (4.6)
$$

and its covariance pattern is

$$
\gamma(s) = \begin{cases} \sigma^2\left[\theta_s + \theta_{s+1}\theta_1 + \theta_{s+2}\theta_2 + \cdots + \theta_q\theta_{q-s}\right], & s = 1, \ldots, q \\ 0 & s > q. \end{cases} \qquad (4.7)
$$

Note that the persistence of ε_t is limited to the horizon corresponding with q.

Finally, an infinite-order MA process specified for y_t is given by

$$y_t = \sum_{j=0}^{\infty} \psi_j \varepsilon_{t-j}$$
$$\equiv \psi(L)\varepsilon_t. \quad (4.8)$$

The Wold Decomposition Theorem holds that any CSSP may be represented as in (4.8), where

$$\sum_{j=0}^{\infty} \psi_j^2 < \infty, \quad (4.9)$$

with the white noise process $\{\varepsilon_t\}$ representing a sequence of one-step-ahead forecast errors:

$$\varepsilon_t = y_t - E_{t-1}(y_t | y_{t-1}, y_{t-2}, \ldots). \quad (4.10)$$

The expectations operator $E_{t-1}(\cdot|\Omega)$ is conditional on information contained in Ω available at time $t-1$. The condition (4.9) is referred to as square summability. It is necessary to insure a finite variance and covariances for y_t:

$$\sigma_y^2 = \sigma^2 \sum_{j=0}^{\infty} \psi_j^2; \quad (4.11)$$

$$\gamma(s) = \sigma^2 \left[\psi_s \psi_0 + \psi_{s+1}\psi_1 + \psi_{s+2}\psi_2 + \cdots\right]. \quad (4.12)$$

Consider now a specification for y_t of the form

$$y_t = \rho y_{t-1} + \varepsilon_t, \qquad |\rho| < 1. \quad (4.13)$$

In this case, y_t is said to follow an autoregressive process of order 1, or AR(1) process. To derive the variance and covariance pattern for y_t implied by (4.13), it is useful obtain an expression for y_t in terms of $\{\varepsilon_t\}$. One way to do so is through recursive substitution. This begins by substituting for y_{t-1} in (4.13), yielding

$$y_t = \rho(\rho y_{t-2} + \varepsilon_{t-1}) + \varepsilon_t$$
$$= \varepsilon_t + \rho\varepsilon_{t-1} + \rho^2 y_{t-2}.$$

Repeated substitution for y_{t-2}, y_{t-3}, and so on yields

$$y_t = \sum_{j=0}^{\infty} \rho^j \varepsilon_{t-j}. \quad (4.14)$$

Notice the role played by the restriction $|\rho| < 1$: this insures satisfaction of the square-summability condition, thus (4.14) constitutes a Wold Representation. For the special case in which $\rho = 1$, $(1 - L)y_t = \varepsilon_t$, and thus y_t is said to be difference-stationary. Square-summability is violated in this case, and the variance of y_t does not exist. In this special case y_t is also said to be integrated, since from (4.14) y_t is obtained by integrating over the set of realizations of $\{\varepsilon_t\}$ observed up to time t.

Given the restriction $|\rho| < 1$, the expressions for σ_y^2 and $\gamma(s)$ in (4.11) and (4.12) specialize to

$$\sigma_y^2 = \frac{\sigma^2}{1-\rho^2}; \tag{4.15}$$

$$\gamma(s) = \rho^s \frac{\sigma^2}{1-\rho^2}, \qquad s = 1, 2, \ldots. \tag{4.16}$$

Correspondingly, $\varphi(s) = \rho^s$. From both (4.14) and (4.16), it is evident that ρ determines the persistence of ε_t: the nearer is ρ to 1, the stronger is the influence of ε_{t-j} on y_t.

Before generalizing beyond the AR(1) case, it is useful to consider a more direct approach to the derivation of (4.14). Rewriting (4.13) as

$$y_t = \rho L y_t + \varepsilon_t,$$

(4.14) can be derived as follows:

$$(1 - \rho L)y_t = \varepsilon_t;$$

$$\begin{aligned} y_t &= \frac{1}{(1-\rho L)}\varepsilon_t \\ &= \sum_{j=0}^{\infty}(\rho^j L^j)\varepsilon_t \\ &= \sum_{j=0}^{\infty}\rho^j \varepsilon_{t-j}. \end{aligned}$$

Think of $(1 - \rho L)$ as a first-order polynomial in the lag operator L. The root of this polynomial is $1/\rho$, which lies outside the unit circle given that $|\rho| < 1$. This is a necessary condition for the stationarity of y_t. Again returning to the special case in which $\rho = 1$, the root of the polynomial is unity, and in this case y_t is said to follow a unit root process.

Generalizing to the AR(p) case, y_t is given by

$$y_t = \rho_1 y_{t-1} + \rho_2 y_{t-2} + \cdots + \rho_p y_{t-p} + \varepsilon_t, \tag{4.17}$$

or

$$(1 - \rho_1 L - \cdots - \rho_p L^p) y_t \equiv \rho(L) y_t = \varepsilon_t. \tag{4.18}$$

Factoring $(1 - \rho_1 L - \cdots - \rho_p L^p)$ as $(1 - \lambda_1 L)(1 - \lambda_2 L)\ldots(1 - \lambda_p L)$, y_t can be expressed as

$$\begin{aligned} y_t &= \left(\frac{1}{\rho(L)}\right) \varepsilon_t \\ &= \left(\frac{1}{1-\lambda_1 L}\right)\left(\frac{1}{1-\lambda_2 L}\right)\cdots\left(\frac{1}{1-\lambda_p L}\right)\varepsilon_t \\ &= \psi(L)\varepsilon_t. \end{aligned} \tag{4.19}$$

So long as the roots $1/\lambda_j$, $j = 1, \ldots, p$ of the polynomial $\rho(L)$ lie outside the unit circle, $\psi(L)$ is square-summable and (4.19) constitutes a Wold Representation.

The persistence of ε_t is determined by the proximity of the smallest root to unity: the closer to unity, the greater is the associated value of λ, and thus the greater is the persistence. If d roots lie exactly on the unit circle, then d applications of the difference operator to y_t, denoted as $(1 - L)^d y_t$, will cancel the d terms $\left(\frac{1}{1-L}\right)$ on the right-hand side of (4.19), and thus $(1 - L)^d\ y_t$ will be stationary. In this case, y_t is said to be integrated of order d, or an I(d) process.

A means for deriving the coefficients of $\psi(L)$ (and thus expressions for σ_y^2 and $\gamma(s)$ using (4.11) and (4.12)) as functions of the coefficients of $\rho(L)$ is provided by the method of undetermined coefficients. This begins by combining (4.8) and (4.18) to obtain

$$\rho(L)^{-1}\varepsilon_t = \psi(L)\varepsilon_t,$$

implying

$$\begin{aligned} 1 &= \rho(L)\psi(L) \\ &= (1 - \rho_1 L - \cdots - \rho_p L^p)(\psi_0 + \psi_1 L + \psi_2 L^2 + \cdots). \end{aligned} \tag{4.20}$$

Both sides of (4.20) may be thought of as infinite-order polynomials in L. Equating the coefficients associated with $L^0, L^1, \ldots$ on both sides of (4.20) yields the following system of equations:

$$
\begin{aligned}
1 &= \psi_0 \\
0 &= \psi_1 - \rho_1 \Rightarrow \psi_1 = \rho_1 \\
0 &= \psi_2 - \rho_1\psi_1 - \rho_2 \Rightarrow \psi_2 = \rho_1^2 + \rho_2 \\
&\cdots \\
0 &= \psi_p - \rho_1\psi_{p-1} - \rho_2\psi_{p-2} - \cdots - \rho_p\psi_0 \\
0 &= \psi_{p+j} - \rho_1\psi_{p+j-1} - \rho_2\psi_{p+j-2} - \cdots - \rho_p\psi_j, \qquad j = 1, 2, \ldots.
\end{aligned} \tag{4.21}
$$

Exercise 4.1

Derive expressions for $\psi_j, j = 0, 1, 2, \ldots$ as functions of the coefficients of $\rho(L)$ for $p = 1, 2,$ and 3.

The specifications for y_t as outlined are encompassed by an ARMA (p, q) model, expressed as

$$
\begin{aligned}
(1 - \rho_1 L - \cdots - \rho_p L^p)y_t &= (1 + \theta_1 L + \cdots + \theta_q L^q)\varepsilon_t, \quad \text{or} \\
\rho(L)y_t &= \theta(L)\varepsilon_t.
\end{aligned} \tag{4.22}
$$

Stationarity is once again determined by the roots of $\rho(L)$. Assuming these lie outside the unit circle, the inversion of $\rho(L)$ yields the Wold Representation

$$
y_t = \left(\frac{\theta(L)}{\rho(L)}\right)\varepsilon_t. \tag{4.23}
$$

Combining (4.8) and (4.23) yields the relationship

$$
\theta(L) = \rho(L)\psi(L), \tag{4.24}
$$

which generalizes (4.20). Accordingly, the method of undetermined coefficients may be applied to (4.24) to obtain expressions for $\psi_j, j = 0, 1, 2, \ldots$ as functions of the coefficients of $\theta(L)$ and $\rho(L)$, again yielding expressions for σ_y^2 and $\gamma(s)$ via (4.11) and (4.12).

Exercise 4.2

Derive expressions for $\psi_j, j=0, 1, 2, \ldots$ as functions of the coefficients of $\rho(L)$ and $\theta(L)$ for $p=1, q=1$.

A numerical algorithm for implementing the method of undetermined coefficients involves the construction of a hypothetical realization of $\{y_t\}_{t=0}^{\infty}$ resulting from a special realization of innovations $\{\varepsilon_t\}_{t=0}^{\infty}$. Specifically, let

$\{y_{-(p+1)}, y_{-(p)}, \ldots y_{-(1)}\} = 0, \varepsilon_0 = 1$, and $\{\varepsilon_t\}_{t=1}^{\infty} = 0$. Then from (4.8), the resulting sequence $\{y_t\}_{t=0}^{\infty}$ is identically $\{\psi_j\}_{j=0}^{\infty}$. From (4.22), the sequence $\{\psi_j\}_{j=0}^{\infty}$ may thus be constructed iteratively as follows:

$$\psi_0 = 1$$
$$\psi_1 = \rho_1 + \theta_1$$
$$\psi_2 = \rho_1\psi_1 + \rho_2 + \theta_2$$
$$\ldots$$
$$\psi_p = \rho_1\psi_{p-1} + \rho_2\psi_{p-2} + \cdots + \rho_p + \theta_p$$
$$\ldots$$
$$\psi_j = \rho_1\psi_{j-1} + \rho_2\psi_{j-2} + \cdots + \rho_p\psi_{j-p} + \theta_j, \tag{4.25}$$

where $\theta_j = 0$ for $j > q$. A plot of the resulting sequence $\{\psi_j\}_{j=0}^{\infty}$ is referred to as an impulse response function, because it traces out the response of y_t to the realization of a representative shock.

We conclude with a brief discussion of estimation. Note from (4.17) that the coefficients of an AR(p) model can be estimated in straightforward fashion using an ordinary least squares (OLS) regression. In the regression, the $(T-p)\times 1$ vector $y = [y_{p+1}, y_{p+2}, \ldots y_T]'$ serves as the dependent variable, and $Ly, L^2y, \ldots, L^Py$ serve as independent variables, where $L^jy = [y_{p+1-j}, y_{p+2-j}, \ldots y_{T-j}]'$, and T denotes the total number of observations of $\{y_t\}$. Moreover, given the assumption of normality for $\{\varepsilon_t\}$, the resulting OLS estimates of $\rho(L)$ coincide with conditional maximum likelihood (ML) estimates, as you will be asked to demonstrate in exercise 4.5 below (where conditioning is on the initial observations $[y_1, y_2, \ldots, y_p]'$).

Estimation is not as straightforward when the specification for y_t contains an MA component. Complication arises from the presence of unobservable variables as explanatory variables for y_t: namely, lagged values of ε_t. But as demonstrated in section 4.3, this complication may be overcome via use of the Kalman filter; see in particular exercise 4.6.[1]

4.1.2 The VAR Model

A vector autoregressive (VAR) model specified for the $m \times 1$ vector X_t is the multivariate analogue of an AR model specified for the single variable

[1] GAUSS's Time Series module is also available for estimating ARMA models. Alternatively, estimation code is available at

http://www.american.edu/academic.depts/cas/econ/gaussres/timeseri/timeseri.htm

y_t. The multivariate analogue to the AR(p) specification (4.18) for X_t is given by

$$\begin{bmatrix} \rho_{11}(L) & \rho_{12}(L) & \dots & \rho_{1m}(L) \\ \rho_{21}(L) & \rho_{22}(L) & \dots & \rho_{2m}(L) \\ \dots & \dots & \dots & \dots \\ \rho_{m1}(L) & \rho_{m2}(L) & \dots & \rho_{mm}(L) \end{bmatrix} \begin{bmatrix} X_{1t} \\ X_{2t} \\ \dots \\ X_{mt} \end{bmatrix} = \begin{bmatrix} \varepsilon_{1t} \\ \varepsilon_{2t} \\ \dots \\ \varepsilon_{mt} \end{bmatrix}, \quad E(\varepsilon_t \varepsilon_t') = \Sigma, \tag{4.26}$$

where

$$\rho_{ij}(L) = (1 + \rho_{ij1} L + \cdots + \rho_{ijp} L^p)$$

is a pth-order polynomial in the lag operator, expressing the influence of X_j on X_i. Defining the lead matrix in (4.26) as $\Phi(L)$, the roots of the VAR representation correspond to the mp factors of the determinant of $\Phi(z)$, z complex. These roots will lie outside the unit circle given stationarity of the individual elements of X_t, thus $\Phi(L)$ may be inverted to obtain a multivariate analogue of the Wold Representation (4.8):

$$X_t = \sum_{j=0}^{\infty} \Psi_j \varepsilon_{t-j}, \tag{4.27}$$

where Ψ_j is $m \times m$.

Covariation patterns between the elements of X_t may be conveniently characterized by writing the VAR in companion form. The companion form of an AR(p) model for a single element X_{it} of X_t is given by

$$\begin{bmatrix} X_{it} \\ X_{it-1} \\ X_{it-2} \\ \dots \\ X_{it-(p+1)} \end{bmatrix} = \begin{bmatrix} \rho_{ii1} & \rho_{ii2} & \rho_{ii3} & \dots & \rho_{iip} \\ 1 & 0 & 0 & \dots & 0 \\ 0 & 1 & 0 & \dots & 0 \\ \dots & \dots & \dots & \dots & \dots \\ 0 & 0 & 0 & \dots 1 & 0 \end{bmatrix} \begin{bmatrix} X_{it-1} \\ X_{it-2} \\ X_{it-3} \\ \dots \\ X_{it-p} \end{bmatrix} + \begin{bmatrix} \varepsilon_{it} \\ 0 \\ 0 \\ \dots \\ 0 \end{bmatrix}. \tag{4.28}$$

Defining the $(mp) \times 1$ vector

$$z_t = [X_{1t}\ X_{1t-1} \dots X_{1t-(p+1)}\ X_{2t}\ X_{2t-1} \\ \dots X_{2t-(p+1)} \dots X_{mt}\ X_{mt-1} \dots X_{mt-(p+1)}]',$$

and the $(mp) \times 1$ vector

$$e_t = [\varepsilon_{1t}\ 0 \dots 0\ \varepsilon_{2t}\ 0 \dots 0\ \varepsilon_{mt}\ 0 \dots 0]',$$

the companion form for the VAR is given by

$$z_t = Az_{t-1} + e_t, \tag{4.29}$$

where the $(mp) \times (mp)$ companion matrix A contains VAR equations in the 1st, $(p+1)^{th}, \ldots,$ and $[(m-1)p+1]^{th}$ rows, and maintains identities between elements of z_t and z_{t-1} in the remaining rows. Note the correspondence between (4.29) and the AR(1) expression for y_t in (4.13).

Exploiting this correspondence, let

$$\Gamma(0) = E(z_t z_t')$$

denote the contemporaneous variance-covariance matrix of z_t, and

$$\Gamma(s) = E(z_t z_{t-s}')$$

the sth-order covariance matrix. From (4.29),

$$\begin{aligned} \Gamma(0) &= E[(Az_{t-1} + e_t)(Az_{t-1} + e_t)'] \\ &= A\Gamma(0)A' + \Sigma, \end{aligned} \tag{4.30}$$

the solution to which is given by

$$vec\,[\Gamma(0)] = [I - A \otimes A]^{-1}\, vec[\Sigma], \tag{4.31}$$

where $\otimes$ denotes the Kronecker product. Further,

$$\begin{aligned} \Gamma(1) &= E(z_t z_{t-1}') \\ &= E((Az_{t-1} + e_t)z_{t-1}') \\ &= A\Gamma(0), \end{aligned}$$

and in general,

$$\begin{aligned} \Gamma(s) &= A\Gamma(s-1) \\ &= A^s\Gamma(0). \end{aligned} \tag{4.32}$$

Note the symmetry between (4.31) and (4.15), and between (4.32) and (4.16).

As with the AR(p) specification, the parameters of the VAR model may be estimated using OLS by rewriting (4.26) in standard regression notation:

$$\Upsilon = \Xi B + u, \tag{4.33}$$

where the $(T-p) \times m$ matrix

$$\Upsilon = [X_1 X_2 \ \dots \ X_m],$$

with

$$X_i = [X_{ip+1} X_{ip+2} \ \dots \ X_{iT}]',$$

the $(T-p) \times (mp)$ matrix Ξ contains in its tth row

$$[X_{1t-1} \ X_{1t-2} \ \dots \ X_{1t-p} \ X_{2t-1} \ X_{2t-2} \ \dots \ X_{2t-p} \\ \dots \ X_{mt-1} \ X_{mt-2} \ \dots \ X_{mt-p}],$$

the $(mp) \times m$ matrix B contains VAR parameters for X_i in its ith column, and the $(T-p) \times m$ matrix u contains the $(T-p) \times 1$ vector of innovations $[\varepsilon_{ip+1} \ \varepsilon_{ip+2} \dots \varepsilon_{iT}]'$ corresponding with the VAR equation for X_i. And as with the AR(p) model, OLS estimates coincide with ML estimates given the assumption of normality for ε_t.[2]

4.2 Summary Statistics

We begin by discussing summary statistics for a single variable y_t. A good initial characterization of y_t is provided by its autocorrelation function, which plots $\varphi(s)$ as a function of s (since $\varphi(s) = \varphi(-s)$, negative values of s are ignored). This plot provides an indication of the persistence of innovations to y_t, because as indicated in (4.12), the greater the persistence (i.e., the greater the horizon over which ψ_j differs from zero), the greater will be the horizon over which autocovariance terms (and thus autocorrelation terms) will differ from zero. The plot also illustrates cyclical patterns followed by y_t.

[2] The collection of procedures contained in `var.src` is available for estimating VAR specifications, constructing the companion matrix A, and calculating $\Gamma(s)$, $s = 0, 1, \dots$.

Estimates of the elements of $\varphi(s)$ may be obtained using the following collection of sample averages:[3]

$$\begin{aligned}
\bar{y} &= \left(\frac{1}{T}\right)\sum_{t=1}^{T} y_t \\
\widehat{\gamma}(0) &= \left(\frac{1}{T}\right)\sum_{t=1}^{T} (y_t - \bar{y})^2 \\
\widehat{\gamma}(s) &= \left(\frac{1}{T}\right)\sum_{t=s+1}^{T} (y_t - \bar{y})(y_{t-s} - \bar{y}) \\
\widehat{\varphi}(s) &= \widehat{\gamma}(s)/\widehat{\gamma}(0).
\end{aligned} \tag{4.34}$$

Alternatively, given estimates of an ARMA specification for y_t, the corresponding Wold Representation of y_t may be constructed using (4.25), which can then be mapped into $\widehat{\varphi}(s)$ using (4.12).

Plots of $\widehat{\varphi}(s)$ (estimated using sample averages) for the four filtered versions of output described in chapter 3 are illustrated in figure 4.1. The four versions were obtained by detrending, differencing, Hodrick-Prescott (H-P) filtering, and band-pass (B-P) filtering; each series represents logged deviations from trend.

Immediately apparent from figure 4.1 is the high degree of persistence exhibited by the detrended series. Recall from figure 3.2 that the level of the series follows broken trend line, indicating a substantial reduction in growth approximately midway through the sample period. Given the removal of an unbroken trend line, the resulting detrended series persistently lies above zero during the first half of the sample period, and below zero during the second half. This persistence translates into the behavior of $\widehat{\varphi}(s)$ depicted in figure 4.1, which decays very slowly, and remains at approximately 0.25 even at the 40-quarter horizon. Plots of $\widehat{\varphi}(s)$ estimated for the alternative versions of y_t reveal a pattern of cyclical behavior: positive autocorrelation over the first four to six quarters gives way to negative autocorrelation until roughly the 16-quarter horizon, indicating predictable movements of y_t above and below trend.

Another useful means of summarizing the persistence and cyclicality of y_t is through the construction of its spectrum. The spectrum was described in detail in chapter 3, section 3.2; here we provide a brief summary. The spectrum $s_y(\omega)$ is a decomposition of the variance of y_t by frequency ω. Frequency, measured in radians, is usefully interpreted through its relationship

[3] The GAUSS command `autocor` performs these calculations.

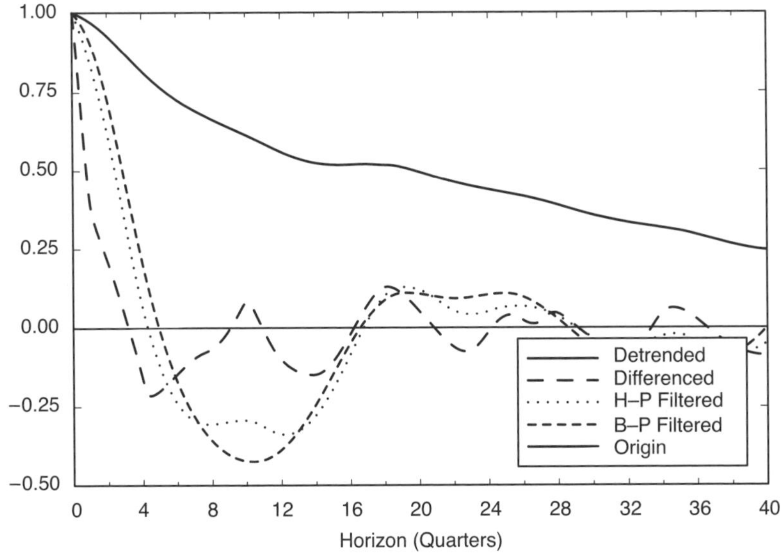

Figure 4.1 Sample autocorrelations of output.

with period p, which measures the number of time periods needed to complete a cycle: $\omega = 2\pi/p$. Thus business cycle frequencies, associated with periods between 6 and 40 quarters, fall within the range $[0.157,\ 1.047]$ in working with quarterly data. The spectrum is closely related to the autocovariance function:

$$s_y(\omega) = \left(\frac{1}{2\pi}\right)\left[\gamma(0) + 2\sum_{\tau=1}^{\infty}\gamma(\tau)\cos(\omega\tau)\right]. \tag{4.35}$$

The integral of $s_y(\omega)$ over the range $[-\pi, \pi]$ yields $\gamma(0)$, and comparisons of the height of $s_y(\omega)$ for alternative values of ω indicate the relative importance of fluctuations at the chosen frequencies in influencing variations in y_t. Recall that because $\cos(\omega\tau)$ is symmetric over $[-\pi, 0]$ and $[0, \pi]$, so too is $s(\omega)$; it is customary to represent $s_y(\omega)$ over $[0, \pi]$.

As is clear from (4.35), the construction of an estimate of $s_y(\omega)$ for y_t is straightforward given estimates $\widehat{\gamma}(s)$. Alternatively, an estimate of $s_y(\omega)$ can be obtained through its relationship with the parameters of an ARMA specification estimated for y_t; the relationship is given by:

$$s_y(\omega) = \left(\frac{\sigma^2}{2\pi}\right)\frac{|\theta(e^{-i\omega})|^2}{|\rho(e^{-i\omega})|^2}, \tag{4.36}$$

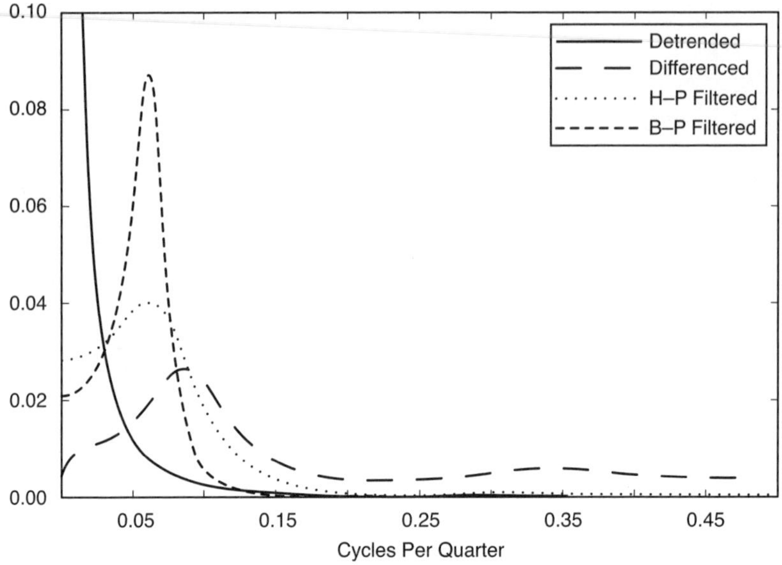

Figure 4.2 Spectra of output.

where

$$e^{-i\omega} = \cos(\omega) - i\sin(\omega),$$

$\sqrt{i} = -1$, and $|\cdot|$ denotes the modulus operator; for example,[4]

$$|\theta(e^{-i\omega})| = \sqrt{\theta(e^{-i\omega})\theta(e^{i\omega})}.$$

Spectra estimated for the four versions of output described above are illustrated in figure 4.2. Also, spectra estimated for the H-P filtered versions of output, consumption, investment, and hours are illustrated in figure 4.3. The estimates were obtained by estimating ARMA models for each series, and constructing $s_y(\omega)$ as in (4.36). In the figures, the horizontal axis is in terms of $\omega/2\pi$: cycles per quarter.

Note how the behavior of the autocorrelation functions depicted in figure 4.1 translate into the behavior of the spectra depicted in figure 4.2. The persistence evident in the detrended series translates as a spike in its corresponding spectrum at zero frequency. (The height of this spectrum

[4] See Harvey (1993) for a derivation of (4.36). The procedure spec_arma.prc can be used to construct $s_y(\omega)$, taking $\rho(L)$ and $\theta(L)$ as inputs.

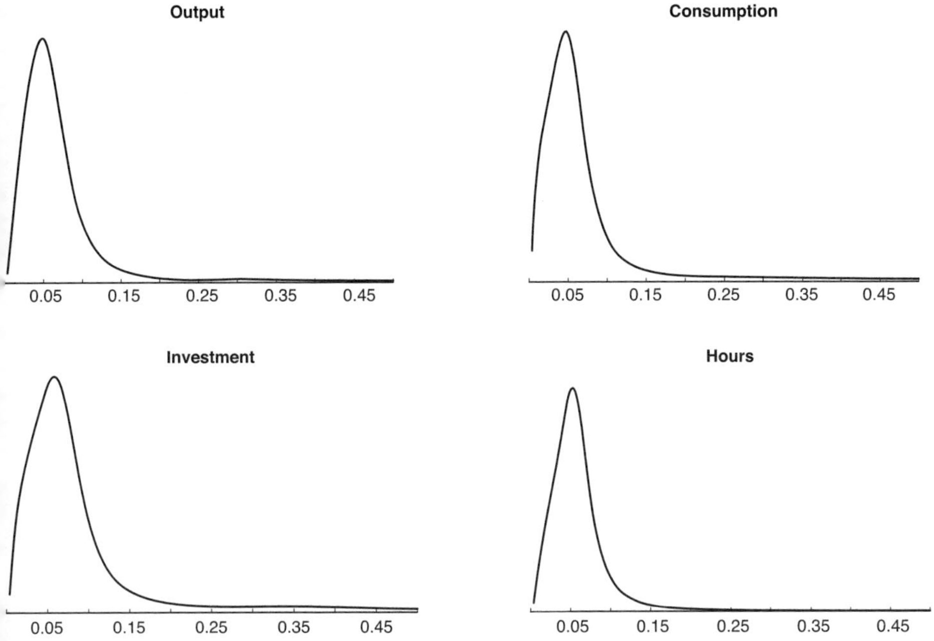

Figure 4.3 Spectra of H-P filtered data.

actually grows unboundedly as ω approaches zero; the spectrum was truncated at 0.1 in the figure to better depict the additional spectra.) The frequency zero corresponds to a period p of infinity, or to a cycle that never repeats. As indicated by its spectrum, innovations with this characteristic dominate the behavior of the detrended series.

For the remaining series, spectral peaks lie within business cycle frequencies (between 1/40 and 1/6 cycles per quarter). In the case of the H-P and B-P filtered series, this is by design, as the characterization of the squared gains corresponding with the H-P and B-P filters provided in chapter 3, section 3.2 illustrate (see in particular figures 3.6 and 3.10). The spectral peak associated with the differenced series is much less pronounced in comparison, and the non-trivial component of the spectrum of this series over the range [0.15, 0.5] reflects the influence of relatively high-frequency fluctuations on the overall behavior of this series.

We conclude the characterization of y_t by recalling the discussion of impulse response functions in section 4.1. Recall that these trace the response of y_t to the realization of a single shock at time 0: $\varepsilon_0 = 1$, $\varepsilon_t = 0$, $t > 0$. Equivalently, these functions plot the coefficients ψ_j, $j = 1, 2, \ldots$ of the Wold Representation of y_t, as expressed in (4.8). Impulse response functions are illustrated for the four H-P filtered series in figure 4.4. Each

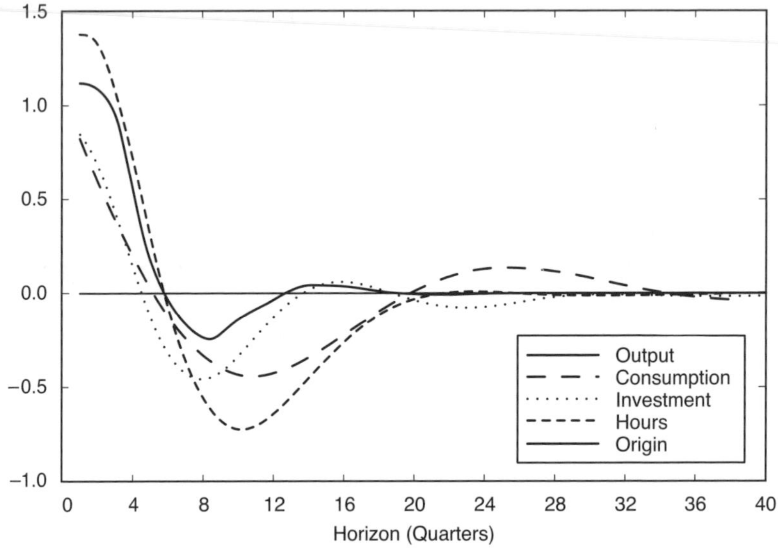

Figure 4.4 Univariate impulse response functions of H-P filtered data.

function was constructed from estimates of an ARMA specification, which were used to construct ψ_j, $j = 1, 2, \ldots$ as in (4.25).[5]

Note how the cyclical nature of the responses mimic the autocorrelation pattern of H-P filtered output in figure 4.1. A positive shock drives each series above trend for approximately four to six quarters; the series then overshoot their trend lines before ultimately recovering at approximately the 20-quarter horizon. Note also the close relationship between the dynamic responses of the series.

We now discuss summary statistics for the collection of variables contained in the $m \times 1$ vector X_t, or when convenient, for the expanded collection of variables contained in the $(mp) \times 1$ vector z_t, constructed from X_t as indicated by the companion form of the VAR specified in (4.29). Patterns of auto- and cross-covariation are usefully characterized using $\Gamma(s) = E(z_t z_t')$, $s = 0, 1, \ldots$. These may be obtained from estimated VAR parameters following (4.30)–(4.32). A collection of statistics frequently of interest in empirical business cycle applications are reported for the differenced, H-P filtered, and B-P filtered data in table 4.1. The detrended data were excluded from the table because the VAR specification estimated for these data contains a unit root, thus the construction of $\Gamma(0)$ via (4.31) is not possible in this case.

[5] The procedure `armaimp.prc` can be used to calculate impulse response functions in this fashion.

TABLE 4.1
Summary statistics estimated from VAR

		Differenced Data			
j	σ_j	$\frac{\sigma_j}{\sigma_y}$	$\varphi(1)$	$\varphi_{j,y}(0)$	$\varphi_{j,y}(1)$
y	0.0099	1.00	0.36	1.00	0.36
c	0.0051	0.51	0.22	0.54	0.42
i	0.0505	5.10	0.14	0.91	0.21
h	0.0091	0.92	0.60	0.69	0.32
		H-P filtered Data			
j	σ_j	$\frac{\sigma_j}{\sigma_y}$	$\varphi(1)$	$\varphi_{j,y}(0)$	$\varphi_{j,y}(1)$
y	0.0177	1.00	0.86	1.00	0.86
c	0.0081	0.46	0.83	0.82	0.75
i	0.0748	4.23	0.79	0.95	0.80
h	0.0185	1.05	0.90	0.83	0.62
		B-P filtered Data			
j	σ_j	$\frac{\sigma_j}{\sigma_y}$	$\varphi(1)$	$\varphi_{j,y}(0)$	$\varphi_{j,y}(1)$
y	0.0184	1.00	0.94	1.00	0.94
c	0.0084	0.46	0.94	0.90	0.85
i	0.0733	3.98	0.92	0.96	0.89
h	0.0193	1.05	0.94	0.87	0.71

The first column of the table reports standard deviations of the individual series, and the second reports standard deviations relative to the standard deviation of output. Note that under all three versions of the data, investment is far more volatile than output (σ_i/σ_y ranges from approximately 4 to 5), whereas consumption is far smoother (σ_c/σ_y is roughly 0.5); the volatility of hours and output are roughly equal. Measures of first-order serial correlation are quite low among the differenced series (particularly for investment: 0.14); while ranging from 0.79 to 0.94 among the H-P and B-P filtered data. Finally, with $\varphi_{j,y}(s)$ denoting the sth-order correlation between variable j and output, note that output is most closely correlated with investment, and that correlation patterns in general are relatively weak among the differenced series in comparison with the H-P and B-P filtered series.

Exercise 4.3

Construct the collection of summary statistics presented in table 4.1 using a version of detrended output obtained by fitting a broken trend to the data. Do this using the following steps.

1. Split the sample into two periods: observations through 1993:IV, and observations from 1994:I–2004:IV. For each, fit a common linear trend to logged output, consumption, and investment; subtract the estimated trend; then recombine the resulting series (use the procedure `ct.prc` for this step).
2. Estimate a VAR representation for the data using $p = 8$, construct the companion matrix A as in (4.29), and then construct $\Gamma(0)$ and $\Gamma(1)$ using (4.30)–(4.32) (use the procedures contained in `var.src` for this step).
3. Obtain $[\sigma_j,\ \frac{\sigma_j}{\sigma_y},\ \varphi(1),\ \varphi_{j,y}(0),\ \varphi_{j,y}(1)]$ from the relevant entries of $\Gamma(0)$ and $\Gamma(1)$.

Spectral representations of the data may also be constructed using VARs. This is accomplished via a multivariate analogue of (4.36). Setting $\theta(L) = 1$, (4.36) characterizes how the spectrum of a single variable is obtained using estimates of an AR(p) model. To obtain the multivariate analogue of (4.36), write the VAR of X_t as

$$X_t = \Upsilon_1 X_{t-1} + \Upsilon_2 X_{t-2} + \cdots + \Upsilon_p X_{t-p} + \varepsilon_t, \tag{4.37}$$

where Υ_j is $k \times k$. Letting

$$\Upsilon(L) = I - \Upsilon_1 L - \cdots - \Upsilon_p L^p,$$

the spectrum of X_t, denoted as $S(\omega)$, is given by[6]

$$S(\omega) = \frac{1}{2\pi}[\Upsilon(e^{-i\omega})'\Sigma^{-1}\Upsilon(e^{-i\omega})]^{-1}. \tag{4.38}$$

The jth diagonal element of $S(\omega)$ contains the spectrum of the jth variable of X_t at frequency ω, $s_j(\omega)$, and the $(i, j)^{\text{th}}$ element of $S(\omega)$ contains the cross spectrum between the ith and j^{th} variables of X_t, $s_{i,j}(\omega)$. Estimates of the spectra for the H-P filtered data produced using (4.38) closely mimic those depicted in figure 4.3, and thus are not reported here.

Finally, impulse response functions may also be constructed using VARs. This is most conveniently accomplished using the companion form of the VAR given by (4.29). Initializing $z_{-1} = 0$, this proceeds by constructing a nonzero initial value e_0, and then constructing $\{z_t\}_{t=0}^{\infty}$ as $z_0 = e_0$, $z_1 = Ae_0$, $z_2 = A^2 e_0, \ldots$ The specification for e_0 is typically chosen to simulate the impact on the system of a one-standard-deviation innovation to the jth variable of the system. If the innovations were all uncorrelated, so that the covariance matrix Σ were diagonal, the specification for e_0 would contain a zero in all but its $[(j-1)p+1]^{\text{th}}$ row, which corresponds to the jth equation of the VAR. This entry would be set to the square root of the

[6] For a derivation, see Hannan (1970). The procedure `spec_var.prc` is available for use in constructing $S(\omega)$ using (4.38).

j^{th} diagonal element of Σ. However, correlation among the innovations implies that an innovation to the jth variable of the system coincides with innovations to additional variables in the system. To capture this, e_0 must be constructed accordingly.

Recall that e_t relates to the system innovations as

$$e_t = [\varepsilon_{1t}\; 0 \ldots 0\; \varepsilon_{2t}\; 0 \ldots 0\; \varepsilon_{mt}\; 0 \ldots 0]';$$

for the moment, it will be convenient to work directly with the vector ε_t. To recap, the problem faced in constructing e_0 is that the elements of ε_t are typically correlated, so that a movement in one component will coincide with movements in additional components. The leading approach to dealing with this involves working with orthogonalized innovations in place of ε_t. Orthogonalized innovations are innovations that are uncorrelated across VAR equations. Let ν_t represent such innovations, so that $E(\nu_t \nu_t') = I$. Defining a matrix P such that

$$P^{-1} \Sigma P'^{-1} = I, \tag{4.39}$$

which implies

$$\Sigma = PP', \tag{4.40}$$

ν_t may be constructed using

$$\nu_t = P^{-1} \varepsilon_t. \tag{4.41}$$

The only problem at this point is that there are many possible specifications of P^{-1} that can be constructed to satisfy (4.40). Here we discuss a leading specification: the Cholesky decomposition of Σ; see Hamilton (1994) for a discussion of alternative decompositions.

The Cholesky decomposition of Σ is a lower-triangular matrix that satisfies (4.40), with diagonal elements containing the square root of the diagonal elements of Σ (i.e., the standard deviations of the elements of ε_t). Consider the construction of ν_0 obtained by introducing into (4.41) a specification of ε_0 containing 1 in its jth row and zeros elsewhere. The resulting specification of ν_0 will contain the jth column of P^{-1}. Using the Cholesky decomposition of Σ for P^{-1}, ν_0 will contain zeros in the first $j-1$ entries, the standard deviation of the jth element of ε_t in the jth row, and non-zero entries in the remaining rows. These latter entries represent the influence of an innovation to the jth equation of the system on innovations to the $(j+1)^{\text{st}}$ through m equations. This reflects the correlation among the innovations. Note however that under this construct the innovation to the jth equation is prevented from influencing the 1st through

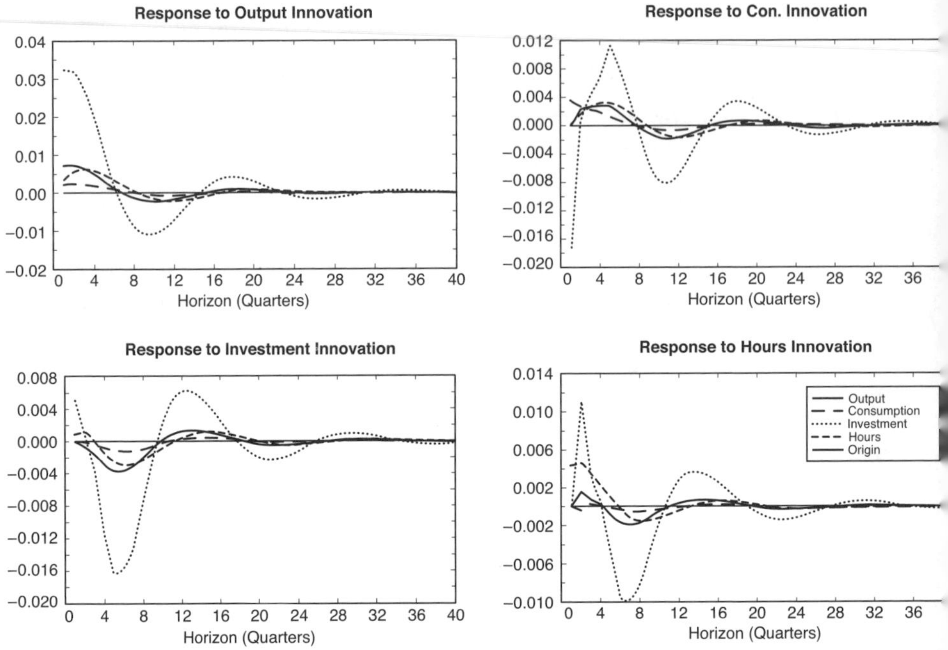

Figure 4.5 System impulse response functions of H-P filtered data.

$(j-1)^{\text{st}}$ equations; thus the ordering of the variables of the system will influence impulse response functions constructed in this manner.

Impulse response functions constructed using the H-P filtered data are illustrated in figure 4.5.[7] The ordering of the variables used to construct the responses is (y, c, i, h). Most striking is the magnitude of the responses of investment to each shock, clearly indicating the high volatility of this series in comparison with the others. Investment initially responds negatively to a positive consumption shock; otherwise, all variables exhibit positive covariation in response to the shocks. Finally, the cyclical patterns described above are once again in evidence here: note in particular that the variables tend to overshoot their targets in returning to pre-shock levels.

As noted, each of the summary statistics we have discussed may be constructed from estimates of ARMA or VAR models, which can themselves be estimated using ML or OLS techniques. An issue involving these estimates regards the choice of lag lengths p and q for these specifications. Often this choice will depend on factors particular to the problem at hand. For example, if the number of available data points is relatively low, parsimony may

[7] A procedure for calculating impulse response functions is included in `var.src`.

be of primary concern. Alternatively, if the objective is to obtain a general feel for the data, as with the examples provided above, it may be preferable to work with relatively liberal specifications. Here, we briefly mention three leading approaches to lag-length specification; for an extended discussion, see Judge et al. (1985).

First is a general-to-specific approach. This involves the sequential testing of exclusion restrictions given an initial specification of a liberally parameterized model. For example, this could involve individual t-tests of the null hypothesis that the qth lag chosen for the MA component of an ARMA model, or the pth lag chosen for the AR component, is zero. Alternatively, sets of exclusion restrictions could be evaluated using a likelihood ratio (LR) test. Letting L_u and L_r denote values of the unrestricted and restricted likelihood functions associated with the model being estimated, the LR test statistic is given by $2\log\,[L_u - L_r]$, which is asymptotically distributed as $\chi^2(k)$, where k denotes the number of restrictions imposed in calculating L_r.

Alternative approaches involve the use of selection criteria that explicitly incorporate penalties for selecting liberal parameterizations. Letting K denote the total number of parameters associated with a given model specification, two leading criteria are the Akaike Information Criterion (AIC) (Akaike, 1974), which delivers the K that minimizes

$$AIC = |\Sigma(K)| + \frac{2K}{T}, \tag{4.42}$$

and the Bayesian Information Criterion (BIC) (Schwarz, 1978), which delivers the K that minimizes

$$BIC = |\Sigma(K)| + \frac{K\log(T)}{T}. \tag{4.43}$$

The notation $\Sigma(K)$ is used to indicate explicitly that the fit of the model, represented by $|\Sigma(K)|$, will improve as K increases: $|\Sigma(K)|$ is decreasing in K. Of course, gains realized by increasing K are countered by increases in the penalty terms.

To this point the discussion has centered on summary statistics designed to characterize the time-series behavior of the collection of observable variables X_t. However, the same collection of statistics may be used to characterize the time-series behavior of model variables. Recall that these are contained in the vector x_t, which has a structural representation given by

$$x_t = Fx_{t-1} + e_t, \qquad E(e_t e_t') = Q. \tag{4.44}$$

Note the similarity of this specification relative to the companion form of the VAR specified for z_t. Exploiting this similarity, we simply note here that each of the summary statistics that can be constructed from VAR estimates can also be constructed for x_t by replacing A and Σ with F and Q. Moreover, because the relationship between model variables and observables is given by the simple linear mapping $X_t = H'x_t$, it is straightforward to align summary statistics obtained from reduced-form specifications with those obtained from structural specifications. The various empirical techniques presented in part II of this book use alternative approaches to aligning statistics and judging their proximity.

We conclude this section with a note regarding measures of the precision with which summary statistics have been estimated. For concreteness, let $\widehat{g(\vartheta)}$ denote the estimate of a given function of the $k \times 1$ vector of parameters ϑ, which summarize a reduced-form model specified for the data. (The replacement of $\widehat{g(\varphi)}$ with $\widehat{g(\mu)}$, so that the discussion is centered on a structural rather than a reduced-form model, yields an analogous discussion.) From a classical statistical perspective, under which parameters are interpreted as fixed and data as random, precision is conveyed by reporting the standard error associated with $\widehat{g(\vartheta)}$. From a Bayesian perspective, under which the data are interpreted as fixed and parameters as random, precision is conveyed by reporting the posterior standard deviation associated with $\widehat{g(\vartheta)}$.

Beginning with the former, because the data used to construct $\widehat{g(\vartheta)}$ are random, and represent one of many possible realizations that could have been obtained, $\widehat{g(\vartheta)}$ is also random. Its variance is referred to as the sampling variance of $g(\vartheta)$, which must typically be estimated. The square root of this estimate is the standard error of $\widehat{g(\vartheta)}$. In some cases analytical expressions for standard errors are available; often they are not. For example, if the vector ϑ is being estimated using an OLS regression of the form

$$y = X\vartheta + e,$$

and $\widehat{g(\vartheta)}$ is a vector representing the OLS estimate of ϑ, then the associated standard errors of the individual elements of $\widehat{g(\vartheta)}$ are the square roots of the diagonal elements of

$$Var(\widehat{\vartheta}) = \widehat{\sigma}^2(X'X)^{-1}, \qquad \widehat{\sigma}^2 = \left(\frac{1}{T}\right)\sum_{t=1}^{T}\widehat{e_t}^2, \qquad \widehat{e_t} = y - X\widehat{\vartheta}.$$

When $g(\vartheta)$ represents a nonlinear function of ϑ, analytical expressions for the standard error of $\widehat{g(\vartheta)}$ are generally unavailable. One remedy for this is use of the Delta method. Consider a first-order Taylor Series approximation of $\widehat{g(\vartheta)}$ around the true value ϑ:

$$\widehat{g(\vartheta)} \approx g(\vartheta) + \left(\frac{\partial g(\vartheta)}{\partial \vartheta}\right)' (\widehat{\vartheta} - \vartheta). \tag{4.45}$$

If $g(\vartheta)$ is a scalar, $(\frac{\partial g(\vartheta)}{\partial \vartheta})'$ is $1 \times k$ and $(\widehat{\vartheta} - \vartheta)$ is $k \times 1$. If $g(\vartheta)$ is an $\ell \times 1$ vector, $(\frac{\partial g(\vartheta)}{\partial \vartheta})'$ is an $\ell \times k$ Jacobian matrix, with $(i,j)^{\text{th}}$ element given by the derivative of the ith row of $g(\vartheta)$ with respect to the jth element of ϑ. By Slutsky's Theorem (e.g., as presented in Greene, 2003), if $\widehat{\vartheta}$ is a consistent estimate of ϑ, then $g(\widehat{\vartheta})$ will be a consistent estimator of $g(\vartheta)$, with variance given by

$$Var[\,\widehat{g(\vartheta)}] \approx \left(\frac{\partial g(\vartheta)}{\partial \vartheta}\right)' Var(\widehat{\vartheta}) \left(\frac{\partial g(\vartheta)}{\partial \vartheta}\right). \tag{4.46}$$

The standard errors associated with the individual elements of $\widehat{g(\vartheta)}$ are thus the square roots of the diagonal elements of $Var[\,\widehat{g(\vartheta)}]$.

Alternatively, if expressions for $\frac{\partial g(\vartheta)}{\partial \vartheta}$ are difficult to obtain, standard errors may be calculated using numerical approximation methods, such as the method of Monte Carlo. This involves generating artificial sample drawings of data from the distribution implied by a parameterized version of their reduced-form model, calculating $\widehat{g(\vartheta)}$ for each artificial drawing, and then computing the variance of $\widehat{g(\vartheta)}$ from the resulting collection of drawings. Once again, square roots of the diagonal elements of the estimated variance of $\widehat{g(\vartheta)}$ serve as estimates of the standard errors of the individual elements of $\widehat{g(\vartheta)}$.

As an example, consider the construction of estimates of σ_j, $\varphi_j(1)$, and $\varphi_{i,j}(s)$ via the use of a VAR specified for X_t, as demonstrated in table 4.1. In this case, a parameterized version of (4.26), or equivalently (4.29), serves as the model used to generate artificial realizations of $\{X_t\}_{t=1}^T$; this model is known as the data generation process in the experiment. Consider the use of (4.29) for this purpose. Using p initial values of $\{X_t\}$ as starting values, implying a specification z_0, a drawing of $\{X_t\}_{t=1}^T$ is obtained using (4.29) first by obtaining a drawing of $\{e_t\}_{t=1}^T$ from a specified distribution, inserting e_1 into (4.29) to obtain

$$z_1 = Az_0 + e_1,$$

and then selecting the 1st, $(p+1)^{\text{th}}, \ldots, [(m-1)p+1]^{\text{th}}$ elements from z_1 to obtain X_1. Repeating this process T times yields $\{X_t\}_{t=1}^T$. This realization is then used to estimate A and Σ, from which $\Gamma(0)$ and $\Gamma(1)$ are constructed using (4.30)–(4.32). Finally, extraction of σ_j, $\varphi_j(1)$, and $\varphi_{i,j}(s)$ from $\Gamma(0)$ and $\Gamma(1)$ yields a Monte Carlo drawing of these statistics.

Denote the ith drawing of these statistics as $\widehat{g(\vartheta)}^i$. The mean and variance of $\widehat{g(\vartheta)}$ calculated over the realization of N Monte Carlo drawings are given by

$$\overline{g(\vartheta)} = \frac{1}{N}\sum_{i=1}^{N} \widehat{g(\vartheta)}^i; \tag{4.47}$$

$$Var(g(\vartheta)) = \frac{1}{N}\sum_{i=1}^{N}[\widehat{g(\vartheta)}^i - \overline{g(\vartheta)}]^2. \tag{4.48}$$

The square root of the diagonal elements of $Var(g(\vartheta))$ provide a single estimate of the standard error of $\widehat{g(\vartheta)}$. Denote this estimate as $s.e.[g(\vartheta)]$. Replication of this process using a total of J Monte Carlo experiments yields J drawings of $s.e.[g(\vartheta)]$. Letting the jth drawing be given by $s.e.[g(\vartheta)]^j$, a natural estimator of $s.e.[g(\vartheta)]$ is the average computed over the J experiments:

$$\overline{s.e.[g(\vartheta)]} = \frac{1}{J}\sum_{j=1}^{J} s.e.[g(\vartheta)]^j. \tag{4.49}$$

The variance of this estimator is calculated as

$$Var\left[\overline{s.e.[g(\vartheta)]}\right] = \frac{1}{J}\sum_{j=1}^{J}\left\{s.e.[g(\vartheta)]^j - \overline{s.e.[g(\vartheta)]}\right\}^2, \tag{4.50}$$

and the standard deviation $s.e.[\overline{s.e.[g(\vartheta)]}]$ is once again the square root of the diagonal elements of the variance.

An assessment of the accuracy of $\overline{s.e.[g(\vartheta)]}$ is provided by its numerical standard error (*nse*). The *nse* associated with any Monte Carlo estimator is given by the ratio of its standard error to the number of Monte Carlo replications (e.g., see Rubinstein, 1981). The *nse* of $\overline{s.e.[g(\vartheta)]}$ is therefore

$$nse\left\{\overline{s.e.[g(\vartheta)]}\right\} = \frac{s.e.\left[\overline{s.e.[g(\vartheta)]}\right]}{\sqrt{J}}. \tag{4.51}$$

A critical step in obtaining Monte Carlo estimates involves the design of the experiment. In the present context the design has three components: parameterization of the DGP (including the distribution chosen for e_t), the specification for z_0, and the specification of the artificial sample size T. Choices for these components in general will depend upon the particular objective of the experiment. But given the goal of constructing standard errors for point estimates of statistics constructed from the parameters of a reduced-form specification, a natural starting point for parameterizing the DGP is to use point estimates obtained using the actual sample. Also, natural choices for z_0 include the unconditional mean of z (zero in this case), or the initial value for z_0 obtained for the actual sample. And a natural choice for T is the actual sample size. Variations along all three dimensions are useful for assessing the sensitivity of results.

Exercise 4.4

Construct a Monte Carlo estimate of standard errors associated with estimates of the spectrum of a single variable y_t obtained using (4.36). Do so using the following steps.

1. Construct an ARMA(1,1) DGP for y_t, using $T=100$, $y_0=0$, $\rho=0.8$, $\theta=-0.3$, and $\varepsilon_t \sim N(0,1)$.
2. Let $g(\vartheta)$ represent the $(n+1)\times 1$ vector of values of the spectrum $s_y(\omega)$, $\omega = 0, \pi/n, 2\pi/n, \ldots, \pi$, $n=40$.
3. For each of 100 realizations of $\{y_t\}$ obtained from the DGP you constructed, estimate an ARMA(2,2) specification, and construct $\widehat{g(\vartheta)}$ by inserting the parameter estimates you obtain in (4.36).
4. Calculate the standard deviation of each element of $\widehat{g(\vartheta)}$ over the 100 drawings you obtained: this yields a single estimate of $s.e.\left[s_y(\omega)\right]$, $\omega = 0, \pi/n, 2\pi/n, \ldots, \pi$.
5. Repeat steps 3 and 4 100 times, and use the resulting 100 drawings of $s.e.\left[s_y(\omega)\right]$ to construct $\overline{s.e.[\,g(\vartheta)]}$, $s.e.\left[\overline{s.e.[\,g(\vartheta)]}\right]$, and $nse\left\{\overline{s.e.[\,g(\vartheta)]}\right\}$.

Under the Bayesian perspective, ϑ (and thus $(g(\vartheta))$ is interpreted as random; inferences regarding $g(\vartheta)$ involve calculations of conditional probabilities associated with alternative values of $g(\vartheta)$. Conditional probabilities are assigned by the posterior distribution associated with $g(\vartheta)$. The posterior distribution reflects the combined influence of a prior distribution specified by the researcher over $g(\vartheta)$, and the conditional likelihood function associated with $g(\vartheta)$ (where conditioning is with respect to the observed data). Point estimates $\widehat{g(\vartheta)}$ are typically given by means or modes of the posterior distribution obtained for $g(\vartheta)$; and the precision of these estimates is typically summarized using posterior standard deviations. Details regarding the Bayesian perspective are provided in chapter 9.

4.3 The Kalman Filter

We now turn to the foundation of full-information analyses of structural models: evaluation of the likelihood function via use of the Kalman filter. For convenience, we begin by repeating the characterization of the DSGE model solution as a collection of stochastic difference equations of the form

$$x_t = F(\mu)x_{t-1} + e_t \tag{4.52}$$

$$e_t = G(\mu)v_t \tag{4.53}$$

$$E(e_t e_t') = G(\mu)E(v_t v_t')G(\mu)' = Q(\mu). \tag{4.54}$$

Again, (4.52)–(4.54) comprise the state system, describing the evolution of the $n \times 1$ vector of model variables x_t. These are mapped into the $m \times 1$ vector of observable variables X_t via either

$$X_t = H(\mu)'x_t \tag{4.55}$$

or

$$X_t = H(\mu)'x_t + u_t, \qquad E(u_t u_t') = \Sigma_u, \tag{4.56}$$

both of which are known as measurement equations. The Kalman filter can be used to build likelihood functions based on various specifications of the measurement system, under the assumption of normality for $\{e_t\}$ and $\{u_t\}$.[8] Departures from normality, and from the linear structure considered here, prompt us to an alternative known as the particle filter, which is outlined in chapter 11. Here we present a general overview of the Kalman filter, and then make specific presentations for three leading specifications.

4.3.1 *Overview*

Full-information analyses entail calculations of the probability or likelihood associated with the realization of an observed sample $X \equiv \{X_t\}_{t=1}^T$. The Kalman filter is an algorithm designed to execute this calculation recursively, following the recursive nature of its associated structural model.

The idea behind the algorithm is to produce assessments of the conditional probability associated with the time-t observation X_t, given the history of past realizations $X^{t-1} \equiv \{X_j\}_{j=1}^{t-1}$. Denote this probability as $L(X_t|X^{t-1})$, with $L(X_1|X^0)$ denoting the unconditional likelihood associated with X_1. The sequence of conditional likelihoods $\{L(X_t|X^{t-1})\}_{t=1}^T$

[8] The GAUSS procedure `kalman.prc` is available for performing the calculations described in this section.

are independent across time, thus the likelihood associated with X is given by the product of the individual conditional likelihoods:

$$L(X) = \prod_{t=1}^{T} L(X_t|X^{t-1}).$$

Regarding the structure of $L(X_t|X^{t-1})$, this is most simply described for the case in which each of the elements of x_t is observable, so that $X_t \equiv x_t$. Conditional on $\{x_j\}_{j=1}^{t-1}$, from (4.52) we observe that the optimal forecast of x_t is given by

$$\widehat{x}_t = F(\mu)x_{t-1},$$

and the difference between the forecasted and observed value of x_t serves as the inferred value of e_t:

$$\widehat{e}_t = x_t - F(\mu)x_{t-1}.$$

The conditional likelihood associated with the observation of x_t can thus be assessed as the likelihood assigned to $\widehat{e}_t$ by its assumed probability distribution (say, p_e):

$$L(X_t|X^{t-1}) = p_e(\widehat{e}_t).$$

The details are slightly more complicated when certain elements of x_t are unobservable, but the basic idea is the same: conditional likelihoods represent probabilities associated with the realization of observables at time t, given the sequence of variables that were observed previously.

4.3.2 The Filter without Measurement Errors

When the measurement system is given by (4.55), then (4.52)–(4.55) are referred to as a state-space representation. The associated likelihood function is obtained by making a distributional assumption for $\{e_t\}$. As noted, we proceed here under the assumption of normality.

Consider the objective of calculating the value of the likelihood function for a given value of μ, which implies values for $[F(\mu), G(\mu), Q(\mu), H(\mu)]$ (hereafter, we revert to the notation under which the dependence of F, etc. on μ is taken as given). To establish intuition for how this is achieved given the presence of unobservable variables in x_t, consider first the simpler case in which each variable is instead observable, as in the previous subsection. In this case, the system consists of (4.52)–(4.54); likelihood evaluation is achieved via the iterative evaluation of a sequence of conditional distributions for x_t, given x_{t-1}. The iteration begins by inserting x_1 into its unconditional distribution, which is $N(0, Q)$:

$$L(x_1|\mu) = (2\pi)^{-n/2}|Q^{-1}|^{1/2} \exp\left[-\frac{1}{2}(x_1' Q^{-1} x_1)\right].$$

Then for x_t, $t = 2, \dots, T$, the iteration continues by inserting x_t into its conditional (on x_{t-1}) distribution, which is $N(Fx_{t-1}, Q)$:

$$L(x_t|\mu) = (2\pi)^{-n/2}|Q^{-1}|^{1/2} \\ \times \exp\left[-\frac{1}{2}(x_t - Fx_{t-1})' Q^{-1}(x_t - Fx_{t-1})\right].$$

Finally, the sample likelihood is the product of the individual likelihoods:

$$L(x|\mu) = \prod_{t=1}^{T} L(x_t|\mu).$$

Exercise 4.5

Map the $AR(p)$ process specified for the univariate time series y_t in (4.17) into a representation of the form given in (4.52)–(4.54). Next, show that OLS and ML estimates of $\rho(L)$ coincide.

For the case in which x_t includes unobservables, the Kalman filter adds an additional step to this iterative process. This involves making an inference regarding the most likely specification for x_t, given the sequence of observations on $\{X_j\}$, $j = 1, \dots t$.

Let $x_{t|t-1}$ be the conditional expectation of x_t given observations

$$\{X_1, \dots, X_{t-1}\},$$

and

$$P_{t|t-1} = E[(x_t - x_{t|t-1})(x_t - x_{t|t-1})']$$

be its associated covariance matrix. The iterative process begins with the calculation of their initial (unconditional) values, given by

$$x_{1|0} = 0, \qquad P_{1|0} = FP_{1|0}F' + Q \\ \rightarrow vec(P_{1|0}) = (I - F \otimes F')^{-1} vec(Q). \tag{4.57}$$

These are used to construct associated values for $X_{1|0}$, given by

$$X_{1|0} = H'x_{1|0} = 0, \tag{4.58}$$

$$\Omega_{1|0} = E[(X_1 - X_{1|0})(X_1 - X_{1|0})'] \\ = H'P_{1|0}H. \tag{4.59}$$

These serve as inputs for the likelihood function of X_1, which is $N(X_{1|0}, \Omega_{1|0})$:

$$L(X_1|\mu) = (2\pi)^{-m/2}|\Omega_{1|0}^{-1}|^{1/2} \exp\left[-\frac{1}{2}(X_1'\Omega_{1|0}{}^{-1}X_1)\right]. \tag{4.60}$$

Finally, the unconditional values $[x_{1|0}, P_{1|0}]$ are updated to take into account information conveyed by the observation of X_1. The updates yield conditional values $x_{1|1} \equiv x_1$ and $P_{1|1} \equiv P_1$:

$$x_{1|1} = x_{1|0} + P_{1|0}H\Omega_{1|0}^{-1}(X_1 - X_{1|0}) \tag{4.61}$$

$$P_{1|1} = P_{1|0} - P_{1|0}H\Omega_{1|0}^{-1}H'P_{1|0}. \tag{4.62}$$

Having accomplished initialization, the iterations involving X_t, $t = 2, \ldots T$ are identical. First, $x_{t|t-1}$ and $P_{t|t-1}$ are constructed:

$$x_{t|t-1} = Fx_{t-1} \tag{4.63}$$

$$P_{t|t-1} = FP_{t|t-1}F' + Q$$

$$\rightarrow vec(P_{t|t-1}) = (I - F \otimes F')^{-1}vec(Q). \tag{4.64}$$

These serve as inputs for the construction of $[X_{t|t-1}, \Omega_{t|t-1}]$:

$$X_{t|t-1} = H'x_{t|t-1} \tag{4.65}$$

$$\begin{aligned}\Omega_{t|t-1} &= E[(X_t - X_{t|t-1})(X_t - X_{t|t-1})'] \\ &= H'P_{t|t-1}H.\end{aligned} \tag{4.66}$$

These then facilitate the calculation of the likelihood function for X_t, which is $N(X_{t|t-1}, \Omega_{t|t-1})$:

$$\begin{aligned}L(X_t|\mu) &= (2\pi)^{-m/2}|\Omega_{t|t-1}^{-1}|^{1/2} \\ &\quad\times \exp\left[\frac{-1}{2}(X_t - X_{t|t-1})'\Omega_{t|t-1}{}^{-1}(X_t - X_{t|t-1})\right].\end{aligned} \tag{4.67}$$

Finally, X_t is fed into the updating system, yielding

$$x_{t|t} = x_{t|t-1} + P_{t|t-1}H\Omega_{t|t-1}^{-1}(X_t - X_{t|t-1}) \tag{4.68}$$

$$P_{t|t} = P_{t|t-1} - P_{t|t-1}H\Omega_{t|t-1}^{-1}H'P_{t|t-1}. \tag{4.69}$$

The sample likelihood is once again the product of the individual likelihoods:

$$L(X|\mu) = \prod_{t=1}^{T} L(X_t|\mu). \tag{4.70}$$

It is often the case that the time-series behavior of certain unobserved elements of x_t are of independent interest. It is possible to infer this behavior as a by-product of the likelihood evaluation process by obtaining what are known as smoothed estimates of the unobservables: $\{\widehat{x}_{t|T}\}_{t=1}^{T}$. As indicated above, the steps of the Kalman filter yield values of

$$\{x_{t|t}\}_{t=1}^{T}, \{x_{t+1|t}\}_{t=0}^{T-1}, \{P_{t|t}\}_{t=1}^{T} \text{ and } \{P_{t+1|t}\}_{t=0}^{T-1}.$$

These values may be used to construct $\{\widehat{x}_{t|T}\}_{t=1}^{T}$, as follows. The smoothed estimate $\widehat{x}_{T|T}$ is simply the last entry of $\{x_{t|t}\}_{t=1}^{T}$. Next, the quantity $J_t = P_{t|t}F'P_{t+1|t}$ is computed so that the series $\{J_t\}_{t=1}^{T-1}$ is available. This allows the computation of

$$\widehat{x}_{T-1|T} = \widehat{x}_{T-1|T-1} + J_{T-1}(\widehat{x}_{T|T} - \widehat{x}_{T|T-1}), \tag{4.71}$$

which can be used for $t = T - 2$ to compute

$$\widehat{x}_{T-1|T} = \widehat{x}_{T-1|T-1} + J_{T-1}(\widehat{x}_{T|T} - \widehat{x}_{T|T-1}). \tag{4.72}$$

Proceeding recursively in this manner yields the sequence of interest

$$\{\widehat{x}_{t|T}\}_{t=1}^{T},$$

with associated covariance given by

$$P_{t|T} = P_{t|t} + J_t(P_{t+1|T} - P_{t+1|t})J_t'. \tag{4.73}$$

Exercise 4.6

Repeat Steps 1–3 of the previous exercise using the ARMA model for y_t specified in (4.22), given $p = q = 1$.

4.3.3 The Filter with Measurement Errors

When there is measurement error associated with the observation of X_t, the measurement system is given by (4.56). The likelihood function is obtained in this case by making a distributional assumption for $\{e_t\}$ and the $m \times 1$ vector of measurement errors $\{u_t\}$. Once again, we proceed here under the assumption of normality for both e_t and u_t.[9] In addition, we assume that the measurement errors u_t are serially uncorrelated; in section 4.3.4 we consider the case in which this assumption is generalized.

Relative to the case in which there is no measurement error, many of the computations required to build the likelihood function remain the

[9] The GAUSS procedure `kalmanm.prc` is available for performing the calculations described in this section.

same. The main difference is that the initial unconditional values at which the filter begins are altered slightly. This implies changes in the updating formulae used in the construction of the likelihood function. In particular, $\Omega_{1|0}$ is now given by

$$\begin{aligned}\Omega_{1|0} &= E[(X_1 - X_{1|0})(X_1 - X_{1|0})'] \\ &= H'P_{1|0}H + \Sigma_u;\end{aligned} \tag{4.74}$$

analogously, $\Omega_{t|t-1}$ is given by:

$$\begin{aligned}\Omega_{t|t-1} &= E[(X_t - X_{t|t-1})(X_t - X_{t|t-1})'] \\ &= H'P_{t|t-1}H + \Sigma_u.\end{aligned} \tag{4.75}$$

The calculation of the likelihood function for X_t, which continues to be $N(X_{t|t-1}, \Omega_{t|t-1})$, is facilitated by replacing (4.66) by (4.75). Finally, smoothed estimates are obtained using exactly the same process described above, with (4.75) replacing (4.66) prior to the computation of (4.71)–(4.73).

Exercise 4.7

Consider the following model relating consumption (y_t) to income (z_t), taste shocks (x_t), and subject to an error in measurement (ε_t)

$$y_t = a_1 z_t + u_2 x_t + \varepsilon_t, \quad \varepsilon_t \sim N(0, \sigma^2).$$

Assume that taste shocks follow an AR(1) specification given by

$$x_t = \rho x_{t-1} + \epsilon_t, \quad \epsilon_t \sim N(0, \varsigma^2).$$

1. Specify the model in state-space form.
2. Initialize the Kalman filter.
3. Specify the likelihood function of the model expressed in Kalman filter form.

4.3.4 Serially Correlated Measurement Errors

As a final case, suppose that the measurement errors in (4.56) are serially correlated, obeying:

$$u_t = \Gamma u_{t-1} + \xi_t \tag{4.76}$$

$$E(\xi_t \xi_t') = \Sigma_\xi. \tag{4.77}$$

Sargent (1989) demonstrated the evaluation of DSGE models featuring diagonal specifications for the $m \times m$ matrices Γ and Σ_ξ, and Ireland

(2004b) demonstrated an extension to the non-diagonal case. In either case, the evaluation of the likelihood function associated with (4.52)–(4.54), (4.56), and (4.76)–(4.77) turns out to be identical to the case in which the observation equation is given by (4.55), and thus the system has no measurement error. To see why, consider an augmentation of the state system given by

$$\zeta_t = \begin{bmatrix} x_t \\ u_t \end{bmatrix} \quad \text{and} \quad \gamma_t = \begin{bmatrix} G\upsilon_t \\ \xi_t \end{bmatrix}. \tag{4.78}$$

Given this augmentation, the state-space representation may be written as

$$\zeta_t = \Theta_0 \zeta_{t-1} + \gamma_t \tag{4.79}$$

$$X_t = \Theta_1 \zeta_t \tag{4.80}$$

$$\Theta_0 = \begin{bmatrix} F & 0 \\ 0 & \Gamma \end{bmatrix}, \quad \Theta_1 = \begin{bmatrix} H \\ I \end{bmatrix}' \tag{4.81}$$

$$Q' = E(\gamma_t \gamma_t') = \begin{bmatrix} Q & 0 \\ 0 & \Sigma_\xi \end{bmatrix}, \tag{4.82}$$

which is exactly in the form of (4.52)–(4.55). Thus replacing F and H with Θ_0 and Θ_1 in section 4.3.2 enables the construction of the likelihood function; likewise, this replacement enables the calculation of smoothed estimates of ζ_t.

As a preview of issues to be discussed in chapter 8, we conclude this chapter by noting that in the absence of restrictions on the matrices (F, G, H, Q), the likelihood function can take on the same value for more than one set of values for μ. This is known as an identification problem. There are several ways to address this problem, one of which involves restricting (F, G, H, Q) on the basis of theoretical restrictions on μ, which then map into restrictions on (F, G, H, Q). Beyond this issue, we also note that in addition to likelihood evaluation and smoothing, the Kalman filter can be used to conduct a battery of model diagnostics. We discuss these and related issues in chapter 8, paying particular attention to peculiarities that arise in the context of the analysis of DSGE models.

Chapter 5

DSGE Models: Three Examples

Example is the School of Mankind, and they will learn at no other.

—Edmund Burke, *Thoughts on the Cause of the Present Discontents*

CHAPTER 2 PROVIDED background for preparing structural models for empirical analysis. Recall that the first step of the preparation stage is the construction of a linear approximation of the structural model under investigation, which takes the form

$$Ax_{t+1} = Bx_t + Cv_{t+1} + D\eta_{t+1}.$$

This chapter demonstrates the completion of this first step for three prototypical model environments that will serve as examples throughout the remainder of the text. This will set the stage for part II, which outlines and demonstrates alternative approaches to pursuing empirical analysis. (For guidance regarding the completion of this step for a far broader range of models than those considered here, see Hansen and Sargent, 2005.)

The first environment is an example of a simple real business cycle (RBC) framework, patterned after that of Kydland and Prescott (1982). The foundation of models in the RBC tradition is a neoclassical growth environment, augmented with two key features: a labor-leisure trade-off that confronts decision makers, and uncertainty regarding the evolution of technological progress. The empirical question Kydland and Prescott (1982) sought to address was the extent to which such a model, bereft of market imperfections and featuring fully flexible prices, could account for observed patterns of business cycle activity while capturing salient features of economic growth. This question continues to serve as a central focus of this active literature; overviews are available in the collection of papers presented in Barro (1989) and Cooley (1995).

Viewed through the lens of an RBC model, business cycle activity is interpretable as reflecting optimal responses to stochastic movements in the evolution of technological progress. Such interpretations are not without controversy. Alternative interpretations cite the existence of market imperfections, costs associated with the adjustment of prices, and other nominal and real frictions as potentially playing important roles in influencing business cycle behavior, and giving rise to additional sources of business cycle fluctuations. Initial skepticism of this nature was voiced by Summers (1986), and the collection of papers contained in Mankiw and Romer (1991) provide an overview of DSGE models that highlight the role of, for example, market imperfections in influencing aggregate economic behavior. As a complement to the RBC environment, the second environment presented here (that of Ireland, 2004a) provides an example of a model within this neo-Keynesian tradition. Its empirical purpose is to simultaneously evaluate the role of cost, demand, and productivity shocks in driving business cycle fluctuations. Textbook references for models within this tradition are Benassy (2002) and Woodford (2003).

The realm of empirical applications pursued through the use of DSGE models extends well beyond the study of business cycles. The third environment serves as an example of this point: it is a model of asset-pricing behavior adopted from Lucas (1978). The model represents financial assets as tools used by households to optimize intertemporal patterns of consumption in the face of exogenous stochastic movements in income and dividends earned from asset holdings. Viewed through the lens of this model, two particular features of asset-pricing behavior have proven exceptionally difficult to explain. First, LeRoy and Porter (1981) and Shiller (1981) used versions of the model to underscore the puzzling volatility of prices associated with broad indexes of assets (such as the Standard & Poor's 500), highlighting what has come to be known as the "volatility puzzle." Second, Mehra and Prescott (1985) and Weil (1989) used versions of the model to highlight the puzzling dual phenomenon of a large gap observed between aggregate returns on risky and riskless assets, coupled with exceptionally low returns yielded by riskless assets. These features came to be known as the "equity premium" and "risk-free rate" puzzles. The texts of Shiller (1989), Campbell, Lo and MacKinlay (1997), and Cochrane (2001) provide overviews of literatures devoted to analyses of these puzzles.

In addition to the references cited above, a host of introductory graduate-level textbooks serve as useful references for the specific example models considered here, and for a wide range of extensions. A partial listing includes Sargent (1987a,b), Stokey and Lucas (1989), Blanchard and Fischer (1998), Romer (2001), and Ljungqvist and Sargent (2004).

5.1 Model I: A Real Business Cycle Model

5.1.1 Environment

The economy consists of a large number of identical households; aggregate economic activity is analyzed by focusing on a representative household.

The household's objective is to maximize U, the expected discounted flow of utility arising from chosen streams of consumption and leisure:

$$\max_{c_t, l_t} \qquad U = E_0 \sum_{t=0}^{\infty} \beta^t u(c_t, l_t). \tag{5.1}$$

In (5.1), E_0 is the expectations operator conditional on information available at time 0, $\beta \in (0, 1)$ is the household's subjective discount factor, $u(\cdot)$ is an instantaneous utility function, and c_t and l_t denote levels of consumption and leisure chosen at time t.

The household is equipped with a production technology that can be used to produce a single good y_t. The production technology is represented by

$$y_t = z_t f(k_t, n_t), \tag{5.2}$$

where k_t and n_t denote quantities of physical capital and labor assigned by the household to the production process, and z_t denotes a random disturbance to the productivity of these inputs to production (that is, a productivity or technology shock).

Within a period, the household has one unit of time available for division between labor and leisure activities:

$$1 = n_t + l_t. \tag{5.3}$$

In addition, output generated at time t can be either consumed or used to augment the stock of physical capital available for use in the production process in period $t + 1$. That is, output can be either consumed or invested:

$$y_t = c_t + i_t, \tag{5.4}$$

where i_t denotes the quantity of investment. Finally, the stock of physical capital evolves according to

$$k_{t+1} = i_t + (1 - \delta)k_t, \tag{5.5}$$

where $\delta \in (0, 1)$ denotes the depreciation rate. The household's problem is to maximize (5.1) subject to (5.2)–(5.5), taking k_0 and z_0 as given.

Implicit in the specification of the household's problem are two sets of trade-offs. One is a consumption/savings trade-off: from (5.4), higher consumption today implies lower investment (savings), and thus from (5.5), less capital available for production tomorrow. The other is a labor/leisure trade-off: from (5.3), higher leisure today implies lower labor today and thus lower output today.

In order to explore quantitative implications of the model, it is necessary to specify explicit functional forms for $u(\cdot)$ and $f(\cdot)$, and to characterize the stochastic behavior of the productivity shock z_t. We pause before doing so to make some general comments. As noted, an explicit goal of the RBC literature is to begin with a model specified to capture important characteristics of economic growth, and then to judge the ability of the model to capture key components of business cycle activity. From the model builder's perspective, the former requirement serves as a constraint on choices regarding the specifications for $u(\cdot)$, $f(\cdot)$, and the stochastic process of z_t. Three key aspects of economic growth serve as constraints in this context: over long time horizons the growth rates of $\{c_t, i_t, y_t, k_t\}$ are roughly equal (balanced growth), the marginal productivity of capital and labor (reflected by relative factor payments) are roughly constant over time, and $\{l_t, n_t\}$ show no tendencies for long-term growth.

Beyond satisfying this constraint, functional forms chosen for $u(\cdot)$ are typically strictly increasing in both arguments, twice continuously differentiable, strictly concave, and satisfy

$$\lim_{c \to 0} \frac{\partial u(c_t, l_t)}{\partial c_t} = \lim_{l \to 0} \frac{\partial u(c_t, l_t)}{\partial l_t} = \infty. \tag{5.6}$$

Functional forms chosen for $f(\cdot)$ typically feature constant returns to scale and satisfy similar limit conditions.

Finally, we note that the inclusion of a single source of uncertainty in this framework, via the productivity shock z_t, implies that the model carries nontrivial implications for the stochastic behavior of a single corresponding observable variable. For the purposes of this chapter, this limitation is not important; however, it will motivate the introduction of extensions of this basic model in part II.

FUNCTIONAL FORMS

The functional forms presented here enjoy prominent roles in the macroeconomics literature. Instantaneous utility is of the constant relative risk aversion (CRRA) form:

$$u(c_t, l_t) = \left(\frac{c_t^{\varphi} l_t^{1-\varphi}}{1-\phi} \right)^{1-\phi}, \tag{5.7}$$

or when $\phi = 1$, $u(\cdot) = \log(\cdot)$. The parameter $\phi > 0$ determines two attributes: it is the coefficient of relative risk aversion, and also determines the intertemporal elasticity of substitution, given by $\frac{1}{\phi}$ (for textbook discussions, see e.g., Blanchard and Fischer, 1998; or Romer, 2006). Note that the larger is ϕ, the more intense is the household's interest in maintaining a smooth consumption/leisure profile. Also, $\varphi \in (0, 1)$ indicates the importance of consumption relative to leisure in determining instantaneous utility.

Next, the production function is of the Cobb-Douglas variety:

$$y_t = z_t k_t^{\alpha} n_t^{1-\alpha}, \tag{5.8}$$

where $\alpha \in (0,1)$ represents capital's share of output. Finally, the log of the technology shock is assumed to follow a first-order autoregressive, or AR(1), process:

$$\log z_t = (1-\rho)\log(\overline{z}) + \rho \log z_{t-1} + \varepsilon_t \tag{5.9}$$

$$\varepsilon_t \sim NID(0,\sigma^2), \quad \rho \in (-1,1). \tag{5.10}$$

The solution to the household's problem may be obtained via standard application of the theory of dynamic programming (e.g., as described in detail in Stokey and Lucas, 1989; and briefly in chapter 10 of this book). Necessary conditions associated with the household's problem expressed in general terms are given by

$$\frac{\partial u(c_t, l_t)}{\partial l_t} = \left\{\frac{\partial u(c_t, l_t)}{\partial c_t}\right\} \times \left\{\frac{\partial f(k_t, n_t)}{\partial n_t}\right\} \tag{5.11}$$

$$\frac{\partial u(c_t, l_t)}{\partial c_t} = \beta E_t \left\{\frac{\partial u(c_{t+1}, l_{t+1})}{\partial c_{t+1}}\left[\frac{\partial f(k_{t+1}, n_{t+1})}{\partial k_{t+1}} + (1-\delta)\right]\right\}. \tag{5.12}$$

The intratemporal optimality condition (5.11) equates the marginal benefit of an additional unit of leisure time with its opportunity cost: the marginal value of the foregone output resulting from the corresponding reduction in labor time. The intertemporal optimality condition (5.12) equates the marginal benefit of an additional unit of consumption today with its opportunity cost: the discounted expected value of the additional utility tomorrow that the corresponding reduction in savings would have generated (higher output plus undepreciated capital).

Consider the qualitative implications of (5.11) and (5.12) for the impact of a positive productivity shock on the household's labor/leisure and consumption/savings decisions. From (5.11), higher labor productivity implies a higher opportunity cost of leisure, prompting a reduction in leisure time in favor of labor time. From (5.12), the curvature in the household's utility function carries with it a consumption-smoothing objective. A positive productivity shock serves to increase output, thus affording an increase in consumption; however, because the marginal utility of consumption is decreasing in consumption, this drives down the opportunity cost of savings. The greater is the curvature of $u(\cdot)$, the more intense is the consumption-smoothing objective, and thus the greater will be the intertemporal reallocation of resources in the face of a productivity shock.

Dividing (5.11) by the expression for the marginal utility of consumption, and using the functional forms introduced above, these conditions can be written as

$$\left(\frac{1-\varphi}{\varphi}\right)\frac{c_t}{l_t} = (1-\alpha)z_t\left(\frac{k_t}{n_t}\right)^{\alpha} \tag{5.13}$$

$$\begin{aligned} &c_t^{\varphi(1-\phi)-1}l_t^{(1-\varphi)(1-\phi)} \\ &\quad = \beta E_t\left\{c_{t+1}^{\varphi(1-\phi)-1}l_{t+1}^{(1-\varphi)(1-\phi)}\left[\begin{array}{c}\alpha z_{t+1}\left(\frac{n_{t+1}}{k_{t+1}}\right)^{1-\alpha} \\ +(1-\delta)\end{array}\right]\right\}. \end{aligned} \tag{5.14}$$

5.1.2 *The Nonlinear System*

Collecting components, the system of nonlinear stochastic difference equations that comprise the model is given by

$$\left(\frac{1-\varphi}{\varphi}\right)\frac{c_t}{l_t} = (1-\alpha)z_t\left(\frac{k_t}{n_t}\right)^{\alpha} \tag{5.15}$$

$$c_t^{\kappa}l_t^{\lambda} = \beta E_t\left\{c_{t+1}^{\kappa}l_{t+1}^{\lambda}\left[\alpha z_{t+1}\left(\frac{n_{t+1}}{k_{t+1}}\right)^{1-\alpha} + (1-\delta)\right]\right\} \tag{5.16}$$

$$y_t = z_t k_t^{\alpha} n_t^{1-\alpha} \tag{5.17}$$

$$y_t = c_t + i_t \tag{5.18}$$

$$k_{t+1} = i_t + (1-\delta)k_t \tag{5.19}$$

$$1 = n_t + l_t \tag{5.20}$$

$$\log z_t = (1-\rho)\log(\overline{z}) + \rho\log z_{t-1} + \varepsilon_t, \tag{5.21}$$

where

$$\kappa = \varphi(1-\phi) - 1$$

and

$$\lambda = (1-\varphi)(1-\phi).$$

Steady states of the variables $\{y_t, c_t, i_t, n_t, l_t, k_t, z_t\}$ may be computed analytically from this system. These are derived by holding z_t to its steady state value $\overline{z}$, which we set to 1:

$$\begin{aligned}
\frac{\overline{y}}{\overline{n}} &= \eta, \\
\frac{\overline{c}}{\overline{n}} &= \eta - \delta\theta, \\
\frac{\overline{i}}{\overline{n}} &= \delta\theta, \\
\overline{n} &= \frac{1}{1 + \left(\frac{1}{1-\alpha}\right)\left(\frac{1-\varphi}{\varphi}\right)\left[1 - \delta\theta^{1-\alpha}\right]}, \qquad (5.22) \\
\overline{l} &= 1 - \overline{n}, \\
\frac{\overline{k}}{\overline{n}} &= \theta,
\end{aligned}$$

where

$$\begin{aligned}
\theta &= \left(\frac{\alpha}{1/\beta - 1 + \delta}\right)^{\frac{1}{1-\alpha}} \\
\eta &= \theta^{\alpha}.
\end{aligned}$$

Note that in steady state the variables $\{y_t, c_t, i_t, k_t\}$ do not grow over time. Implicitly, these variables are represented in the model in terms of deviations from trend, and steady state values indicate the relative heights of trend lines. To incorporate growth explicitly, consider an alternative specification of z_t:

$$z_t = z_0(1+g)^t e^{\omega_t}, \qquad (5.23)$$

$$\omega_t = \rho\omega_{t-1} + \varepsilon_t. \qquad (5.24)$$

Note that, absent shocks, the growth rate of z_t is given by g, and that removal of the trend component $(1+g)^t$ from z_t yields the specification for $\log z_t$ given by (5.21). Further, the reader is invited to verify that under this specification for z_t, $\{c_t, i_t, y_t, k_t\}$ will have a common growth rate given by $\frac{g}{1-\alpha}$. Thus the model is consistent with the balanced-growth requirement, and as specified, all variables are interpreted as being measured in terms of deviations from their common trend.

One subtlety is associated with the issue of trend removal that arises in dealing with the dynamic equations of the system. Consider the law of motion for capital (5.19). Trend removal here involves division of both sides of (5.19) by $\left(1+\frac{g}{1-\alpha}\right)^{t}$; however, the trend component associated with k_{t+1} is $\left(1+\frac{g}{1-\alpha}\right)^{t+1}$, so the specification in terms of detrended variables is

$$\left(1+\frac{g}{1-\alpha}\right)k_{t+1} = i_t + (1-\delta)k_t. \tag{5.25}$$

Likewise, a residual trend factor will be associated with c_{t+1} in the intertemporal optimality condition (5.16). Because c_{t+1} is raised to the power

$$\kappa = \varphi(1-\phi) - 1,$$

the residual factor is given by $\left(1+\frac{g}{1-\alpha}\right)^{\kappa}$:

$$c_t^{\kappa} l_t^{\lambda} = \beta E_t \times \left\{\left(1+\frac{g}{1-\alpha}\right)^{\kappa} c_{t+1}^{\kappa} l_{t+1}^{\lambda}\left[\alpha z_{t+1}\left(\frac{n_{t+1}}{k_{t+1}}\right)^{1-\alpha} + (1-\delta)\right]\right\}. \tag{5.26}$$

With κ negative (insured by $\frac{1}{\phi} < 1$, i.e., an inelastic intertemporal elasticity of substitution specification), the presence of g provides an incentive to shift resources away from $(t+1)$ towards t.

Exercise 5.1

Rederive the steady state expressions (5.22) by replacing (5.19) with (5.25), and (5.16) with (5.26). Interpret the intuition behind the impact of g on the expressions you derive.

5.1.3 Linearization

The linearization step involves taking a log-linear approximation of the model at steady state values. In this case, the objective is to map (5.15)–(5.21) into the linearized system

$$Ax_{t+1} = Bx_t + C\upsilon_{t+1} + D\eta_{t+1}$$

for eventual empirical evaluation. Regarding D, dropping E_t from the Euler equation (5.16) introduces an expectations error in the model's second equation, therefore

$$D = [0\ 1\ 0\ 0\ 0\ 0\ 0]'.$$

Likewise, the presence of the productivity shock in the model's seventh equation (5.21) implies

$$C = [0\ 0\ 0\ 0\ 0\ 0\ 1]'.$$

Regarding A and B, using the solution methodology discussed in chapter 2, these can be constructed by introducing the following system of equations into a gradient procedure (where time subscripts are dropped so that, e.g., $y = y_t$ and $y' = y_{t+1}$):

$$0 = \log\left(\frac{1-\varphi}{\varphi}\right) + \log c' - \log l' - \log(1-\alpha) - \log z'$$

$$- \alpha \log k + \alpha \log n' \tag{5.27}$$

$$0 = \kappa \log c + \lambda \log l - \log \beta - \kappa \log c' - \lambda \log l' \tag{5.28}$$

$$- \log\left[\alpha \exp(\log z') \frac{\exp[(1-\alpha)\log n']}{\exp[(1-\alpha)\log k']} + (1-\delta)\right]$$

$$0 = \log y' - \log z' - \alpha \log k - (1-\alpha)\log n' \tag{5.29}$$

$$0 = \log y' - \log\{\exp[\log(c')] + \exp[\log(i')]\} \tag{5.30}$$

$$0 = \log k' - \log\{\exp[\log(i')] + (1-\delta)\exp[\log(k)]\} \tag{5.31}$$

$$0 = -\log\{\exp[\log(n')] + \exp[\log(l')]\} \tag{5.32}$$

$$0 = \log z' - \rho \log z. \tag{5.33}$$

The mapping from (5.15)–(5.21) to (5.27)–(5.33) involves four steps. First, logs of both sides of each equation are taken; second, all variables not converted into logs in the first step are converted using the fact, for example, that $y = \exp(\log(y))$; third, all terms are collected on the right-hand side of each equation; fourth, all equations are multiplied by -1. Derivatives taken with respect to $\log y'$, and so on evaluated at steady state values yield A, and derivatives taken with respect to $\log y$, and so on yield $-B$. Note that capital installed at time t is not productive until period $t+1$; thus k rather than k' appears in (5.29).

Having obtained A, B, C, and D, the system can be solved using any of the solution methods outlined in chapter 2 to obtain a system of the form

$$x_{t+1} = F(\mu)x_t + e_{t+1}.$$

This system can then be evaluated empirically using any of the methods described in part II.

Exercise 5.2

With x_t given by

$$x_t = \left[\log\frac{y_t}{\overline{y}}, \log\frac{c_t}{\overline{c}}, \log\frac{i_t}{\overline{i}}, \log\frac{n_t}{\overline{n}}, \log\frac{l_t}{\overline{l}}, \log\frac{k_t}{\overline{k}}, \log\frac{z_t}{\overline{z}}\right]'$$

and

$$\mu = [\alpha\ \beta\ \phi\ \varphi\ \delta\ \rho\ \sigma]' = [0.33\ 0.975\ 2\ 0.5\ 0.06\ 0.9\ 0.01]',$$

show that the steady state values of the model are $\overline{y} = 0.9$, $\overline{c} = 0.7$, $\overline{i} = 0.2$, $\overline{n} = 0.47$, $\overline{l} = 0.53$, and $\overline{k} = 3.5$ (and take as granted $\overline{z} = 1$). Next, use a numerical gradient procedure to derive

$$A = \begin{bmatrix} 0 & 1 & 0 & 0.33 & -1 & 0 & -1 \\ 0 & 1.5 & 0 & -0.12 & 0.5 & 0 & -0.17 \\ 1 & 0 & 0 & -0.67 & 0 & 0 & -1 \\ 1 & -0.77 & -0.23 & 0 & 0 & 0 & 0 \\ 0 & 0 & -0.18 & 0 & 0 & 1 & 0 \\ 0 & 0 & 0 & -0.47 & -0.53 & 0 & 0 \\ 0 & 0 & 0 & 0 & 0 & 0 & 1 \end{bmatrix}$$

$$B = \begin{bmatrix} 0 & 0 & 0 & 0 & 0 & 0.33 & 0 \\ 0 & 1.5 & 0 & 0 & 0.5 & -0.9 & 0 \\ 0 & 0 & 0 & 0 & 0 & 0.33 & 0 \\ 0 & 0 & 0 & 0 & 0 & 0 & 0 \\ 0 & 0 & 0 & 0 & 0 & 0.77 & 0 \\ 0 & 0 & 0 & 0 & 0 & 0 & 0 \\ 0 & 0 & 0 & 0 & 0 & 0 & 0.9 \end{bmatrix}.$$

Exercise 5.3

Rederive the matrices A and B given the explicit incorporation of growth in the model. That is, derive A and B using the steady state expressions obtained in Exercise 5.1, and using (5.25) and (5.26) in place of (5.19) and (5.16).

5.2 Model II: Monopolistic Competition and Monetary Policy

This section outlines a model of imperfect competition featuring "sticky" prices. The model includes three sources of aggregate uncertainty: shocks to demand, technology, and the competitive structure of the economy. The model is due to Ireland (2004a), who designed it to determine how the apparent role of technology shocks in driving business-cycle fluctuations is influenced by the inclusion of these additional sources of uncertainty.

From a pedagogical perspective, the model differs in two interesting ways relative to the RBC model outlined above. Whereas the linearized RBC model is a first-order system of difference equations, the linearized version of this model is a second-order system. However, recall from chapter 2 that it is possible to represent a system of arbitrary order using the first-order form taken by

$$Ax_{t+1} = Bx_t + C\upsilon_{t+1} + D\eta_{t+1},$$

given appropriate specification of the elements of x_t. Second, the problem of mapping implications carried by a stationary model into the behavior of non-stationary data is revisited from an alternative perspective than that adopted in the discussion of the RBC model. Specifically, rather than assuming the actual data follow stationary deviations around deterministic trends, here the data are modeled as following drifting random walks; stationarity is induced via differencing rather than detrending.

5.2.1 Environment

The economy once again consists of a continuum of identical households. Here, there are two distinct production sectors: an intermediate-goods sector and a final-goods sector. The former is imperfectly competitive: it consists of a continuum of firms that produce differentiated products that serve as factors of production in the final-goods sector. Although firms in this sector have the ability to set prices, they face a friction in doing so. Finally, there is a central bank.

HOUSEHOLDS

The representative household maximizes lifetime utility defined over consumption, money holdings, and labor:

$$\max_{c_t, m_t, n_t} \quad U = E_0 \sum_{t=0}^{\infty} \beta^t \left\{ a_t \log c_t + \log \frac{m_t}{p_t} - \frac{n_t^{\xi}}{\xi} \right\} \tag{5.34}$$

$$s.t. \quad p_t c_t + \frac{b_t}{r_t} + m_t = m_{t-1} + b_{t-1} + \tau_t + w_t n_t + d_t, \tag{5.35}$$

where $\beta \in (0,1)$ and $\xi \geq 1$. According to the budget constraint (5.35), the household divides its wealth between holdings of bonds b_t and money m_t; bonds mature at the gross nominal rate r_t between time periods. The household also receives transfers τ_t from the monetary authority and works n_t hours in order to earn wages w_t to finance its expenditures. Finally, the household owns an intermediate-goods firm, from which it receives a dividend payment d_t. Note from (5.34) that the household is subject to an exogenous demand shock a_t that affects its consumption decision.

Recognizing that the instantaneous marginal utility derived from consumption is given by $\frac{a_t}{c_t}$, the first-order conditions associated with the household's choices of labor, bond holdings, and money holdings are given by

$$\left(\frac{w_t}{p_t}\right)\left(\frac{a_t}{c_t}\right) = n_t^{\xi-1} \tag{5.36}$$

$$\beta E_t\left\{\left(\frac{1}{p_{t+1}}\right)\left(\frac{a_{t+1}}{c_{t+1}}\right)\right\} = \left(\frac{1}{r_t p_t}\right)\left(\frac{a_t}{c_t}\right) \tag{5.37}$$

$$\left(\frac{m_t}{p_t}\right)^{-1} + \beta E_t\left\{\left(\frac{1}{p_{t+1}}\right)\left(\frac{a_{t+1}}{c_{t+1}}\right)\right\} = \left(\frac{1}{p_t}\right)\left(\frac{a_t}{c_t}\right). \tag{5.38}$$

Exercise 5.4

Interpret how (5.36)–(5.38) represent the optimal balancing of trade-offs associated with the household's choices of n, b, and m.

FIRMS

There are two types of firms: one produces a final consumption good y_t, which sells at price p_t; the other is a continuum of intermediate-goods firms that supply inputs to the final-good firm. The output of the ith intermediate good is given by y_{it}, which sells at price p_{it}. The intermediate goods combine to produce the final good via a constant elasticity of substitution (CES) production function. The final-good firm operates in a competitive environment and pursues the following objective:

$$\max_{y_{it}} \quad \Pi_t^F = p_t y_t - \int_0^1 p_{it} y_{it}\, di \tag{5.39}$$

$$s.t. \quad y_t = \left\{\int_0^1 y_{it}^{\frac{\theta_t - 1}{\theta_t}}\, di\right\}^{\frac{\theta_t}{\theta_t - 1}}. \tag{5.40}$$

The solution to this problem yields a standard demand for intermediate inputs and a price aggregator:

$$y_{it} = y_t\left\{\frac{p_{it}}{p_t}\right\}^{-\theta_t} \tag{5.41}$$

$$p_t = \left\{\int_0^1 p_{it}^{1-\theta_t}\, di\right\}^{\frac{1}{1-\theta_t}}. \tag{5.42}$$

Notice that θ_t is the markup of price above marginal cost; randomness in θ_t provides the notion of a cost-push shock in this environment.

Intermediate-goods firms are monopolistically competitive. Because the output of each firm enters the final-good production function symmetrically, the focus is on a representative firm. The firm is owned by the representative household, thus its objectives are aligned with the household's. It manipulates the sales price of its good in pursuit of these objectives, subject to a quadratic adjustment cost:

$$\max_{p_{it}} \quad \Pi^I_{it} = E_0 \sum_{t=0}^{\infty} \beta^t \left(\frac{a_t}{c_t}\right)\left(\frac{d_t}{p_t}\right), \tag{5.43}$$

$$s.t. \quad y_{it} = z_t n_{it} \tag{5.44}$$

$$y_{it} = y_t \left\{\frac{p_{it}}{p_t}\right\}^{-\theta_t} \tag{5.45}$$

$$\chi(p_{it}, p_{it-1}) = \frac{\phi}{2}\left[\frac{p_{it}}{\overline{\pi} p_{it-1}} - 1\right]^2 y_t, \quad \phi > 0, \tag{5.46}$$

where $\overline{\pi}$ is the gross inflation rate targeted by the monetary authority (described below), and the real value of dividends in (5.43) is given by

$$\frac{d_t}{p_t} = \left\{\frac{p_{it} y_{it} - w_t n_{it}}{p_t} - \chi(p_{it}, p_{it-1})\right\}. \tag{5.47}$$

The associated first-order condition can be written as

$$\begin{aligned}
&(\theta_t - 1)\left(\frac{p_{it}}{p_t}\right)^{-\theta_t} \frac{y_t}{p_t} \\
&= \theta_t \left(\frac{p_{it}}{p_t}\right)^{-\theta_t - 1} \frac{w_t}{p_t}\frac{y_t}{z_t}\frac{1}{p_t} - \left\{\phi\left[\frac{p_{it}}{\overline{\pi} p_{it-1}} - 1\right]\frac{y_t}{\overline{\pi} p_{it-1}} - \beta\phi \right. \\
&\left. \times E_t\left(\frac{a_{t+1}}{a_t}\frac{c_t}{c_{t+1}}\left(\frac{p_{it+1}}{\overline{\pi} p_{it}} - 1\right)\frac{y_{t+1} p_{it+1}}{\overline{\pi} p_{it}^2}\right)\right\}.
\end{aligned} \tag{5.48}$$

The left-hand side of (5.48) reflects the marginal revenue to the firm generated by an increase in price; the right-hand side reflects associated marginal costs. Under perfect price flexibility ($\phi = 0$) there is no dynamic component to the firm's problem; the price-setting rule reduces to

$$p_{it} = \frac{\theta_t}{\theta_t - 1}\frac{w_t}{z_t},$$

which is a standard markup of price over marginal cost $\frac{w_t}{z_t}$. Under "sticky prices" ($\phi > 0$) the marginal cost of an increase in price has two additional components: the direct cost of a price adjustment, and an expected discounted cost of a price change adjusted by the marginal utility to the households of conducting such a change. Empirically, the estimation of ϕ is of particular interest: this parameter plays a central role in distinguishing this model from its counterparts in the RBC literature.

THE MONETARY AUTHORITY

The monetary authority chooses the nominal interest rate according to a Taylor Rule. With all variables expressed in terms of logged deviations from steady state values, the rule is given by

$$\widetilde{r}_t = \rho_r \widetilde{r}_{t-1} + \rho_\pi \widetilde{\pi}_t + \rho_g \widetilde{g}_t + \rho_o \widetilde{o}_t + \varepsilon_{rt}, \qquad \varepsilon_{rt} \sim iidN(0, \sigma_r^2), \qquad (5.49)$$

where $\widetilde{\pi}_t$ is the gross inflation rate, $\widetilde{g}_t$ is the gross growth rate of output, and $\widetilde{o}_t$ is the output gap (defined below). The ρ_i parameters denote elasticities. The inclusion of $\widetilde{r}_{t-1}$ as an input into the Taylor Rule allows for the gradual adjustment of policy to demand and technology shocks, for example, as in Clarida, Gali, and Gertler (2000).

The output gap is the logarithm of the ratio of actual output y_t to capacity output $\widehat{y}_t$. Capacity output is defined to be the "efficient" level of output, which is equivalent to the level of output chosen by a benevolent social planner who solves:

$$\max_{\widehat{y}_t, n_{it}} \qquad U^S = E_0 \sum_0^\infty \beta^t \left\{ a_t \log \widehat{y}_t - \frac{1}{\xi} \left(\int_0^1 n_{it} \, di \right)^\xi \right\} \qquad (5.50)$$

$$s.t. \qquad \widehat{y}_t = z_t \left(\int_0^1 n_{it}^{\frac{\theta_t - 1}{\theta_t}} \, di \right)^{\frac{\theta_t}{\theta_t - 1}}. \qquad (5.51)$$

The symmetric solution to this problem is simply

$$\widehat{y}_t = a_t^{\frac{1}{\xi}} z_t. \qquad (5.52)$$

STOCHASTIC SPECIFICATION

In addition to the monetary policy shock ε_{rt} introduced in (5.49), the model features a demand shock a_t, a technology shock z_t, and a cost-push shock θ_t. The former is *iid*; the latter three evolve according to

$$\log(a_t) = (1 - \rho_a) \log(\overline{a}) + \rho_a \log(a_{t-1}) + \varepsilon_{at}, \qquad \overline{a} > 1 \qquad (5.53)$$

$$\log(z_t) = \log(\overline{z}) + \log(z_{t-1}) + \varepsilon_{zt}, \qquad \overline{z} > 1 \qquad (5.54)$$

$$\log(\theta_t) = (1 - \rho_\theta) \log(\overline{\theta}) + \rho_\theta \log(\theta_{t-1}) + \varepsilon_{\theta t}, \qquad \overline{\theta} > 1, \qquad (5.55)$$

with $|\rho_i| < 1$, $i = a, \theta$. Note that the technology shock is non-stationary: it evolves as a drifting random walk. This induces similar behavior in the model's endogenous variables, and necessitates the use of an alternative to the detrending method discussed above in the context of the RBC model. Here, stationarity is induced by normalizing model variables by z_t. For the corresponding observable variables, stationarity is induced by differencing rather than detrending: the observables are measured as deviations of growth rates (logged differences of levels) from sample averages. Details are provided in the linearization step discussed below.

The model is closed through two additional steps. The first is the imposition of symmetry among the intermediate-goods firms. Given that the number of firms is normalized to one, symmetry implies:

$$y_{it} = y_t, \qquad n_{it} = n_t, \qquad p_{it} = p_t, \qquad d_{it} = d_t. \tag{5.56}$$

The second is the requirement that the money and bond markets clear:

$$m_t = m_{t-1} + \tau_t \tag{5.57}$$

$$b_t = b_{t-1} = 0. \tag{5.58}$$

5.2.2 *The Nonlinear System*

In its current form, the model consists of twelve equations: the household's first-order conditions and budget constraint, the aggregate production function, the aggregate real dividends paid to the household by its intermediate-goods firm, the intermediate-goods firm's first-order condition, the stochastic specifications for the structural shocks, and the expression for capacity output. Following Ireland's (2004a) empirical implementation the focus is on a linearized reduction to an eight-equation system consisting of an IS curve, a Phillips curve, the Taylor Rule (specified in linearized form in (5.49)), the three exogenous shock specifications, and definitions for the growth rate of output and the output gap.

The reduced system is recast in terms of the following normalized variables:

$$\ddot{y}_t = \frac{y_t}{z_t}, \quad \ddot{c}_t = \frac{c_t}{z_t}, \quad \ddot{\hat{y}}_t = \frac{\hat{y}_t}{z_t}, \qquad \pi_t = \frac{p_t}{p_{t-1}},$$

$$\ddot{d}_t = \frac{(d_t/p_t)}{z_t}, \qquad \ddot{w}_t = \frac{(w_t/p_t)}{z_t}, \qquad \ddot{m}_t = \frac{(m_t/p_t)}{z_t}, \quad \ddot{z}_t = \frac{z_t}{z_{t-1}}.$$

Using the expression for real dividends given by (5.47), the household's budget constraint in equilibrium is rewritten as

$$\ddot{y}_t = \ddot{c}_t + \frac{\phi}{2}\left(\frac{\pi_t}{\overline{\pi}} - 1\right)^2 \ddot{y}_t. \tag{5.59}$$

Next, the household's first-order condition (5.37) is written in normalized form as

$$\frac{a_t}{\ddot{c}_t} = \beta r_t E_t \left\{ \frac{a_{t+1}}{\ddot{c}_{t+1}} \times \frac{1}{\ddot{z}_{t+1}} \times \frac{1}{\pi_{t+1}} \right\}. \tag{5.60}$$

Next, the household's remaining first-order conditions, the expression for the real dividend payment (5.47) it receives, and the aggregate production function can be combined to eliminate wages, money, labor, dividends, and capacity output from the system. Having done this, we then introduce the expression for the output gap into the system:

$$o_t \equiv \frac{y_t}{\widehat{y}_t} = \frac{\ddot{y}_t}{a_t^{\frac{1}{\xi}}}. \tag{5.61}$$

Finally, normalizing the first-order condition of the intermediate-goods firm and the stochastic specifications leads to the following nonlinear system:

$$\ddot{y}_t = \ddot{c}_t + \frac{\phi}{2}\left(\frac{\pi_t}{\overline{\pi}} - 1\right)^2 \ddot{y}_t \tag{5.62}$$

$$\frac{a_t}{\ddot{c}_t} = \beta r_t E_t \left\{ \frac{a_{t+1}}{\ddot{c}_{t+1}} \times \frac{1}{\ddot{z}_{t+1}} \times \frac{1}{\pi_{t+1}} \right\} \tag{5.63}$$

$$\begin{aligned} 0 = 1 - \theta_t + \theta_t \frac{\ddot{c}_t}{a_t} \ddot{y}_t^{\xi-1} - \phi\left(\frac{\pi_t}{\overline{\pi}} - 1\right)\frac{\pi_t}{\overline{\pi}} \\ + \beta\phi E_t \left\{ \frac{\ddot{c}_t a_{t+1}}{\ddot{c}_{t+1} a_t}\left(\frac{\pi_{t+1}}{\overline{\pi}} - 1\right)\frac{\pi_{t+1}}{\overline{\pi}}\frac{\ddot{y}_{t+1}}{\ddot{y}_t} \right\} \end{aligned} \tag{5.64}$$

$$g_t = \frac{\ddot{z}_t \ddot{y}_t}{\ddot{y}_{t-1}} \tag{5.65}$$

$$o_t = \frac{y_t}{\widehat{y}_t} = \frac{\ddot{y}_t}{a_t^{\frac{1}{\xi}}} \tag{5.66}$$

$$\log(a_t) = (1 - \rho_a)\log(\overline{a}) + \rho_a \log(a_{t-1}) + \varepsilon_{at} \tag{5.67}$$

$$\log(\theta_t) = (1 - \rho_\theta)\log(\overline{\theta}) + \rho_\theta \log(\theta_{t-1}) + \varepsilon_{\theta t} \tag{5.68}$$

$$\log(\ddot{z}_t) = \log(\overline{z}) + \varepsilon_{zt} \tag{5.69}$$

Along with the Taylor Rule, this is the system to be linearized.

5.2.3 Linearization

Log-linearization proceeds with the calculation of steady state values of the endogenous variables:

$$\overline{r} = \frac{\overline{z}}{\beta}\overline{\pi},$$

$$\overline{c} = \overline{y} = \left(\overline{a}\frac{\overline{\theta}-1}{\overline{\theta}}\right)^{\frac{1}{\xi}},$$

$$\overline{o} = \left(\frac{\overline{\theta}-1}{\overline{\theta}}\right)^{\frac{1}{\xi}}; \tag{5.70}$$

(5.62)–(5.69) are then log-linearized around these values. As with model I, this can be accomplished through the use of a numerical gradient procedure. However, as an alternative to this approach, here we follow Ireland (2004a) and demonstrate the use of a more analytically oriented procedure. In the process, it helps to be mindful of the re-configuration Ireland worked with: an IS curve, a Phillips curve, the Taylor Rule, the shock processes, and definitions of the growth rate of output and the output gap.

As a first step, the variables appearing in (5.62)–(5.69) are written in logged form. Log-linearization of (5.62) then yields

$$\widetilde{y}_t \equiv \log\left(\frac{\ddot{y}_t}{\overline{y}}\right) = \widetilde{c}_t,$$

because the partial derivative of $\widetilde{y}_t$ with respect to $\widetilde{\pi}_t$ (evaluated at steady state) is zero. (Recall our notational convention: tildes denote logged deviations of variables from steady state values.) Hence upon linearization, this equation is eliminated from the system, and $\widetilde{c}_t$ is replaced by $\widetilde{y}_t$ in the remaining equations.

Next, recalling that $E_t(\widetilde{z}_{t+1}) = 0$, log-linearization of (5.63) yields

$$0 = \widetilde{r}_t - E_t\widetilde{\pi}_{t+1} - (E_t\widetilde{y}_{t+1} - \widetilde{y}_t) + E_t\widetilde{y}_{t+1} - \widetilde{a}_t. \tag{5.71}$$

Relating output and the output gap via the log-linearization of (5.66),

$$\widetilde{y}_t = \frac{1}{\xi}\widetilde{a}_t + \widetilde{o}_t, \tag{5.72}$$

the term $E_t(\widetilde{y}_{t+1}) - \widetilde{y}_t$ can be substituted out of (5.71), yielding the IS curve:

$$\widetilde{o}_t = E_t\widetilde{o}_{t+1} - (\widetilde{r}_t - E_t\widetilde{\pi}_{t+1}) + (1 - \xi^{-1})(1 - \rho_a)\widetilde{a}_t. \tag{5.73}$$

Similarly, log-linearizing (5.64) and eliminating $\widetilde{y}_t$ using (5.72) yields the Phillips curve:

$$\widetilde{\pi}_t = \beta E_t \widetilde{\pi}_{t+1} + \psi \widetilde{o}_t - \widetilde{e}_t, \tag{5.74}$$

where $\psi = \frac{\xi(\theta-1)}{\phi}$ and $\widetilde{e}_t = \frac{1}{\phi}\widetilde{\theta}_t$. This latter equality is a normalization of the cost-push shock; like the cost-push shock itself, the normalized shock follows an AR(1) process with persistence parameter $\rho_\theta = \rho_e$, and innovation standard deviation $\sigma_e = \frac{1}{\phi}\sigma_\theta$.

The resulting IS and Phillips curves are forward looking: they include the one-step-ahead expectations operator. However, prior to empirical implementation, Ireland augmented these equations to include lagged variables of the output gap and inflation in order to enhance the empirical coherence of the model. This final step yields the system he analyzed. Dropping time subscripts and denoting, for example, $\widetilde{o}_{t-1}$ as $\widetilde{o}^-$, the system is given by

$$\widetilde{o} = \alpha_o \widetilde{o}^- + (1-\alpha_o)E_t\widetilde{o}' - (\widetilde{r} - E_t\widetilde{\pi}') + (1-\xi^{-1})(1-\rho_a)\widetilde{a} \tag{5.75}$$

$$\widetilde{\pi} = \beta\alpha_\pi\widetilde{\pi}^- + \beta(1-\alpha_\pi)E_t\widetilde{\pi}' + \psi\widetilde{o} - \widetilde{e} \tag{5.76}$$

$$\widetilde{g}' = \widetilde{y}' - \widetilde{y} + \widetilde{z}' \tag{5.77}$$

$$\widetilde{o}' = \widetilde{y}' - \xi^{-1}\widetilde{a}' \tag{5.78}$$

$$\widetilde{r}' = \rho_r\widetilde{r} + \rho_\pi\widetilde{\pi}' + \rho_g\widetilde{g}' + \rho_o\widetilde{o}' + \varepsilon_r' \tag{5.79}$$

$$\widetilde{a}' = \rho_a\widetilde{a} + \varepsilon_a' \tag{5.80}$$

$$\widetilde{e}' = \rho_e\widetilde{e} + \varepsilon_e' \tag{5.81}$$

$$\widetilde{z}' = \varepsilon_z' \tag{5.82}$$

where the structural shocks

$$\upsilon_t = \{\varepsilon_{rt}, \varepsilon_{at}, \varepsilon_{et}, \varepsilon_{zt}\}$$

are *iidN* with diagonal covariance matrix Σ. The additional parameters introduced are $\alpha_o \in [0,1]$ and $\alpha_\pi \in [0,1]$; setting $\alpha_o = \alpha_\pi = 0$ yields the original microfoundations.

The augmentation of the IS and Phillips curves with lagged values of the output gap and inflation converts the model from a first- to a second-order system. Thus a final step is required in mapping this system into the first-order specification

$$Ax_{t+1} = Bx_t + C\upsilon_{t+1} + D\eta_{t+1}.$$

This is accomplished by augmenting the vector x_t to include not only contemporaneous observations of the variables of the system, but also to include lagged values of the output gap and inflation:

$$x_t \equiv [\,\widetilde{o}_t \quad \widetilde{o}_{t-1} \quad \widetilde{\pi}_t \quad \widetilde{\pi}_{t-1} \quad \widetilde{y}_t \quad \widetilde{r}_t \quad \widetilde{g}_t \quad \widetilde{a}_t \quad \widetilde{e}_t \quad \widetilde{z}_t]'.$$

This also requires the introduction of two additional equations into the system: $\widetilde{\pi}' = \widetilde{\pi}'$ and $\widetilde{o}' = \widetilde{o}'$. Specifying these as the final two equations of the system, the corresponding matrices A and B are given by

$$A = \begin{bmatrix} -(1-\alpha_0) & 1 & -1 & 0 & 0 & 0 & 0 & 0 & 0 & 0 \\ 0 & -\psi & -\beta(1-\alpha_\pi) & 1 & 0 & 0 & 0 & 0 & 0 & 0 \\ 0 & 0 & 0 & 0 & -1 & 0 & 1 & 0 & 0 & -1 \\ 1 & 0 & 0 & 0 & -1 & 0 & 0 & \xi^{-1} & 0 & 0 \\ -\rho_0 & 0 & -\rho_\pi & 0 & 0 & 1 & -\rho_g & 0 & 0 & 0 \\ 0 & 0 & 0 & 0 & 0 & 0 & 0 & 1 & 0 & 0 \\ 0 & 0 & 0 & 0 & 0 & 0 & 0 & 0 & 1 & 0 \\ 0 & 0 & 0 & 0 & 0 & 0 & 0 & 0 & 0 & 1 \\ 0 & 0 & 0 & 1 & 0 & 0 & 0 & 0 & 0 & 0 \\ 0 & 1 & 0 & 0 & 0 & 0 & 0 & 0 & 0 & 0 \end{bmatrix}, \tag{5.83}$$

$$B = \begin{bmatrix} 0 & \alpha_o & 0 & 0 & 0 & -1 & 0 & (1-\xi^{-1})(1-\rho_a) & 0 & 0 \\ 0 & 0 & 0 & \beta\alpha_\pi & 0 & 0 & 0 & 0 & -1 & 0 \\ 0 & 0 & 0 & 0 & -1 & 0 & 0 & 0 & 0 & 0 \\ 0 & 0 & 0 & 0 & 0 & 0 & 0 & 0 & 0 & 0 \\ 0 & 0 & 0 & 0 & 0 & \rho_r & 0 & 0 & 0 & 0 \\ 0 & 0 & 0 & 0 & 0 & 0 & 0 & \rho_a & 0 & 0 \\ 0 & 0 & 0 & 0 & 0 & 0 & 0 & 0 & \rho_e & 0 \\ 0 & 0 & 0 & 0 & 0 & 0 & 0 & 0 & 0 & 0 \\ 0 & 0 & 1 & 0 & 0 & 0 & 0 & 0 & 0 & 0 \\ 1 & 0 & 0 & 0 & 0 & 0 & 0 & 0 & 0 & 0 \end{bmatrix}. \tag{5.84}$$

Further, defining $\eta_t = [\eta_{1t} \;\; \eta_{2t}]'$, where

$$\eta_{1t+1} = E_t\widetilde{o}_{t+1} - \widetilde{o}_{t+1}$$

and

$$\eta_{2t+1} = E_t\widetilde{\pi}_{t+1} - \widetilde{\pi}_{t+1},$$

the matrices C and D are given by

$$C = \begin{bmatrix} & 0_{4x4} & & \\ 1 & 0 & 0 & 0 \\ 0 & 1 & 0 & 0 \\ 0 & 0 & 1 & 0 \\ 0 & 0 & 0 & 1 \\ & 0_{2x4} & & \end{bmatrix}, \qquad D = \begin{bmatrix} -(1-\alpha_0) & -1 \\ 0 & -\beta(1-\alpha_\pi) \\ & 0_{2x8} \end{bmatrix}. \tag{5.85}$$

The final step needed for empirical implementation is to identify the observable variables of the system. For Ireland, these are the gross growth rate of output g_t, the gross inflation rate π_t, and the nominal interest rate r_t (all measured as logged ratios of sample averages). Under the assumption that output and aggregate prices follow drifting random walks, g_t and π_t are stationary; the additional assumption of stationarity for r_t is all that is necessary to proceed with the analysis.

Exercise 5.5

Solve the linearized system (5.75)–(5.82) using any of the methods outlined in chapter 2. Note that the vector of deep parameters is now given by:

$$\mu = [\overline{z}\,\overline{\pi}\ \beta\ \omega\ \theta\ \phi\ \alpha_x\ \alpha_\pi\ \rho_r\ \rho_\pi\ \rho_g\ \rho_x\ \rho_a\ \rho_\theta\ \sigma_a\ \sigma_\theta\ \sigma_z\ \sigma_r]'.$$

Exercise 5.6

Consider the following CRRA form for the instantaneous utility function for model II:

$$u\left(c_t, \frac{m_t}{p_t}, n_t\right) = a_t \frac{c_t^\lambda}{\lambda} + \log \frac{m_t}{p_t} - \frac{n_t^\xi}{\xi}.$$

1. Derive the nonlinear system under this specification.
2. Sketch the linearization of the system via a numerical gradient procedure.

5.3 Model III: Asset Pricing

The final model is an adaptation of Lucas' (1978) one-tree model of asset-pricing behavior. Alternative versions of the model have played a prominent role in two important strands of the empirical finance literature. The first, launched by LeRoy and Porter (1981) and Shiller (1981) in the context of single-asset versions of the model, concerns the puzzling degree of volatility exhibited by prices associated with aggregate stock indexes. The second, launched by Mehra and Prescott (1985) in the context of a multi-asset version of the model, and subsequently underscored by Weil (1989), concerns the puzzling coincidence of a large gap observed between the returns of risky and risk-free assets, and a low average risk-free return. Resolutions to both puzzles have been investigated using alternate preference specifications. After outlining single- and multi-asset versions of the model given a generic specification of preferences, alternative functional forms are introduced. Overviews of the role of preferences in the equity-premium literature are provided by Kocherlakota (1996); Campbell, Lo, and MacKinlay (1997); and Cochrane (2001); and in the stock-price volatility literature by Shiller (1989) and DeJong and Ripoll (2004).

5.3.1 Single-Asset Environment

The model features a continuum of identical households and a single risky asset. Shares held during period $(t-1)$, s_{t-1}, yield a dividend payment d_t at time t; time-t share prices are p_t. Households maximize expected lifetime utility by financing consumption c_t from an exogenous stochastic dividend stream, proceeds from sales of shares, and an exogenous stochastic endowment q_t. The utility maximization problem of the representative household is given by

$$\max_{c_t} \qquad U = E_0 \sum_{t=0}^{\infty} \beta^t u(c_t), \tag{5.86}$$

where $\beta \in (0,1)$ again denotes the discount factor, and optimization is subject to

$$c_t + p_t(s_t - s_{t-1}) = d_t s_{t-1} + q_t. \tag{5.87}$$

Because households are identical, equilibrium requires $s_t = s_{t-1}$ for all t, and thus

$$c_t = d_t s_t + q_t = d_t + q_t$$

(hereafter, s_t is normalized to 1). Combining this equilibrium condition with the household's necessary condition for a maximum yields the pricing equation

$$p_t = \beta E_t \left[\frac{u'(d_{t+1} + q_{t+1})}{u'(d_t + q_t)} (d_{t+1} + p_{t+1}) \right]. \tag{5.88}$$

From (5.88), following a shock to either d_t or q_t, the response of p_t depends in part upon the variation of the marginal rate of substitution between t and $t+1$. This in turn depends upon the instantaneous utility function $u(\cdot)$. The puzzle identified by LeRoy and Porter (1981) and Shiller (1981) is that p_t is far more volatile than what (5.88) would imply, given the observed volatility of d_t.

The model is closed by specifying stochastic processes for (d_t, q_t). These are given by

$$\log d_t = (1-\rho_d)\log(\overline{d}) + \rho_d \log(d_{t-1}) + \varepsilon_{dt} \tag{5.89}$$

$$\log q_t = (1-\rho_q)\log(\overline{q}) + \rho_q \log(q_{t-1}) + \varepsilon_{qt}, \tag{5.90}$$

with $|\rho_i| < 1$, $i = d, q$, and

$$\begin{bmatrix} \varepsilon_{dt} \\ \varepsilon_{qt} \end{bmatrix} \sim iidN(0, \Sigma). \tag{5.91}$$

5.3.2 Multi-Asset Environment

An n-asset extension of the environment leaves the household's objective function intact, but modifies its budget constraint to incorporate the potential for holding n assets. As a special case, Mehra and Prescott (1985) studied a two-asset specification, including a risk-free asset (ownership of government bonds) and risky asset (ownership of equity). In this case, the household's budget constraint is given by

$$c_t + p_t^e(s_t^e - s_{t-1}^e) + p_t^f s_t^f = d_t s_{t-1}^e + s_{t-1}^f + q_t, \tag{5.92}$$

where p_t^e denotes the price of the risky asset, s_t^e represents the number of shares held in the asset during period $t-1$, and p_t^f and s_t^f are analogous for the risk-free asset. The risk-free asset pays one unit of the consumption good at time t if held at time $t-1$ (hence the loading factor of 1 associated with s_{t-1}^f on the right-hand side of the budget constraint).

First-order conditions associated with the choice of the assets are analogous to the pricing equation (5.88) established in the single-asset specification. Rearranging slightly:

$$\beta E_t \left\{ \frac{u'(c_{t+1})}{u'(c_t)} \times \frac{p_{t+1}^e + d_t}{p_t^e} \right\} = 1 \tag{5.93}$$

$$\beta E_t \left\{ \frac{u'(c_{t+1})}{u'(c_t)} \times \frac{1}{p_t^f} \right\} = 1. \tag{5.94}$$

Defining gross returns associated with the assets as

$$r_{t+1}^e = \frac{p_{t+1}^e + d_t}{p_t^e}$$

$$r_{t+1}^f = \frac{1}{p_t^f},$$

Mehra and Prescott's identification of the equity premium puzzle centers on

$$\beta E_t \left\{ \frac{u'(c_{t+1})}{u'(c_t)} r^f_{t+1} \right\} = 1 \tag{5.95}$$

$$E_t \left\{ \frac{u'(c_{t+1})}{u'(c_t)} \left[r^e_{t+1} - r^f_{t+1} \right] \right\} = 0, \tag{5.96}$$

where (5.96) is derived by subtracting (5.94) from (5.93). The equity premium puzzle has two components. First, taking $\{c_t\}$ as given, the average value of $r^e - r^f$ is quite large: given CRRA preferences, implausibly large values of the risk-aversion parameter are needed to account for the average difference observed in returns. Second, given a specification of $u(c)$ that accounts for (5.96), and again taking $\{c_t\}$ as given, the average value observed for r^f is far too low to reconcile with (5.95). This second component, as emphasized by Weil (1989), is the risk-free rate puzzle.

5.3.3 *Alternative Preference Specifications*

As noted, alternative preference specifications have been considered for their potential in resolving both puzzles. Here, in the context of the single-asset environment, three forms for the instantaneous utility function are presented in anticipation of the empirical applications to be presented in part II: CRRA preferences, habit/durability preferences, and self-control preferences. The presentation follows that of DeJong and Ripoll (2004), who sought to evaluate empirically the ability of these preference specifications to make headway in resolving the stock-price volatility puzzle.

CRRA

Once again, CRRA preferences are parameterized as

$$u(c_t) = \frac{c_t^{1-\gamma}}{1-\gamma}, \tag{5.97}$$

thus $\gamma > 0$ measures the degree of relative risk aversion, and $1/\gamma$ the intertemporal elasticity of substitution. The equilibrium pricing equation is given by

$$p_t = \beta E_t \left[\frac{(d_{t+1} + q_{t+1})^{-\gamma}}{(d_t + q_t)^{-\gamma}} (d_{t+1} + p_{t+1}) \right]. \tag{5.98}$$

Notice that, *ceteris paribus*, a relatively large value of γ will increase the volatility of price responses to exogenous shocks, at the cost of decreasing the correlation between p_t and d_t (due to the heightened role assigned to

q_t in driving price fluctuations). Because $\{d_t\}$ and $\{q_t\}$ are exogenous, their steady states $\overline{d}$ and $\overline{q}$ are simply parameters. Normalizing $\overline{d}$ to 1 and defining $\eta = \frac{\overline{q}}{\overline{d}}$, so that $\eta = \overline{q}$, the steady state value of consumption (derived from the budget constraint) is $\overline{c} = 1 + \eta$. And from the pricing equation,

$$\begin{aligned} \overline{p} &= \frac{\beta}{1-\beta}\overline{d} \\ &= \frac{\beta}{1-\beta}. \end{aligned} \tag{5.99}$$

Letting $\beta = 1/(1+r)$, where r denotes the household's discount rate, (5.99) implies $\overline{p}/\overline{d} = 1/r$. Thus as the household's discount rate increases, its asset demand decreases, driving down the steady state price level. Empirically, the average price/dividend ratio observed in the data serves to pin down β under this specification of preferences.

Exercise 5.7

Linearize the pricing equation (5.98) around the model's steady state values.

HABIT/DURABILITY

Following Ferson and Constantinides (1991) and Heaton (1995), an alternative specification of preferences that introduces habit and durability into the specification of preferences is parameterized as

$$u(h_t) = \frac{h_t^{1-\gamma}}{1-\gamma}, \tag{5.100}$$

with

$$h_t = h_t^d - \alpha h_t^h, \tag{5.101}$$

where $\alpha \in (0,1)$, h_t^d is the household's durability stock, and h_t^h its habit stock. The stocks are defined by,

$$h_t^d = \sum_{j=0}^{\infty} \delta^j c_{t-j} \tag{5.102}$$

$$\begin{aligned} h_t^h &= (1-\theta)\sum_{j=0}^{\infty} \theta^j h_{t-1-j}^d \\ &= (1-\theta)\sum_{j=0}^{\infty} \theta^j \sum_{i=0}^{\infty} \delta^i c_{t-1-i} \end{aligned} \tag{5.103}$$

where $\delta \in (0,1)$ and $\theta \in (0,1)$. Thus the durability stock represents the flow of services from past consumption, which depreciates at rate δ. This parameter also represents the degree of intertemporal substitutability of consumption. The habit stock can be interpreted as a weighted average of the durability stock, where the weights sum to one. Notice that more recent durability stocks, or more recent flows of consumption, are weighted relatively heavily; thus the presence of habit captures intertemporal consumption complementarity. The variable h_t represents the current level of durable services net of the average of past services; the parameter α measures the fraction of the average of past services that is netted out. Notice that if $\delta = 0$, there would be only habit persistence, whereas if $\alpha = 0$ only durability survives. Finally, when $\theta = 0$, the habit stock includes only one lag. Thus estimates of these parameters are of particular interest empirically.

Using the definitions of durability and habit stocks, h_t becomes

$$h_t = c_t + \sum_{j=1}^{\infty} \left[\delta^j - \alpha(1-\theta) \sum_{i=0}^{j-1} \delta^i \theta^{j-i-1} \right] c_{t-j}$$

$$\equiv \sum_{j=0}^{\infty} \Phi_j c_{t-j}, \tag{5.104}$$

where $\Phi_0 \equiv 1$. Thus for these preferences, the pricing equation is given by

$$p_t = \beta E_t \frac{\sum_{j=0}^{\infty} \beta^j \Phi_j \left(\sum_{i=0}^{\infty} \Phi_i c_{t+1+j-i} \right)^{-\gamma}}{\sum_{j=0}^{\infty} \beta^j \Phi_j \left(\sum_{i=0}^{\infty} \Phi_i c_{t+j-i} \right)^{-\gamma}} (d_{t+1} + p_{t+1}), \tag{5.105}$$

where as before $c_t = d_t + q_t$ in equilibrium.

To see how the presence of habit and durability can potentially influence the volatility of the prices, rewrite the pricing equation as

$$p_t = \beta E_t \frac{(c_{t+1} + \Phi_1 c_t + \Phi_2 c_{t-1} + \cdots)^{-\gamma}}{(c_t + \Phi_1 c_{t-1} + \Phi_2 c_{t-2} + \cdots)^{-\gamma}}$$

$$\frac{+\beta \Phi_1 (c_{t+2} + \Phi_1 c_{t+1} + \Phi_2 c_t + \cdots)^{-\gamma} + \cdots}{+\beta \Phi_1 (c_{t+1} + \Phi_1 c_t + \Phi_2 c_{t-1} + \cdots)^{-\gamma} + \cdots} (d_{t+1} + p_{t+1}). \tag{5.106}$$

When there is a positive shock to say q_t, c_t increases by the amount of the shock, say σ_q. Given (5.89)–(5.90), c_{t+1} would increase by $\rho_q \sigma_q$, c_{t+2} would increase by $\rho_q^2 \sigma_q$, and so on. Now, examine the first term in parenthesis in both the numerator and the denominator. First, in the denominator c_t will grow by σ_q. Second, in the numerator $c_{t+1} + \Phi_1 c_t$ goes up by $(\rho_q + \Phi_1)\,\sigma_q \lesseqgtr \sigma_q$. Thus, whether the share price p_t increases by more than in the standard CRRA case depends ultimately on whether $\rho_q + \Phi_1 \lesseqgtr 1$. Notice that if $\Phi_j = 0$ for $j > 0$, (5.106) reduces to the standard CRRA utility case. If we had only habit and not durability, then $\Phi_1 < 0$, and thus the response of prices would be greater than in the CRRA case. This result is intuitive: habit captures intertemporal complementarity in consumption, which strengthens the smoothing motive relative to the time-separable CRRA case.

Alternatively, if there was only durability and not habit, then $0 < \Phi_1 < 1$, but one still would not know whether $\rho + \Phi_1 \lesseqgtr 1$. Thus with only durability, we cannot judge how the volatility of p_t would be affected: this will depend upon the sizes of ρ and Φ_1. Finally, we also face indeterminacy under a combination of both durability and habit: if α is large and δ is small enough to make $\rho + \Phi_1 < 1$, then we would get increased price volatility. Thus this issue is fundamentally quantitative. Finally, with respect to the steady state price, note from (5.106) that it is identical to the CRRA case.

Exercise 5.8

Given that the pricing equation under Habit/Durability involves an infinite number of lags, truncate the lags to 3 and linearize the pricing equation (5.106) around its steady state.

SELF-CONTROL PREFERENCES

Consider next a household that every period faces a temptation to consume all of its wealth. Resisting this temptation imposes a self-control utility cost. To model these preferences we follow Gul and Pesendorfer (2004), who identified a class of dynamic self-control preferences. In this case, the problem of the household can be formulated recursively as

$$W(s,P) = \max_{s'}\{u(c) + v(c) + \beta E W(s',P')\} - \max_{\widetilde{s}'} v(\widetilde{c}), \qquad (5.107)$$

where $P = (p, d, q)$, $u(\cdot)$ and $v(\cdot)$ are Von Neuman-Morgenstern utility functions, $\beta \in (0,1)$, $\widetilde{c}$ represents temptation consumption, and s' denotes share holdings in the next period. Whereas $u(\cdot)$ is the momentary utility function, $v(\cdot)$ represents temptation. The problem is subject to the following budget constraints:

$$c = ds + q - p(s' - s) \qquad (5.108)$$

$$\widetilde{c} = ds + q - p(\widetilde{s}' - s). \qquad (5.109)$$

In (5.107), $v(c) - \max_{\widetilde{s}'} v(\widetilde{c}) \leq 0$ represents the disutility of self-control given that the agent has chosen c. With $v(c)$ specified as strictly increasing, the solution for $\max_{\tilde{s}'} v(\tilde{c})$ is simply to drive $\tilde{c}$ to the maximum allowed by the constraint

$$\tilde{c} = ds + q - p(\tilde{s}' - s),$$

which is attained by setting $\tilde{s}' = 0$. Thus the problem is written as

$$W(s, P) = \max_{s'}\{u(c) + v(c) + \beta E W(s', P')\} - v(ds + q + ps) \quad (5.110)$$

subject to

$$c = ds + q - p(s' - s). \quad (5.111)$$

The optimality condition reads

$$\left[u'(c) + v'(c)\right] p = \beta E W'(s', P'), \quad (5.112)$$

and since

$$W'(s, P) = \left[u'(c) + v'(c)\right](d + p) - v'(ds + q + ps)(d + p), \quad (5.113)$$

the optimality condition becomes

$$\left[u'(c) + v'(c)\right] p = \beta E \left[u'(c') + v'(c') - v'(d's' + q' + p's')\right](d' + p'). \quad (5.114)$$

Combining this expression with the equilibrium conditions $s = s' = 1$ and $c = d + q$ yields

$$p = \beta E \left\{ (d' + p') \left[\frac{u'(d' + q') + v'(d' + q') - v'(d' + q' + p')}{u'(d + q) + v'(d + q)} \right] \right\}. \quad (5.115)$$

Notice that when $v(\cdot) = 0$, there is no temptation, and the pricing equation reduces to the standard case. Otherwise, the term $u'(d' + q') + v'(d' + q') - v'(d' + q' + p')$ represents tomorrow's utility benefit from saving today. This corresponds to the standard marginal utility of wealth tomorrow $u'(d' + q')$, plus the term $v'(d' + q') - v'(d' + q' + p')$ which represents the derivative of the utility cost of self-control with respect to wealth.

DeJong and Ripoll (2004) assume the following functional forms for the momentary and temptation utility functions:

$$u(c) = \frac{c^{1-\gamma}}{1-\gamma} \quad (5.116)$$

$$v(c) = \lambda \frac{c^{\phi}}{\phi}, \quad (5.117)$$

with $\lambda > 0$, which imply the following pricing equation:

$$p = \beta E\left\{[d' + p']\left[\frac{(d' + q')^{-\gamma} + \lambda(d' + q')^{\phi-1} - \lambda(d' + q' + p')^{\phi-1}}{(d + q)^{-\gamma} + \lambda(d + q)^{\phi-1}}\right]\right\}. \tag{5.118}$$

The concavity/convexity of $v(\cdot)$ plays an important role in determining implications of this preference specification for the stock-price volatility issue. To understand why, rewrite (5.118) as

$$p = \beta E\left\{[d' + p'] \times \left[\frac{\frac{(d'+q')^{-\gamma}}{(d+q)^{-\gamma}} + \lambda(d + q)^{\gamma}\left[(d' + q')^{\phi-1} - (d' + q' + p')^{\phi-1}\right]}{1 + \lambda(d + q)^{\phi-1+\gamma}}\right]\right\}. \tag{5.119}$$

Suppose $\phi > 1$, so that $v(\cdot)$ is convex, and consider the impact on p of a positive endowment shock. This increases the denominator, while decreasing the term

$$\lambda(d + q)^{\gamma}[(d' + q')^{\phi-1} - (d' + q' + p')^{\phi-1}]$$

in the numerator. Both effects imply that relative to the CRRA case, in which $\lambda = 0$, this specification *reduces* price volatility in the face of an endowment shock, which is precisely the opposite of what one would like to achieve in seeking to resolve the stock-price volatility puzzle.

The mechanism behind this reduction in price volatility is as follows: a positive shock to d or q increases the household's wealth today, which has three effects. The first ("smoothing") captures the standard intertemporal motive: the household would like to increase saving, which drives up the share price. Second, there is a "temptation" effect: with more wealth today, the feasible budget set for the household increases, which represents more temptation to consume, and less willingness to save. This effect works opposite to the first, and reduces price volatility with respect to the standard case. Third, there is the "self-control" effect: due to the assumed convexity of $v(\cdot)$, marginal self-control costs also increase, which reinforces the second effect. As shown above, the last two effects dominate the first, and thus under convexity of $v(\cdot)$ the volatility is reduced relative to the CRRA case.

In contrast, price volatility would not necessarily be reduced if $v(\cdot)$ is concave, and thus $0 < \phi < 1$. In this case, when d or q increases, the term

$$\lambda(d+q)^{\gamma}[(d'+q')^{\phi-1} - (d'+q'+p')^{\phi-1}]$$

increases. On the other hand, if $\phi - 1 + \gamma > 0$, that is, if the risk-aversion parameter $\gamma > 1$, the denominator also increases. If the increase in the numerator dominates that in the denominator, then higher price volatility can be observed than in the CRRA case.

To understand this effect, note that the derivative of the utility cost of self-control with respect to wealth is positive if $v(\cdot)$ is concave:

$$v'(d'+q') - v'(d'+q'+p') > 0.$$

This means that as agents get wealthier, self-control costs become lower. This explains why it might be possible to get higher price volatility in this case. The mechanism behind this result still involves the three effects discussed above: smoothing, temptation, and self-control. The difference is on the latter effect: under concavity, self-control costs are *decreasing* in wealth. This gives the agent an incentive to save *more* rather than less. If this self-control effect dominates the temptation effect, then these preferences will produce higher price volatility.

Notice that when $v(\cdot)$ is concave, conditions need to be imposed to guarantee that $W(\cdot)$ is strictly concave, so that the solution corresponds to a maximum (e.g., see Stokey and Lucas, 1989). In particular, the second derivative of $W(\cdot)$ must be negative:

$$-\gamma(d+q)^{-\gamma-1} + \lambda(\phi-1)[(d+q)^{\phi-2} - (d+q+p)^{\phi-2}] < 0 \tag{5.120}$$

which holds for any d, q, and $p > 0$, and for $\gamma > 0$, $\lambda > 0$, and $0 < \phi < 1$. The empirical implementation in part II of this book proceeds under this set of parameter restrictions.

Finally, from the optimality conditions under self-control preferences, steady-state temptation consumption is

$$\bar{\tilde{c}} = 1 + \eta + \bar{p}.$$

From (5.118), the steady-state price in this case is given by

$$\begin{aligned}\bar{p} &= \beta(1+\bar{p}) \\ &\quad \times \left[\frac{(1+\eta)^{-\gamma} + \lambda(1+\eta)^{\phi-1} - \lambda(1+\eta+\bar{p})^{\phi-1}}{(1+\eta)^{-\gamma} + \lambda(1+\eta)^{\phi-1}}\right].\end{aligned} \tag{5.121}$$

Regarding (5.121), the left-hand-side is a 45-degree line. The right-hand side is strictly concave in $\bar{p}$, has a positive intercept, and a positive slope that is less than one at the intercept. Thus (5.121) yields a unique positive solution for $\overline{p}$ for any admissible parameterization of the model. (In practice, (5.121) can be solved numerically, e.g., using GAUSS's quasi-Newton algorithm NLSYS; see Judd, 1998, for a presentation of alternative solution algorithms.) An increase in λ causes the function of $\overline{p}$ on the right-hand side of (5.121) to shift down and flatten, thus $\overline{p}$ is decreasing in λ. The intuition for this is again straightforward: an increase in λ represents an intensification of the household's temptation to liquidate its asset holdings. This drives down its demand for asset shares, and thus $\overline{p}$. Note the parallel between this effect and that generated by an increase in r, or a decrease in β, which operates analogously in both (5.99) and (5.121).

Exercise 5.9

Solve for $\overline{p}$ in (5.121) using $\beta = 0.96$, $\gamma = 2$, $\lambda = 0.01$, $\eta = 10$, $\phi = 0.4$. Linearize the asset-pricing equation (5.119) using the steady state values for $(\overline{p}, \overline{d}, \overline{q})$ implied by these parameter values.

Part II

Empirical Methods

When you come to a fork in the road, take it.
—Yogi Berra

Chapter 6

Calibration

Models are to be used, not believed.
—Henri Theil, *Principles of Econometrics*

6.1 Historical Origins and Philosophy

With their seminal analysis of business cycles, Kydland and Prescott (1982) capped a paradigm shift in the conduct of empirical work in macroeconomics. They did so using a methodology that enabled them to cast the DSGE model they analyzed as the centerpiece of their empirical analysis. The analysis contributed towards the Nobel Prize in Economics they received in 2004, and the methodology has come to be known as a calibration exercise.[1] Calibration not only remains a popular tool for analyzing DSGEs, but has also served as the building block for subsequent methodologies developed towards this end. Thus it provides a natural point of departure for our presentation of these methodologies.

Although undoubtedly an empirical methodology, calibration is distinct from the branch of econometrics under which theoretical models are represented as complete probability models that can be estimated, tested, and used to generate predictions using formal statistical procedures. Haavelmo (1944) provided an early and forceful articulation of this latter approach to econometrics, and in 1989 received the Nobel Prize in Economics "... for his clarification of the probability theory foundations of econometrics and his analyses of simultaneous economic structures." (Bank of Sweden, 1989) Henceforth, we will refer to this as the probability approach to econometrics.

Regarding Haavelmo's "... analyses of simultaneous economic structures," otherwise known as systems-of-equations models, at the time of his work this was the most sophisticated class of structural models that could be subjected to formal empirical analysis. As characterized by Koopmans (1949), such models include equations falling into one of four classes:

[1] Specifically, Kydland and Prescott received the Nobel Prize "for their contributions to dynamic macroeconomics: the time consistency of economic policy and the driving forces behind business cycles." (Bank of Sweden, 2004)

identities (e.g., the national income accounting identity), institutional rules (e.g., tax rates), technology constraints (e.g., a production function), and behavioral equations (e.g., a consumption function relating consumption to disposable income). For a textbook presentation of systems-of-equations models, see Sargent (1987a).

This latter class of equations distinguishes systems-of-equations models from DSGE models. Behavioral equations cast endogenous variables as *ad hoc* functions of additional variables included in the model. An important objective in designing these specifications is to capture relationships between variables observed from historical data. Indeed, econometric implementations of such models proceed under the assumption that the parameters of the behavioral equations are fixed, and thus may be estimated using historical data; the estimated models are then used to address quantitative questions. Such analyses represented state-of-the-art practice in econometrics into the 1970s.

In place of behavioral equations, DSGE models feature equations that reflect the pursuit of explicit objectives (e.g., the maximization of lifetime utility) by purposeful decision makers (e.g., representative households). For example, the RBC model presented in chapter 5 features two such equations: the intratemporal optimality condition that determines the labor-leisure trade-off; and the intertemporal optimality condition that determines the consumption-investment trade-off. The parameters in these equations reflect either the preferences of the decision maker (e.g., discount factors, intertemporal elasticities of substitution, etc.) or features of their environment (e.g., capital's share of labor in the production technology).

Two important developments ultimately ended the predominance of the systems-of-equations approach. The first was empirical: systems-of-equations models suffered "... spectacular predictive failure ..." in the policy guidance they provided during the episode of stagflation experienced during the early 1970s (Kydland and Prescott, 1991a, p. 166). Quoting Lucas and Sargent (1979):

> In the present decade, the U.S. economy has undergone its first major depression since the 1930's, to the accompaniment of inflation rates in excess of 10 percent per annum. ... These events ... were accompanied by massive government budget deficits and high rates of monetary expansion, policies which, although bearing an admitted risk of inflation, promised according to modern Keynesian doctrine rapid real growth and low rates of unemployment. That these predictions were wildly incorrect and that the doctrine on which they were based is fundamentally flawed are now simple matters of fact, involving no novelties in economic theory. [p. 1]

The second development was theoretical: the underlying assumption that the parameters of behavioral equations in such models are fixed was recognized as being inconsistent with optimizing behavior on the part of purposeful decision makers. This is the thrust of Lucas' (1976) critique of policy evaluation based on systems-of-equations models:

> ... given that the structure of an econometric model consists of optimal decision rules of economic agents, and that optimal decision rules vary systematically with changes in the structure of series relevant to the decision maker, it follows that any change in policy will systematically alter the structure of econometric models. [p. 41]

Or as summarized by Lucas and Sargent (1979):

> The casual treatment of expectations is not a peripheral problem in these models, for the role of expectations is pervasive in them and exerts a massive influence on their dynamic properties. ... The failure of existing models to derive restrictions on expectations from any first principles grounded in economic theory is a symptom of a deeper and more general failure to derive behavioral relationships from any consistently posed dynamic optimization problem. ... There are, therefore, ... theoretical reasons for believing that the parameters identified as structural by current macroeconomic methods are not in fact structural. That is, we see no reason to believe that these models have isolated structures which will remain invariant across the class of interventions that figure in contemporary discussions of economic policy. [pp. 5-6]

In consequence, Lucas (1976) concludes that "... simulations using these models can, in principle, provide no useful information as to the actual consequences of alternative economic policies." [p. 20] In turn, again referring to the predictive failure of these models during the stagflation episode of the 1970s, Lucas and Sargent (1979) conclude that "... the difficulties are *fatal*: that modern macroeconomic models are of *no* value in guiding policy and that this condition will not be remedied by modifications along any line which is currently being pursued." [p. 2]

Two leading reactions to these developments ensued. First, remaining in the tradition of the probability approach to econometrics, the methodological contributions of Sims (1972) and Hansen and Sargent (1980) made possible the imposition of theoretical discipline on reduced-form models of macroeconomic activity. DSGE models featuring rational decision makers provided the source of this discipline, and the form of the discipline most commonly took the form of "cross-equation restrictions" imposed on vector autoregressive (VAR) models. This development represents an intermediate step towards the implementation of DSGE models in empirical applications, because reduced-form models serve as the focal point of such analyses. Moreover, early empirical applications spawned by this development proved to be disappointing, because rejections of particular parametric implementations of the restrictions were commonplace (e.g., see Hansen and Sargent, 1981; Hansen and Singleton 1982, 1983; and Eichenbaum 1983). The second reaction was the development of the modern calibration exercise.

In place of estimation and testing, the goal in a calibration exercise is to use a parameterized structural model to address a specific quantitative question. The model is constructed and parameterized subject to the constraint that it mimic features of the actual economy that have been identified a priori. Questions fall under two general headings. They may involve the ability of the model to account for an additional set of features of the actual economy; that is, they may involve assessments of fit. Alternatively, they may involve assessments of the theoretical implications of changes in economic policy. This characterization stems from Kydland and Prescott (1991a, 1996), who traced the historical roots of the use of calibration exercises as an empirical methodology, and outlined their view of what such exercises entail.

Kydland and Prescott (1991a) identify calibration as embodying the approach to econometrics articulated and practiced by Frisch (1933a,b). Regarding articulation, this is provided by Frisch's (1933a) editorial opening the inaugural issue of the flagship journal of the Econometric Society: *Econometrica*. As stated in its constitution, the main objective of the Econometric Society is to

> ... promote studies that aim at a unification of the theoretical-quantitative and empirical-quantitative approach to economic problems and that are penetrated by constructive and rigorous thinking. ... Any activity which promises ultimately to further such unification of theoretical and factual studies in economics shall be within the sphere of interest of the Society. [p. 1]

Such studies personified Frisch's vision of econometrics: "This mutual penetration of quantitative economic theory and statistical observation is the essence of econometrics." [p. 2]

Of course, this vision was also shared by the developers of the probability approach to econometrics. To quote Haavelmo (1944): "The method of econometric research aims, essentially, at a conjunction of economic theory and actual measurements, using the theory and technique of statistical inference as a bridge pier." [p. iii] However, in practice Frisch pursued this vision without strict adherence to the probability approach: for example, his (1933b) analysis of the propagation of business-cycle shocks was based on a production technology with parameters calibrated on the basis of micro data. This work contributed towards the inaugural Nobel Prize in Economics he shared with Jan Tinbergen in 1969:

> Let me take, as an example, Professor Frisch's pioneer work in the early thirties involving a dynamic formulation of the theory of cycles. He demonstrated how a dynamic system with difference and differential equations for investments

> and consumption expenditure, with certain monetary restrictions, produced a damped wave movement with wavelengths of 4 and 8 years. By exposing the system to random disruptions, he could demonstrate also how these wave movements became permanent and uneven in a rather realistic manner. Frisch was before his time in the building of mathematical models, and he has many successors. The same is true of his contribution to methods for the statistical testing of hypotheses. [Lundberg, 1969]

In their own analysis of business cycles, Kydland and Prescott (1982) eschewed the probability approach in favor of a calibration experiment that enabled them to cast the DSGE model they analyzed as the focal point of their empirical analysis. (Tools for working with general-equilibrium models in static and nonstochastic settings had been developed earlier by Shoven and Whalley, 1972; and Scarf and Hansen, 1973.) It is tempting to view this as a decision made due to practical considerations, because formal statistical tools for implementing DSGE models empirically had yet to be developed. However, an important component of Kydland and Prescott's advocacy of calibration is based on a criticism of the probability approach. For example, writing with specific reference to calibration exercises involving real business cycle models, Prescott (1986) makes the case as follows:

> The models constructed within this theoretical framework are necessarily highly abstract. Consequently, they are necessarily false, and statistical hypothesis testing will reject them. This does not imply, however, that nothing can be learned from such quantitative theoretical exercises. [p. 10]

A similar sentiment was expressed earlier by Lucas (1980): "Any model that is well enough articulated to give clear answers to the questions we put to it will necessarily be artificial, abstract, patently 'unreal.'" [p. 696] As another example, in discussing Frisch's (1970) characterization of the state of econometrics, Kydland and Prescott (1991a) offer the following observation:

> In this review (Frisch) discusses what he considers to be 'econometric analysis of the genuine kind' (p. 163), and gives four examples of such analysis. None of these examples involve the estimation and statistical testing of some model. None involve an attempt to discover some true relationship. All use a model, which is an abstraction of a complex reality, to address some clear-cut question or issue. [p. 162]

In sum, the use of calibration exercises as a means for facilitating the empirical implementation of DSGE models arose in the aftermath of the demise of systems-of-equations analyses. Estimation and testing are purposefully de-emphasized under this approach, yet calibration exercises are decidedly an empirical tool, in that they are designed to provide concrete answers to quantitative questions. We now describe their implementation.

6.2 Implementation

Enunciations of the specific methodology advocated by Kydland and Prescott for implementing calibration exercises in applications to DSGE models are available in a variety of sources (e.g., Kydland and Prescott 1991a, 1996; Prescott 1986, 2006; and Cooley and Prescott 1995). Here we begin by outlining the five-step procedure presented by Kydland and Prescott (1996). We then discuss its implementation in the context of the notation established in part I of this book.

The first step is to pose a question, which will fall under one of two general headings: questions may involve assessments of the theoretical implications of changes in policy (e.g., the potential welfare gains associated with a given tax reform), or they may involve assessments of the ability of a model to mimic features of the actual economy. Kydland and Prescott characterize the latter class of questions as follows:

> Other questions are concerned with the testing and development of theory. These questions typically ask about the quantitative implications of theory for some phenomena. If the answer to these questions is that the predictions of theory match the observations, theory has passed that particular test. If the answer is that there is a discrepancy, a deviation from theory has been documented. [pp. 70–71]

The second step is to use "well-tested theory" to address the question: "With a particular question in mind, a researcher needs some strong theory to carry out a computational experiment: that is, a researcher needs a theory that has been tested through use and found to provide reliable answers to a class of questions." [p. 72] This step comes with a caveat: "We recognize, of course, that although the economist should choose a well-tested theory, every theory has some issues and questions that it does not address well." [p. 72]

Of course, this caveat does not apply exclusively to calibration exercises: as simplifications of reality, all models suffer empirical shortcomings along certain dimensions, and any procedure that enables their empirical implementation must be applied with this problem in mind. The point here is that the chosen theory must be suitably developed along the dimensions of relevance to the question at hand. To take the example offered by Kydland and Prescott: "In the case of neoclassical growth theory . . . it fails spectacularly when used to address economic development issues. . . . This does not preclude its usefulness in evaluating tax policies and in business cycle research." [p. 72]

The third step involves the construction of the model economy: "With a particular theoretical framework in mind, the third step in conducting a computational experiment is to construct a model economy. Here, key issues are the amount of detail and the feasibility of computing the equilibrium process." [p. 72] Regarding this last point, the more detailed and complex is a given model, the harder it is to analyze; thus in the words of Solow (1956): "The art of successful theorizing is to make the inevitable simplifying assumptions in such a way that the final results are not very sensitive." [p. 65] So in close relation with step two, the specific model chosen for analysis is ideally constructed to be sufficiently rich for addressing the question at hand without being unnecessarily complex. For example, Rowenhorst (1991) studied versions of an RBC model with and without the "time-to-build" feature of the production technology included in the model analyzed by Kydland and Prescott (1982). (Under "time to build," current investments yield productive capital only in future dates.) His analysis demonstrated that the time-to-build feature was relatively unimportant in contributing to the propagation of technology shocks; today, time-to-build rarely serves as a central feature of RBC models.

Beyond ease of analysis, model simplicity has an additional virtue: it is valuable for helping to disentangle the importance of various features of a given specification for generating a particular result. Consider the simultaneous inclusion of a set of additional features to a baseline model with known properties. Given the outcome of an interesting modification of the model's properties, the attribution of importance to the individual features in generating this result is at minimum a significant challenge. In contrast, analysis of the impact of the individual features in isolation or in smaller subsets is a far more effective means of achieving attribution. It may turn out that each additional feature is necessary for achieving the result; alternatively, certain features may turn out to be unimportant and usefully discarded.

These first three steps apply quite broadly to empirical applications; the fourth step, the calibration of model parameters, does not:

> Generally, some economic questions have known answers, and the model should give an approximately correct answer to them if we are to have any confidence in the answer given to the question with unknown answer. Thus, data are used to calibrate the model economy so that it mimics the world as closely as possible along a limited, but clearly specified, number of dimensions. [p. 74]

Upon offering this definition, calibration is then distinguished from estimation: "Note that calibration is not an attempt at assessing the size of something: it is not estimation." [p. 74] Moreover:

> It is important to emphasize that the parameter values selected are not the ones that provide the best fit in some statistical sense. In some cases, the presence of a particular discrepancy between the data and the model economy is a test of the

theory being used. In these cases, absence of that discrepancy is grounds to reject the use of the theory to address the question. [p. 74]

Although in general this definition implies no restrictions on the specific dimensions of the world used to pin down parameter values, certain dimensions have come to be applied rather extensively in a wide range of applications. Long-run averages such as the share of output paid to labor, and the fraction of available hours worked per household, both of which have been remarkably stable over time, serve as primary examples. In addition, empirical results obtained in micro studies conducted at the individual or household level are often used as a means of pinning down certain parameters. For example, the time-allocation study of Ghez and Becker (1975), conducted using panel data on individual allocations of time to market activities, was used by Cooley and Prescott (1995) to determine the relative weights assigned to consumption and leisure in the instantaneous utility function featured in the RBC model they analyzed.

The final step is to run the experiment. Just how this is done depends upon the question at hand, but at a minimum this involves the solution of the model, for example, as outlined in chapter 2. Using the notation established in part I of this book, the model solution yields a state-space representation of the form

$$x_{t+1} = F(\mu)x_t + G(\mu)\upsilon_{t+1} \tag{6.1}$$

$$X_t = H(\mu)'x_t \tag{6.2}$$

$$E(e_t e_t') = G(\mu)E(\upsilon_t \upsilon_t')G(\mu)' \equiv Q(\mu). \tag{6.3}$$

Recall that x_t represents the full set of variables included in the model, represented as deviations from steady state values; X_t represents the collection of associated observable variables, represented analogously; and μ contains the structural parameters of the model.

At this point it is useful to distinguish between two versions of X_t. We will denote model versions as X_t^M, and the actual data as X_t. In the context of this notation, the calibration step involves the specification of the individual elements of μ. Representing the real-world criteria used to specify μ as $\Omega(\{X_t\}_{t=1}^T)$, the calibration step involves the choice of μ such that

$$\Omega(\{X_t^M\}_{t=1}^T) = \Omega(\{X_t\}_{t=1}^T). \tag{6.4}$$

If the question posed in the calibration exercise is to compare model predictions with an additional collection of features of the real world, then denoting these additional features as $\Phi(\{X_t\}_{t=1}^T)$, the question is addressed via comparison of $\Phi(\{X_t\}_{t=1}^T)$ and $\Phi(\{X_t^M\}_{t=1}^T)$. Depending upon the specification of $\Phi(\cdot)$, $\Phi(\{X_t^M\}_{t=1}^T)$ may either be calculated analytically or via simulation.

As noted above, Kydland and Prescott characterize exercises of this sort as a means of facilitating the "... testing and development of theory." [p. 70] As will be apparent in chapter 7, wherein we present generalized and simulated method-of-moment procedures, such exercises are closely related to moment-matching exercises, which provide a powerful means of estimating models and evaluating their ability to capture real-world phenomena. The only substantive difference lies in the level of statistical formality upon which comparisons are based.

If the question posed in the exercise involves an assessment of the theoretical implications of a change in policy, then once again the experiment begins with the choice of μ such that (6.4) is satisfied. In this case, given that μ contains as a subset of elements parameters characterizing the nature of the policy under investigation, then the policy change will be reflected by a new specification μ', and thus $X_t^{M'}$. The question can then be cast in the form of a comparison between $\Phi(\{X_t^M\}_{t=1}^T)$ and $\Phi(\{X_t^{M'}\}_{t=1}^T)$. Examples of both sorts of exercises follow.

6.3 The Welfare Cost of Business Cycles

We begin with an example of the first sort, based on an exercise conducted originally by Lucas (1987), and updated by Lucas (2003). The question involves a calculation of the potential gains in welfare that could be achieved through improvements in the management of business-cycle fluctuations. In particular, consider the availability of a policy capable of eliminating all variability in consumption, beyond long-term growth. Given risk aversion on the part of consumers, the implementation of such a policy will lead to an improvement in welfare. The question is: to what extent?

A quantitative answer to this question is available from a comparison of the utility derived from consumption streams $\{c_t^A\}$ and $\{c_t^B\}$ associated with the implementation of alternative policies A and B. Suppose the latter is preferred to the former, so that

$$U(\{c_t^A\}) < U(\{c_t^B\}).$$

To quantify the potential welfare gains to be had in moving from A to B, or alternatively, the welfare cost associated with adherence to policy A, Lucas proposed the calculation of λ such that

$$U(\{(1+\lambda)c_t^A\}) = U(\{c_t^B\}). \tag{6.5}$$

In this way, welfare costs are measured in units of a percentage of the level of consumption realized under policy A.

Lucas' implementation of this question entailed a comparison of the expected discounted lifetime utility derived by a representative consumer from two alternative consumption streams: one that mimics the behavior of actual postwar consumption, and one that mimics the deterministic growth pattern followed by postwar consumption. Under the first, consumption is stochastic, and obeys

$$c_t = Ae^{\mu t}e^{-\frac{1}{2}\sigma^2}\varepsilon_t, \tag{6.6}$$

where $\log \varepsilon_t$ is distributed as $N(0, \sigma^2)$. Under this distributional assumption for ε_t,

$$E(\varepsilon_t^m) = e^{\frac{1}{2}\sigma^2 m^2}, \tag{6.7}$$

and thus

$$E(c_t) = Ae^{\mu t}, \tag{6.8}$$

the growth rate of which is μ. Under the second, consumption is deterministic, and at time t is given by $Ae^{\mu t}$, as in (6.8).

Modeling the lifetime utility generated by a given consumption stream $\{c_t\}$ as

$$E_0 \sum_{t=0}^{\infty} \beta^t \frac{c_t^{1-\gamma}}{1-\gamma}, \tag{6.9}$$

where β is the consumer's discount factor and γ measures the consumer's degree of relative risk aversion, Lucas' welfare comparison involves the calculation of λ such that

$$E_0 \sum_{t=0}^{\infty} \beta^t \frac{[(1+\lambda)c_t]^{1-\gamma}}{1-\gamma} = \sum_{t=0}^{\infty} \beta^t \frac{(Ae^{\mu t})^{1-\gamma}}{1-\gamma}, \tag{6.10}$$

with the behavior of c_t given by (6.6). Given (6.7),

$$E_0(\varepsilon_t^{1-\gamma}) = e^{\frac{1}{2}(1-\gamma)^2\sigma^2},$$

and thus (6.10) simplifies to

$$(1+\lambda)^{1-\gamma} e^{\frac{1}{2}(1-\gamma)^2\sigma^2} = 1. \tag{6.11}$$

Finally, taking logs and using the approximation $\log(1+\lambda) \approx \lambda$, the comparison reduces to

$$\lambda = \frac{1}{2}\sigma^2\gamma. \tag{6.12}$$

TABLE 6.1
Welfare Costs, CRRA Preferences

γ	λ	\$/person, 2004
0.5	0.00023	\$5.86
1	0.00045	\$11.72
1.5	0.00068	\$17.59
2	0.00090	\$23.45
2.5	0.00113	\$29.31

Thus the calculation of λ boils down to this simple relationship involving two parameters: σ^2 and γ. The former can be estimated directly as the residual variance in a regression of $\log c_t$ on a constant and trend. Using annual data on real per capita consumption spanning 1947–2001, Lucas (2003) estimated σ^2 as $(0.032)^2$. Extending these data through 2004 yields an estimate of $(0.030)^2$; the data used for this purpose are contained in the file `weldat.txt`, available at the textbook Web site.

Regarding the specification of γ, Lucas (2003) appeals to an intertemporal optimality condition for consumption growth μ that is a standard feature of theoretical growth models featuring consumer optimization (e.g., see Barro and Sala-i-Martin, 2004):

$$\mu = \frac{1}{\gamma}(r - \rho), \tag{6.13}$$

where r is the after-tax rate of return generated by physical capital and ρ is the consumer's subjective discount rate. In this context, $\frac{1}{\gamma}$ represents the consumer's intertemporal elasticity of substitution. With r averaging approximately 0.05 in postwar data, μ estimated as 0.023 in the regression of $\log c_t$ on a constant and trend, and ρ restricted to be positive, an upper bound for γ is approximately 2.2, and a value of 1 is often chosen as a benchmark specification.

Table 6.1 reports values of λ calculated for alternative specifications of γ, based on the estimate $\sigma^2 = (0.030)^2$. It also reports the associated (chain-weighted 2000) dollar value of per capita consumption in 2004.

As these figures indicate, potential welfare gains offered by the complete elimination of cyclical fluctuations in consumption are strikingly low: as high as only \$29.31 per person given $\gamma = 2.5$, and only \$11.71 given $\gamma = 1$. They led Lucas (2003) to two conclusions. First, the figures serve as a tribute to the success of the stabilization policies that have been implemented over the postwar period: the policies have not left much room for improvement. Second, efforts designed to deliver further gains in stabilization have little to offer in generating further improvements in welfare.

Lucas' (1987) analysis prompted an extensive literature that grew out of efforts to analyze the robustness of these figures; a summary of this literature is provided by Lucas (2003). For example, one prominent strand of this literature involves investigations of robustness to departures from the representative-agent framework (e.g., as pursued by Krusell and Smith, 1999). Such departures enable the calculation of differential welfare effects for, for example, low-income households, who may suffer disproportionately from cyclical uncertainty. Another prominent strand involves departures from the CRRA specification chosen for instantaneous utility. Lucas' (2003) reading of this literature led him to conclude that his original calculations have proven to be remarkably robust. Here we demonstrate an extension that underscores this conclusion, adopted from Otrok (2001).

Otrok's extension involves the replacement of the CRRA specification for instantaneous utility with the habit/durability specification introduced in chapter 5. Otrok's analysis was conducted in the context of a fully specified RBC model featuring a labor/leisure trade-off, along with a consumption/investment trade-off. The parameters of the model were estimated using Bayesian methods discussed in chapter 9. Here, we adopt Otrok's estimates of the habit/durability parameters in pursuit of calculations of λ akin to those made by Lucas (1987, 2003) for the CRRA case.

Recall that under habit/durability preferences, instantaneous utility is given by

$$u(h_t) = \frac{h_t^{1-\gamma}}{1-\gamma}, \tag{6.14}$$

with

$$h_t = h_t^d - \alpha h_t^h, \tag{6.15}$$

where $\alpha \in (0,1)$, h_t^d is the household's durability stock, and h_t^h its habit stock. The stocks are defined by

$$h_t^d = \sum_{j=0}^{\infty} \delta^j c_{t-j} \tag{6.16}$$

$$h_t^h = (1-\theta)\sum_{j=0}^{\infty} \theta^j h_{t-1-j}^d$$

$$= (1-\theta)\sum_{j=0}^{\infty} \theta^j \sum_{i=0}^{\infty} \delta^i c_{t-1-i} \tag{6.17}$$

where $\delta \in (0,1)$ and $\theta \in (0,1)$. Substituting for h_t^d and h_t^h in (6.15) thus yields

$$h_t = c_t + \sum_{j=1}^{\infty} \left[\delta^j - \alpha(1-\theta) \sum_{i=0}^{j-1} \delta^i \theta^{j-i-1} \right] c_{t-j}$$

$$\equiv \sum_{j=0}^{\infty} \Phi_j c_{t-j}, \tag{6.18}$$

where $\Phi_0 \equiv 1$.

Combining (6.14) and (6.18) with (6.10), Lucas' welfare comparison in this case involves the calculation of λ such that

$$E_0 \sum_{t=0}^{\infty} \beta^t \frac{\left[(1+\lambda) \left\{ \sum_{j=0}^{\infty} \Phi_j c_{t-j} \right\} \right]^{1-\gamma}}{1-\gamma}$$

$$= \sum_{t=0}^{\infty} \beta^t \frac{\left(\sum_{j=0}^{\infty} \Phi_j A e^{\mu t - j} \right)^{1-\gamma}}{1-\gamma}, \tag{6.19}$$

where once again the behavior of c_t is given by (6.6). In this case, a convenient analytical expression for λ is unavailable, due to the complicated nature of the integral needed to calculate the expectation on the left-hand side of (6.19). Hence we proceed in this case by approximating λ numerically.

The algorithm we use for this purpose takes the collection of parameters that appear in (6.19) and (6.6), including λ, as given. The parameters (A, μ, σ^2), dictating the behavior of consumption, were obtained once again from an OLS regression of log c_t on a constant and trend; the parameters $(\beta, \gamma, \alpha, \delta, \theta)$ were obtained from Otrok (2001), and a grid of values was specified for λ. Because Otrok's estimates were obtained using postwar quarterly data on per capita consumption, defined as the consumption of nondurables and services, we re-estimated (A, μ, σ^2) using this alternative measure of consumption. The series is contained in `ycih.txt`, available at the textbook Web site. It is slightly more volatile than the annual measure of consumption considered by Lucas: the estimate of σ^2 it yields is $(0.035)^2$.

Given a specification of parameters, the right-hand side of (6.19) may be calculated directly, subject to two approximations. First, for each value of t, the infinite-order expression $\sum_{j=0}^{\infty} \Phi_j A e^{\mu t - j}$ must be calculated using a finite-ordered approximation. It turns out that under the range of values for $(\beta, \gamma, \alpha, \delta, \theta)$ estimated by Otrok, the corresponding sequence $\{\Phi_j\}$ decays rapidly as j increases, reaching approximately zero for $j = 6$; we set an upper bound of $J = 10$ to be conservative. Second, the infinite time horizon over which the discounted value of instantaneous utility is aggregated must also be truncated. It turns out that summation over approximately a 1,500-period time span provides an accurate approximation of the infinite time horizon; we worked with an upper bound of $T = 3,000$ to be conservative.

Using the same upper limits J and T, an additional approximation is required to calculate the expectation that appears on the left-hand side of (6.19). This is accomplished via use of a technique known as numerical integration. Full details on the general use of this technique are provided in chapter 9. In the present application, the process begins by obtaining a simulated realization of $\{u_t\}_{t=1}^{T}$ from an $N(0, \sigma^2)$ distribution, calculating $\{\varepsilon_t\}_{t=1}^{T}$ using $\varepsilon_t = e^{u_t}$, and then inserting $\{\varepsilon_t\}_{t=1}^{T}$ into (6.6) to obtain a simulated drawing of $\{c_t\}_{t=1}^{T}$. Using this drawing, the corresponding realization of the discounted value of instantaneous utility is calculated. These steps deliver the value of a single realization of lifetime utility. Computing the average value of realized lifetime utilities calculated over many replications of this process yields an approximation of the expected value of lifetime utility. The results reported below were obtained using 1,000 replications of this process. (A discussion of the accuracy with which this calculation approximates the actual integral we seek is provided in chapter 9.)

Finally, to determine the value of λ that satisfies (6.19), the left-hand side of this equation was approximated over a sequence of values specified for λ; the specific sequence we used began at 0 and increased in increments of 0.000025. Given the risk aversion implied by the habit/durability specification, the left-hand side of (6.19) is guaranteed to be less than the right-hand side given $\lambda = 0$; and as λ increases, the left-hand side increases, ultimately reaching the value of the right-hand side. The value of λ we seek in the approximation is the value that generates equality between the two sides.

Results of this exercise are reported in table 6.2 for nine specifications of $(\beta, \gamma, \alpha, \delta, \theta)$. The first is referenced as a baseline: these correspond with median values of the marginal posterior distributions Otrok calculated for each parameter: 0.9878, 0.7228, 0.446, 0.1533, 0.1299. Next, sensitivity to the specification of γ is demonstrated by re-specifying γ first at the 5% quantile value of its marginal posterior distribution, then at its 95% quantile value. The remaining parameters were held fixed at their median values given the re-specification of γ. Sensitivity to the specifications of α, δ, and θ is demonstrated analogously. Finally, a modification of the baseline under which $\gamma = 1$ is reported, to facilitate a closer comparison of Lucas' estimate of λ obtained under CRRA preferences given $\gamma = 1$.

Under Otrok's baseline parameterization, λ is estimated as 0.00275. In terms of the annual version of consumption considered by Lucas,

TABLE 6.2
Welfare Costs, Habit/Durability Preferences

Parameterization	λ	*\$/Person, 2004*
Baseline	0.000275	\$7.15
$\gamma = 0.5363$	0.000225	\$5.85
$\gamma = 0.9471$	0.000400	\$10.40
$\theta = 0.0178$	0.000375	\$9.75
$\theta = 0.3039$	0.000200	\$5.20
$\alpha = 0.2618$	0.000275	\$7.15
$\alpha = 0.6133$	0.000400	\$10.40
$\delta = 0.0223$	0.000425	\$11.05
$\delta = 0.3428$	0.000175	\$4.55
$\gamma = 1$	0.000550	\$14.30

Note: Baseline estimates are $(\beta, \gamma, \alpha, \delta, \theta) = (0.9878, 0.7228, 0.446, 0.1533, 0.1299)$.

this corresponds with a consumption cost of \$7.15/person in 2004. For the modification of the baseline under which $\gamma = 1$, the cost rises to \$14.30/person, which slightly exceeds the cost of \$11.72/person calculated using CRRA preferences given $\gamma = 1$. The estimated value of λ is most sensitive to changes in δ, which determines the persistence of the flow of services from past consumption in contributing to the durability stock. However, even in this case the range of estimates is modest: \$4.55/person given $\delta = 0.3428$; \$11.05/person given $\delta = 0.0223$. These results serve to demonstrate the general insensitivity of Lucas' results to this particular modification of the specification of instantaneous utility; as characterized by Otrok: "... it is a result that casts doubt that empirically plausible modifications to preferences alone could lead to large costs of consumption volatility." [p. 88]

Exercise 6.1

Recalculate the welfare cost of business cycles for the CRRA case given a relaxation of the log-Normality assumption for $\{\varepsilon_t\}$. Do so using the following steps.

1. Using the consumption data contained in `weldat.txt`, regress the log of consumption on a constant and trend. Use the resulting parameter estimates to specify (A, μ, σ^2) in (6.6), and save the resulting residuals in the vector u.
2. Construct a simulated realization of $\{c_t\}_{t=0}^{T}$, $T = 3,000$, by obtaining random drawings (with replacement) of the individual elements of u. For each of the t drawings u_t you obtain, calculate $\varepsilon_t = e^{u_t}$; then insert the resulting drawing $\{\varepsilon_t\}_{t=0}^{T}$ into (6.6) to obtain $\{c_t\}_{t=0}^{T}$.

3. Using the drawing $\{c_t\}_{t=0}^{T}$, calculate $\sum_{t=0}^{T}\beta^t \frac{[(1+\lambda)c_t]^{1-\gamma}}{1-\gamma}$ using $\beta = 0.96$, $\gamma = 0.5,\ 1,\ 1.5,\ 2$ (recalling that for $\gamma = 1$, $\frac{x^{1-\gamma}}{1-\gamma} = \ln(x)$), and $\lambda = 0$, $0.000025, \ldots, 0.0001$.
4. Repeat steps 2 and 3 1,000 times, and record the average values of $\sum_{t=0}^{T}\beta^t \frac{[(1+\lambda)c_t]^{1-\gamma}}{1-\gamma}$ you obtain as approximations of $E_0 \sum_{t=0}^{T}\beta^t \frac{[(1+\lambda)c_t]^{1-\gamma}}{1-\gamma}$.
5. Calculate the right-hand side of (6.10) using the estimates of A and μ obtained in step 1. Do so for each value of γ considered in step 3.
6. For each value of γ, find the value of λ that most closely satisfies (6.10). Compare the values you obtain with those reported in table 6.1. Are Lucas' original calculations robust to departures from the log-Normality assumption adopted for $\{\varepsilon_t\}$?

Exercise 6.2

Using the baseline estimates of the habit/durability specification reported in table 6.2, evaluate the robustness of the estimates of λ reported in table 6.2 to departures from the log-Normality assumption adopted for $\{\varepsilon_t\}$. Do so using simulations of $\{c_t\}_{t=0}^{T}$ generated as described in step 2 of the exercise 6.1. Once again, are the results reported in table 6.2 robust to departures from the log-Normality assumption adopted for $\{\varepsilon_t\}$?

6.4 Productivity Shocks and Business Cycle Fluctuations

As an example of an experiment involving a question of fit, we calibrate the RBC model presented in chapter 5, section 5.1.1, and examine the extent to which it is capable of accounting for aspects of the behavior of output, consumption, investment, and hours introduced in chapters 3 and 4 (the data are contained in `ycih.txt`, available at the textbook Web site). Reverting to the notation used in the specification of the model, the parameters to be calibrated are as follows: capital's share of output α; the subjective discount factor $\beta = \frac{1}{1+\varrho}$, where ϱ is the subjective discount rate; the degree of relative risk aversion ϕ; consumption's share (relative to leisure) of instantaneous utility φ; the depreciation rate of physical capital δ; the AR parameter specified for the productivity shock ρ; and the standard deviation of innovations to the productivity shock σ.

Standard specifications of β result from the association of the subjective discount rate ϱ with average real interest rates: roughly 4%–5% on an annual basis, or 1%–1.25% on a quarterly basis. As a baseline, we select a rate of 1%, implying $\beta = \frac{1}{1.01} = 0.99$. The parameterization of the CRRA parameter was discussed in the previous section; as a baseline, we set $\phi = 1.5$, and consider $[0.5, 2.5]$ as a plausible range of alternative values.

We use the long-run relationship observed between output and investment to identify plausible parameterizations of α and δ. Recall that steady state values of $\frac{\overline{y}}{\overline{n}}$ and $\frac{\overline{i}}{\overline{n}}$ are given by

$$\frac{\overline{y}}{\overline{n}} = \eta,$$
$$\frac{\overline{i}}{\overline{n}} = \delta\theta,$$

where

$$\theta = \left(\frac{\alpha}{\varrho + \delta}\right)^{\frac{1}{1-\alpha}},$$
$$\eta = \theta^{\alpha}.$$

Combining these expressions yields the relationship

$$\alpha = \left(\frac{\delta + \varrho}{\delta}\right)\frac{\overline{i}}{\overline{y}}. \tag{6.20}$$

Using the sample average of 0.175 as a measure of $\frac{\overline{i}}{\overline{y}}$, and given $\varrho = 0.01$, a simple relationship is established between α and δ.

Before illustrating this relationship explicitly, we use a similar step to identify a plausible range of values for φ. Here we use the steady state expression for $\overline{n}$, the fraction of discretionary time spent on job-market activities:

$$\overline{n} = \frac{1}{1 + \left(\frac{1}{1-\alpha}\right)\left(\frac{1-\varphi}{\varphi}\right)[1 - \delta\theta^{1-\alpha}]}. \tag{6.21}$$

According to the time-allocation study of Ghez and Becker (1975), which is based on household survey data, $\overline{n}$ is approximately 1/3. Using this figure in (6.21), and exploiting the fact that $\frac{\overline{c}}{\overline{y}} = [1 - \delta\theta^{1-\alpha}]$ (the sample average of which is 0.825), we obtain the following relationship between α and φ:

$$\varphi = \frac{1}{1 + \frac{2(1-\alpha)}{\overline{c}/\overline{y}}}. \tag{6.22}$$

In sum, using sample averages to pin down $\frac{\overline{i}}{\overline{y}}$, $\frac{\overline{c}}{\overline{y}}$, and $\overline{n}$, we obtain the relationships between α, δ, and φ characterized by (6.20) and (6.22).

TABLE 6.3
Trade-Offs Between δ, α, and φ

δ	α	φ
0.010	0.35	0.39
0.015	0.29	0.37
0.020	0.26	0.36
0.025	0.24	0.35
0.030	0.23	0.35
0.035	0.22	0.35
0.040	0.22	0.35

Note: The moments used to establish these trade-offs are $\frac{\overline{i}}{\overline{y}} = 0.175$, $\frac{\overline{c}}{\overline{y}} = 0.825$, and $\overline{n} = 1/3$.

Table 6.3 presents combinations of these parameters for a grid of values specified for δ over the range $[0.01, 0.04]$, implying a range of annual depreciation rates of $[4\%, 16\%]$. As a baseline, we specify $\delta = 0.025$ (10% annual depreciation), yielding specifications of $\alpha = 0.24$ and $\varphi = 0.35$ that match the empirical values of $\frac{\overline{i}}{\overline{y}}$, $\frac{\overline{c}}{\overline{y}}$, and $\overline{n}$. Regarding the specification of α, this is somewhat lower than the residual value attributed to capital's share given the measure of labor's share calculated from National Income and Product Accounts (NIPA) data. In the NIPA data, labor's share is approximately $2/3$, implying the specification of $\alpha = 1/3$. The reason for the difference in this application is the particular measure of investment we use (real gross private domestic investment). Using the same measure of investment over the period 1948:I–1995:IV, DeJong and Ingram (2001) obtain an estimate of $\alpha = 0.23$ (with a corresponding estimate of $\delta = 0.02$) using Bayesian methods described in chapter 9.

The final parameters to be established are those associated with the behavior of the productivity shock z_t: ρ and σ. We obtain these by first measuring the behavior of z_t implied by the specification of the production function, coupled with the observed behavior of output, hours, and physical capital. Given this measure, we then estimate the AR parameters directly via OLS.

Regarding physical capital, the narrow definition of investment we use must be taken into account in measuring the corresponding behavior of capital. We do so using a tool known as the perpetual inventory method. This involves the input of $\{i_t\}_{t=1}^{T}$ and k_0 into the law of motion of capital

$$k_{t+1} = i_t + (1 - \delta)k_t \tag{6.23}$$

to obtain a corresponding sequence $\{k_t\}_{t=1}^{T}$. A measure of k_0 may be obtained in four steps: divide both sides of (6.23) by y_t; use beginning-of-sample averages to measure the resulting ratios $\frac{\overline{x}}{\overline{y}}$, $\overline{x} = \overline{i}, \overline{k}$; solve for

$$\frac{\overline{k}}{\overline{y}} = \frac{1}{\delta}\frac{\overline{i}}{\overline{y}}; \tag{6.24}$$

and finally, multiply $\frac{1}{\delta}\frac{\overline{i}}{\overline{y}}$ by y_0. The results reported here are based on the specification of $\frac{\overline{i}}{\overline{y}}$ obtained using an eight-period, or two-year sample average.

Given this measure of $\{k_t\}_{t=1}^{T}$, $\log z_t$ is derived following Solow (1957) as the unexplained component of $\log y_t$ given the input of $\log k_t$ and $\log n_t$ in the production function:

$$\log z_t = \log y_t - \alpha \log k_t - (1-\alpha)\log n_t. \tag{6.25}$$

For this reason, z_t is often referred to as a Solow residual. Finally, we apply the Hodrick-Prescott (H-P) filter to each variable, and estimate ρ and σ using the HP-filtered version of z_t. The resulting estimates are 0.78 and 0.0067.

Having parameterized the model, we characterize its implications regarding the collection of moments reported for the HP-filtered data in table 4.1. Moments calculated using both the model and data are reported in table 6.4.

As these results indicate, the model performs well in characterizing the patterns of serial correlation observed in the data, and also replicates the patterns of volatility observed for consumption and investment relative to output: the former is quite smooth relative to the latter. However, it performs poorly in characterizing the relative volatility of hours, which are roughly equally as volatile as output in the data, but only 1/3 as volatile in the model. Figure 6.1 illustrates this shortcoming by depicting the time-series paths followed by output and hours in the actual data, along with paths followed by counterparts simulated from the model. The simulated hours series is far smoother than the corresponding output series.

The standard RBC model's characterization of the volatility of hours is a well-known shortcoming, and has prompted many extensions that improve upon its performance along this dimension. Examples include specifications featuring indivisible labor hours (Hansen, 1985; Rogerson, 1988; Kydland and Prescott, 1991b); home production (Benhabib, Rogerson, and Wright, 1991; Greenwood and Hercowitz, 1991); labor hoarding (Burnside, Eichenbaum, and Rebelo, 1993; Burnside and Eichenbaum,

TABLE 6.4
Moment comparison

			H-P filtered Data		
j	σ_j	$\frac{\sigma_j}{\sigma_y}$	$\varphi(1)$	$\varphi_{j,y}(0)$	$\varphi_{j,y}(1)$
y	0.0177	1.00	0.86	1.00	0.86
c	0.0081	0.46	0.83	0.82	0.75
i	0.0748	4.23	0.79	0.95	0.80
n	0.0185	1.05	0.90	0.83	0.62
			RBC Model		
	σ_j	$\frac{\sigma_j}{\sigma_y}$	$\varphi(1)$	$\varphi_{j,y}(0)$	$\varphi_{j,y}(1)$
y	0.0207	1.00	0.87	1.00	0.87
c	0.0101	0.48	0.94	0.96	0.93
i	0.0752	3.63	0.81	0.98	0.79
n	0.0076	0.366	0.78	0.97	0.76

Notes: $\varphi(1)$ denotes first-order serial correlation; $\varphi_{j,y}(l)$ denotes l^{th} order correlation between variables j and y. Model moments based on the parameterization

$$\mu = [\alpha\ \beta\ \phi\ \varphi\ \delta\ \rho\ \sigma]' = [0.24\ 0.99\ 1.5\ 0.35\ 0.025\ 0.78\ 0.0067]'.$$

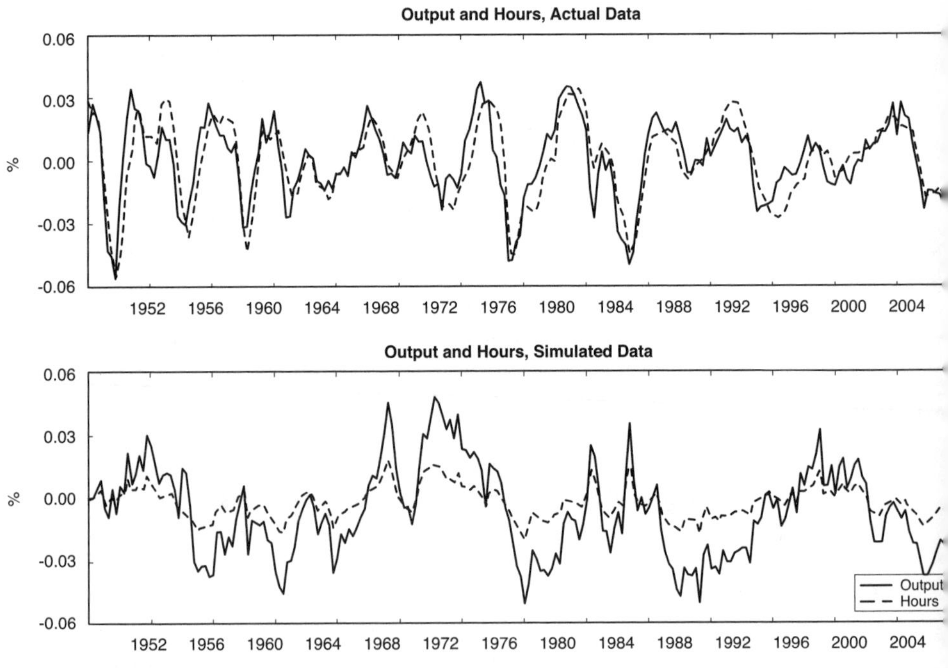

Figure 6.1 Comparisons of output and hours.

1997); fiscal disturbances (McGrattan, 1994); and skill-acquisition activities (Einarsson and Marquis, 1997; Perli and Sakellaris, 1998; and DeJong and Ingram, 2001). Thus this example serves as a prime case study for the use of calibration experiments as a means of facilitating the "... testing and development of theory," as advocated by Kydland and Prescott (1996, p. 70).

Exercise 6.3

Reconstruct table 6.4 by using the alternative combinations of values specified for δ, α, and φ listed in table 6.3. Also, consider 0.5 and 2.5 as alternative specifications of ϕ. Are the results of table 6.4 materially altered by any of the alternative choices you considered?

Exercise 6.4

Reconduct the calibration exercise of this section using the extension of the RBC model outlined in chapter 5, section 5.1.1 that explicitly incorporates long-term growth. Pay careful attention to the fact that equations (6.20) and (6.22), used to restrict the parameterizations of δ, α, and φ, will be altered given this extension. So too will be (6.24), which was used to specify k_0. Once again, are the results of table 6.4 materially altered given this extension of the model?

6.5 The Equity Premium Puzzle

The calibration experiment of Mehra and Prescott (1985) also serves as a prime case study involving the testing and development of theory. The test they conducted sought to determine whether the asset-pricing model presented in chapter 5, section 5.3.2, is capable of characterizing patterns of returns generated by relatively risky assets (equity) and riskless assets (Treasury bills). The data they considered for this purpose consist of the annual real return on the Standard and Poor's 500 composite index, the annualized real return on Treasury bills, and the growth rate of real per capita consumption on non-durables and services. The time span of their data is 1889–1978; here we demonstrate a brief replication of their study using data updated through 2004. The original data set is contained in `mpepp.txt`, and the updated data set is contained in `mpeppext.txt`; both are available at the textbook Web site.

As characterized in chapter 5, section 5.3.2, Mehra and Prescott's statement of the equity premium puzzle amounts to a presentation of the empirical incompatibility of the following equations, derived in a two-asset environment:

$$\beta E_t\left\{\frac{u'(c_{t+1})}{u'(c_t)}r^f_{t+1}-1\right\}=0 \tag{6.26}$$

$$E_t\left\{\frac{u'(c_{t+1})}{u'(c_t)}\left[r^e_{t+1}-r^f_{t+1}\right]\right\}=0, \tag{6.27}$$

where r^f_{t+1} and r^e_{t+1} denote the gross returns associated with a risk-free and risky asset. The difference $r^e_{t+1}-r^f_{t+1}$ is referred to as the equity premium. Sample averages (standard deviations) of r^f_{t+1} and r^e_{t+1} are 0.8% (5.67%) and 6.98% (16.54%) in the data ending in 1978, and 1.11% (5.61%) and 7.48% (16.04%) in the data ending through 2004. Thus equity returns are large and volatile relative to risk-free returns. The question is: can this pattern of returns be reconciled with the attitudes towards risk embodied by the CRRA preference specification?

Given CRRA preferences, with γ representing the risk-aversion parameter, the equations are given by

$$\beta E_t\left\{\left(\frac{c_{t+1}}{c_t}\right)^{-\gamma}r^f_{t+1}-1\right\}=0 \tag{6.28}$$

$$E_t\left\{\left(\frac{c_{t+1}}{c_t}\right)^{-\gamma}\left[r^e_{t+1}-r^f_{t+1}\right]\right\}=0. \tag{6.29}$$

Here, we use sample averages to estimate the expectations represented in (6.28) and (6.29), and seek to determine whether it is possible to specify γ in order to jointly account for each equation, given $\beta=0.99$. The results of this exercise are presented in table 6.5.

Note that for a specification of γ between 0 and 0.5, it is possible to account for the first equation. The reason for the requirement of such a low value is that in addition to characterizing attitudes towards risk, γ plays the role of determining the household's intertemporal elasticity of substitution, given by $1/\gamma$. The presence in the data of a relatively large average consumption growth rate (1.83% in the data ending in 1978, and 1.79% in the data ending in 2004), coupled with the low average returns generated by the risk-free rate, implies a highly elastic intertemporal substitution parameter, and thus a low value of γ. Of course, the specification of a smaller value for β requires an even lower value for γ; thus $\beta=0.99$ represents nearly a best-case scenario along this dimension.

In turn, a large specification of γ is required to account for the second equation. In fact, the sample average first becomes negative given $\gamma=20$.

TABLE 6.5
The Equity Premium and Risk-Free Rate Puzzles

γ	$\beta\overline{\left(\frac{c_{t+1}}{c_t}^{-\gamma} r^f_{t+1}\right)} - 1$	$\overline{\left(\frac{c_{t+1}}{c_t}\right)^{-\gamma}\left[r^e_{t+1} - r^f_{t+1}\right]}$
0	0.001	0.064
0.5	−0.007	0.062
1	−0.015	0.060
1.5	−0.023	0.059
2	−0.030	0.057
2.5	−0.037	0.056
3	−0.044	0.054

Notes: $\overline{x}$ denotes the sample mean of x. Results obtained using $\beta = 0.99$.

The reason is that the relatively large premium associated with returns generated by the risky asset implies substantial risk aversion on the part of households. This in turn implies a highly inelastic intertemporal elasticity of substitution given CRRA preferences, which is inconsistent with the first equation. Thus the puzzle.

Mehra and Prescott's (1985) statement of the puzzle spawned an enormous literature seeking to determine whether alterations of preferences or additional features of the environment are capable of accounting for this behavior. Surveys of this literature are given by Kocherlakota (1996) and Mehra and Prescott (2003). Certainly these efforts have served to make headway towards a resolution; however, the conclusion of both surveys is that the equity premium remains a puzzle.

Exercise 6.5

Replicate the calculations presented in table 6.5 using the baseline parameterization of the habit/durability specification presented in section 6.3. Does this modification represent progress in resolving the puzzle? Ponder the intuition behind your findings.

6.6 Critiques and Extensions

6.6.1 Critiques

As noted, Kydland and Prescott's (1982) use of a calibration exercise to implement the DSGE model they studied represents a pathbreaking advance in the conduct of empirical work in macroeconomic applications. Moreover, as illustrated in the applications above, calibration exercises can certainly serve as an effective means of making headway in empirical applications involving general-equilibrium models. At a minimum, they are well-suited for conveying a quick initial impression regarding the empirical strengths and weaknesses of a given model along specific dimensions chosen by the researcher. This latter attribute is particularly important, in that it provides an effective means of discovering dimensions along which extensions to the model are most likely to bear fruit.

This being said, the lack of statistical formality associated with calibration exercises imposes distinct limitations upon what can be learned and communicated via their use. Moreover, the particular approach advocated by Kydland and Prescott (as presented in section 6.2) for addressing empirical questions in the absence of a formal statistical framework has been criticized on a variety of fronts. We conclude this chapter by summarizing certain aspects of this criticism, and discussing some closely related extensions to calibration that retain the general spirit of the exercise.

In the preface to his (1944) articulation of the probability approach to econometrics, Haavelmo opened with a criticism of the approach that prevailed at the time. The criticism is striking in its applicability to calibration exercises devoted to questions regarding fit (the included quotation marks and italics are Haavelmo's):

> So far, the common procedure has been, first to construct an economic theory involving *exact* functional relationships, then to compare this theory with some actual measurements, and, finally, "to judge" whether the correspondence is "good" or "bad." Tools of statistical inference have been introduced, in some degree, to support such judgements, e.g., the calculation of a few standard errors and multiple-correlation coefficients. The application of such simple "statistics" has been considered legitimate, while, at the same time, the adoption of definite probability models has been deemed a crime in economic research, a violation of the very nature of economic data. That is to say, it has been considered legitimate to use some of the *tools* developed in statistical theory *without* accepting the very *foundation* upon which statistical theory is built. For *no tool developed in the theory of statistics has any meaning* - except, perhaps, for descriptive purposes - *without being referred to some stochastic scheme.* [p. iii]

Our interpretation of the thrust of this criticism is that in the absence of statistical formality, communication regarding the results of an experiment is problematic. Judgments of "good" or "bad", or as Kydland and Prescott (1996, p. 71) put it, judgments of whether "... the predictions of theory match the observations ... ," are necessarily subjective. In applications such as Mehra and Prescott's (1985) identification of the equity premium puzzle, empirical shortcomings are admittedly fairly self-evident. But in evaluating marginal gains in empirical performance generated by various modifications of a baseline model, the availability of coherent and objective reporting mechanisms is invaluable. No such mechanism is available in conducting calibration exercises.

Reacting to Kydland and Prescott (1996), Sims (1996) makes a similar point:

> Economists can do very little experimentation to produce crucial data. This is particularly true of macroeconomics. Important policy questions demand opinions from economic experts from month to month, regardless of whether professional consensus has emerged on the questions. As a result, economists normally find themselves considering many theories and models with legitimate claims to matching the data and predicting the effects of policy. We have to deliver recommendations or accurate descriptions of the nature of the uncertainty about the consequences of alternative policies, despite the lack of a single accepted theory. [p. 107]

Moreover:

> Axiomatic arguments can produce the conclusion that anyone making decisions under uncertainty must act as if that agent has a probability distribution over the uncertainty, updating the probability distribution by Bayes' rule as new evidence accumulates. People making decisions whose results depend on which of a set of scientific theories is correct should therefore be interested in probabilistic characterizations of the state of the evidence. [p. 108]

These observations lead him to conclude:

> ... formal statistical inference is not necessary when there is no need to choose among competing theories among which the data do not distinguish decisively. But if the data do not make the choice of theory obvious, and if decisions depend on the choice, experts can report and discuss their conclusions reasonably only using notions of probability. [p. 110]

Regarding the problem of choosing among given theories, there is no doubt that from a classical hypothesis testing perspective, under which one model is posed as the null hypothesis, this is complicated by the fact that the models in question are "necessarily false." But this problem is not unique to the analysis of DSGE models, as the epigram to this chapter by Theil implies. Moreover, this problem is not an issue given the adoption of a Bayesian perspective, under which model comparisons involve calculations of the relative probability assigned to alternative models, conditional on the observed data. Under this perspective, there is no need for the declaration of a null model; rather, all models are treated symmetrically, and none are assumed a priori to be "true." Details regarding this approach are provided in chapter 9.

Also in reaction to Kydland and Prescott (1996), Hansen and Heckman (1996) offer additional criticisms. For one, they challenge the view that calibration experiments involving questions of fit are to be considered as distinct from estimation: "... the distinction drawn between calibrating and estimating the parameters of a model is artificial at best." [p. 91] Their reasoning fits nicely with the description provided in section 6.1 of the means by which the specification of μ is achieved via use of (6.4); and the means by which judgements of fit are achieved via comparisons of $\Phi(\{X_t\}_{t=1}^T)$ with $\Phi(\{X_t^M\}_{t=1}^T)$:

> Econometricians refer to the first stage as *estimation* and the second stage as *testing*. ... From this perspective, the Kydland-Prescott objection to mainstream econometrics is simply a complaint about the use of certain loss functions for describing the fit of a model to the data or for producing parameter estimates. [p. 92]

In addition, Hansen and Heckman call into question the practice of importing parameter estimates obtained from micro studies into macroeconomic models. They do so on two grounds. First, such parameter estimates are associated with uncertainty. In part this uncertainty can be conveyed by reporting corresponding standard errors, but in addition, model uncertainty plays a substantial role (a point emphasized by Sims). Second, "... it is only under very special circumstances that a micro parameter ... can be 'plugged into' a representative consumer model to produce an empirically concordant aggregate model." [p. 88] As an example of such a pitfall, they cite Houthakker (1956), who demonstrated that the aggregation of Leontief micro production technologies yields an aggregate Cobb-Douglas production function.

These shortcomings lead Hansen and Heckman and Sims to similar conclusions. To quote Hansen and Heckman:

> Calibration should only be the starting point of an empirical analysis of general-equilibrium models. In the absence of firmly established estimates of key parameters, sensitivity analyses should be routine in real business cycle simulations. Properly used and qualified simulation methods can be an important source of information and an important stimulus to high-quality empirical economic research. [p. 101]

And to quote Sims:

> A focus on solving and calibrating models, rather than carefully fitting them to data, is reasonable at a stage where solving the models is by itself a major research task. When plausible theories have been advanced, though, and when decisions depend on evaluating them, more systematic collection and comparison of evidence cannot be avoided. [p. 109]

It is precisely in the spirit of these sentiments that we present the additional material contained in Part II of this book.

6.6.2 Extensions

We conclude this chapter by presenting two extensions to the basic calibration exercise. In contrast to the extensions presented in the chapters that follow, the extensions presented here are distinct in that they do not entail an estimation stage. Instead, both are designed to provide measures of fit for calibrated models.

The first extension is due to Watson (1993), who proposed a measure of fit based on the size of the stochastic error necessary for reconciling discrepancies observed between the second moments corresponding to the model under investigation and those corresponding with the actual data. Specifically, letting X_t denote the $m \times 1$ vector of observable variables corresponding with the model, and Υ_t their empirical counterparts, Watson's measure is based on the question: how much error U_t would have to be added to X_t so that the autocovariances of $X_t + U_t$ are equal to the autocovariances of Υ_t?

To quantify this question, recall from chapter 4 that the sth-order autocovariance of a mean-zero covariance-stationary stochastic process z_t is given by the $m \times m$ matrix

$$E(z_t z_{t-s}') \equiv \Gamma_z(s).$$

Therefore the sth-order autocovariance of $U_t = \Upsilon_t - X_t$ is given by

$$\Gamma_U(s) = \Gamma_\Upsilon(s) + \Gamma_X(s) - \Gamma_{X\Upsilon}(s) - \Gamma_{\Upsilon X}(s), \tag{6.30}$$

where

$$\Gamma_{X\Upsilon}(s) = E(X_t \Upsilon_{t-s}'),$$

and

$$\Gamma_{X\Upsilon}(s) = \Gamma_{\Upsilon X}(-s)'.$$

With the autocovariance generating function (ACGF) of z_t given by

$$A_z(e^{-i\omega}) = \sum_{s=-\infty}^{\infty} \Gamma_z(s) e^{-i\omega s}, \tag{6.31}$$

where i is complex and $\omega \in [0, 2\pi]$ represents a particular frequency, the ACGF of U_t implied by (6.30) is given by

$$\begin{aligned} A_U(e^{-i\omega}) = {} & A_\Upsilon(e^{-i\omega}) + A_X(e^{-i\omega}) \\ & - A_{X\Upsilon}(e^{-i\omega}) - A_{X\Upsilon}(e^{i\omega})', \end{aligned} \tag{6.32}$$

where

$$A_{X\Upsilon}(e^{i\omega})' = A_{\Upsilon X}(e^{-i\omega}).$$

As discussed in chapter 4, it is straightforward to construct $A_{\Upsilon}(e^{-i\omega})$ and $A_X(e^{-i\omega})$ given observations on Υ_t and a model specified for X_t. However, absent theoretical restrictions imposed upon $A_{X\Upsilon}(e^{-i\omega})$, and absent joint observations on (Υ_t, X_t), the specification of $A_{X\Upsilon}(e^{-i\omega})$ is arbitrary. Watson overcame this problem by proposing a restriction on $A_{X\Upsilon}(e^{-i\omega})$ that produces a lower bound for the variance of U_t, or in other words, a best-case scenario for the model's ability to account for the second moments of the data.

To characterize the restriction, it is useful to begin with the implausible but illustrative case in which X_t and Υ_t are serially uncorrelated. In this case, the restriction involves minimizing the size of the covariance matrix of U_t, given by

$$\Sigma_U = \Sigma_{\Upsilon} + \Sigma_X - \Sigma_{X\Upsilon} - \Sigma_{\Upsilon X}. \tag{6.33}$$

Because there is no unique measure of the size of Σ_U, Watson proposes the minimization of the trace of $W\Sigma_U$, where W is an $m \times m$ weighting matrix that enables the researcher to assign alternative importance to linear combinations of the variables under investigation. If W is specified as the identity matrix, then each individual variable is treated as equally important. If alternatively the researcher is interested in $G\Upsilon_t$ and GX_t, then W can be chosen as $G'G$, since

$$tr(G\Sigma_U G') = tr(G'G\Sigma_U).$$

Given W, Watson shows that

$$\Sigma_{X\Upsilon} = C_X V U' C_{\Upsilon}' \tag{6.34}$$

is the unique specification of $\Sigma_{X\Upsilon}$ that minimizes $tr(W\Sigma_U)$. In (6.34), C_X and C_{Υ} are arbitrary $m \times m$ matrix square roots of Σ_X and Σ_{Υ} (e.g., $\Sigma_X = C_X C_X'$, an example of which is the Cholesky decomposition), and the matrices U and V are obtained by computing the singular value decomposition of $C_{\Upsilon}' W C_X$. Specifically, the singular value decomposition of $C_{\Upsilon}' W C_X$ is given by

$$C_{\Upsilon}' W C_X = USV', \tag{6.35}$$

where U is an $m \times k$ orthonormal matrix (i.e., $U'U$ is the $k \times k$ identity matrix), S is a $k \times k$ matrix, and V is a $k \times k$ orthonormal matrix.[2]

[2] In GAUSS, Cholesky decompositions can be obtained using the command `chol`, and singular value decompositions can be obtained using the command `svd1`.

For the general case in which X_t and Υ_t are serially correlated, Watson's minimization objective translates directly from $\Sigma_{X\Upsilon}$ to $A_{X\Upsilon}(e^{-i\omega})$. Recall from chapter 4 the relationship between ACGFs and spectra; in the multivariate case of interest here, the relationship is given by

$$s_z(\omega) = \left(\frac{1}{2\pi}\right) \sum_{s=-\infty}^{\infty} \Gamma_z(s) e^{-i\omega s}, \qquad \omega \in [-\pi, \pi]. \tag{6.36}$$

With $C_X(\omega)$ now denoting the matrix square root of $s_X(\omega)$ calculated for a given specification of ω, etc., the specification of $A_{X\Upsilon}(e^{-i\omega})$ that minimizes $tr(W\Sigma_U)$ is given by

$$A_{X\Upsilon}(e^{-i\omega}) = C_X(\omega) V(\omega) U'(\omega) C'_\Upsilon(\omega), \tag{6.37}$$

where $U(\omega)$ and $V(\omega)$ are as indicated in (6.35).

In this way, the behavior of the minimum-variance stochastic process U_t can be analyzed on a frequency-by-frequency basis. As a summary of the overall performance of the model, Watson proposes a relative mean square approximation error (RMSAE) statistic, analogous to a lower bound on $1 - R^2$ statistics in regression analyses (lower is better):

$$r_j(\omega) = \frac{A_U(e^{-i\omega})_{jj}}{A_\Upsilon(e^{-i\omega})_{jj}}, \tag{6.38}$$

where $A_U(e^{-i\omega})_{jj}$ denotes the jth diagonal element of $A_U(e^{-i\omega})$.

As an illustration, figure 6.2 closely follows Watson by demonstrating the application of his procedure to the RBC model presented in section 6.4, parameterized as indicated in table 6.4. Following Watson, the figure illustrates spectra corresponding to first differences of both the model variables and their empirical counterparts. This is done to better accentuate behavior over business-cycle frequencies (i.e., frequencies between 1/40 and 1/6 cycles per quarter). The data were also HP-filtered, and W was specified as the 4×4 identity matrix.[3]

The striking aspect of this figure is that the model fails to capture the spectral peaks observed in the data over business-cycle frequencies. Given this failure, associated RMSAE statistics are decidedly anticlimactic. Nevertheless, RMSAEs calculated for output, consumption, investment, and hours over the [1/40, 1/6] frequency range are given by 0.18, 0.79, 0.15, and 0.66; thus the model's characterization of consumption and hours over this range is seen to be particularly poor.

[3] Three GAUSS procedures were used to produce this figure: `modspec.prc`, `dataspec.prc`, and `errspec.prc`. All are available at the textbook Web site.

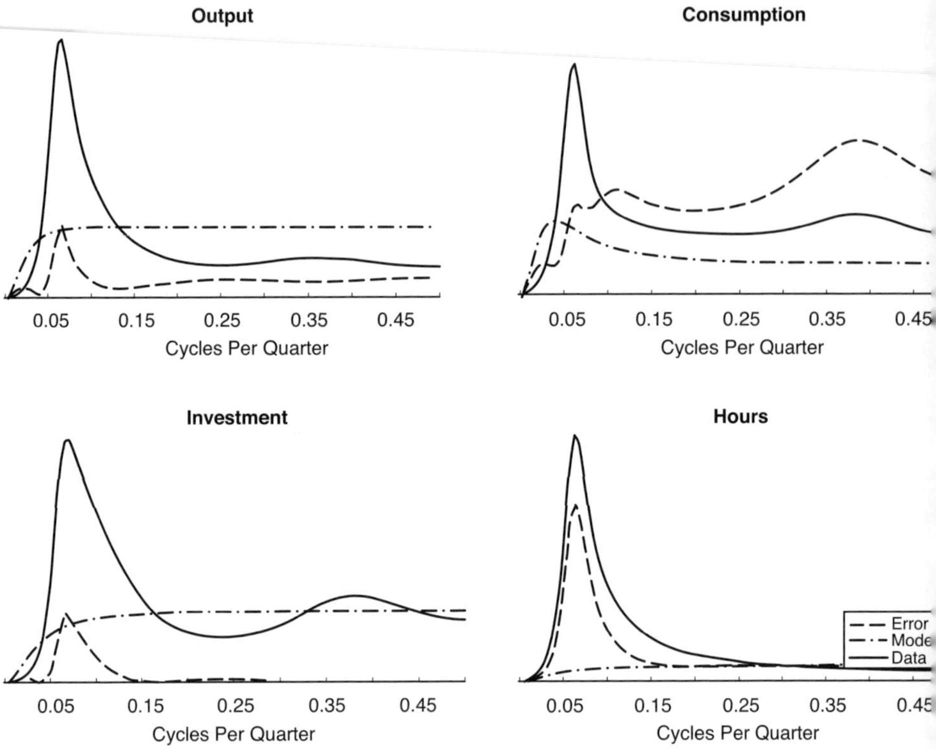

Figure 6.2 Decomposition of spectra.

Watson's demonstration of the failure of the standard RBC model to produce spectral peaks prompted several efforts devoted to determining whether plausible modifications of the model are capable of improving empirical performance along this dimension. For example, Wen (1998) obtained an affirmative answer to this question by introducing two modifications: an employment externality, under which the level of aggregate employment has an external affect on sectoral output; and the specification of habit formation in the enjoyment of leisure activities. So too did Otrok (2001), for the model (described in section 6.3) he used to analyze the welfare cost of business cycles. Thus the results of figure 6.2 do not provide a general characterization of the empirical performance of RBC models along this dimension.

The second extension is due to related work by Canova (1995) and DeJong, Ingram, and Whiteman (1996). Each study proposed the replacement of a single set of values specified over μ with a prior distribution $\pi(\mu)$. The distribution induced by $\pi(\mu)$ over a collection of empirical targets chosen by the researcher is then constructed and compared with a corresponding distribution calculated from the actual data. For example, the collection of moments featured in table 6.4 used to evaluate the RBC model presented in section 6.4 represents a common choice of empirical targets. Reverting to the notation used in section 6.2, hereafter we represent the selected targets as Ω.

The difference between these studies lies in the empirical distributions over Ω they use. DeJong et al. worked with posterior distributions over Ω obtained from the specification of a vector autoregressive (VAR) model for the actual data; Canova worked with sampling distributions. Methodologies available for calculating posterior distributions are not presented in this book until chapter 9, so details regarding the implementation of the extension proposed by DeJong et al. are not provided here. Instead, we present an algorithm for calculating sampling distributions over Ω induced by a VAR specification for the data, and thus for implementing Canova's measure of fit. This represents a specialization of the Monte Carlo method presented in chapter 4, section 4.2, as a means of approximating standard errors numerically.

Using the notation of chapter 4, let the VAR specified for X_t be given by

$$X_t = \Upsilon_1 X_{t-1} + \Upsilon_2 X_{t-2} + \cdots + \Upsilon_p X_{t-p} + \varepsilon_t, \qquad E(\varepsilon_t \varepsilon_t') = \Sigma. \tag{6.39}$$

The algorithm takes as inputs OLS estimates $\widehat{\Upsilon}_j, j = 1, \ldots, p, \widehat{\Sigma}$, estimated residuals $\{\widehat{\varepsilon}_t\}$, and the first p observations of X_t, which serve as starting values. Given these inputs, a simulated drawing $\widetilde{X}_{p+1}$ can be constructed by obtaining an artificial drawing $\widetilde{\varepsilon}_p$ from a given distribution, and evaluating the right-hand side of (6.39) using $\{X_1, X_2, \ldots, X_{p-1}, X_p\}$ and $\widetilde{\varepsilon}_p$. Next, $\widetilde{X}_{p+2}$ is constructed by obtaining a second drawing $\widetilde{\varepsilon}_{p+1}$, and evaluating the right-hand side of (6.39) using $\{X_2, X_3, \ldots, X_p, \widetilde{X}_{p+1}\}$ and $\widetilde{\varepsilon}_p$. Performing T replications of this process yields an artificial drawing $\{\widetilde{X}_t\}$. (The influence of the initial observations $\{X_1, X_2, \ldots, X_{p-1}, X_p\}$ can be reduced by obtaining $T + T'$ drawings of $\widetilde{X}_t$, and discarding the first T' drawings in constructing $\{\widetilde{X}_t\}$.) For each of J replications of this process, a collection of J estimates of Ω is calculated; the resulting distribution of Ω approximates the sampling distribution we seek.

There are two common general methods for obtaining artificial drawings $\widetilde{\varepsilon}_t$. One method involves a distributional assumption for $\{\varepsilon_t\}$, parameterized by $\widehat{\Sigma}$. For example, let $\widehat{S}$ denote the Cholesky decomposition of $\widehat{\Sigma}$. Then under the assumption of Normality for $\{\varepsilon_t\}$, drawings $\widetilde{\varepsilon}_t$ may be obtained using $\widetilde{\varepsilon}_t = \widehat{S}\,\widetilde{u}$, where $\widetilde{u}$ represents an $m \times 1$ vector of independent $N(0,1)$ random variables. Alternatively, $\widetilde{\varepsilon}_t$ may be obtained as a drawing (with replacement) from the collection of residuals $\{\widehat{\varepsilon}_t\}$.

Let the distribution obtained for the ith element of Ω be given by $S(\Omega_i)$, and let $[a, b]_i$ denote the range of values for Ω_i derived by subtracting and adding one standard deviation of $S(\Omega_i)$ to the mean value of $S(\Omega_i)$. Also, let $\pi(\Omega_i)$ denote the prior distribution over Ω_i induced by $\pi(\mu)$. Then Canova's measure of fit along this dimension of the target space is the proportion $\pi(\Omega_i)$ that lies within $[a, b]_i$:

$$f_i = \int_{a_i}^{b_i} \pi(\Omega_i) d\Omega_i. \tag{6.40}$$

Thus $f_i \in [0, 1]$, and the greater is the proportion of $\pi(\Omega_i)$ contained in the range $[a, b]_i$, the closer f_i will be to 1. A measure of fit related to that proposed by DeJong et al. is obtained by replacing the range $[a, b]_i$ with an analogous coverage interval corresponding to a posterior distribution specified over Ω_i.

Exercise 6.6

Using the RBC model presented in section 6.4, calculate f_i for the collection of moments analyzed in table 6.4. Use a 6-lag VAR specified for the data to construct $[a, b]_i$ for each moment. Do so using the version of the Monte Carlo algorithm described above under which artificial drawings $\widetilde{\varepsilon}_t$ are obtained as drawings (with replacement) from the collection of residuals $\{\widehat{\varepsilon}_t\}$. Finally, use the following prior distribution specified over the elements of $\mu : \beta \sim U[0.988, 0.9925]$; $\delta \sim U[0.01, 0.04]$; $\rho \sim U[0.75, 0.81]$, and U denoting the uniform distribution. (Uniform drawings of, e.g., β over $[\underline{\beta}, \overline{\beta}]$ may be obtained using the transformation $\widetilde{\beta} = \underline{\beta} + (\overline{\beta} - \underline{\beta})\widetilde{u}$, where $\widetilde{u}$ is a drawing from a $U[0, 1]$ distribution.) Given a drawing of δ and $\varrho = 1/\beta - 1$, calculate the corresponding value of α using (6.20), and the corresponding value of φ using (6.22). Throughout, hold σ fixed at 0.0067.

Chapter 7

Matching Moments

Know the right moment.
—The Seven Sages, from Diogenes Luertius, *Lives of Eminent Philosophers*

7.1 Overview

In the previous chapter, we characterized calibration as an exercise under which a set of empirical targets is used to pin down the parameters of the model under investigation, and a second set of targets is used to judge the model's empirical performance. Here we present a collection of procedures that establish a statistical foundation upon which structural models can be parameterized and evaluated. Under these procedures, parameterization is accomplished via estimation, and empirical performance is assessed via hypothesis testing.

As with calibration, the focus of these procedures remains on a set of empirical targets chosen by the researcher. Thus we broadly characterize their implementation as involving the matching of moments (although our use of the term moments extends rather liberally to include empirical targets such as spectra and impulse response functions). But in contrast with calibration, these procedures involve the adoption of a classical statistical perspective under which the model under investigation is interpreted as a potential data generation process from which the actual data, and thus the moments used to characterize the data, were realized. As discussed in chapter 4, statistical uncertainty associated with the realization of these moments is represented by their corresponding standard errors.

In the estimation stage, moment-matching procedures seek to determine the parameterization μ that best enables the underlying structural model to match a collection of preselected moments. The parameterization $\widehat{\mu}$ that accomplishes this objective is interpreted as an estimate of the actual value of these parameters. Because the estimate $\widehat{\mu}$ is a function of the data, it too is associated with statistical uncertainty, represented in the form of standard errors. In the testing stage, the goal is to determine whether the collection of moments selected as targets can plausibly be interpreted as a random drawing from the underlying structural model. If the probability associated with this outcome falls below a preselected threshold, or critical value, the model is rejected as a potential data generating process; otherwise it is accepted. Typically, moment-matching procedures accomplish estimation and testing simultaneously, through a process known as over-identification.

Because the procedures described in this chapter accomplish estimation and testing on the basis of a preselected collection of moments, rather than on the full range of statistical implications associated with the model under investigation, they are often referred to as limited-information procedures. This characteristic is at once a strength and a weakness. The full range of statistical implications associated with a given model is conveyed by its corresponding likelihood function. By working instead with a collection of moments, these procedures entail a loss of efficiency that can sometimes be problematic in working with small sample sizes. Also, resulting inferences can potentially be sensitive to the particular collection of moments chosen for the analysis. On the other hand, the establishment of a likelihood function involves an assumption regarding the distribution from which the structural shocks υ_t have been realized. Unless they require a simulation step, moment-matching procedures require no such assumption, and are therefore not subject to potential concerns regarding mis-specification along this dimension.

Moment-matching procedures date at least to Pearson (1894), and a wide range of specific alternatives remain in use today. Here we focus on three: the Generalized Method of Moments (GMM), the Simulated Method of Moments (SMM), and Indirect Inference (II). General textbook discussions are available, for example, in Hamilton (1994) and Greene (2003) (for GMM), and Gourieroux and Monfort (1996) (for SMM and II). Applications of these procedures to DSGE models are discussed in Adda and Cooper (2003).

This chapter is organized as follows. In order to help establish intuition, section 7.2 presents each procedure in relatively general terms. Section 7.3 then discusses their implementation in the specific context of analyses involving DSGE models. Finally, section 7.4 presents an example application to the RBC model introduced in chapter 5, section 5.1.

7.2 Implementation

7.2.1 The Generalized Method of Moments

Although moment-based estimation procedures have enjoyed a long tradition, their continued prominence stems from the work of Hansen (1982), who generalized their use to applications involving serially correlated stochastic processes, and established their asymptotic properties. Our presentation here closely follows his original development; as noted, in section 7.3 we then specialize the discussion of implementation in applications involving DSGE models.[1]

Let z_t denote an $a \times 1$ vector of variables observed at time t, and let $f(z_t,\theta)$ denote an $r \times 1$ vector-valued function. The $q \times 1$ vector of parameters θ have a true but unknown value θ_0 that is to be estimated. When evaluated at θ_0, the unconditional expectation of $f(z_t,\theta)$ satisfies

$$E[f(z_t,\theta_0)] = 0, \tag{7.1}$$

which are known as orthogonality conditions. The idea behind GMM estimation is to choose parameter estimates $\widehat{\theta}$ such that the sample analogs of (7.1) are as close as possible to zero. Denote these analogs as

$$g(Z,\theta) = \frac{1}{T}\sum_{t=1}^{T} f(z_t,\theta), \tag{7.2}$$

where

$$Z = [z'_T, z'_{T-1}, \dots, z'_1]'$$

is a $(T \times a) \times 1$ vector containing the observed data.

As stated, the specification of $\widehat{\theta}$ involves the minimization of the r-valued function $g(Z,\theta)$ with respect to the $q \times 1$ vector θ. If $q > r$, then the possibility arises that multiple specifications of $\widehat{\theta}$ will yield $g(Z,\widehat{\theta}) = 0$, and we are said to be faced with an identification problem. This problem is circumvented by augmenting $f(z_t,\theta)$ so that $r \geq q$. For the case in which $r = q$, it may be possible to choose $\widehat{\theta}$ such that $g(Z,\widehat{\theta}) = 0$. This is known as the just-identified case. Otherwise, when $r > q$, it will not be possible in general to achieve $g(Z,\widehat{\theta}) = 0$. In this case, the objective is to choose $\widehat{\theta}$ in such a way to make $g(Z,\widehat{\theta})$ as close as possible to zero, in a manner made precise below. This is known as the over-identified case. The case of over-identification is of particular interest, because it enables a formal test of the null hypothesis that the orthogonality conditions are in fact consistent with the data generation process from which Z was realized.

[1] GAUSS code for performing the GMM estimation and testing procedures described here is available at
http://www.american.edu/academic.depts/cas/econ/gaussres/GMM/GMM.HTM
The code was prepared by Lars Hansen, John Heaton, and Masao Ogaki, which they designed specifically to estimate the asset-pricing model analyzed by Hansen and Singleton (1982). Details for adopting the code in pursuit of alternative applications is provided in supporting documentation available at this Web site.

Given $r \geq q$, the GMM estimate $\widehat{\theta}$ is obtained as the solution to a quadratic minimization problem of the form

$$\min_{\theta} \quad \Gamma(\theta) = g(Z,\theta)' \times \Omega \times g(Z,\theta), \tag{7.3}$$

where Ω is a positive-definite weighting matrix. (Techniques available for minimizing objective functions such as (7.3) are discussed in detail in chapter 8.) This weighting matrix determines the relative importance of the individual components of $g(Z,\theta)$ in determining $\widehat{\theta}$. Following Hansen (1982), the optimal weighting matrix Ω^* is that which minimizes the asymptotic variance of $\widehat{\theta}$. This optimal weighting matrix turns out to be given by the inverse of the variance-covariance matrix Σ associated with the sample mean $g(Z,\theta)$: $\Omega^* = \Sigma^{-1}$. Intuitively, the optimal weighting matrix serves to decrease the influence on $\widehat{\theta}$ of elements of $g(Z,\theta)$ that provide relatively imprecise estimates of their population analogues $Ef(z_t,\theta)$. We now characterize a sequential procedure for constructing an estimate $\widehat{\Omega}^*$ of the optimal weighting matrix.

The asymptotic variance-covariance matrix of the sample mean $g(Z,\theta)$ is given by

$$\Sigma = \lim_{T\to\infty} T\, E\left[g(Z,\theta_0) g(Z,\theta_0)' \right]. \tag{7.4}$$

Notice that Σ is a function of the unknown value of θ_0, and thus must be estimated. For the case in which $f(z_t,\theta_0)$ is serially uncorrelated, a consistent estimator for Σ is given by

$$\widehat{\Sigma} = \frac{1}{T}\sum_{t=1}^{T} f(z_t,\widehat{\theta}) f(z_t,\widehat{\theta})', \tag{7.5}$$

where $\widehat{\theta}$ is any consistent estimate of θ_0. For the case in which $f(z_t,\theta_0)$ is serially correlated, a consistent estimator for Σ is given by

$$\widehat{\Sigma} = \widehat{\Gamma}_0 + \sum_{\nu=1}^{s} \left(1 - \frac{\nu}{s+1}\right) (\widehat{\Gamma}_\nu + \widehat{\Gamma}'_\nu), \tag{7.6}$$

where estimates of the νth-order covariance matrices, $\nu = 0, \ldots, s$ are given by

$$\widehat{\Gamma}_\nu = \frac{1}{T} \sum_{t=\nu+1}^{T} f(z_t,\widehat{\theta}) f(z_{t-\nu},\widehat{\theta})'. \tag{7.7}$$

This latter estimator for Σ is due to Newey and West (1987a).

Notice that the estimates $\widehat{\Sigma}$ given in (7.5) and (7.6) are both functions of $\widehat{\theta}$, which in turn is obtained using a weighting matrix ideally constructed as $\Omega^* = \widehat{\Sigma}^{-1}$. Due to this circularity, an iterative procedure is typically used in constructing $\widehat{\theta}$ and $\widehat{\Sigma}$. This begins by obtaining an initial estimate $\widehat{\theta}^0$ using an identity matrix for Ω in (7.3), and then obtaining an estimate $\widehat{\Sigma}^0$ by inserting $\widehat{\theta}^0$ into either (7.5) or (7.6). Next, $\widehat{\theta}^1$ is derived by substituting $[\widehat{\Sigma}^0]^{-1}$ for Ω in (7.3), and $\widehat{\Sigma}^1$ is derived by inserting $\widehat{\theta}^1$ into either (7.5) or (7.6). Repeating this process until the estimates $\widehat{\theta}$ and $\widehat{\Sigma}$ converge yields optimal GMM estimates of θ_0 and Σ.

If the orthogonality conditions (7.1) are in fact consistent with the data generation process from which Z was realized, then by the law of large numbers the limiting distribution of $g(Z,\theta_0)$ is given by

$$\sqrt{T}g(Z,\theta_0) \rightarrow N(0,\Sigma). \tag{7.8}$$

In turn, under mild regularity conditions established by Hansen (1982), the limiting distribution of $\widehat{\theta}$ is given by

$$\sqrt{T}(\widehat{\theta} - \theta_0) \rightarrow N(0, V), \tag{7.9}$$

where

$$V = (D\Sigma^{-1}D')^{-1},$$

and D' is a $q \times r$ gradient matrix:

$$D' = \frac{\partial g(Z,\theta)}{\partial \theta'}, \tag{7.10}$$

with $(i,j)^{\text{th}}$ element containing the derivative of the ith component of $g(Z,\theta)$ with respect to the jth component of θ. Letting $\widehat{D}$ denote the evaluation of D obtained using $\widehat{\theta}$, V may be estimated using[2]

$$\widehat{V} = (\widehat{D}\widehat{\Sigma}^{-1}\widehat{D}')^{-1}. \tag{7.11}$$

Given $\widehat{\theta}$ and $\widehat{V}$, tests of various sorts of parameter restrictions are straightforward to conduct. Consider the following three classes of restrictions. First, the statistical significance of the difference between an individual element θ^j and a hypothesized value $\overline{\theta}^j$ may be evaluated using the t-statistic

$$t^j = \frac{\widehat{\theta}^j - \overline{\theta}^j}{\widehat{\sigma}_{\theta^j}}, \tag{7.12}$$

[2] The GAUSS command `gradp` is available for use in constructing D.

where $\widehat{\sigma}_{\theta j}$ is the standard error of $\widehat{\theta}^j$, or the square root of the jth diagonal element of $\widehat{V}$. Under the null hypothesis that $\widehat{\theta}^j = \overline{\theta}^j$, t^j is distributed as Student's-t with $T-1$ degrees of freedom; large values of t^j are assigned low probabilities, or p-values, under this distribution. When p-values lie below a pre-specified critical value, the null hypothesis is rejected; otherwise it is accepted.

Second, following Newey and West (1987b), tests of joint sets of restrictions imposed upon θ may be conducted using GMM counterparts to likelihood-based tests. Consider a collection of restrictions imposed upon θ of the form

$$\gamma(\theta) = 0, \tag{7.13}$$

where $\gamma(\theta)$ is an l-valued differentiable function, with $l < q$. Then letting $\widehat{\theta}_R$ denote the value of θ that minimizes $\Gamma(\theta)$ subject to (7.13), the null hypothesis that the restrictions in fact hold can be tested using the GMM analogue to the likelihood ratio statistic:

$$LR = \Gamma(\widehat{\theta}_R) - \Gamma(\widehat{\theta}). \tag{7.14}$$

Under the null, LR is distributed as $\chi^2(l)$. As the gap between the restricted and unrestricted objective functions widens, LR increases, and its associated p-value falls. As with the t-test, if the p-value falls below a pre-specified critical value the null is rejected; otherwise it is accepted. Regarding the specification chosen for Ω in estimating $\widehat{\theta}_R$, this should be the optimal weighting matrix $\widehat{\Sigma}^{-1}$ used to estimate $\widehat{\theta}$, because $\widehat{\theta}$ is a consistent estimator of θ_0 regardless of whether the restrictions (7.13) in fact hold. Finally, regarding implementation, consider the case in which (7.13) can be rewritten as

$$\theta = r(\omega), \tag{7.15}$$

where ω is an ℓ-vector such that $\ell = q - l$. Then $\Gamma(\widehat{\theta}_R)$ can be calculated by optimizing over ω, and setting $\widehat{\theta}_R = r(\widehat{\omega})$.

Third, consider a test designed to assess the stability of θ over the sample period. Following Andrews and Fair (1988), this can be conducted as follows. Let T_0 denote a potential date at which θ undergoes a structural change. Also, let $(\widehat{\theta}_1, \widehat{V}_1)$ and $(\widehat{\theta}_2, \widehat{V}_2)$ denote estimates of (θ, V) obtained over the sub-samples $[1, T_0]$ and $[T_0 + 1, T]$. Finally, let $\pi = T_0/T$ denote the fraction of observations contained in the first subsample. Then the null hypothesis of structural stability (i.e., $\theta_1 = \theta_2$) can be evaluated using a Wald test:

$$\lambda = T(\widehat{\theta}_1 - \widehat{\theta}_2)'[\pi^{-1}\widehat{V}_1 + (1-\pi^{-1})\widehat{V}_2]^{-1}(\widehat{\theta}_1 - \widehat{\theta}_2). \tag{7.16}$$

Under the null, λ is distributed as $\chi^2(q)$; once again, the null is rejected if the p-value associated with λ falls below a pre-specified critical value. However, if a systematic search is conducted over a range of potential break dates, then the test statistic associated with any one potential break date (e.g., the date at which the largest value of λ is obtained) will no longer be appropriately interpreted as being distributed as $\chi^2(q)$. Andrews (1993) reports relevant distributions for λ in this case.

For the case in which $r > q$, so that the model is over-identified, Hansen (1982) derives a test of the null hypothesis that the orthogonality conditions (7.1) are consistent with the data generation process from which Z was obtained. Recall that under the null, $\sqrt{T}g(Z,\theta_0)$ is asymptotically distributed as $N(0,\Sigma)$. Thus replacing (θ_0,Σ) with their estimated values $(\widehat{\theta},\widehat{\Sigma})$, under the null the test statistic

$$J = \left[\sqrt{T}g(Z,\widehat{\theta})\right]' \widehat{\Sigma}^{-1}\left[\sqrt{T}g(Z,\widehat{\theta})\right] \tag{7.17}$$

is distributed as $\chi^2(r-q)$, where note that the degrees of freedom are given by the difference between the number of moment conditions and the number of parameters determined by these conditions.

To further enhance the intuition behind the GMM approach to estimation, consider the following three examples. First, following Hamilton (1994), consider the implementation of GMM in the context of an ordinary least squares (OLS) regression model. Specifically, consider a regression model of the form

$$y_t = w_t'\beta + \varepsilon_t, \tag{7.18}$$

where y_t is a single time series and w_t is a $d \times 1$ matrix of explanatory variables. Moment conditions for this model are derived under the assumption that the residuals $\{\varepsilon_t\}$ are orthogonal to the explanatory variables: $E(w_t\varepsilon_t) = 0$. Under this assumption, the true value β_0 satisfies the $d \times 1$ system of equations

$$E\left[w_t(y_t - w_t'\beta_0)\right] = 0. \tag{7.19}$$

Thus the analog for $f(z_t,\theta_0)$ in (7.1) in the linear regression context is $w_t(y_t - w_t'\beta_0)$. Notice that β is a $d \times 1$ vector, so that we are working in the context of the just-identified case. Therefore, the GMM estimate $\widehat{\beta}$ is obtained as the vector of parameters that sets the sample average of (7.19) equal to zero:

$$g(Z,\beta) = \frac{1}{T}\sum_{t=1}^{T} w_t(y_t - w_t'\widehat{\beta}) = 0, \tag{7.20}$$

where

$$Z = [y_T \sim w_T', y_{T-1} \sim w_{T-1}', \ldots, y_1 \sim w_1']'.$$

Rearranging (7.20) and solving for $\widehat{\beta}$ yields the familiar least squares expression

$$\widehat{\beta} = \left[\sum_{t=1}^{T} w_t w_t'\right]^{-1} \left[\sum_{t=1}^{T} w_t y_t\right]. \tag{7.21}$$

Proceeding under the assumption that $\{\varepsilon_t\}$ is serially uncorrelated, the estimate $\widehat{\Sigma}$ is given by

$$\begin{aligned}\widehat{\Sigma} &= \frac{1}{T}\sum_{t=1}^{T}[w_t(y_t - w_t'\widehat{\beta})][w_t(y_t - w_t'\widehat{\beta})]' \\ &= \widehat{\sigma}^2 \frac{1}{T}\sum_{t=1}^{T} w_t w_t', \end{aligned} \tag{7.22}$$

where

$$\widehat{\sigma}^2 = \frac{1}{T}\sum_{t=1}^{T}(y_t - w_t'\widehat{\beta})(y_t - w_t'\widehat{\beta})'.$$

Finally,

$$\begin{aligned}\widehat{D}' &= \frac{\partial}{\partial \widehat{\beta}'}\frac{1}{T}\sum_{t=1}^{T} w_t(y_t - w_t'\widehat{\beta}) \\ &= \frac{1}{T}\sum_{t=1}^{T} w_t w_t', \end{aligned} \tag{7.23}$$

and thus

$$\begin{aligned}\widehat{V} &= \left[\left(\frac{1}{T}\sum_{t=1}^{T} w_t w_t'\right)\left(\widehat{\sigma}^2 \frac{1}{T}\sum_{t=1}^{T} w_t w_t'\right)^{-1}\left(\frac{1}{T}\sum_{t=1}^{T} w_t w_t'\right)\right]^{-1} \\ &= \widehat{\sigma}^2\left(\frac{1}{T}\sum_{t=1}^{T} w_t w_t'\right)^{-1}. \end{aligned}$$

Exercise 7.1

As a second example, in the context of the regression model (7.18), suppose that the orthogonality assumption $E(w_t \varepsilon_t) = 0$ is inappropriate, due to the presence of endogenous variables included among the elements of w_t. In this case, assume the availability of a $d \times 1$ collection of instrumental variables u_t that are correlated with w_t but orthogonal to ε_t. Using the collection of d orthogonality conditions $E[u_t(y_t - w_t'\beta_0)] = 0$, obtain the corresponding GMM estimates $(\widehat{\beta}, \widehat{V})$, once again under the assumption that $\{\varepsilon_t\}$ is serially uncorrelated. The estimates you obtain are known as instrumental variable (IV) estimates.

As a third example, consider the case in which (7.1) specializes to

$$E[f(z_t, \theta_0)] = E\begin{Bmatrix} [f_1(w_t, \theta_0)]\, u_t \\ [f_2(w_t, \theta_0)]\, u_t \\ \cdots \\ [f_m(w_t, \theta_0)]\, u_t \end{Bmatrix} = 0, \tag{7.24}$$

where u_t is an $\ell \times 1$ vector of instruments. In this case,

$$z_t = [w_t', u_t']',$$

and the number of orthogonality conditions is $r = m\ell$. Although a specialization of (7.1), (7.24) is nevertheless quite general, and in fact encompasses the full range of applications to analyses involving DSGE models discussed in section 7.3.

We conclude this subsection with three comments, made in the context of GMM applications cast in the form of (7.24). First, cases in which the number of orthogonality conditions r exceeds q (the dimensionality of the parameter vector θ) are in no way guaranteed to be free from identification problems. Symptoms of such problems include the attainment of large standard errors associated with particular elements of θ. The presence of large standard errors indicates that the objective function is relatively insensitive to alternative specifications of θ along certain dimensions, and thus that a wide range of alternative parameterizations represent roughly equally plausible estimates of θ_0. Potential remedies for this problem involve adjustments to $\{f_i(w_t, \theta_0)\}_{i=1}^{m}$ and/or u_t, the goal being to produce orthogonality conditions that are more informative regarding the parameterization of θ. We caution, though, that remedies simply involving expansions of the instruments included in u_t can cause additional problems, as Tauchen (1986) and Kocherlakota (1990) have illustrated. In particular, applying GMM estimation and testing procedures to artificial data simulated from asset-pricing models, they show that the small-sample performance of estimators and tests based on parsimonious specifications of u_t is superior to tests based on profligate specifications, both in terms of the accuracy of parameter estimates and rejection rates obtained in applications of the J test in (7.17). Further discussion of identification problems, cast in the context of maximum-likelihood estimation, is provided in chapter 8.

Second, depending upon the specific context of the empirical exercise, the researcher will often have considerable leeway regarding the specification of (7.24), in terms of both $\{f_i(w_t, \theta_0)\}_{i=1}^m$ and u_t. The results of the exercise may depend sensitively upon the particular specification that has been chosen. For example, in the context of the specification of the regression model (7.18), coefficient estimates associated with particular elements of w_t may depend sensitively upon the inclusion or exclusion of additional variables in w_t. As we shall see in section 7.3, it is often the case in working with DSGE models that the specification of $\{f_i(w_t, \theta_0)\}_{i=1}^m$ is determined rather directly by the particular question the model has been designed to address, or by the specification of the model itself. In addition, theoretical considerations can also be helpful in specifying u_t. However, guidance from theory rarely obviates the need for sensitivity analysis.

Third, we have noted that because GMM estimates are not based upon distributional assumptions regarding random disturbances included in the model, they are not subject to mis-specification along this dimension. However, they are of course sensitive to the validity and effectiveness of u_t as instruments. Simultaneity between $f_i(w_t, \theta_0)$ and individual elements of u_{it} has long been known to produce bias in the resulting estimates of θ, but bias can also result from the use of instruments that are weakly correlated with the elements of w_t, a point made dramatically by Nelson and Startz (1990a,b) (for a survey of problems associated with weak instruments, see Stock, Wright, and Yogo, 2002). Once again, guidance from theory is often helpful in identifying appropriate specifications of u_t, particularly in applications involving DSGE models; but to repeat: this guidance rarely obviates the need for sensitivity analysis.

7.2.2 The Simulated Method of Moments

In certain applications, it may be the case that orthogonality conditions associated with the model under investigation cannot be assessed analytically. In such cases, the work of McFadden (1986), Pakes and Pollard (1989), Lee and Ingram (1991) and Duffie and Singleton (1993) has demonstrated that moment-matching estimation and testing procedures based on model simulations retain asymptotic characteristics akin to those based on analytical calculations. Here, we present a straightforward means of implementing so-called SMM procedures. For a general textbook presentation, see Gourieroux and Monfort (1996).

Consider a collection of empirical targets contained in the $r \times 1$ vector $h(z_t)$, where as in section 7.2.1 z_t denotes an $a \times 1$ vector of variables observed at time t. Let y_t denote an $a \times 1$ vector of model variables that correspond directly to their empirical counterparts z_t, and $h(y_t, \theta)$ denote the theoretical counterparts to $h(z_t)$. Under GMM, $E[h(y_t, \theta)]$ is calculated analytically; under SMM this need not be the case. Instead, all that is required is the ability to simulate $\{y_t\}$ using a parameterization of the structural model under investigation (model simulation is discussed in section 7.3). Proceeding under the usual assumption that the model has been specified for stationary versions of the data, the sample average

$$h(\Upsilon,\theta) = \frac{1}{N}\sum_{i=1}^{N} h(y_t,\theta), \tag{7.25}$$

where

$$\Upsilon = [y'_N, y'_{N-1}, \ldots, y'_1],$$

is an asymptotically consistent estimator of $E[h(y_t,\theta)]$. The idea behind SMM estimators is to use sample averages in place of population averages in evaluating implications of the structural model regarding $h(y_t,\theta)$.

SMM estimation proceeds under the hypothesis that there exists a parameterization of the structural model θ_0 under which

$$Eh(z_t) = Eh(y_t,\theta_0); \tag{7.26}$$

the objective is to choose parameter estimates $\widehat{\theta}$ that come as close as possible to satisfying this equality. In terms of the notation used in discussing the GMM estimator, $f(z_t,\theta_0)$ in (7.1) is given by

$$f(z_t,\theta_0) = h(z_t) - h(y_t,\theta_0), \tag{7.27}$$

and the sample analogue $g(Z,\theta)$ in (7.2) is given by

$$g(Z,\theta) = \left(\frac{1}{T}\sum_{t=1}^{T} h(z_t)\right) - \left(\frac{1}{N}\sum_{i=1}^{N} h(y_t,\theta)\right). \tag{7.28}$$

Having made these adjustments to $f(z_t,\theta_0)$ and $g(Z,\theta)$, estimation and hypothesis testing proceed as described in section 7.2.1, with a minor modification needed for the weighting matrix Ω in (7.3). The optimal weighting matrix Ω^* is once again given by the inverse of the variance-covariance matrix Σ associated with the sample mean of $g(Z,\theta)$. Under the null hypothesis (7.26), the sample means of $h(z_t)$ and $h(y_t,\theta)$ in (7.28) are identical. Moreover, the empirical and artificial samples $\{z_t\}$ and $\{y_t\}$ are independent. Thus because $g(Z,\theta)$ is a linear combination of independent sample means, its variance-covariance matrix is given by

$$\Sigma(1 + T/N).$$

Note that as the artificial sample size N increases relative to T, the covariance matrix of $g(Z,\theta)$ converges to its GMM counterpart. This is true because as N increases, the influence of the numerical error associated with the use of a sample average to approximate $E[h(y_t, \theta)]$ decreases. See chapter 9 for a discussion of numerical errors. For the reasons outlined there, the specification of $N = 10,000$ is standard, because it is associated with a numerical standard error of 1% of the standard error associated with the simulated moment.

With the adjustment

$$\Omega^* = \Sigma(1 + T/N),$$

estimation and testing via GMM and SMM proceed identically. To briefly summarize, the objective function used to estimate $\widehat{\theta}$ is given by

$$\min_{\theta} \quad \Gamma(\theta) = g(Z, \theta)' \times [\Sigma(1 + T/N)]^{-1} \times g(Z, \theta),$$

where Σ is given by either

$$\Sigma = \frac{1}{T} \sum_{t=1}^{T} f(z_t, \theta) f(z_t, \theta)'$$

or

$$\Sigma = \Gamma_0 + \sum_{\nu=1}^{s} \left(1 - \frac{\nu}{s+1}\right) (\Gamma_\nu + \Gamma'_\nu),$$

$$\Gamma_\nu = \frac{1}{T} \sum_{t=\nu+1}^{T} f(z_t, \theta) f(z_{t-\nu}, \theta)'.$$

The circular relationship between θ and Σ once again necessitates an iterative estimation procedure under which an initial estimate $\widehat{\theta}^0$ is obtained using an identity matrix for Σ, $\widehat{\theta}^0$ is used to construct $\widehat{\Sigma}^0$, and the process is repeated until the estimates $\widehat{\theta}$ and $\widehat{\Sigma}$ converge.

Under mild regularity conditions, the limiting distribution of $\widehat{\theta}$ is once again given by

$$\sqrt{T}(\widehat{\theta} - \theta_0) \rightarrow N(0, V), \tag{7.29}$$

where

$$V = (D \Sigma^{-1} D')^{-1},$$

and D' is a $q \times r$ gradient matrix:

$$D' = \frac{\partial g(Z, \theta)}{\partial \theta'}. \tag{7.30}$$

With $\widehat{D}$ denoting the evaluation of D obtained using $\widehat{\theta}$, V is estimated using

$$\widehat{V} = (\widehat{D}\widehat{\Sigma}^{-1}\widehat{D}')^{-1}. \tag{7.31}$$

Finally, the null hypothesis (7.26) can be evaluated using a modification of Hansen's (1982) J statistic:

$$J = \left[\sqrt{T}g(Z,\widehat{\theta})\right]' \left[\widehat{\Sigma}(1+T/N)\right]^{-1} \left[\sqrt{T}g(Z,\widehat{\theta})\right],$$

which is distributed asymptotically as $\chi^2(r-q)$.

7.2.3 Indirect Inference

Although it is becoming increasingly common to address specific empirical questions using structural models, reduced-form models remain a workhorse for empirical practitioners. The use of structural specifications to account for and help interpret findings obtained using reduced-form models is the objective of the indirect inference methodology, which is the subject of this sub-section. The goal of indirect inference is to determine whether data simulated from a given structural model can be used to replicate estimates obtained using actual data in a given reduced-form analysis. If so, then a structural interpretation for the reduced-form phenomenon can be offered. Note that indirect inference amounts to a moment-matching exercise, in which estimates obtained in the reduced-form analysis serve as target moments. An attractive feature of this approach to structural estimation is that clear guidance regarding relevant moments is available a priori: this is provided by the reduced-form exercise for which a structural interpretation is sought. The method of indirect inference was developed by Gourieroux, Monfort, and Renault (1993) and Smith (1993); a general textbook presentation is available in Gourieroux and Monfort (1996).

Once again, let z_t and y_t denote $a \times 1$ vectors of actual and model variables. In this case, the empirical target is an $r \times 1$ vector of reduced-form parameters δ. To match the notation used in characterizing SMM, let $\delta(z_t)$ denote the true value of δ, and $\delta(y_t,\theta)$ its theoretical counterpart (Gourieroux et al. (1993) refer to $\delta(y_t,\theta)$ as the binding function). Indirect inference proceeds under the hypothesis that there exists a parameterization of the structural model θ_0 under which

$$\delta(z_t) = \delta(y_t,\theta_0). \tag{7.32}$$

The sample analogue of $\delta(z_t)$, denoted as $\delta(Z)$, is obtained by estimating δ using the actual data $Z = [z'_T, z'_{T-1}, \ldots, z'_1]'$:

$$\delta(Z) = \arg\max_{\delta} \Delta(Z, \delta). \tag{7.33}$$

In (7.33), $\Delta(Z,\delta)$ represents the objective function used to estimate δ. For example, $\Delta(Z,\delta)$ could represent the likelihood function associated with the reduced-form model under investigation, in which case $\delta(Z)$ would represent the maximum-likelihood estimate of δ. Alternatively, $\Delta(Z,\delta)$ could represent the negative of quadratic objective functions associated with OLS, IV, GMM, or SMM estimators. In turn, let $\delta(\Upsilon,\theta)$ denote an estimate of δ obtained using a simulated realization of artificial data $\Upsilon = [y'_T, y'_{T-1}, \ldots, y'_1]'$:

$$\delta(\Upsilon,\theta) = \arg\max_{\delta} \Delta(\Upsilon, \delta). \tag{7.34}$$

Note that the sample sizes of Υ and Z are identical. Letting Υ^j denote the jth of S realizations of Υ, the sample analogue of $\delta(y_t,\theta)$, denoted as $\delta_S(\Upsilon,\theta)$, is obtained by averaging over $\delta(\Upsilon^j,\theta)$:

$$\delta_S(\Upsilon,\theta) = \frac{1}{S}\sum_{j=1}^{S} \delta(\Upsilon^j,\theta). \tag{7.35}$$

Given these sample analogues, $g(Z,\theta)$ is in this case given by

$$g(Z,\theta) = \delta(Z) - \delta_S(\Upsilon,\theta). \tag{7.36}$$

In turn, the objective function used to obtain the estimate $\widehat{\theta}$ is given by

$$\begin{aligned} \min_{\theta} \quad \Gamma(\theta) &= g(Z,\theta)' \times \Omega^* \times g(Z,\theta) \\ &= [\delta(Z) - \delta_S(\Upsilon,\theta)]' \times \Omega^* \times [\delta(Z) - \delta_S(\Upsilon,\theta)]. \end{aligned} \tag{7.37}$$

Once again, Ω^* denotes the optimal weighting matrix given by the inverse of the variance-covariance matrix Σ associated with $g(Z,\theta)$. We now turn to a characterization of this matrix.

Under certain regularity conditions Gourieroux et al. (1993) demonstrate that the indirect inference estimator is consistent and asymptotically Normal (for fixed S, as $T \to \infty$):

$$\sqrt{T}(\widehat{\theta} - \theta_0) \to N(0, W(S,\Omega)). \tag{7.38}$$

The asymptotic variance-covariance matrix $W(S,\Omega)$ is given by

$$\left(1+\frac{1}{S}\right)\left(\frac{\partial\delta(y_t,\theta)'}{\partial\theta}\Omega\frac{\partial\delta(y_t,\theta)}{\partial\theta'}\right)^{-1}\frac{\partial\delta(y_t,\theta)'}{\partial\theta}\Omega J_0^{-1}(I_0-K_0)J_0^{-1}\Omega$$
$$\times\frac{\partial\delta(y_t,\theta)}{\partial\theta'}\left(\frac{\partial\delta(y_t,\theta)'}{\partial\theta}\Omega\frac{\partial\delta(y_t,\theta)}{\partial\theta'}\right)^{-1}, \tag{7.39}$$

where

$$J_0 = p\lim -\frac{\partial^2\Delta(\Upsilon,\delta)}{\partial\delta\partial\delta'} \tag{7.40}$$

$$I_0 = \lim Var\left[\sqrt{T}\frac{\partial\Delta(\Upsilon,\delta)}{\partial\delta}\right] \tag{7.41}$$

$$K_0 = \lim Var\left[E\left(\sqrt{T}\frac{\partial\Delta(Z,\delta)}{\partial\delta}\right)\right]. \tag{7.42}$$

This expression simplifies considerably when evaluated using the optimal weighting matrix Ω^*, which once again is defined as that which minimizes W. This is given by

$$\Omega^* = J_0(I_0-K_0)^{-1}J_0. \tag{7.43}$$

Substituting Ω^* into (7.39), the asymptotic variance-covariance matrix $W(S,\Omega)$ becomes

$$W(S,\Omega)=\left(1+\frac{1}{S}\right)\left[\left(\frac{\partial^2\Delta(\Upsilon,\delta)}{\partial\theta\partial\delta'}\right)(I_0-K_0)^{-1}\left(\frac{\partial^2\Delta(\Upsilon,\delta)}{\partial\delta\partial\theta'}\right)\right]^{-1}. \tag{7.44}$$

Finally, J_0 may be estimated using

$$\widehat{J}_0 = -\frac{\partial^2\Delta(\Upsilon,\delta_S(\Upsilon,\widehat{\theta}))}{\partial\delta\partial\delta'}, \tag{7.45}$$

$\frac{\partial^2\Delta(\Upsilon,\delta)}{\partial\theta\partial\delta'}$ may be estimated using

$$\frac{\partial^2\Delta(\Upsilon,\delta_S(\Upsilon,\widehat{\theta}))}{\partial\widehat{\theta}\partial\delta'}, \tag{7.46}$$

and $I_0 - K_0$ may be estimated using

$$\widehat{\Xi}=\frac{T}{S}\sum_{s=1}^{S}\left(\frac{\partial\Delta(\Upsilon,\delta_S(\Upsilon,\widehat{\theta}))}{\partial\delta}-\frac{1}{S}\sum_{s=1}^{S}\frac{\partial\Delta(\Upsilon,\delta_S(\Upsilon,\widehat{\theta}))}{\partial\delta}\right)$$
$$\times\left(\frac{\partial\Delta(\Upsilon,\delta_S(\Upsilon,\widehat{\theta}))}{\partial\delta}-\frac{1}{S}\sum_{s=1}^{S}\frac{\partial\Delta(\Upsilon,\delta_S(\Upsilon,\widehat{\theta}))}{\partial\delta_S}\right)'. \tag{7.47}$$

Once again, we face a circularity involving θ and Ω^*. A by-now familiar algorithm for dealing with this circularity is as follows. Specify an identity matrix for Ω^0, and estimate θ^0 using (7.37). Next, use θ^0 to construct $\delta_S(\Upsilon,\theta^0)$ using (7.35). Finally, use $\delta_S(\Upsilon,\theta^0)$ to construct $\widehat{J}_0^0$ using (7.45) and $\widehat{\Xi}^0$ using (7.47); substitute these estimates into (7.43) to obtain Ω^{*0}. Iterate over these steps until $\widehat{\theta}$ converges, and use the final estimate to construct $W(S,\Omega^*)$ using (7.46) and (7.47).

Having obtained $\widehat{\theta}$ and Ω^*, a J-type test can be used to assess the null hypothesis (7.32). The test statistic in this case is given by

$$J = \left[\delta(Z) - \delta_S(\Upsilon,\widehat{\theta})\right]' \times \Omega^* \times \left[\delta(Z) - \delta_S(\Upsilon,\widehat{\theta})\right], \tag{7.48}$$

which is once again distributed asymptotically as $\chi^2(r-q)$.

7.3 Implementation in DSGE Models

7.3.1 Analyzing Euler Equations

We now discuss three contexts in which the estimation procedures described in section 7.2 can be used to analyze DSGE models (a fourth context is introduced briefly, and described in detail in chapter 11). The first concerns applications involving the set of Euler equations associated with the theoretical model under investigation. Such applications were pioneered by Hansen and Singleton (1982), working in the context of the multi-asset pricing environment introduced in chapter 5, section 5.3. For a survey of the enormous literature spawned by this work, see Hansen and West (2002).

As we have seen in part I the Euler equations associated with a given DSGE model take the form of a collection of first-order nonlinear expectational difference equations. Let these equations be represented by the $m \times 1$ system

$$E_t \Psi(x_{t+1}, x_t) = 0, \tag{7.49}$$

where the full set of model variables are contained in the $n \times 1$ vector x_t, and E_t is the expectations operator conditional on information available to the model's decision makers at time t. Assuming that this information includes the collection of variables contained in the $\ell \times 1$ vector of instruments u_t, then it will also be the case that

$$E\{[\Psi(x_{t+1}, x_t)]\, u_t\} = 0, \tag{7.50}$$

where $E\{\}$ denotes the unconditional expectations operator. Note that this expression is precisely in terms of the specialization of the GMM orthogonality conditions given in (7.24). Implementation of the GMM estimator in this context is therefore straightforward.

Consider as an example the asset-pricing model analyzed by Mehra and Prescott (1985). Letting r^e and r^f denote returns associated with a risky and risk-free asset, and c denote consumption, the Euler equations under consideration are given by

$$\beta E_t \left\{ \frac{u'(c_{t+1})}{u'(c_t)} r^f_{t+1} - 1 \right\} = 0 \tag{7.51}$$

$$E_t \left\{ \frac{u'(c_{t+1})}{u'(c_t)} \left[r^e_{t+1} - r^f_{t+1} \right] \right\} = 0. \tag{7.52}$$

Under the assumption that preferences follow the CRRA specification

$$u(c_t) = \frac{c_t^{1-\gamma}}{1-\gamma}, \tag{7.53}$$

the Euler equations become

$$E_t \left\{ \beta \left(\frac{c_{t+1}}{c_t} \right)^{-\gamma} r^f_{t+1} - 1 \right\} = 0 \tag{7.54}$$

$$E_t \left\{ \left(\frac{c_{t+1}}{c_t} \right)^{-\gamma} \left[r^e_{t+1} - r^f_{t+1} \right] \right\} = 0. \tag{7.55}$$

In terms of the notation in (7.24),

$$w_t = \left[c_t/c_{t-1}, r^f_t, r^e_t \right]'$$

and

$$\theta = [\gamma, \beta]'.$$

Valid instruments include a constant, and lagged values of consumption growth and returns. For an early example of an application of this estimation strategy in the context of an RBC framework, see Christiano and Eichenbaum (1992).

7.3.2 Analytical Calculations Based on Linearized Models

The second context involves applications to fully specified linearized models. Here, we discuss situations in which implications conveyed by the model regarding the selected empirical targets can be calculated analytically. Recall that the state-space representation we use in this context is given by

$$x_{t+1} = F(\mu)x_t + e_{t+1}, \qquad E(e_{t+1}e'_{t+1}) = Q(\mu), \tag{7.56}$$

where the $k \times 1$ vector μ contains the model's structural parameters. One of two measurement equations maps x_t into observable variables X_t:

$$X_t = H(\mu)' x_t, \tag{7.57}$$

or

$$X_t = H(\mu)' x_t + u_t, \qquad E(u_t u_t') = \Sigma_u, \tag{7.58}$$

where u_t represents measurement error. Hereafter, the dependence of F, Q, H, and Σ_u on μ is suppressed to simplify notation.

Given this representation, a wide range of empirical targets can be calculated analytically. Chapter 4 described three sets of targets that have received considerable attention in the context of analyzing DSGE models: covariance terms (e.g., Kydland and Prescott, 1982); spectra (e.g., Watson, 1993; Diebold, Ohanian, and Berkowitz, 1998); and impulse response functions (e.g., Christiano, Eichenbaum, and Evans, 2005). The calculation of these targets using vector autoregressive (VAR) representations estimated using actual data was discussed in chapter 4; here we briefly discuss their construction for the theoretical analogues contained in X_t.

Regarding covariance terms, let

$$\Gamma(0) = E(x_t x_t')$$

denote the contemporaneous variance-covariance matrix of x_t, and

$$\Gamma(s) = E(x_t x_{t-s}')$$

the sth-order covariance matrix. From (7.56),

$$\begin{aligned}\Gamma(0) &= E[(Fx_{t-1} + e_t)(Fx_{t-1} + e_t)'] \\ &= F\Gamma(0)F' + Q, \end{aligned} \tag{7.59}$$

the solution to which is given by

$$vec[\Gamma(0)] = [I - F \otimes F]^{-1} \, vec[Q], \tag{7.60}$$

where $\otimes$ denotes the Kronecker product. Further,

$$\begin{aligned}\Gamma(1) &= E(x_t x_{t-1}') \\ &= E((Fx_{t-1} + e_t)x_{t-1}') \\ &= F\Gamma(0),\end{aligned}$$

and in general,

$$\begin{aligned}\Gamma(s) &= F\Gamma(s-1) \\ &= F^s\Gamma(0).\end{aligned} \tag{7.61}$$

Thus for the $m \times 1$ vector observable variables X_t, we have

$$\begin{aligned}\Gamma_X(0) &= E\left(X_t X_t'\right) \\ &= E\left[(H'x_t + u_t)(H'x_t + u_t)'\right] \\ &= H'\Gamma(0)H + \Sigma_u, \qquad (7.62)\end{aligned}$$

where $\Sigma_u = 0$ in the absence of measurement error. And since $\{u_t\}$ is serially uncorrelated,

$$\begin{aligned}\Gamma_X(s) &= EX_t X_{t-s}' \\ &= H'\Gamma(s)H.\end{aligned}$$

Regarding spectra, let $S(\omega)$ denote the spectral matrix of x_t evaluated at frequency ω. That is, the jth diagonal element of $S(\omega)$ contains the spectrum of the jth variable of x_t at frequency ω, $s_j(\omega)$, and the $(i,j)^{\text{th}}$ element of $S(\omega)$ contains the cross spectrum between the ith and j^{th} variables of x_t, $s_{i,j}(\omega)$. Then from Hannan (1970), $S(\omega)$ is given by

$$S(\omega) = \frac{1}{2\pi}\left[(I - Fe^{-i\omega})' Q^{-1} (I - Fe^{-i\omega})\right]^{-1}, \qquad (7.63)$$

where I is the $n \times n$ identity matrix. And since $\{u_t\}$ is serially uncorrelated, the spectral matrix of X_t is proportional to

$$S_X(\omega) = H'S(\omega)H. \qquad (7.64)$$

Regarding impulse response functions, given an initial impulse e_0, the responses of x_t are given by $x_0 = e_0$, $x_1 = Fe_0$, $x_2 = F^2 e_0$, and so on. The corresponding j-step response of the observables is

$$X_j = H'F^j e_0.$$

Recall that the relationship between e_t and the structural shocks υ_t is given by

$$e_t = G\upsilon_t,$$

thus the j-step response to a structural innovation υ_0 is given by

$$X_j = H'F^j G\upsilon_0.$$

When using impulse response functions as an empirical target, a major challenge involves the identification of an empirical counterpart to υ_0. To illustrate this point, consider a pth-order VAR specified for the $m \times 1$ vector of observations of actual data z_t that corresponds with the $m \times 1$ vector of model variables X_t:

$$z_t = \Upsilon_1 z_{t-1} + \Upsilon_2 z_{t-2} + \cdots + \Upsilon_p z_{t-p} + \varepsilon_t, \qquad E\varepsilon_t \varepsilon_t' = \Sigma_\varepsilon \tag{7.65}$$

$$= \Upsilon_1 z_{t-1} + \Upsilon_2 z_{t-2} + \cdots + \Upsilon_p z_{t-p} + P\nu_t, \tag{7.66}$$

$$PP' = \Sigma_\varepsilon, \qquad E\nu_t \nu_t' = I, \tag{7.67}$$

where Υ_j is $k \times k$, and P is a lower-triangular matrix that accomplished the Cholesky decomposition $PP' = \Sigma_\varepsilon$. As illustrated in chapter 4, it is straightforward to construct impulse response functions based upon this specification for a given orthogonalized impulse ν_0. The challenge is to construct ν_0 in such a way that it is credibly identified with its structural counterpart υ_0. The quest for such an identification involves the construction of what are known as identified VARs, the use of which dates to Sims (1980); see Watson (1994) for a survey, and Hamilton (1994) for a textbook discussion.

As Fernandez-Villaverde, Rubio-Ramirez, and Sargent (2005) note with understatement, "The process of reverse engineering a subset of economic shocks from the innovations to a VAR is known to be fraught with hazards." [p. 3] However, they have developed a means of determining conditions under which this reverse engineering process can be accomplished. In fact, their procedure illustrates conditions under which a mapping from structural parameters μ to the VAR parameters (7.65) can be induced. A related procedure for achieving reverse engineering, or as they characterize it, for solving the "invertibility problem," has been developed by Sims and Zha (2005).

Here we provide a sketch of Fernandez-Villaverde et al.'s reverse engineering procedure. To do so, we must modify the notation used to represent the linearized DSGE model. Let s_t denote the collection of state variables included in the model, and $w_t = [\upsilon_t', u_t']'$ contain the structural shocks and measurement errors associated with the observation of X_t. Then the representation we seek is given by

$$s_{t+1} = As_t + Bw_t, \tag{7.68}$$

$$X_t = Cs_t + Dw_t. \tag{7.69}$$

Once again, the dependence of $[A, B, C, D]$ upon μ is suppressed to simplify the notation. Measurement errors play no role in determining the law of motion for s_t, and thus

$$Bw_t = [B_1 \;\; 0] \begin{bmatrix} \upsilon_t \\ u_t \end{bmatrix}.$$

In contrast, both structural shocks and measurement error may play a role in determining the observable variables X_t, and thus in general,

$$Dw_t = [D_1 \quad D_2] \begin{bmatrix} \upsilon_t \\ u_t \end{bmatrix}.$$

Now, when D is square and D^{-1} exists, we can rearrange (7.69) as

$$w_t = D^{-1}(X_t - Cs_t).$$

Substituting for w_t in (7.68) then yields

$$s_{t+1} = (A - BD^{-1}C)s_t + BD^{-1}X_t.$$

Representing s_t as Ls_{t+1}, where L is the lag operator, write this equation as

$$[I - (A - BD^{-1}C)L]s_{t+1} = BD^{-1}X_t. \qquad (7.70)$$

If the eigenvalues of $(A - BD^{-1}C)$ are strictly less than unity in modulus, then the inverse of $[I - (A - BD^{-1}C)L]$ yields a square-summable polynomial in L, and thus s_{t+1} can be written as

$$s_{t+1} = \sum_{j=0}^{\infty}(A - BD^{-1}C)^j BD^{-1}X_{t-j}.$$

Lagging this expression by one period, and substituting for $BD^{-1}X_t s_t$ in (7.69), we obtain

$$X_t = C\sum_{j=0}^{\infty}(A - BD^{-1}C)^j BD^{-1}X_{t-j-1} + Dw_t. \qquad (7.71)$$

Comparing (7.65) and (7.71), we see that the representation of X_t stemming from the model is an infinite-order VAR, with the mapping from structural innovations to VAR disturbances given by

$$Dw_t = P\nu_t.$$

To reiterate, the two conditions that yielded this mapping are that D is square and invertible, and the eigenvalues of $(A - BD^{-1}C)$ are strictly less than unity in modulus. The largest eigenvalue associated with $(A - BD^{-1}C)$ determines the rate of decay of the lag coefficients $(A - BD^{-1}C)^j$ in (7.71), and thus the extent to which a the finite-ordered specification (7.65) serves as an adequate approximation of (7.71).

A recent empirical application involving the use of identified VARs involves assessments of the impact of technology shocks in driving the behavior of hours worked (depicted in figure 3.1). Interest in this topic follows Gali (1999), who used an identified VAR to show that hours tend to fall following the realization of positive productivity shocks. Because this evidence poses a severe challenge to the real-business-cycle paradigm, its identification has spawned a large literature.

One response to this evidence has involved investigations of whether various modifications to standard RBC environments are useful in helping take the evidence into account (e.g., Christiano and Todd, 1996; Boldrin, Christiano, and Fisher, 2001; and Francis and Ramey, 2003). An alternative response has involved challenges to the robustness of this evidence to the specification of the VAR upon which it is based. This latter line of investigation has shown the evidence to be fragile along at least two dimensions.

First, Christiano, Eichenbaum, and Vigfusson (2003) have shown that if hours are treated as being stationary in levels rather than in first differences (as Gali assumed), then the direction of the response in hours to productivity shocks is reversed. (For a discussion of difficulties associated with appropriate characterizations of stationarity, see chapter 3, section 3.1.)

Second, Chari, Kehoe, and McGrattan (2005) have shown that the evidence can stem spuriously from the specification of a lag structure in the VAR that is not sufficiently rich to capture the dynamic behavior of the data it is meant to characterize. In particular, they show that specification errors associated with technology shocks identified using parsimoniously specified VARs tend to be large. Moreover, in experiments involving artificial data simulated from various DSGE models, they show more generally that VARs can have difficulties in identifying patterns of impulse responses consistent with those present in the models from which the data were obtained. The breadth of the applicability of this critique is surely a topic for future research. We now characterize means by which such simulation exercises can be conducted.

7.3.3 Simulations Involving Linearized Models

The third context again involves applications to fully specified linearized models. But in this case, we discuss situations in which implications conveyed by the model regarding the selected empirical targets must be calculated via simulations.

The recursive nature of DSGE models renders the task of model simulation straightforward (for details regarding the accuracy of simulations involving DSGE models, see Santos and Peralta-Alva, 2005). Two inputs are required to generate a simulation of $\{x_t\}_{t=1}^T$ for a given model parameterization μ. First is a specification of the initial state vector s_0, which can be taken either as known or as a realization obtained from an underlying distribution. The stationary nature of the model (typically induced by an appropriate transformation of variables) renders this distinction as unimportant in simulations designed to characterize the asymptotic properties of the model. Because the remaining variables in x_t are a function of the state variable, the specification of s_0 serves to determine x_0. Second is a drawing of structural shocks $\{\upsilon_t\}_{t=1}^T$, and if appropriate, a drawing of measurement errors $\{u_t\}_{t=1}^T$, from distributions specified for these processes. A random number generator is used to obtain these drawings. Note that unlike estimates obtained using GMM, simulation-based estimates are not distribution-free: inferences will be conditional on the distributions specified for υ_t and u_t.

Given x_0 and $\{\upsilon_t\}_{t=1}^T$, $\{x_t\}_{t=1}^T$ is constructed via recursive substitution using (7.56): $x_1 = Fx_0 + e_1$, $x_2 = Fx_1 + e_2$, and so on, where $e_t = G\upsilon_t$. Next, $\{x_t\}_{t=1}^T$ and $\{u_t\}_{t=1}^T$ combine in (7.58) to yield a simulated realization $\{X_t\}_{t=1}^T$. Finally, the function of interest is computed from this simulated realization, and a single simulation step has been completed. To eliminate the influence of the starting value chosen for s_0, a burn-in phase can be implemented. This involves merely discarding the first, say 1,000 artificial realizations obtained for $\{x_t\}_{t=1}^T$.

7.3.4 Simulations Involving Nonlinear Approximations

The fourth context involves applications to nonlinear approximations to DSGE models. Chapter 11 is devoted exclusively to a discussion of empirical applications involving nonlinear approximations, and so we postpone a detailed description until that point. Here we briefly sketch the simulation process (analytical calculations will rarely be feasible in this context).

To briefly establish notation, let s_t again denote the vector of state variables contained in x_t, with law of motion determined by

$$s_t = f(s_{t-1}, \upsilon_t), \tag{7.72}$$

where υ_t continues to represent structural shocks. Further, let c_t denote the vector of control variables contained in x_t. These are determined according to the policy rule

$$c_t = c(s_t), \tag{7.73}$$

which is derived as the solution to the optimization problem facing the decision makers included in the model. Finally, for empirical implementation, (7.72) and (7.73) are mapped into observables X_t by the observation equation

$$
\begin{aligned}
X_t &= \widetilde{g}(s_t, c_t, \upsilon_t, u_t) \\
&\equiv g(s_t, u_t),
\end{aligned}
\tag{7.74}
$$

where u_t continues to represent measurement error. The parameterizations of $f(s_{t-1}, \upsilon_t)$, $c(s_t)$, and $g(s_t, u_t)$, along with the distributions governing the stochastic behavior of υ_t and u_t, are determined by the structural parameters μ.

Like its linearized counterpart, this nonlinear model representation is recursive, so the task of model simulation remains relatively straightforward. The list of inputs to the simulation process once again includes a specification of the initial state vector s_0, and distributions specified for υ_t and u_t. Given these inputs, model simulation proceeds as in the linear case. From (7.72), s_0 and $\{\upsilon_t\}_{t=1}^T$ yield $\{s_t\}_{t=1}^T$ directly. Using this series as an input to the policy function (7.73) yields $\{c_t\}_{t=1}^T$. Then $\{s_t\}_{t=1}^T$ and $\{c_t\}_{t=1}^T$ combine to form $\{x_t\}_{t=1}^T$ ($x_t \equiv (s_t', c_t')$), which combined with $\{u_t\}_{t=1}^T$ maps into X_t as in (7.74). Functions of interest are computed using the simulated realizations of $\{X_t\}_{t=1}^T$, which completes the simulation step.

7.4 Empirical Application: Matching RBC Moments

In chapter 6, section 6.4, we presented a calibration exercise designed to illustrate the ability of the RBC model introduced in chapter 5, section 5.1 to match a collection of moments summarizing the time-series behavior of output, consumption, investment, and labor hours. Here, we formalize this illustration statistically by conducting a moment-matching exercise. Specifically, we estimate the parameters of the model using various combinations of the moments reported in table 6.4 as targets, and then compare predictions conveyed by the model estimates regarding the moments with their empirical counterparts.

Moments corresponding with the data were measured by estimating a six-lag VAR, and mapping the resulting coefficient estimates into moment measures as indicated in chapter 4, section 4.1.2 (the data are contained in `ycih.txt`, available at the textbook Web site). Associated standard errors were obtained using the delta method, as indicated in chapter 4, section 4.2. Moments corresponding with the model were measured as indicated above in section 7.3.2.

To begin, table 7.1 reports point estimates and associated standard errors of the full collection of moments we consider, along with moments obtained using the baseline model parameterization used in the calibration

TABLE 7.1
Baseline Moment Comparison

Moment	*Point Estimate*	*Standard Error*	*Model Moment*	t–*Stat*
σ_y	0.0177	0.0019	0.0207	−1.64
σ_c	0.0081	0.0008	0.0101	−2.38
σ_i	0.0748	0.0070	0.0752	−0.06
σ_n	0.0185	0.0021	0.0076	5.14
$\varphi_y(1)$	0.8642	0.0199	0.8681	−0.20
$\varphi_c(1)$	0.8318	0.0293	0.9448	−3.85
$\varphi_i(1)$	0.7891	0.0307	0.8066	−0.57
$\varphi_n(1)$	0.8992	0.0144	0.7829	8.05
$\varphi_{y,c}(0)$	0.8237	0.0379	0.9626	−3.67
$\varphi_{y,i}(0)$	0.9502	0.0101	0.9842	−3.39
$\varphi_{y,n}(0)$	0.8342	0.0241	0.9702	−5.65
$\varphi_{y,c}(1)$	0.7467	0.0436	0.9281	−4.16
$\varphi_{y,i}(1)$	0.7991	0.0355	0.7941	0.014
$\varphi_{y,n}(1)$	0.6230	0.0396	0.7597	−3.45

Notes: $\varphi(1)$ denotes first-order serial correlation; $\varphi_{j,y}(l)$ denotes l^{th} order correlation between variables j and y. Model moments based on the parameterization

$$\theta = [\alpha\ \beta\ \phi\ \varphi\ \delta\ \rho\ \sigma]' = [0.24\ 0.99\ 1.5\ 0.35\ 0.025\ 0.78\ 0.0067]'.$$

exercise. To convey the statistical significance of differences between the two sets of moment calculations, table 7.1 also reports associated t-statistics: differences between the empirical and model moments, divided by associated standard errors.

Immediately apparent from the table is the poor performance of the model in characterizing hours: the t-statistics associated with σ_n, $\varphi_n(1)$, $\varphi_{y,n}(0)$ and $\varphi_{y,n}(1)$ all lie above 3 in absolute value, and range as high as 8. This poor performance was also clearly evident in the calibration exercise. What was not evident in the calibration exercise, but emerges from table 7.1, is that the performance in characterizing consumption is also disappointing: t-statistics associated with σ_c, and so on, all exceed 2 in absolute value, and range above 4. In contrast, the model's characterization of investment is solid, with only the t-statistic associated with $\varphi_{y,i}(0)$ exceeding 1. The question we now address is: can the model's performance be improved by conducting an estimation step?

We facilitate estimation using the GMM approach outlined in section 7.2.1. Specifically, in this case

$$\theta = [\alpha\ \beta\ \phi\ \varphi\ \delta\ \rho\ \sigma]',$$

the entries of $g(Z,\theta)$ contain differences between empirical and model moments, the weighting matrix Ω is the inverse of the variance-covariance

TABLE 7.2
Parameter estimates

Parameter	*Calibrated Value*	*All*	*C Subset*	*I Subset*	*N Subset*
α	0.24	0.1871	0.1927	0.2480	0.1946
		(8.52*e*-6)	(2.94*e*-4)	(0.005)	(2.46*e*-5)
β	0.99	0.9989	0.9987	0.9899	0.9990
	[0.9877, 0.999]	(2.09*e*-8)	(2.18*e*-5)	(1.51*e*-6)	(1.41*e*-6)
δ	0.025	0.0152	0.0126	0.0242	0.0100
	[0.01, 0.04]	(1.06*e*-5)	(8.60*e*-6)	(0.0002)	(1.50*e*-8)
ϕ	1.5	0.5022	2.2512	1.5123	0.6143
	[0.5, 2.5]	(2.55*e*-4)	(0.3228)	(0.0070)	(0.2510)
φ	0.35	0.3367	0.3383	0.3543	0.3388
		(2.34*e*-6)	(8.09*e*-5)	(0.0001)	(6.84*e*-6)
ρ	0.78	0.8690	0.6000	0.7805	0.8839
	[0.6, 0.95]	(0.0101)	(0.1324)	(0.3838)	(0.0623)
σ	0.0067	0.0052	0.0092	0.0067	0.0010
	(0,0.01]	(2.65*e*-4)	(0.0007)	(0.0012)	(0.0005)

Notes: Brackets reported under calibrated parameter values indicate range restrictions. Parentheses reported under parameter estimates indicate standard errors. Moments included under J Subset are σ_y, σ_j, $\varphi_j(1)$, $\varphi_{y,j}(0)$ and $\varphi_{y,j}(1)$, $j = c, i, n$.

associated with the empirical moment estimates, and estimates $\widehat{\theta}$ are obtained as the solution to

$$\min_{\theta} \quad \Gamma(\theta) = g(Z,\theta)' \times \Omega \times g(Z,\theta).$$

Minimization was accomplished using GAUSS's derivative-based software package `optmum`; details regarding the algorithms it implements are provided in chapter 8.

Table 7.2 reports parameter estimates obtained using four alternative sets of empirical moments as targets: the full set of moments, and three subsets designed to capture the relationship between output and the three remaining variables, each in isolation: σ_y, σ_j, $\varphi_j(1)$, $\varphi_{y,j}(0)$, and $\varphi_{y,j}(1)$, $j = c, i, n$. In all cases, parameter estimates were restricted to the following ranges of values deemed to be reasonable a priori: the discount factor $\beta \in [0.9877, 0.999]$, implying a restriction on average real interest rates between 0.1% and 1.25% on a quarterly basis; the CRRA parameter $\phi \in [0.5, 2.5]$; the depreciation rate $\delta \in [0.01, 0.04]$, implying annual depreciation rates between 4% and 16%; the AR coefficient $\rho \in [0.6, 0.95]$; and the innovation standard deviation $\sigma \in (0, 0.01]$. In addition, the capital-share parameter α, along with φ, which indicates the importance of consumption relative to leisure in the instantaneous utility specification, were restricted to insure that steady state values of $\frac{i}{y}$, $\frac{c}{y}$, and n match their long-run empirical counterparts (measured as sample averages):

$$\alpha = \left(\frac{\delta + \varrho}{\delta}\right)\frac{\bar{i}}{\bar{y}},$$

$$\varphi = \frac{1}{1 + \frac{2(1-\alpha)}{\bar{c}/\bar{y}}},$$

where $\varrho = 1/\beta - 1$. Details regarding the derivation of these restrictions are provided in chapter 6, section 6.4, and details regarding the imposition of range restrictions on β, and so on are provided in chapter 8, section 8.4.

Note that the estimates obtained using the "I Subset" of moments are quite close to the parameter values specified under the calibration exercise. This reflects the relatively strong performance of the calibrated model in characterizing the behavior of investment in general. For the remaining collection of estimates, α is estimated in the neighborhood of 0.19, substantially below its calibrated value of 0.24; β is estimated at or near its upper-bound value of 0.999; δ is estimated between 0.01 and 0.015, at or near its lower-bound value of 0.01; estimates of ϕ and ρ tend to be relatively imprecise and vary substantially over their restricted ranges; estimates of φ lie close to its calibrated value of 0.35; and estimates of σ also exhibit substantial variability. Finally, note that in seeking to account for the behavior of consumption, we obtain a relatively high estimate of the CRRA parameter ϕ (2.25) and low estimate of the AR parameter ρ (at its lower bound of 0.6). In contrast, we obtain the reverse pattern of estimates in seeking to account for the behavior of hours: the estimate of ϕ we obtain is relatively low (0.61), and the estimate of ρ is relatively high (0.88). As a result, the joint characterization of these series appears particularly problematic.

The correspondence between these parameter estimates and their targeted moments is reported in table 7.3. In addition to point estimates, discrepancies with empirical counterparts are again reported using t-statistics.

Regarding the results obtained using the full collection of moments, the estimation step is seen to have generated little payoff: performance along the investment dimension remains solid, but is at best marginally improved relative to the results reported in table 7.1 along the consumption and hours dimensions. In targeting the consumption moments in isolation, the model's performance clearly improves, but remains disappointing: t-statistics remain above 2 for all moments besides $\varphi_{y,c}(1)$. Little change in

TABLE 7.3
Moment Comparisons Using Model Estimates

Moment	*All*	*C Subset*	*I Subset*	*N Subset*
σ_y	0.0220 (−2.33)	0.0217 (−2.15)	0.0205 (−1.54)	0.0019 (7.00)
σ_c	0.0112 (−4.25)	0.0101 (−2.35)	XX	XX
σ_i	0.0782 (−0.49)	XX	0.0691 (0.81)	XX
σ_n	0.0081 (4.89)	XX	XX	0.0013 (8.08)
$\varphi_y(1)$	0.9119 (−2.40)	XX	XX	XX
$\varphi_c(1)$	0.9825 (−5.14)	0.9029 (−2.42)	XX	XX
$\varphi_i(1)$	0.8377 (−1.58)	XX	0.8061 (−0.56)	XX
$\varphi_n(1)$	0.8095 (6.21)	XX	XX	0.8118 (6.05)
$\varphi_{y,c}(0)$	0.9198 (−2.54)	0.9116 (−2.32)	XX	XX
$\varphi_{y,i}(0)$	0.9609 (−1.07)	XX	0.9779 (−2.76)	XX
$\varphi_{y,n}(0)$	0.9261 (−3.81)	XX	XX	0.8202 (0.58)
$\varphi_{y,c}(1)$	0.9399 (−4.43)	0.8196 (−1.67)	XX	XX
$\varphi_{y,i}(1)$	0.8049 (−0.16)	XX	0.7887 (0.29)	XX
$\varphi_{y,n}(1)$	0.7473 (−3.14)	XX	XX	0.6490 (−0.66)

Notes: $\varphi(1)$ denotes first-order serial correlation; $\varphi_{j,y}(l)$ denotes l^{th} order correlation between variables j and y. t-statistics indicating discrepancies with empirical counterparts provided in parentheses. XX denotes unestimated moment.

performance along the investment dimension results when targeting the investment moments in isolation. Finally, a mixed picture emerges when targeting the hours moments in isolation: the characterizations of $\varphi_{y,n}(0)$ and $\varphi_{y,n}(1)$ improve significantly, at the cost of substantially deteriorated characterizations of σ_y, σ_n, and $\varphi_n(1)$.

In sum, we draw two conclusions from this exercise. First, although the standard RBC model is well-known to have difficulties in characterizing the behavior of hours, we have also found its performance along the consumption dimension to be disappointing. Second, it is apparent that improvements in the overall performance of the model cannot be attained merely through adjustments in its parameterization: dramatic improvements in performance do not result from an optimization step.

Of course, these results should not be viewed as an indictment of the empirical performance of RBC models in general. State-of-the-art specifications featuring, for example, time-to-build production processes, non-convexities associated with adjustments to labor and capital inputs, and so on, have been developed to improve upon the performance of the baseline specification we have considered. (The collection of papers in Cooley, 1995, provide a good overview of developments on this front. See also the collection of papers in Sustek, 2005.) Instead, we have offered this exercise as an illustration of the ability of moment-matching exercises to highlight particular dimensions along which the model under investigation succeeds or fails to capture relevant facets of the data it has been designed to characterize. This sort of information is particularly valuable in helping to pinpoint trouble spots, and thus in providing guidance for pursuing fruitful extensions.

Chapter 8

Maximum Likelihood

8.1 Overview

Chapters 6 and 7 presented limited-information methods for evaluating DSGE models. This chapter and the next present full-information alternatives: the classical (chapter 8) and Bayesian (chapter 9) approaches to likelihood analysis. Under these methods, the DSGE model under investigation is viewed as providing a complete statistical characterization of the data, in the form of a likelihood function. As described in chapter 4, section 4.3, the source of the likelihood function is the corresponding state-space representation of the observable data, coupled with a distributional assumption for the stochastic innovations included in the model.

Two features of full-information analyses distinguish them from the moment-based procedures presented previously. First is the requirement of a distributional assumption for the stochastic innovations: inferences obtained under such analyses are jointly conditional upon the model and the underlying distributional assumption. Second, the basis of inference is on the full range of empirical implications conveyed by the model, rather than on a subset of implications conveyed by the collection of moments chosen by the researcher.

The distinction between classical and Bayesian approaches to likelihood analysis can be cast succinctly in terms of whether the data or parameters are interpreted by the researcher as random variables. (For more elaborate treatments of this distinction, see, e.g., Berger and Wolpert, 1988; or Poirier, 1995.) Under the classical approach, parameters are interpreted as fixed (but unknown), and the data are interpreted as the realization of a random drawing from the corresponding likelihood function. Given the realization of a drawing of data, parameter estimates are chosen as those that maximize the likelihood function; uncertainty regarding the specific values estimated for the parameters is conveyed by reporting associated standard errors. Uncertainty regarding parameter estimates arises from the fact that the realized data represent one of many possible realizations that could have been obtained from the likelihood function. Because parameter estimates are a function of the corresponding data, randomness in the data imparts randomness in the parameter estimates.

Under the classical approach, the empirical plausibility of a given model may be assessed using formal hypothesis testing procedures. Such procedures begin with the designation of a parameterized version of the model as the null hypothesis, or in other words, as the stochastic process from which the observed data have been realized. The likelihood function corresponding with the null hypothesis is then used to assess the probability that the observed data could have in fact been generated by the null model. If the probability lies above a prespecified threshold, or critical value, the null hypothesis is not rejected, and the model is deemed to have passed the test; otherwise the parameterized model is rejected as a plausible candidate for representing the true data generation process.

Under the Bayesian approach, parameters are interpreted as random and the data as fixed. In estimation, the objective is to make conditional probabilistic statements regarding the parameters of the model, where conditioning is with respect to the observed data. The probabilistic interpretation of the parameters enables the formal incorporation of a priori views regarding their specification. These views are introduced though the specification of a prior distribution; coupling this distribution with the likelihood function via Bayes' Rule yields a posterior distribution for the parameters. Means or modes of the posterior distribution typically provide point estimates of the parameters, and uncertainty associated with these estimates are typically conveyed using posterior standard deviations.

Inferences regarding the empirical support assigned by the data to a particular model involve comparisons of the conditional probability associated with the model relative to probabilities associated with alternative models. As with estimation, conditioning is once again made with respect to the data, and probability calculations are based on posterior distributions. In contrast to the classical approach, no one model is maintained as the null hypothesis to be accepted or rejected as the true data generation process. Instead, judgments regarding the empirical plausibility of competing models are based upon assessments of their relative conditional probabilities.

In sum, the assessment of a given model under the classical approach to likelihood analysis involves the following question: how plausible are the observed data, given the maintained null hypothesis? Under the Bayesian approach, the question is: how plausible is a given model relative to competing alternatives, given the observed data? This chapter provides details regarding the implementation of the classical approach. (For general textbook discussions of the classical approach to likelihood analysis, see, e.g., Amemiya, 1985; Hamilton, 1999; Harvey, 1994; or Greene, 2003.) The key component of implementation involves the maximization of likelihood functions associated with state-space representations. Chapter 9 then provides details regarding the implementation of the Bayesian approach.

8.2 Introduction and Historical Background

Chapter 4 provided details regarding the evaluation of the likelihood function $L(X|\mu)$ associated with the state-space representation of a given DSGE model. To reestablish notation, recall that the $k \times 1$ vector μ contains the model's structural parameters, and X represents the T observations of the $m \times 1$ vector of observable variables X_t. The likelihood function is a multiplicative product over the time-t data points X_t:

$$L(X|\mu) = \prod_{t=1}^{T} L(X_t|\mu). \tag{8.1}$$

Given this structure, it is convenient in practice to work with the log-likelihood function $\log L(X|\mu)$, which is additive over time-t data points:

$$\log L(X|\mu) = \sum_{t=1}^{T} \log L(X_t|\mu). \tag{8.2}$$

Convenience aside, details regarding implementation apply equally to $L(X|\mu)$ and $\log L(X|\mu)$: Because the logarithmic transform is monotonic, the maximum of the log-likelihood function corresponds to that of the likelihood function.

With the $n \times 1$ vector x_t denoting the full collection of model variables, the state-space representation of the model is given by:

$$x_t = F(\mu)x_{t-1} + e_t \tag{8.3}$$

$$e_t = G(\mu)\upsilon_t \tag{8.4}$$

$$E\left(e_t e_t'\right) = G(\mu)E\left(\upsilon_t \upsilon_t'\right) G(\mu)' = Q(\mu). \tag{8.5}$$

The associated measurement equation is given either by

$$X_t = H(\mu)' x_t \tag{8.6}$$

or

$$X_t = H(\mu)' x_t + u_t. \tag{8.7}$$

The matrices $(F(\mu),\ G(\mu),\ Q(\mu),\ H(\mu))$ represent the parameters of the state-space representation; given a specification of μ, they are derived via the model-solution techniques presented in chapter 2. Hereafter, the ability to calculate $\log L(X|\mu)$ for a particular specification of μ, via use of the Kalman filter, is taken as granted.[1]

As noted, the classical approach to estimation involves the maximization of $\log L(X|\mu)$ with respect to μ. Let this maximum-likelihood (ML)

[1] The GAUSS procedure `kalman.prc` is available for this purpose.

estimator be denoted as $\widehat{\mu}$. Because $\widehat{\mu}$ is a function of X, it is interpretable as a random variable, thus there is uncertainty associated with the information it conveys regarding the true value of μ. This uncertainty is conveyed by reporting associated standard errors.

For a heuristic description of the means by which $\widehat{\mu}$ and associated standard errors may be obtained, note that the log-likelihood function is a particular example of a more general function $f(\mu)$. For the case in which μ is 1×1, the first-order condition associated with the maximization of $f(\mu)$ is given by $f'(\mu) = 0$, and the second-order condition is $f''(\mu) < 0$, implying that the function decreases when moving away from $\widehat{\mu}$. (Here we take for granted the existence of a single optimizing value $\widehat{\mu}$; departures from this case are discussed in section 8.5.) When $|f''(\widehat{\mu})|$ is large, the function decreases rapidly in moving away from $\widehat{\mu}$, and thus $\widehat{\mu}$ has been identified with a relatively high degree of precision. For the case in which μ is $k \times 1$, the same first-order condition applies, except that $f'(\mu)$ is the $k \times 1$ gradient vector associated with $f(\mu)$; the second-order condition is that the $k \times k$ matrix of second derivatives (the Hessian associated with $f(\mu)$) is negative definite when evaluated at $\widehat{\mu}$. The larger in absolute value is the jth diagonal element of the Hessian, the more rapidly $f(\widehat{\mu})$ decreases in moving away from $\widehat{\mu}_j$.

For the specific case in which the function of interest is the log-likelihood function, the theory of maximum likelihood states that under suitable regularity conditions, the ML estimator $\widehat{\mu}$ is consistent and distributed asymptotically as Normal (e.g., see Amemiya, 1985):

$$\widehat{\mu} \rightarrow N(\mu^*, (T\Im)^{-1}), \tag{8.8}$$

where μ^* is the true but unknown value of μ and $\Im$ is the Hessian associated with $\log L(X|\mu)$. The presence of T^{-1} in the asymptotic covariance matrix offsets the dependence of $\Im$ on T:

$$\Im(\mu) = -T^{-1}\frac{\partial^2 \log L(X|\mu)}{\partial\mu\partial\mu'}. \tag{8.9}$$

Substituting (8.9) into (8.8), T is eliminated, yielding the asymptotic covariance matrix

$$\Sigma_\mu = \left[-\frac{\partial^2 \log L(X|\mu)}{\partial\mu\partial\mu'}\right]^{-1}. \tag{8.10}$$

Evaluating (8.10) at $\widehat{\mu}$ yields an estimate of the covariance matrix $\widehat{\Sigma_\mu}$ associated with $\widehat{\mu}$, the diagonal elements of which are associated standard errors, $\widehat{\sigma_\mu}$. Following the logic of the heuristic description, if the log-likelihood function falls sharply in moving away from $\widehat{\mu}_j$, its corresponding standard error $\widehat{\sigma_{\mu_j}}$ will be small, and $\widehat{\mu}_j$ will be tightly identified. Before moving to a discussion of techniques for maximizing $\log L(X|\mu)$ and computing Hessians, we pause to provide historical perspective on their application to DSGE models.

The mapping of DSGE models into likelihood functions specified over μ was pioneered by Sargent (1989). A key obstacle that must be overcome in developing any such mapping involves what is known as the stochastic singularity problem: DSGE models carry nontrivial implications for the stochastic behavior of only as many observable variables as there are sources of uncertainty included in the model. With fewer sources of uncertainty than observables, various linear combinations of variables will be predicted to be deterministic, and departures from this prediction will render likelihood analysis untenable (for elaboration, see Ingram, Kocherlakota, and Savin, 1994).

Sargent overcame this obstacle by working with the measurement equation (8.7), which features the measurement errors u_t. The errors were alternatively taken as being serially uncorrelated, or as following a VAR(1) specification:

$$E(u_t u_t') = \Sigma_u, \text{ or} \tag{8.11}$$

$$u_t = \Gamma u_{t-1} + \xi_t, \qquad E(\xi_t \xi_t') = \Sigma_\xi. \tag{8.12}$$

In the first case, Σ_u was restricted to be diagonal; in the second, Γ and Σ_ξ were also restricted to be diagonal; these restrictions insure that the measurement errors associated with the individual elements of X_t are uncorrelated.[2] In both cases, the stochastic singularity problem is resolved through the attribution of departures from the deterministic behavior implied for linear combinations of the observables to measurement errors associated with their observation. Subsequent studies that used this approach to the problem include Altug (1989), McGrattan (1994), and McGrattan, Rogerson, and Wright (1997).

Ingram, Kocherlakota, and Savin (1994) advocate an alternative resolution to the stochastic singularity problem. Their approach involves the specification of a model featuring as many structural shocks as there are observable variables; this has become known as the multiple-shock approach. Their motivation for this approach, cast in the context of an RBC framework, is that the real world features many more sources of stochastic uncertainty that can be captured through the specification of a catchall total factor productivity shock. Examples of studies that have used

[2] The GAUSS procedures `kalmanm.prc` and `kalman.prc` are available for evaluating likelihood functions associated with state-space representations augmented with (8.11) and (8.12), as described in chapter 4, section 4.3.

this approach include DeJong, Ingram, and Whiteman (2000a,b); DeJong and Ingram (2001); and Otrok (2001).

An alternative to the multiple-shock approach has been proposed by Ireland (2004b), who recognized the potential for a broader interpretation (beyond measurement error) of the role played by u_t in (8.7). Ireland's so-called hybrid approach follows Sargent (1989) in assuming the VAR(1) process (8.12) for u_t, but relaxes the restriction that the matrices Γ and Σ_ξ be diagonal. Beyond this relatively straightforward extension, Ireland's contribution lies in the observation that u_t can play a role in addressing the model-specification issues that have led some researchers to reject the use of statistical formalism in analyzing DSGE models. A broad discussion of these issues is provided in chapter 6, but the crux of the problem is summarized by Prescott (1986): "The models constructed within this theoretical framework are necessarily highly abstract. Consequently, they are necessarily false, and statistical hypothesis testing will reject them." [p. 10] But as Ireland notes, beyond capturing measurement error, u_t can be "... interpreted more liberally as capturing all of the movements and co-movements in the data that the real business cycle model, because of its elegance and simplicity, cannot explain. In this way, the hybrid model [...] combines the power of the DSGE model with the flexibility of a VAR." [p. 1210] Under this interpretation, u_t plays the role that residuals play in empirical applications involving reduced-form specifications. Their inclusion in the specification of a DSGE model thus provides explicit recognition that the model is not designed to capture the full extent of variation observed in the data.

8.3 A Primer on Optimization Algorithms

We now characterize numerical methods for obtaining ML estimates. Several optimization algorithms exist for this purpose; here we discuss two classes: simplex and derivative-based algorithms. (For more comprehensive textbook overviews of optimization algorithms, see Judd, 1998; Hamilton, 1999; and Harvey, 1999.) In practice, most algorithms are designed to minimize the function of interest. Therefore, hereafter we consider the objective of calculating the $\widehat{\mu}$ that minimizes $f(\mu) = -\log L(X|\mu)$.

The algorithms we present require two inputs: a procedure that takes μ as an input and delivers $f(\mu)$ as output, and an initial value specified for μ. Given these inputs, simplex algorithms deliver as output parameter estimates $\widehat{\mu}$ and the corresponding value of the likelihood function $f(\widehat{\mu})$; in addition, derivative-based methods also deliver $\widehat{\Sigma_\mu}$. (Given the use of a simplex method, an additional step, described below, is required to produce $\widehat{\Sigma_\mu}$.)

In this section, we proceed under the assumption that $f(\mu)$ is well-behaved. In particular, we assume that it is continuous and monotonic in μ, and contains a global minimum. Deviations from this rosy scenario are discussed in section 8.4.

8.3.1 Simplex Methods

Simplex algorithms are designed to minimize $f(\mu)$, $\mu \in \Re^k$ via the use of "triangularization" techniques, which involve the construction and manipulation of simplexes. With μ being $k \times 1$, a simplex Δ is a $k+1$ collection of specific specifications of μ: $(\mu_1, \ldots, \mu_{k+1})$. The specifications are referred to as vertices. For example, given $k = 2$, Δ is a triangle; and given $k = 3$, Δ is a pyramid.

Simplex algorithms are iterative procedures designed to manipulate the shape and location of simplexes over the parameter space, with the ultimate goal of producing a degenerate simplex at the optimal value $\widehat{\mu}$. Many specific algorithms exist for this purpose; here we present a popular version developed by Nelder and Mead (1965). Further details regarding this algorithm are provided by Lagarias et al. (1998), who detailed its convergence properties in low-dimensional applications; we follow their discussion closely here.[3]

The basic idea behind any simplex algorithm is to search by trial and error for "lower ground" on the likelihood surface. Starting from a given point, the first step in a typical algorithm is to determine a local neighborhood over which an additional move is contemplated. Technically, this amounts to the construction of a simplex. The second step is to make a move within this local neighborhood, from which a new local neighborhood is established and probed. Depending upon the particular conditions encountered at a given point, the size and shape of the selected local neighborhood can vary substantially. The evolution of simplexes that results from the exploration of the likelihood surface is suggestive of the movements of an amoeba gliding through a fluid.

Relative to derivative-based algorithms, simplex algorithms are attractive because they do not require that the likelihood surface be differentiable. In the context of evaluating DSGE models, this is a particularly important consideration because analytical expressions for derivatives are rarely available; and the calculation of numerical derivatives can be inaccurate

[3] GAUSS code for implementing this algorithm is available through the American University archive at
http://www.american.edu/academic.depts/cas/econ/gaussres/GAUSSIDX.HTM
It is also available at the GAUSS software archive http://faculty.washington.edu/rons/

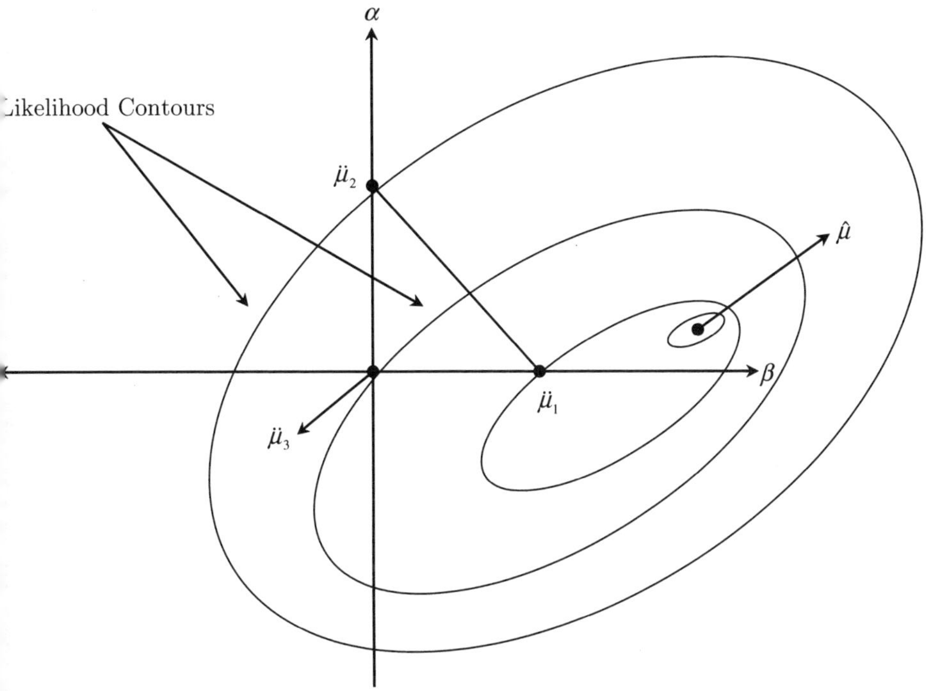

Figure 8.1 Initial Δ^0 for Nelder–Mead algorithm.

(particularly in working with numerical approximations of the likelihood function, as with the particle filter described in chapter 11).

We begin with a heuristic description of the two-dimensional case. As noted, in this case the simplex is a triangle with three vertices. Let $\mu = (\beta, \alpha)$, and denote starting values as $\mu^0 = (\beta^0, \alpha^0)$. These map into an initial triangle Δ^0 as follows: $\ddot{\mu}_1^0 = (\beta_0^0, 0)$, $\ddot{\mu}_2^0 = (0, \alpha_0^0)$, and $\ddot{\mu}_3^0 = (0, 0)$; a graphical characterization is provided in figure 8.1.

Using this initial specification, an iteration designed to generate a new triangle that lies closer to the minimum value $\widehat{\mu}$ is performed. Subsequent iterations have the same objective, thus the designation of μ^0 as the initial specification of μ is unimportant; hereafter superscripts denoting iteration numbers will be suppressed. The first step of the iteration is to relabel (if necessary) the vertices so that $f(\mu_1) \leq f(\mu_2) \leq f(\mu_3)$. Note from figure 8.1 that, given the likelihood contours, it is in fact the case that $f(\ddot{\mu}_1) \leq f(\ddot{\mu}_3) \leq f(\ddot{\mu}_2)$; thus the vertices are relabeled as $\mu_1 = (\beta_0^0, 0)$, $\mu_2 = (0, 0)$, and $\mu_3 = (0, \alpha_0^0)$, achieving $f(\mu_1) \leq f(\mu_2) \leq f(\mu_3)$.

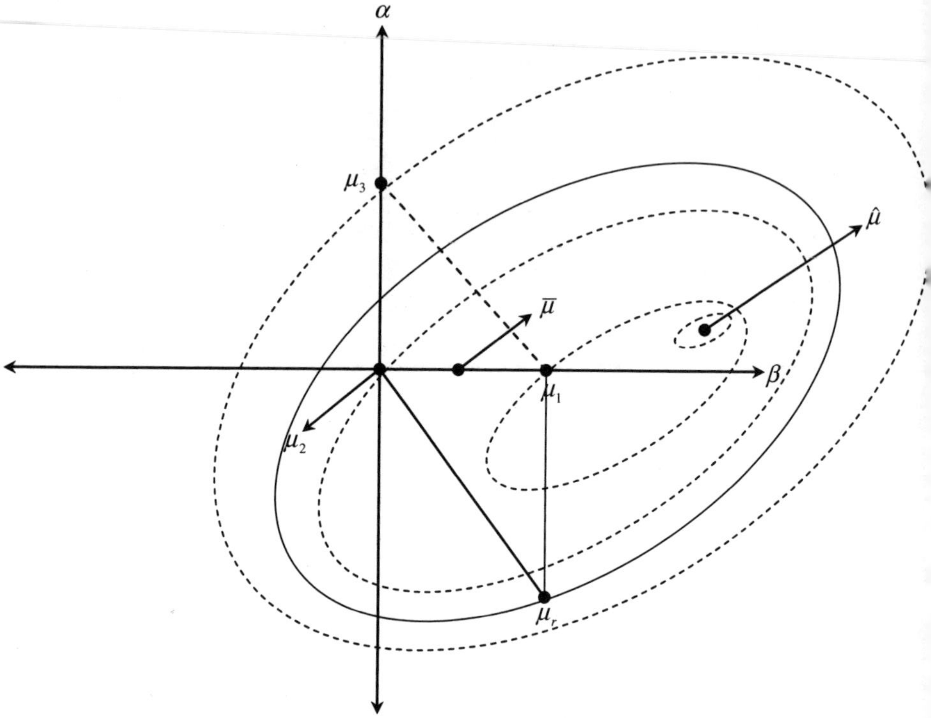

Figure 8.2 Reflection point.

Given this rearrangement, a reflection point μ_r is calculated:

$$\mu_r = \overline{\mu} + (\overline{\mu} - \mu_3), \quad \overline{\mu} = \frac{\mu_1 + \mu_2}{2}. \tag{8.13}$$

The reflection point, along with the relabeled vertices, is depicted in figure 8.2. (The initial simplex is drawn with dashed lines in all of the subsequent figures in this chapter.)

The next step involves taking either a "shrink step" or a "nonshrink step," depending upon contingencies involving the reflection point. We first describe contingencies under which a nonshrink step is taken. If these fail, a shrink step is taken.

Several possibilities fall under the heading of a nonshrink step. First, if $f(\mu_1) \leq f(\mu_r) < f(\mu_2)$, so that μ_r is superior to the next-to-worst vertex associated with the previous iteration, but inferior to the best vertex, the worst point (here μ_3) is discarded and replaced with μ_r; the simplex constructed using (μ_1, μ_2, μ_r) is then passed to the next iteration and the current iteration terminates.

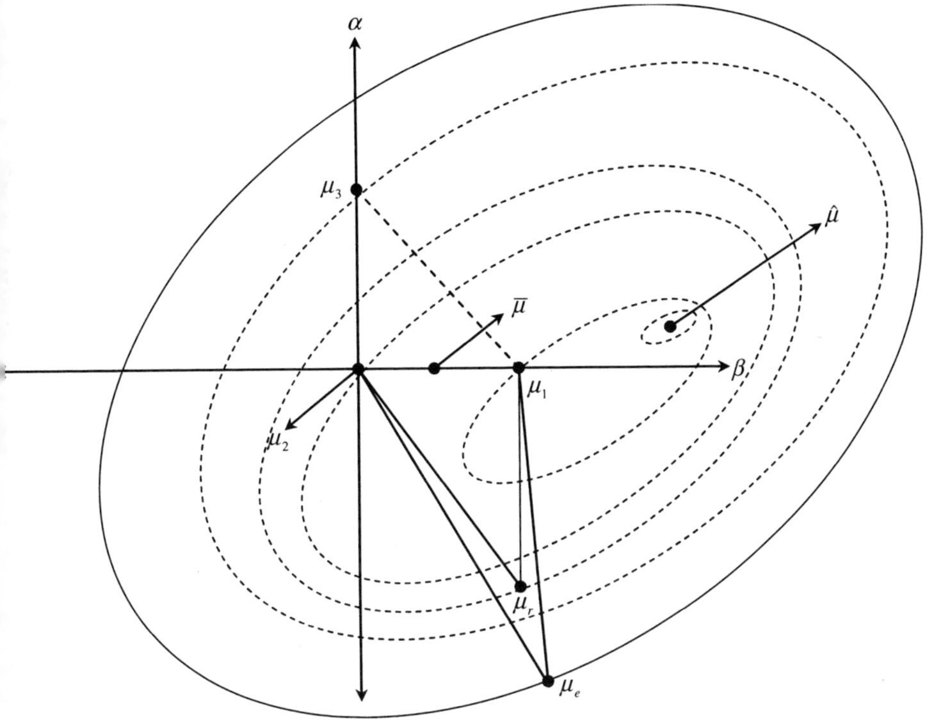

Figure 8.3 Expansion point.

If $f(\mu_1) \leq f(\mu_r) < f(\mu_2)$ does not hold, as is true with the scenario depicted in figure 8.2, two alternative possibilities arise. If $f(\mu_r) < f(\mu_1)$, an expansion step is taken; if instead $f(\mu_r) \geq f(\mu_2)$, a contraction step is taken. Both fall under the heading of a nonshrink step. In the former case, the algorithm attempts to improve upon μ_r by computing

$$\mu_e = \overline{\mu} + 2(\mu_r - \overline{\mu}). \tag{8.14}$$

If this indeed turns out to be an improvement, μ_e is accepted in favor of μ_r and the simplex constructed using (μ_1, μ_2, μ_e) is passed to the next iteration. Otherwise μ_r is retained and the simplex constructed using (μ_1, μ_2, μ_r) is passed to the next iteration. In the example depicted in figure 8.3, the expansion point would not be accepted.

If $f(\mu_r) \geq f(\mu_2)$, the algorithm proceeds to a contraction step, of which there are two types. An outside contraction is conducted if $f(\mu_3) > f(\mu_r) \geq f(\mu_2)$; that is, if μ_r is better than the worse vertex but inferior

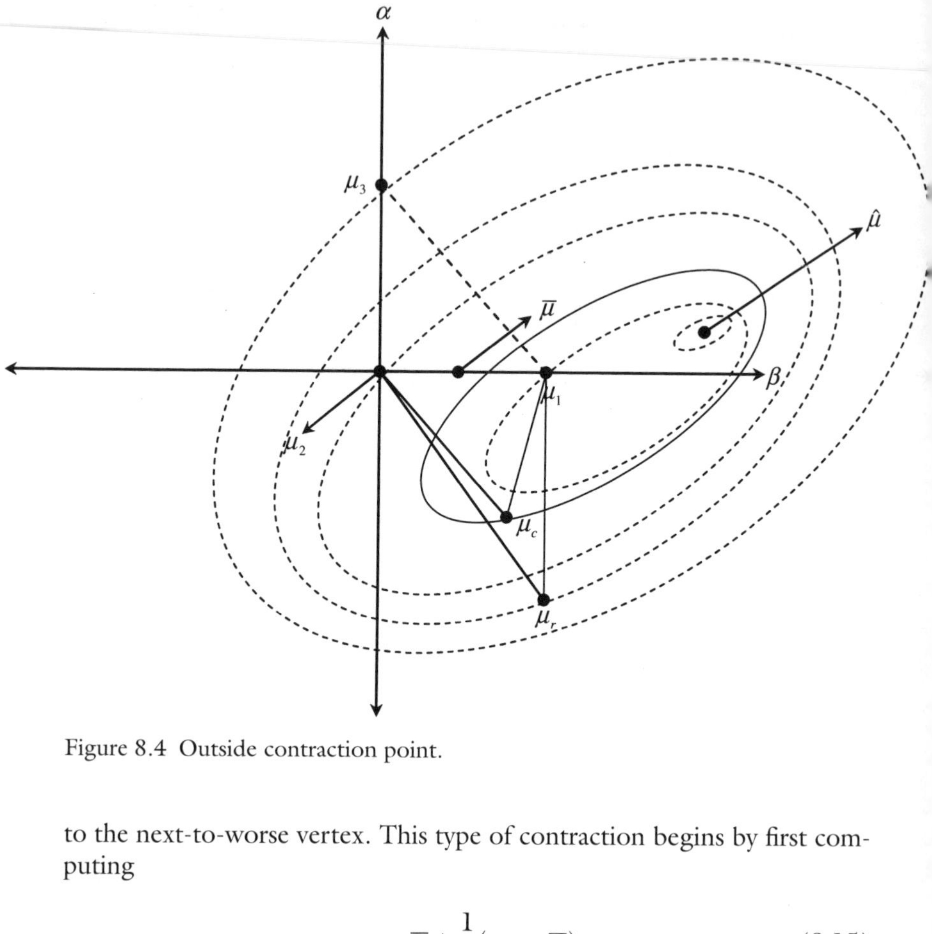

Figure 8.4 Outside contraction point.

to the next-to-worse vertex. This type of contraction begins by first computing

$$\mu_c = \overline{\mu} + \frac{1}{2}(\mu_r - \overline{\mu}). \tag{8.15}$$

If $f(\mu_c) \leq f(\mu_r)$, as is the case in the example depicted in figure 8.4, the new simplex computed using (μ_1, μ_2, μ_c) is passed to the next iteration. Alternatively, if $f(\mu_c) > f(\mu_r)$, then μ_c is discarded. In this case the algorithm moves to a shrink step, described below. Note that the rejection of an outside contraction leads to a shrink step even though the reflection point has improved over the worst point μ_3, a property of the Nelder-Mead method noted by Lagarias et al. (1998).

An inside contraction is performed for the case in which $f(\mu_r) \geq f(\mu_3)$. This is performed by computing

$$\mu_{cc} = \overline{\mu} - \frac{1}{2}(\mu_r - \mu_3). \tag{8.16}$$

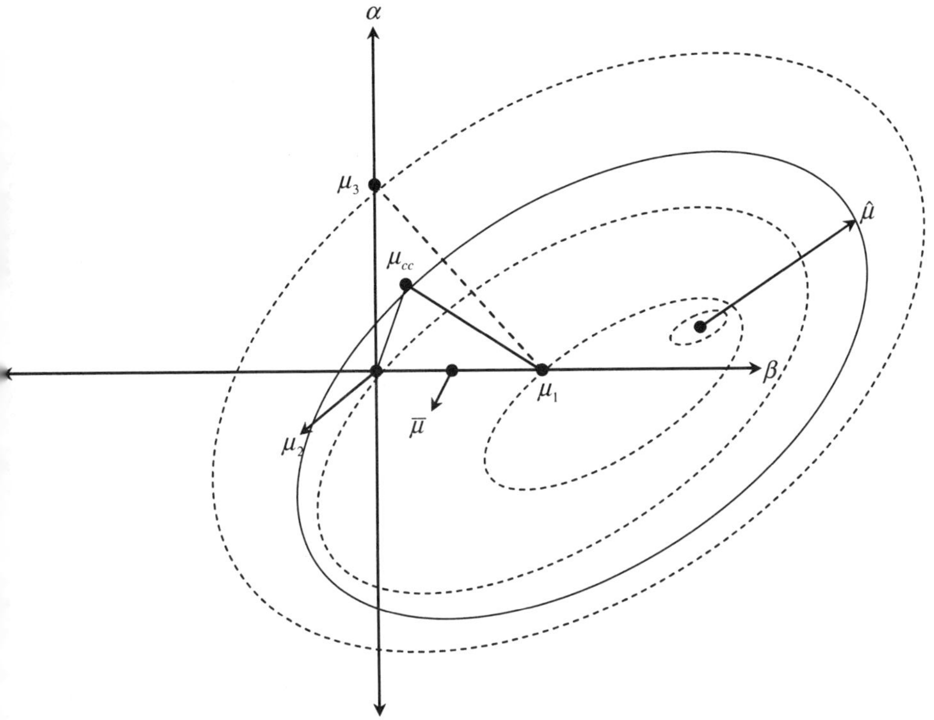

Figure 8.5 Inside contraction point.

If $f(\mu_{cc}) < f(\mu_3)$, the simplex constructed using (μ_1, μ_2, μ_{cc}) is passed to the next iteration; otherwise the algorithm proceeds to a shrink step. An inside contraction point is depicted in figure 8.5.

If the algorithm reaches a shrink step, two new vertices are constructed:

$$\nu_l = \mu_1 + \frac{1}{2}(\mu_l - \mu_1),\ l = 2, 3. \tag{8.17}$$

This results in the simplex constructed using (μ_1, ν_2, ν_3), which is passed to the next iteration. This simplex is depicted for the example in figure 8.6.

The full range of possibilities outlined above for the completion of a single iteration are illustrated in the flow chart depicted in figure 8.7. As illustrated by the two-dimensional example, the objective of an iteration is to create a new simplex that comes closer to containing $\widehat{\mu}$ as an exclusive element.

We now indicate briefly how the iteration process extends to the k-dimensional case. Under the first step of the ith iteration in the k-dimensional

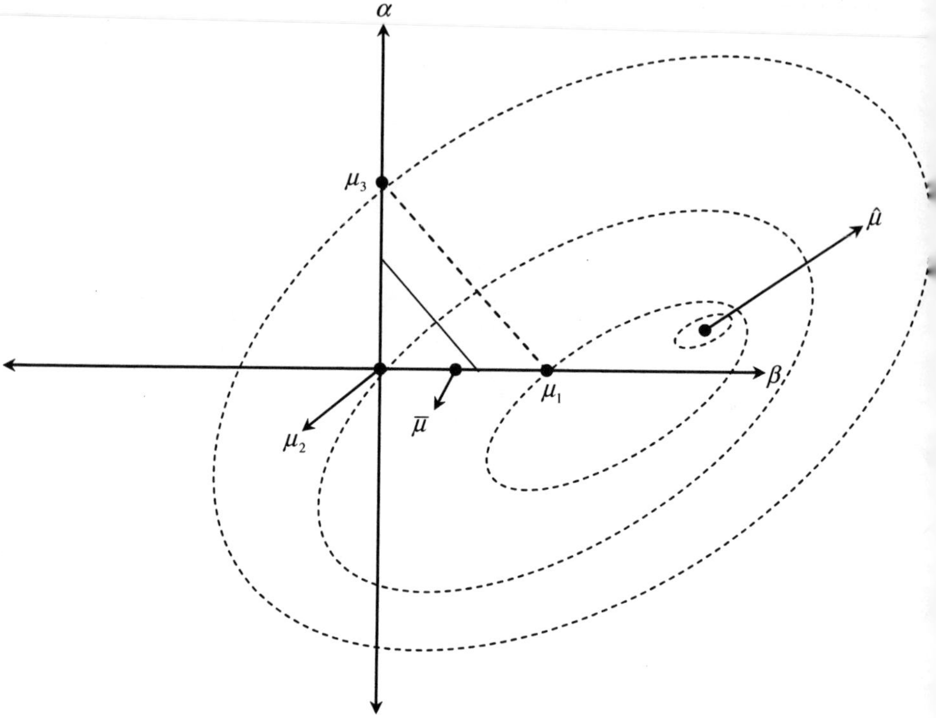

Figure 8.6 Shrink step.

case, the vertices of the simplex $\Delta_k^{(i)}$, denoted as $\mu_1^{(i)}, \ldots, \mu_{k+1}^{(i)}$, are ordered such that

$$f(\mu_1^{(i)}) \leq \cdots \leq f(\mu_{k+1}^{(i)}). \tag{8.18}$$

(Under the first iteration, μ_{k+1}^0 is typically chosen as the zero vector.) Once again subsuming iteration numbers, the next step involves the computation of a reflection point:

$$\mu_r = \overline{\mu} + \rho(\overline{\mu} - \mu_{k+1}), \tag{8.19}$$

$$\overline{\mu} = \frac{\sum_{j=1}^{k} \mu_j}{k}, \qquad \rho > 0. \tag{8.20}$$

If $f(\mu_1) \leq f(\mu_r) < f(\mu_k)$, μ_{k+1} is replaced by μ_r and the resulting simplex is passed to the next iteration. Otherwise if $f(\mu_r) < f(\mu_1)$, an expansion point is computed as

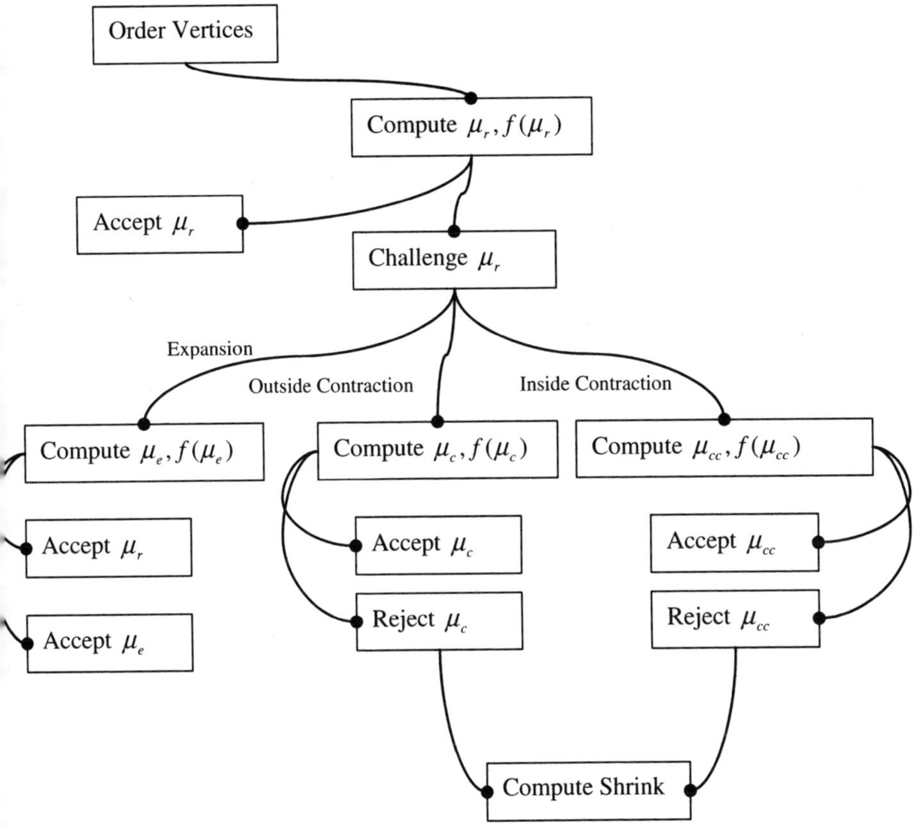

Figure 8.7 Flow chart for simplex method iteration.

$$\begin{aligned} \mu_e &= \overline{\mu} + \chi(\mu_r - \overline{\mu}) \\ &= (1 + \rho\chi)\overline{\mu} - \rho\mu_{k+1}, \qquad \chi > \rho. \end{aligned} \tag{8.21}$$

If $f(\mu_e) < f(\mu_r)$, μ_e replaces μ_r; otherwise μ_r is retained and the resulting simplex is passed to the next iteration.

If instead $f(\mu_r) \geq f(\mu_k)$, one of two types of a contraction is performed. If $f(\mu_k) \leq f(\mu_r) < f(\mu_{k+1})$, an outside contraction point is computed:

$$\begin{aligned} \mu_c &= \overline{\mu} + \gamma(\mu_r - \overline{\mu}) \\ &= (1 + \rho\gamma)\overline{\mu} - \rho\gamma\mu_{k+1}, \qquad \gamma \in (0, 1). \end{aligned} \tag{8.22}$$

If $f(\mu_c) \leq f(\mu_r)$, μ_c is accepted; otherwise a shrink step is performed. If instead $f(\mu_r) \geq f(\mu_{k+1})$, an inside contraction point is computed:

$$\begin{aligned} \mu_{cc} &= \overline{\mu} - \gamma(\overline{\mu} - \mu_{k+1}) \\ &= (1-\gamma)\overline{\mu} + \gamma\mu_{k+1} \longrightarrow f(\mu_{c'}). \end{aligned} \tag{8.23}$$

If $f(\mu_{cc}) < f(\mu_{k+1})$, μ_{cc} is accepted; otherwise a shrink step is performed.

If a shrink step is required, a new set of points

$$\nu_l = \mu_1 + \sigma(\mu_l - \mu_1), \qquad \sigma \in (0,1), \qquad l = 1, \ldots, k+1$$

is computed, resulting in the simplex constructed using $(\mu_1, \nu_2, \ldots, \nu_{k+1})$. Upon completion of an iteration, a new iteration begins with the reordering of vertices as indicated in (8.18). Note that the simplex procedure we have described for the k-dimensional case is governed by the set of parameters $(\rho, \chi, \gamma, \sigma)$. Values of these parameters corresponding to the Nelder-Mead simplex are given by

$$\rho = 1, \; \chi = 2, \; \gamma = \frac{1}{2}, \; \sigma = \frac{1}{2}. \tag{8.24}$$

For cases in which ties result in the comparisons described above, Lagarias et al. propose two tie-breaking rules: one for shrink steps and one for nonshrink steps. Under the former, if there is a tie between the best point retained (μ_1) and any one of the new points, the best point is retained for the next iteration. Specifically:

$$f(\mu_1^{(i)}) = \min\left\{f(\nu_2^{(i)}), \ldots, f(\nu_{k+1}^{(i)})\right\} \rightarrow \mu_1^{(i+1)} = \mu_1^{(i)}. \tag{8.25}$$

Under the latter, the worst vertex $\mu_{k+1}^{(i)}$ is dropped in favor of an accepted point, say $\varpi^{(i)}$, and if there is a tie with any of the remaining vertices, the accepted point takes position m in the vertices of the simplex $\Delta^{(i+1)}$, where

$$m = \max_{0 \leq n \leq k} \{m | f(\varpi^{(i)}) < f(\mu_{n+1}^{(i)})\}. \tag{8.26}$$

The remaining vertices retain their positions.

Regarding convergence, two tolerance measures are set in order to determine whether a minimum has been reached. The first measure is with respect to the "diameter" of the simplex $\Delta_k^{(i)}$:

$$diam(\Delta_k^{(i)}) = \max_{l \neq m} \left\| \mu_l^{(i)} - \mu_m^{(i)} \right\|, \tag{8.27}$$

$$\left\| \mu_l^{(i)} - \mu_m^{(i)} \right\| = \sqrt{\sum\nolimits_{j=1}^{k} (\mu_{l,j}^{(i)} - \mu_{m,j}^{(i)})^2}. \tag{8.28}$$

When this diameter reaches a predetermined level, typically equalling 10^{-4}, the first criterion has been reached. The second measure is with respect to the function values $f^{(i)}$. When iterations reach a point such that the difference $f^{(i+1)}(\mu_1^{i+1}) - f^{(i)}(\mu_1^i)$ reaches a predetermined level, again typically equalling 10^{-4}, the iterations are terminated and the algorithm is declared to have converged. The vertex μ_1 obtained in the final iteration is taken as the estimate $\widehat{\mu}$.

The output of non-derivative-based methods is a vector of estimates $\widehat{\mu}$ and the corresponding log-likelihood value $f(\widehat{\mu}) = \log L(X|\widehat{\mu})$. The associated covariance matrix

$$\widehat{\Sigma}_\mu = \left[-\frac{\partial^2 \log L(X|\widehat{\mu})}{\partial \widehat{\mu} \partial \widehat{\mu}'} \right]^{-1} \tag{8.29}$$

must typically be computed numerically. This may be achieved using a nested gradient-calculation procedure. Specifically, letting $\iota(\widehat{\mu})$ denote the gradient of $\log L(X|\mu)$ calculated at $\widehat{\mu}$, $\widehat{\Sigma}_\mu$ may be obtained by calculating the gradient of $\iota(\widehat{\mu})$ at $\widehat{\mu}$.[4]

We conclude by noting that because simplex methods do not rely on the calculation of derivatives in seeking a minimum, they tend to converge relatively quickly in comparison to their derivative-based counterparts. Also, they are not as susceptible to problems arising from the presence of discontinuities in the likelihood surface. Although they do not naturally produce standard errors as by-products of their search methodology, this can be overcome using finite-difference methods (see Judd, 1998, for a discussion of numerical approaches to computing gradients and Hessians). Alternatively, Harvey (1999) suggests that such methods can be used to identify attractive initial values for μ, which can then be fed into derivative-based methods to obtain estimated standard errors. We now turn to a discussion of these methods.

8.3.2 Derivative-Based Methods

Derivative-based methods are patterned after the heuristic characterization of function optimization provided in section 8.2. (Several versions of derivative-based methods exist. For textbook discussions, see Judd, 1998; Hamilton, 1994; and Harvey, 1999.)[5] Recall that if $\widehat{\mu}$ minimizes $f(\mu)$, it satisfies the first-order condition

[4] The GAUSS procedure `hessp` is available for this purpose.

[5] Code for executing these methods is available in the Maximum Likelihood toolbox of GAUSS.

$$\frac{\partial f}{\partial \mu}|_{\mu=\widehat{\mu}} = \iota(\widehat{\mu}) = 0;$$

and the associated Hessian $\Im(\widehat{\mu})$ is positive definite (provided $\iota(\mu)$ and $\Im(\mu)$ exist and are continuous). Now consider the second-order Taylor Series expansion of the function to be minimized around the "true" value $\widehat{\mu}$:

$$f(\mu) \approx f(\widehat{\mu}) + (\mu - \widehat{\mu})\iota(\widehat{\mu}) + \frac{1}{2}(\mu - \widehat{\mu})'\Im(\widehat{\mu})(\mu - \widehat{\mu}). \tag{8.30}$$

Differentiating this expansion with respect to μ and imposing the first-order condition for a minimum, we obtain the following iterative scheme commonly known as Newton's Method:

$$\mu^{i+1} = \mu^i - \Im^{-1}(\mu^i)\iota(\mu^i). \tag{8.31}$$

Iterations on (8.31) will converge to $\widehat{\mu}$ provided that the Hessian is always positive definitive, a condition that is in no way guaranteed. If the Hessian is ever singular in a given iteration, the scheme will collapse. Alternatively, if the Hessian ever fails to be positive definite the scheme can generate increasing rather than decreasing values of $f(\mu)$. Indeed, if the step size produced by (8.31) turns out to be excessively large, such "overshooting" can occur even if the Hessian is positive definite. Optimization algorithms that incorporate solutions to these problems fall under the general heading of quasi-Newton methods; we now discuss such methods.

In order to overcome problems of "overshooting," an additional parameter known as a step length (λ) is introduced:

$$\mu^{i+1} = \mu^i - \lambda\Im^{-1}(\mu^i)\iota(\mu^i). \tag{8.32}$$

If $\Im$ is positive definite and μ^i is not a minimum, then, as noted by Harvey (1999), there always exists a positive λ such that $f(\mu^{i+1}) < f(\mu^i)$, which helps keep the iterations going until convergence. A common technique for computing λ is the solution to

$$\min_{\lambda} \quad f(\mu^i + \lambda\iota^i), \tag{8.33}$$

which is computed at each iteration.

To avoid problems associated with non-positive definite Hessians, quasi-Newton methods replace $\Im(\mu^i)$ with alternative matrices that mimic the role of the Hessian, but that are guaranteed to be positive definite. Two popular alternatives are due to Broyden, Fletcher, Goldfarb, and Shanno (BFGS) and Davidson, Fletcher, and Powell (DFP). Letting

$$D^i = \Im^{-1}(\mu^i), \quad p = (\mu^{i+1} - \mu^i),$$

and

$$q = \iota(\mu^{i+1}) - \iota(\mu^i),$$

the BFGS alternative constructs D iteratively using

$$D^{i+1} = D^i + \frac{pp'}{p'q}\left[1 + \frac{q'D^i q}{p'q}\right] - \frac{Dqp' + pq'D}{p'q}. \tag{8.34}$$

The DFP alternative constructs D iteratively using

$$D^{i+1} = D^i + \frac{pp'}{p'q} - \frac{Dqq'D}{q'Dq}. \tag{8.35}$$

In both cases, initial specifications of the Hessian are typically chosen as the identity matrix, which is positive definite. Under either alternative, the approximation obtained in the final iteration is used to construct the estimated variance-covariance matrix associated with $\widehat{\mu}$, as indicated in (8.10).

With respect to convergence, two criteria are often simultaneously used. Letting μ^i represent a proposed minimum, the criteria involve comparisons of the minimum elements of $(\mu^{i+1} - \mu^i)$ and $\iota(\mu^i)$ with prespecified thresholds, typically 10^{-4}. Heuristically this translates into a check of whether the sequence of estimates has converged and the first-order condition is satisfied. As noted, because they require the continuous calculations of gradients and Hessians, derivative-based methods tend to be slow to converge relative to simplex methods. However, they do produce estimates of both parameter values and associated standard errors as a by-product of the optimization process, so they are attractive in this regard.

Additional considerations regarding the choice of simplex versus derivative-based methods arise when $f(\mu)$ is not well-behaved, as we have assumed throughout this section. Problems associated with $f(\mu)$ fall into three general categories: discontinuities, local minima, and flat surfaces. We now turn to a discussion of these problems, and methods for overcoming them.

8.4 Ill-Behaved Likelihood Surfaces: Problems and Solutions

The preceding presentations have taken for granted the existence of well-behaved likelihood surfaces. This of course is not always the case in practice, and as noted, implementation can be particularly challenging in applications involving DSGE models. The primary source of complication arises from the fact that although optimization is with respect to μ, the likelihood function itself is parameterized in terms of $(F(\mu),\ G(\mu),\ Q(\mu),\ H(\mu))$, and as we have seen, mappings from μ into the parameters of these matrices tend to be complex, highly nonlinear, and analytically intractable. Here we discuss three classes of problems that can arise in minimizing a function: discontinuities, multiple local minima, and identification.

8.4.1 Problems

Loosely, a likelihood surface contains discontinuities if it features "walls" or "cliffs," so that a small change in a parameter value results in a jump in the value of the function. At such a point the function is not differentiable, thus posing an obvious challenge in the implementation of derivative-based methods. Prepackaged quasi-Newton software routines typically produce as output warnings when discontinuities are encountered. Alternatively, grid plots provide an effective diagnostic tool. In fact, such plots are effective in identifying all three types of problems that can arise in seeking to minimize a function, thus a brief digression is worthwhile.

Grid plots are merely graphical explorations of the likelihood surface. Two-dimensional plots are constructed by fixing all but the jth element μ^j of the parameters at particular values, and tracing $f(\mu)$ over a grid of values specified for μ^j. Three-dimensional plots are constructed analogously by tracing $f(\mu)$ over ranges specified for two elements of μ. Correlations among the elements of μ can pose challenges in effectively constructing and interpreting plots, because they will render particular plots sensitive to values specified for the fixed elements of μ. However, initial estimates of the Hessian can be helpful in identifying key dimensions along which correlations exist, and thus dimensions along which the sensitivity of plots can be usefully explored. Even in cases in which convergence to a minimum appears to have been achieved successfully, the construction of grid plots in the neighborhood of the optimum is an advisable practice.

Discontinuities pose less of a challenge in implementing simplex methods, because the calculation of reflection points, expansion points, and so on are unencumbered by their existence. Due to this fact, Christopher Sims has developed a hybrid optimization algorithm that combines the derivative-based BFGS method with a simplex algorithm that is triggered when discontinuities are encountered.[6]

[6] Software facilitating its implementation is available on his Web site: http://www.princeton.edu/~sims/

When $f(\mu)$ features local minima, the obvious possibility arises that the estimate $\widehat{\mu}$ delivered by either class of optimization routine is not in fact a global minimum. Once again, grid plots constructed using generous ranges for parameters are helpful in detecting such instances. In addition, investigations of the sensitivity of $\widehat{\mu}$ to the use of alternative starting values can be used for this purpose.

Finally, an identification problem is said to exist when alternative specifications of μ yield the same value of $f(\mu)$. Colloquially, identification problems exist if the likelihood function is flat along any dimension of the parameter space. In the context of evaluating state-space representations using the Kalman filter, identification problems are manifested by the inability to invert the matrix $\Omega_{t|t-1}$.

8.4.2 Solutions

Just as DSGE models pose special challenges in the context of maximum-likelihood analysis, they also offer special solutions. In particular, it is most often the case that the elements of μ are subject to a priori restrictions that, when imposed, can be helpful in avoiding the problems mentioned above. For example, parameters representing discount factors, depreciation rates, capital's share of output, and so on, must all lie between zero and one, and moreover, only fractions of this range warrant serious consideration. In other words, guidance from theory is typically available in imposing restrictions on ranges of the parameter space over which optimization searches are conducted. Moreover, the imposition of such restrictions is straightforward via the use of parameter transformations.

Parameter transformations are implemented by establishing relationships of the form

$$\mu = \mu(\omega), \tag{8.36}$$

where ω is $l \times 1$, and optimizing $f(\mu(\omega))$ with respect to ω. Given estimates $(\widehat{\omega}, \widehat{\Sigma}_\omega)$ generated by optimizing over ω, corresponding estimates for μ are given by

$$\widehat{\mu} = \mu(\widehat{\omega}), \qquad \widehat{\Sigma}_\mu = [\mu'(\widehat{\omega})]\widehat{\Sigma}_\omega[\mu'(\widehat{\omega})]', \tag{8.37}$$

where $[\mu'(\widehat{\omega})]$ is the $k \times l$ Jacobian matrix evaluated at $\widehat{\omega}$.

Three goals should be considered in establishing useful parameter transformations. First, the transformations should eliminate the need to impose additional restrictions on ranges for the individual elements ω^j over which the search is to be conducted. Second, the transformations should be made so that $f(\mu(\omega))$ is reasonably responsive to changes in the individual elements ω^j. For example, for a one-to-one mapping between μ^j and ω^j, if $\partial\mu^j/\omega^j$ is nearly zero in the neighborhood of the minimum, it will be difficult for any optimization routine to pin down the minimizing value. Third, the Hessian associated with ω should be "balanced": the sums of its columns (and rows) should be roughly equal. Convergence is greatly enhanced by the use of transformations that help achieve balance.

Parameter transformations of particular relevance are as follows. If it is desired that an individual element μ^j be constrained to lie in the range (a, b), but no information is available regarding where in this range an optimal value might lie, the following logistic transformation is useful:

$$\mu^j = a + \frac{b-a}{1+e^{\omega^j}}. \tag{8.38}$$

A starting value of $\omega_0^j = 0$ will place μ^j at the midpoint between a and b. If it turns out that optimization fails given this specification, it may be the case that it is not well-suited for meeting the second or third goals. For example, if the optimal value of μ^j lies near one of its boundaries, then $\partial\mu^j/\omega^j$ will be nearly zero. In this case it may be useful to introduce an additional parameter χ:

$$\mu^j = a + \frac{b-a}{1+e^{\chi\omega^j}}. \tag{8.39}$$

As illustrated in figure 8.8 (constructed using $a = 0, b = 1$), as χ decreases, $\partial\mu^j/\omega^j$ increases near the boundaries. Problems with balance can also be addressed given the introduction of χ.

Finally, it may also be useful to introduce a centering parameter c:

$$\mu^j = a + \frac{b-a}{1+e^{\chi(\omega^j+c)}}. \tag{8.40}$$

If a good starting value for μ^j is known a priori, denoted μ_0^j, then zero will be a good starting value for ω^j given the specification

$$c = \frac{1}{\chi}\log\left(\frac{b-a}{\mu_0^j - a} - 1\right); \tag{8.41}$$

moreover, $\widehat{\omega^j}$ will be approximately zero if the starting value μ_0^j turned out to lie near $\widehat{\mu^j}$.

For a parameter restricted merely to be positive, a useful transformation is

$$\mu^j = e^{\chi\omega^j}, \tag{8.42}$$

where again χ can be adjusted to deal with cases under which μ^j lies near its boundary, or to help achieve balance.

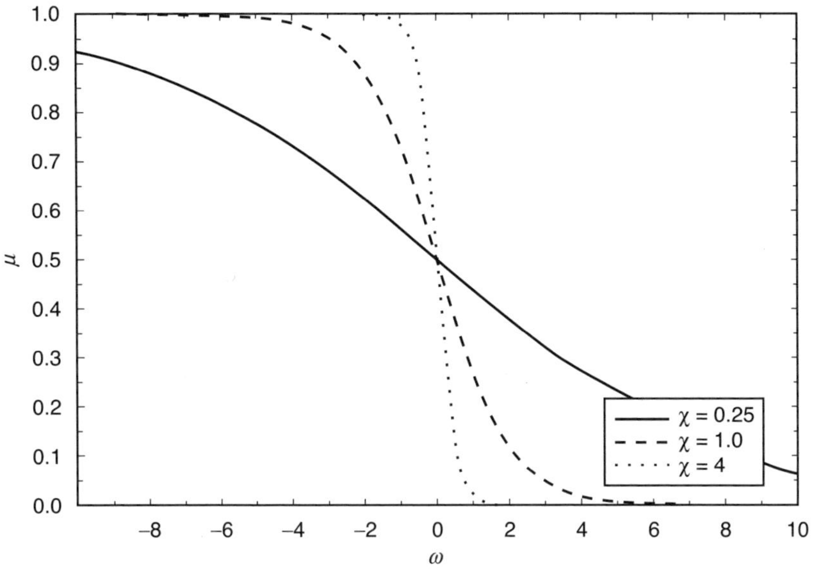

Figure 8.8 Logistic transformations.

If any of the problems mentioned above cannot be overcome by restricting ranges over the elements of μ, four additional potential remedies are available. First, the outcome of calibration or method-of-moments exercises conducted prior to estimation can help with the specification of effective starting values μ_0, or be used to impose additional restrictions for conducting the optimization search. Second, multi-step optimization can be used. The idea here is to split the parameter vector μ into sub-vectors (say, μ^1 and μ^2 for a two-step procedure), and to optimize over each sub-vector in turn. Sequential iteration can help lead to overall convergence. Third, a sub-vector of μ can simply be fixed (e.g., at calibrated values), and optimization conducted over the remaining elements.

Finally, quasi-Bayesian methods can be used in order to help induce curvature in the likelihood function. Such methods involve augmenting the log-likelihood function with a prior distribution specified over μ, denoted by $\pi(\mu)$, and minimizing

$$-\log L(X|\mu) - \log \pi(\mu). \tag{8.43}$$

In this context, $\log \pi(\mu)$ can be thought of a penalty function. Ruge-Murcia (2003) evaluated the use of this approach in the context of estimating a DSGE model via maximum likelihood, and found it useful as a gentle means of imposing a priori restrictions in the exercise.

8.5 Model Diagnostics and Parameter Stability

Having obtained estimates of μ and associated standard errors, model diagnostics can be conducted. Here we discuss four types of diagnostics: tests of restrictions imposed on individual elements of μ, tests of restrictions imposed across multiple elements of μ, tests of the stability of μ over time, and given evidence of temporal parameter instability, a procedure designed to help pinpoint the date at which a structural break is likely to have occurred.

With $\widehat{\sigma}_{\mu^j}$ denoting the standard error associated with $\widehat{\mu}^j$, the statistical significance of the difference between $\widehat{\mu}^j$ and $\overline{\mu}^j$ can be assessed using the t-statistic:

$$t^j = \frac{\widehat{\mu}^j - \overline{\mu}^j}{\widehat{\sigma}_{\mu^j}}. \tag{8.44}$$

The statistic t^j measures the distance of $\widehat{\mu}^j$ from $\overline{\mu}^j$ in units of the estimated standard error $\widehat{\sigma}_{\mu^j}$. Under the null hypothesis that $\mu^j = \overline{\mu}^j$, t^j is distributed as Student's t with $T-1$ degrees of freedom, where T denotes the sample size. Large values of t^j are assigned low probabilities, or p-values, under this distribution; when p-values lie below a pre-specified critical value, the null hypothesis is rejected; otherwise it is accepted.

Consider now a collection of restrictions imposed upon μ of the form

$$g(\mu) = 0, \tag{8.45}$$

where $g(\mu)$ is an l-valued differentiable function, with $l < k$. Letting $\widehat{\mu}_R$ denote the value of μ that minimizes $f(\mu)$ subject to (8.45), the null hypothesis that the restrictions in fact hold can be tested using the likelihood ratio statistic:

$$LR = 2\log\left[L(X|\widehat{\mu}) - L(X|\widehat{\mu}_R)\right]. \tag{8.46}$$

Under the null, LR is distributed as $\chi^2(l)$. As the gap between the unrestricted and restricted likelihood functions widens, LR increases, and once again its associated p-value falls. As with the t-test, if the p-value falls below a pre-specified threshold, the null is rejected; otherwise it is accepted.

Regarding implementation, consider the case in which (8.45) can be rewritten as

$$\mu = r(\omega), \tag{8.47}$$

where ω is an ℓ-vector such that $\ell = k - l$. Then $L(X|\widehat{\mu}_R)$ can be calculated by maximizing over ω, and setting $\widehat{\mu}_R = r(\widehat{\omega})$.

A special adaptation of the *LR* test can be used to conduct tests of temporal parameter stability. Let $\widehat{\mu}_1$ and $\widehat{\mu}_2$ denote parameter estimates obtained over two disjoint but fully inclusive ranges of the sample period. That is, $\widehat{\mu}_1$ is estimated over the time span $[1, t_1]$, and $\widehat{\mu}_2$ is estimated over the time span $[t_1 + 1, T]$. Letting X_1 and X_2 denote respective samples spanning these time intervals, the *LR* test of the null hypothesis that $\mu_1 = \mu_2$ is given by

$$\mathcal{L} = 2\left[\log L(X_1 | \widehat{\mu}_1) + \log L(X_2 | \widehat{\mu}_1) - \log L(X | \widehat{\mu})\right]. \tag{8.48}$$

For the specification of a single candidate breakpoint t_1, $\mathcal{L}$ will be distributed as $\chi^2(k)$, and the null hypothesis can be assessed as described above. However, if the researcher conducts a search over alternative possible break dates, for example, by searching for the date at which the associated p-value is minimized, then the resulting distribution of $\mathcal{L}$ will not be distributed as $\chi^2(k)$. Andrews (1993) and Hansen (1997) have developed formal testing procedures that enable specification searches over t_1, but they are impractical to conduct in this context because they involve calculations of $L(X_1 | \widehat{\mu}_1)$ and $L(X_2 | \widehat{\mu}_2)$ for each candidate break date, and such calculations can be extremely time-consuming in working with DSGE models.

However, progress can be made in this context if in place of a formal test for the occurrence of a break over a range of possible dates, we consider the alternative objective of calculating conditional probabilities associated with the occurrence of a break over a range of dates. For this purpose, a procedure developed by DeJong, Liesenfeld, and Richard (2005a) for timing the occurrence of a *known* break can be adopted. Their procedure is designed for implementation after a rejection of the structural-stability hypothesis generated by a preliminary test is attained, for example, using the testing strategy developed by Andrews (1993) and Hansen (1997). We proceed in this context under the caveat that the results of such a pretest will in general be unavailable.

DeJong et al.'s motivation for developing their procedure is that although the structural stability tests of Andrews and Hansen are effective in identifying the occurrence of breaks, they are ineffective in pinpointing timing. The adoption of the relatively modest objective of calculating conditional probabilities associated with breaks, in place of the objective of seeking to reject the null hypothesis of structural stability, accounts for the relative effectiveness of DeJong et al.'s procedure in pinpointing timing.

The procedure requires two sets of ML estimates: $\widehat{\mu}_1$ calculated over an early portion of the sample $[1, T_1]$, and $\widehat{\mu}_2$ calculated over a late portion of the sample $[T_2 + 1, T]$. The range of dates over which potential break dates are contained is thus $[T_1 + 1, T_2]$. For each $j \in [T_1 + 1, T_2]$, consider a division of the entire sample into two intervals: $\{X_t\}_{t=1}^{j}$ and $\{X_t\}_{t=j+1}^{T}$. The likelihood value associated with this division of the sample is given by

$$L(j) = L(\{X_t\}_{t=1}^{j} \mid \widehat{\mu}_1) \times L_2(\{X_t\}_{t=j+1}^{T} \mid \widehat{\mu}_2). \qquad (8.49)$$

Notice that if there is a distinct difference between the alternative likelihood functions parametrized under $\widehat{\mu}_1$ and $\widehat{\mu}_2$ due to a structural break, then $L(j)$ will be sensitive to changes in j that improve upon or worsen the alignment of the division of the sample with the date at which the break has occurred.

Consider now the ratio of $L(j)$ to the sum of likelihoods calculated for every possible division of the sample between $[T_1 + 1, T_2]$:

$$p(j) = \frac{L(j)}{\sum_{\tau=T_1+1}^{T_2} L(\tau)}. \qquad (8.50)$$

Given the known occurrence of a break between $[T_1 + 1, T_2]$,

$$\sum_{\tau=T_1+1}^{T_2} L(\tau)$$

represents the likelihood associated with the full range of possible scenarios regarding a break, and thus $p(j)$ is appropriately interpreted as the probability associated with a break at date j. Absent the known occurrence of a break, it is still possible to assess the relative size of $p(j)$ across alternative values of j. A relatively flat profile signals the absence of a break, whereas abrupt peaks in the profile indicate potential breaks.

8.6 Empirical Application: Identifying Sources of Business Cycle Fluctuations

To demonstrate the implementation of ML techniques for estimating DSGE models, we build upon Ireland's (2004a) analysis of the New Keynesian model introduced in chapter 5, section 5.2. Recall that this model is an extension of a standard RBC model under which demand shocks, cost-push shocks, and shocks to the central bank's monetary policy function combine with technology shocks in driving business-cycle fluctuations. Using ML estimation techniques, the empirical objective Ireland pursued in estimating this model was to assess the relative importance of these shocks in accounting for fluctuations in output growth, inflation, and the output gap. He pursued this objective by constructing impulse response functions and variance decompositions (introduced in chapter 4), which are designed to measure responses of these series to innovations in the respective shocks.

Here we extend this analysis using the smoothing feature of the Kalman filter introduced in chapter 2. Specifically, conditional on the model estimates obtained by Ireland, we back out the implied time series observations on innovations to the shocks, along with the shocks themselves, and study the behavior of these measured series over stages of the business cycle. In part, our intent is to depict smoothing as an important by-product of full-information analyses based on the Kalman filter. Examples of similar exercises in the RBC literature are given by DeJong, Ingram, and Whiteman (2000a) and Chari, Kehoe, and McGrattan (2004). It bears emphasizing that in any such exercise, inferences regarding the behavior of model unobservables are conditional not only on the behavior of the corresponding observable variables, but also on the specification of the model under investigation.

To be clear regarding our terminology, the demand, cost-push, and technology shocks follow AR representations of the form

$$s_t = \rho_s s_{t-1} + \varepsilon_{st}, \qquad \varepsilon_s \sim N(0, \sigma_s^2). \tag{8.51}$$

When we refer to the shocks themselves, we refer to s_t; when we refer to innovations to the shocks, we refer to ε_{st}. Shocks to the monetary policy function are *iid*, thus there is no distinction between innovations and shocks in this case.

We begin with an overview of Ireland's analysis. Using quarterly data over the period 1948.1–2003.1 on output growth, inflation, and short-term nominal interest rates, Ireland sought to obtain ML estimates of the full set of parameters of the model.[7] Denoting the demand, cost-push, technology, and policy shocks as $(\widetilde{a}, \widetilde{e}, \widetilde{z}, \varepsilon_r)$, the key equations of the model are the IS curve, the Phillips curve, and the Taylor Rule (the full specification of the model is given in chapter 5, section 5.2):

$$\widetilde{o} = \alpha_o \widetilde{o}^- + (1 - \alpha_o) E_t \widetilde{o}' \quad (\widetilde{r} - E_t \widetilde{\pi}') + (1 - \omega)(1 - \rho_a)\widetilde{a} \tag{8.52}$$

$$\widetilde{\pi} = \beta \alpha_\pi \widetilde{\pi}^- + \beta(1 - \alpha_\pi) E_t \widetilde{\pi}' + \psi \widetilde{o} - \widetilde{e}, \tag{8.53}$$

$$\widetilde{r}' = \rho_r \widetilde{r} + \rho_\pi \widetilde{\pi}' + \rho_g \widetilde{g}' + \rho_o \widetilde{o}' + \varepsilon_r'. \tag{8.54}$$

Here, tildes denote logged departures of variables from steady state values, x' denotes the period-$(t+1)$ observation of x, and x^- denotes the period-$(t-1)$ observation of x. Inflation, nominal interest rates, and the output

[7] The data and computer code he used are available at `www2.bc.edu/~irelandp`.

gap are denoted as $(\widetilde{\pi}, \widetilde{r}, \widetilde{o})$, where $\widetilde{o} = \widetilde{y} - \omega\widetilde{a}$, $\widetilde{y}$ denotes output, and ω denotes the inverse of the elasticity of labor supply.

Sample means were removed from the data prior to analysis. In addition, sample means were used to pin down the parameters z and π, which serve to identify steady state values of output growth and inflation: $z = 1.0048$, which matches the averaged annualized growth rate observed for output of 1.95%; and $\pi = 1.0086$, matching the average annual inflation rate of 3.48%. Given the specification of π, the sample mean of nominal interest rates in principle serves to identify the real steady state interest rate, and thus the discount factor β. However, identifying β in this fashion implies an implausible value in excess of 1, which is a manifestation of the risk-free rate puzzle discussed in chapter 5, section 5.3. In response, Ireland broke the link between nominal interest rates and β by fixing β at 0.99, and removing the mean nominal rate of 5.09% from the data irrespective of this specification. Finally, the policy parameter ρ_r was fixed at unity; thus deviations from steady state levels of inflation, output growth, and the output gap have persistent affects on interest rates.

Ireland's initial attempts at estimating the remaining parameters resulted in estimates of ψ, the output-gap parameter in the Phillips curve, that he deemed to be unreasonably small (implying enormous nominal price-adjustment costs). Thus this parameter was also fixed prior to estimating the remaining parameters. The value chosen for this parameter was 0.1, implying that prices on individual goods are reset on average every $3\frac{3}{4}$ quarters. Estimates of the remaining parameters, obtained conditionally on these specifications, are reported in table 8.1, which replicates Ireland's table 1, p. 928.

Regarding behavioral parameters, the small estimate obtained for ω (the inverse of the elasticity of labor supply ξ) implies a highly inelastic labor-supply specification. An implication of this estimate is that the efficient level of output is unresponsive to the demand shock. Next, the estimates of α_o and α_π are both statistically insignificant. Note that these are the parameters associated with lagged values of the output gap in the IS curve, and inflation in the Phillips curve. They were incorporated in the model to investigate whether the allowance for potential backward-looking behavior on the part of decision makers is important for helping characterize the data. The insignificance of these parameters suggests that this allowance turns out to be unimportant. Regarding policy parameters, the estimates obtained for ρ_π and ρ_g indicate the responsiveness of policy to movements in inflation and output growth, whereas the estimate obtained for ρ_o indicates a relative lack of responsiveness to the output gap.

Turning to estimates regarding the shocks, all four standard deviation parameters are estimated as statistically significant, implying a nontrivial empirical role for each shock. Also, the AR parameters estimated for both

TABLE 8.1
ML Estimates

Parameter	*Estimate*	*Standard Error*
ω	0.0617	0.0634
α_0	0.0836	0.1139
α_π	0.0000	0.0737
ρ_π	0.3597	0.0469
ρ_g	0.2536	0.0391
ρ_o	0.0347	0.0152
ρ_a	0.9470	0.0250
ρ_e	0.9625	0.0248
σ_a	0.0405	0.0157
σ_e	0.0012	0.003
σ_z	0.0109	0.0028
σ_r	0.0031	0.003

Note: Source of estimates: Ireland (2004a), table 1, p. 928.

the demand- and cost-push shocks are in the neighborhood of 1, suggesting that innovations to these series are extremely persistent (recall that the technology shock was modeled as having a unit root, and that the policy shock was modelled as being *iid*).

Ireland quantified implications of these parameter estimates for the role played by the shocks in driving cyclical fluctuations by calculating impulse-response functions and forecast-error variance decompositions. Regarding movements in output growth, he found policy shocks to be most influential, accounting for 37% of the errors associated with forecasts of this series over various horizons; in comparison, technology, demand, and cost-push shocks accounted for 25%, 22%, and 15% of this error. In addition, cost-push shocks were found to have the greatest influence on inflation, and demand shocks on nominal interest rates.

We now underscore these findings by demonstrating the smoothing feature of the Kalman filter. Recall from chapter 4, section 4.3, that given a parameterized version of the state-space representation, the time-series observations on the observable variables X_t can be used to obtain smoothed estimates of the unobservables $\{\widehat{x}_{t|T}\}_{t=1}^{T}$, along with innovations to these variables $\{\widehat{e}_{t|T}\}_{t=1}^{T}$. These smoothed time-series observations can be thought of as point estimates of a particular set of functions of the collection of structural parameters μ. As such, standard errors corresponding to these estimates can be constructed using a gradient-based conversion method. Specifically, let the smoothed observation of the jth element of $\{\widehat{x}_{t|T}\}_{t=1}^{T}$ be given by

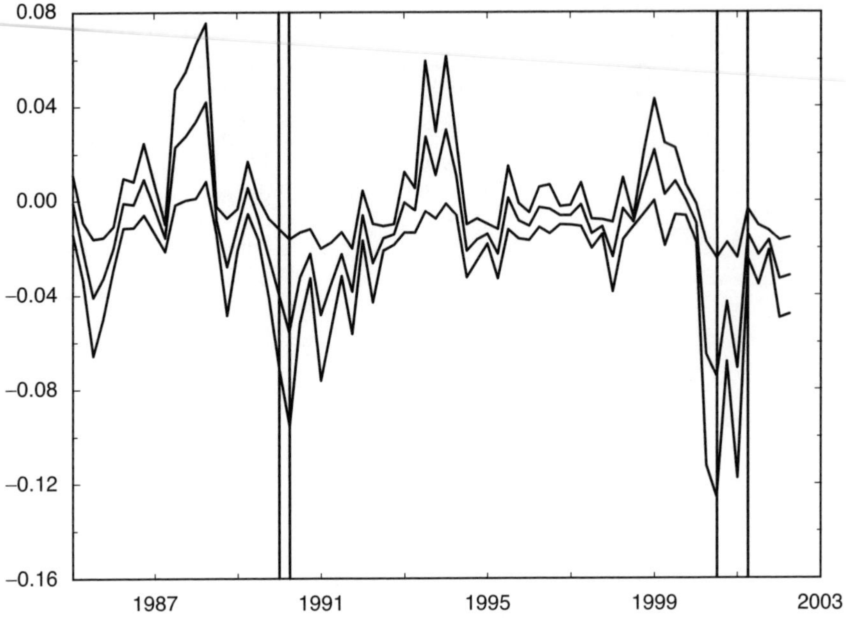

Figure 8.9 Smoothed innovations to the demand-push shock and 95% coverage intervals.

$$\{\widehat{x}^j_{t|T}\}_{t=1}^T = g(\widehat{\mu}). \tag{8.55}$$

Passing this function along with $\widehat{\mu}$ to a gradient-calculation procedure (such as GAUSS's `gradp`) yields as output $g'(\widehat{\mu})$, a $T \times k$ Jacobian matrix evaluated at $\widehat{\mu}$. The standard errors associated with $\widehat{x}^j_{t|T}$ for each date t can then be calculated as the square roots of the diagonal elements of the $T \times T$ matrix $[g'(\widehat{\mu})]\Sigma_\mu[g'(\widehat{\mu})]'$:

$$\{\widehat{\sigma}^j_{t|T}\}_{t=1}^T = \sqrt{diag([g'(\widehat{\mu})]\,\Sigma_\mu\,[g'(\widehat{\mu})]')}. \tag{8.56}$$

Finally, 95% error bands associated with the observations $\{\widehat{x}^j_{t|T}\}_{t=1}^T$ can be constructed as $\{\widehat{x}^j_{t|T}\}_{t=1}^T \pm 2\{\widehat{\sigma}^j_{t|T}\}_{t=1}^T$.

Representative point estimates and error bands obtained for innovations to the demand-shock process are illustrated in figure 8.9 over the period 1985:I–2003:I. Also depicted are NBER-defined recessions, indicated using vertical lines (beginning at business-cycle peaks and ending at troughs). Note, for example, that both recessions observed during this period coincide with the realization of a sequence of negative realizations of these innovations that differ significantly from zero.

The full series of smoothed realizations obtained for the level of the demand shock are depicted in figure 8.10, and their associated innovations are depicted in figure 8.11. Hereafter, standard-error bands are suppressed to aid in the presentation of point estimates, and NBER-dated recessions are illustrated using shaded bars. Note that demand shocks tend to rise systematically as the business cycle moves from trough to peak, and then spike dramatically downwards during recessions. These measurements indicate that, conditional on the estimated model, demand shocks do seem to have played an important role in contributing towards movements over stages of the business cycle.

Smoothed observations of the cost-push shock and associated innovations are depicted in figures 8.12 and 8.13. Relative to the demand shock, movements in this case are less systematic over phases of the business cycle. However, it is interesting to note that large negative values are observed for this shock around 1974 and 1979–1980, which coincide with the realization of significant oil-price shocks.

We next depict observations on the technology shock and its associated innovations in figures 8.14 and 8.15. Befitting its random-walk specification, this series exhibits wide swings that somewhat obfuscate movements at cyclical frequencies. However, the series does exhibit a clear tendency to drop sharply during recessions. Occasionally these drops slightly predate business-cycle peaks; other times the drops coincide almost precisely.

Finally, observations on the policy shock are depicted in figure 8.16. Outside of recessions, the volatility of this series is somewhat lower in the early portion of the sample relative to the latter portion. However, throughout the sample the series shows a tendency to spike upwards during recessions, perhaps signaling purposeful responses of policy to these episodes.

To further explore the systematic nature of movements in these series over phases of the business cycle, we conducted a logit analysis under which we used current and lagged values of innovations to each series as explanatory variables used to model the occurrence of NBER-identified recessions. This follows a similar shock-identification analysis conducted by DeJong, Ingram, and Whiteman (2000a). Specifically, we used as a dependent variable an indicator variable that is assigned the value of unity for dates coinciding with NBER-defined recessions and zero otherwise. We then modeled this series using contemporaneous and four lagged values of innovations to each shock. We considered five model specifications: one each using the individual series as explanatory variables, and one using all four series jointly as explanatory variables. Fitted values of the recession indicator, along with NBER dates, are illustrated in the five panels of figure 8.17.

Using the full set of explanatory variables, we obtained an excellent characterization of the occurrence of recessions. Using 0.75 and 0.5 as ad hoc

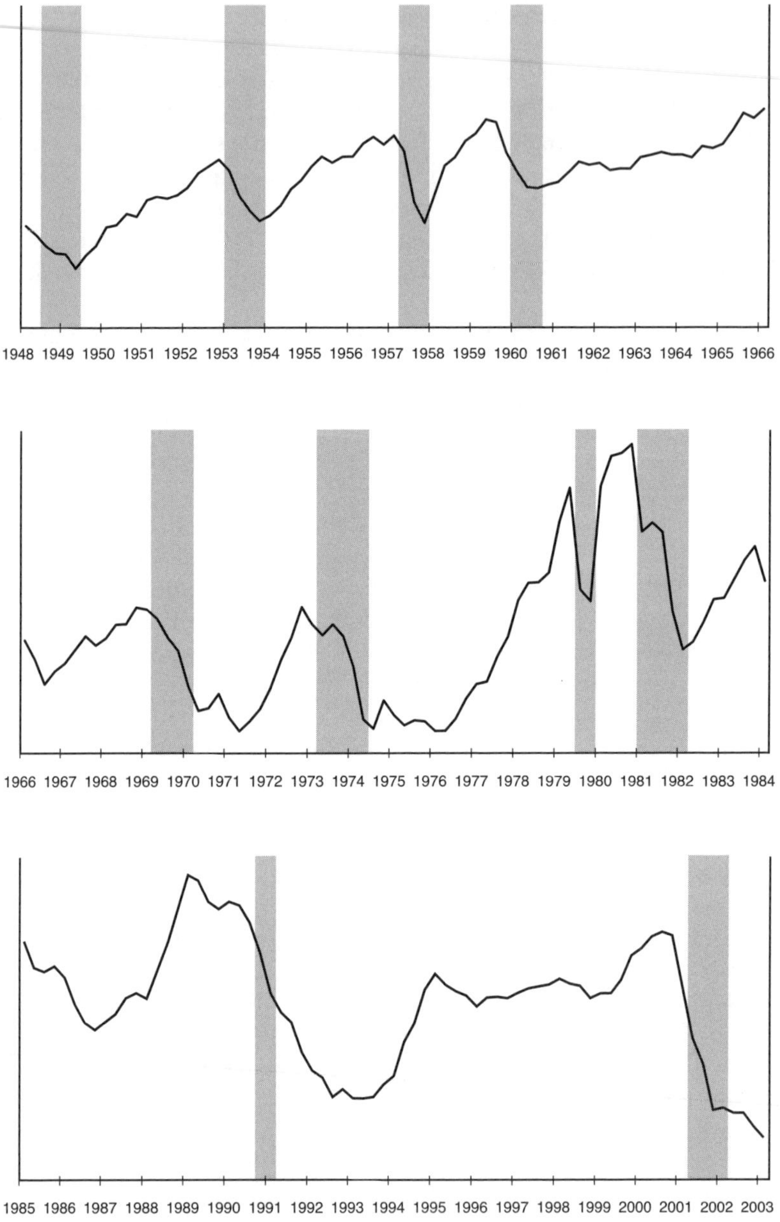

Figure 8.10 Smoothed demand shock.

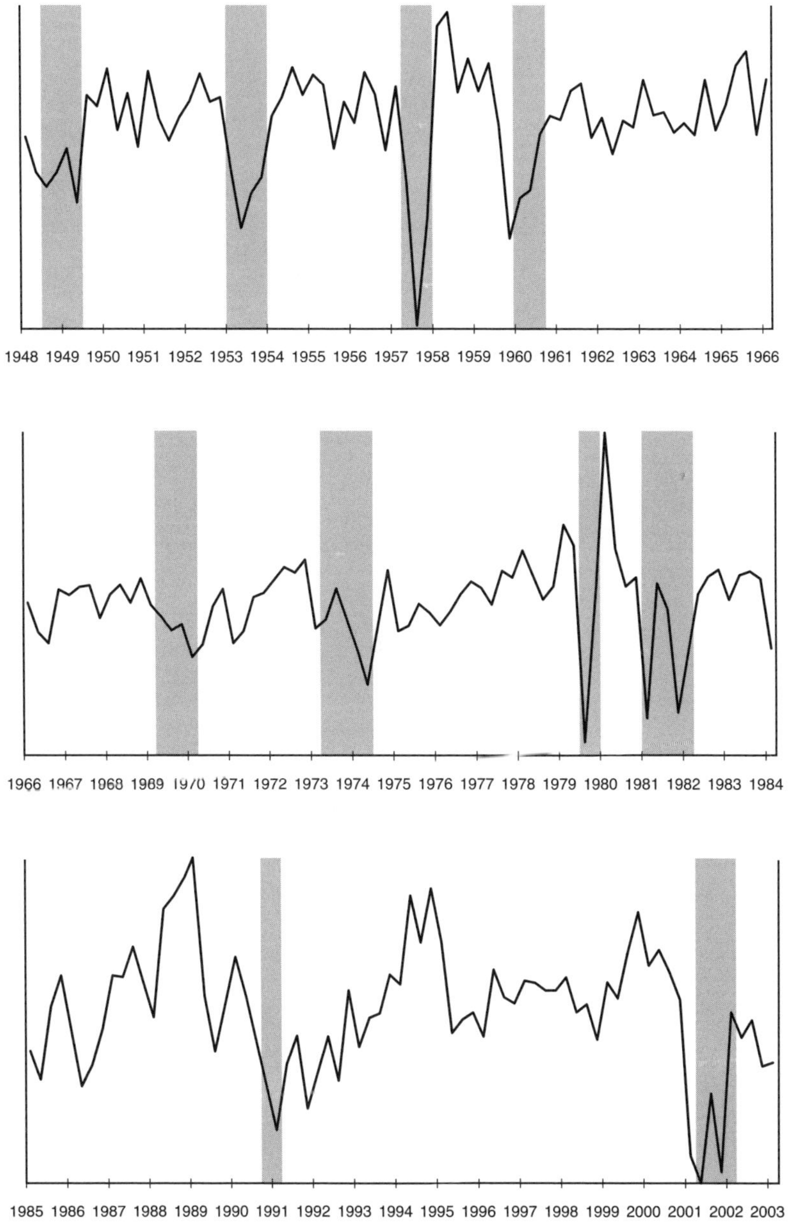

Figure 8.11 Smoothed innovations to the demand shock.

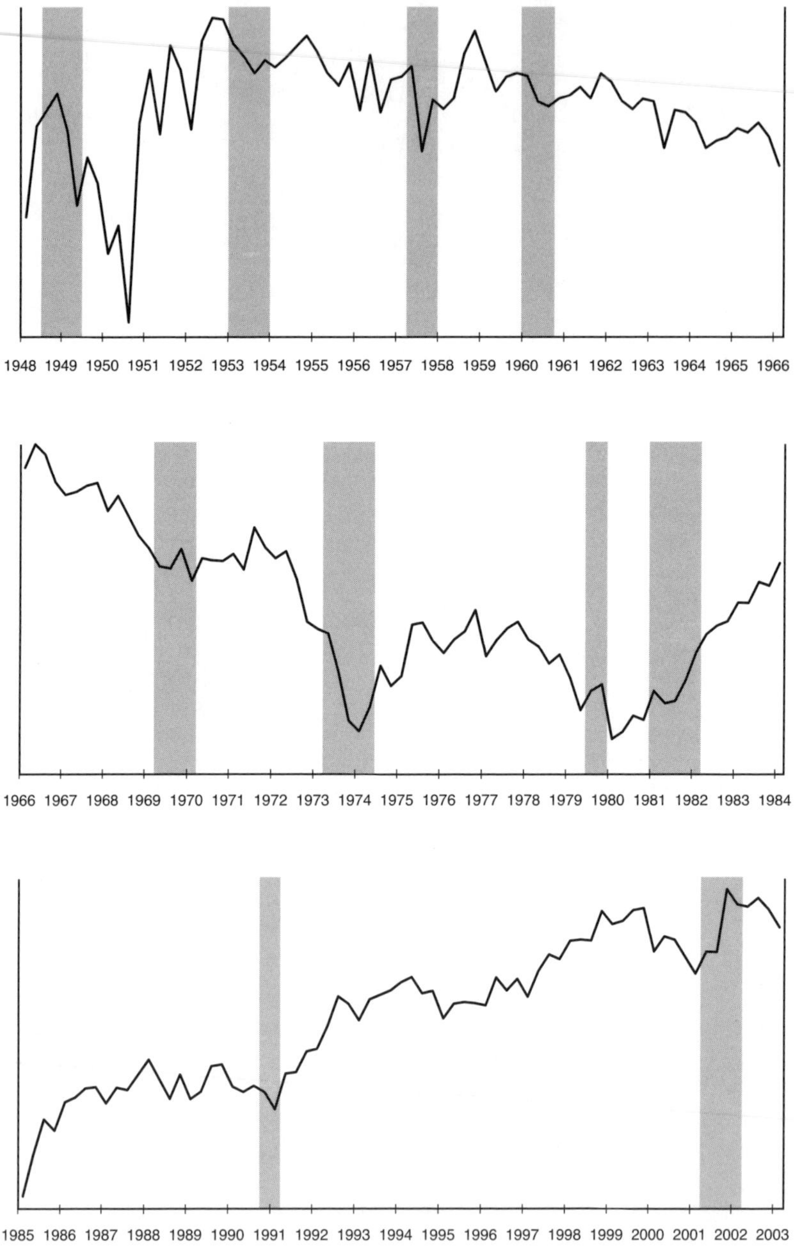

Figure 8.12 Smoothed cost-push shock.

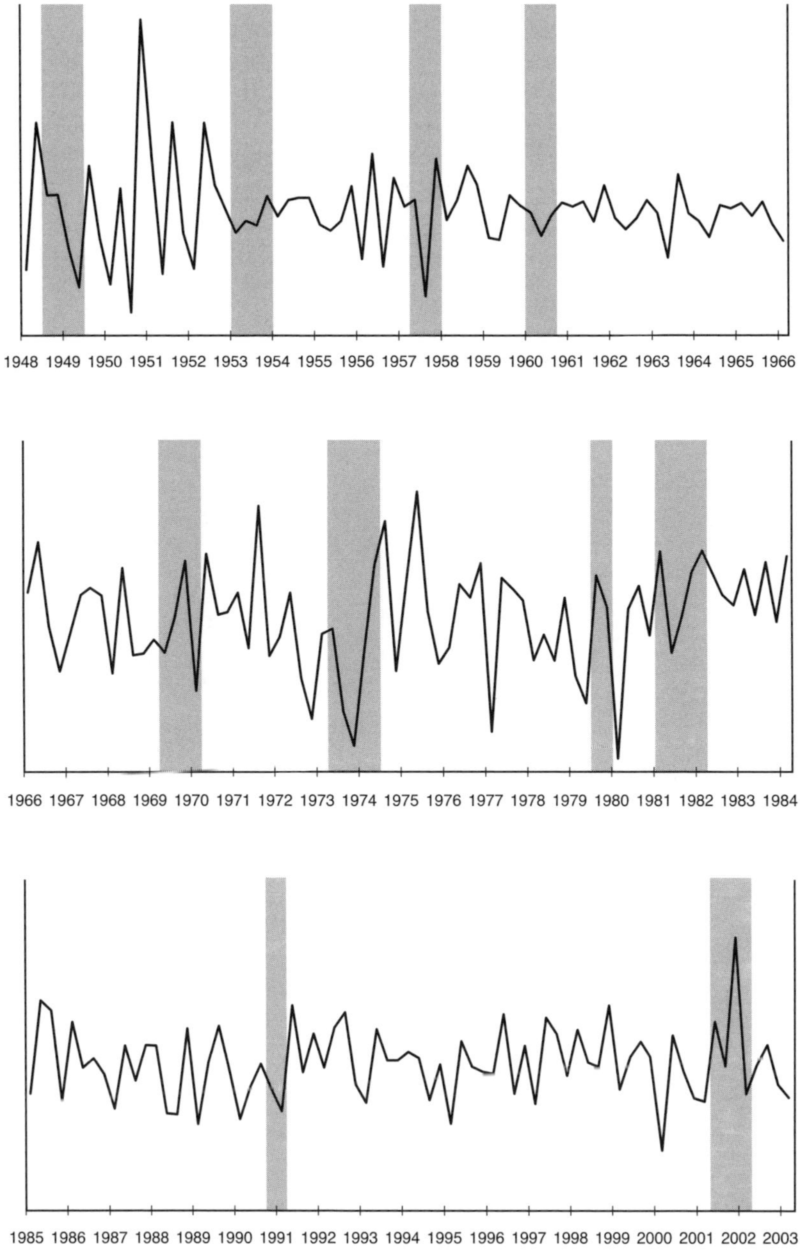

Figure 8.13 Smoothed innovations to the cost-push shock.

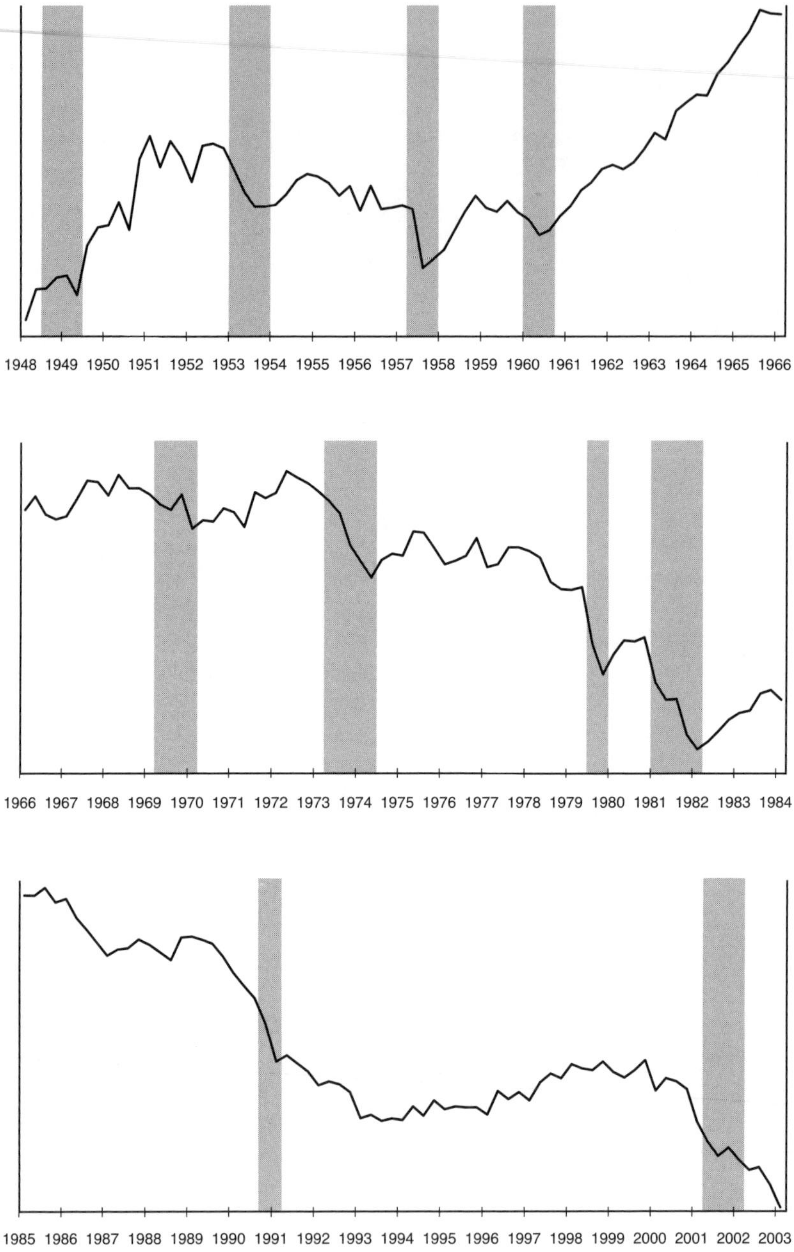

Figure 8.14 Smoothed technology shock.

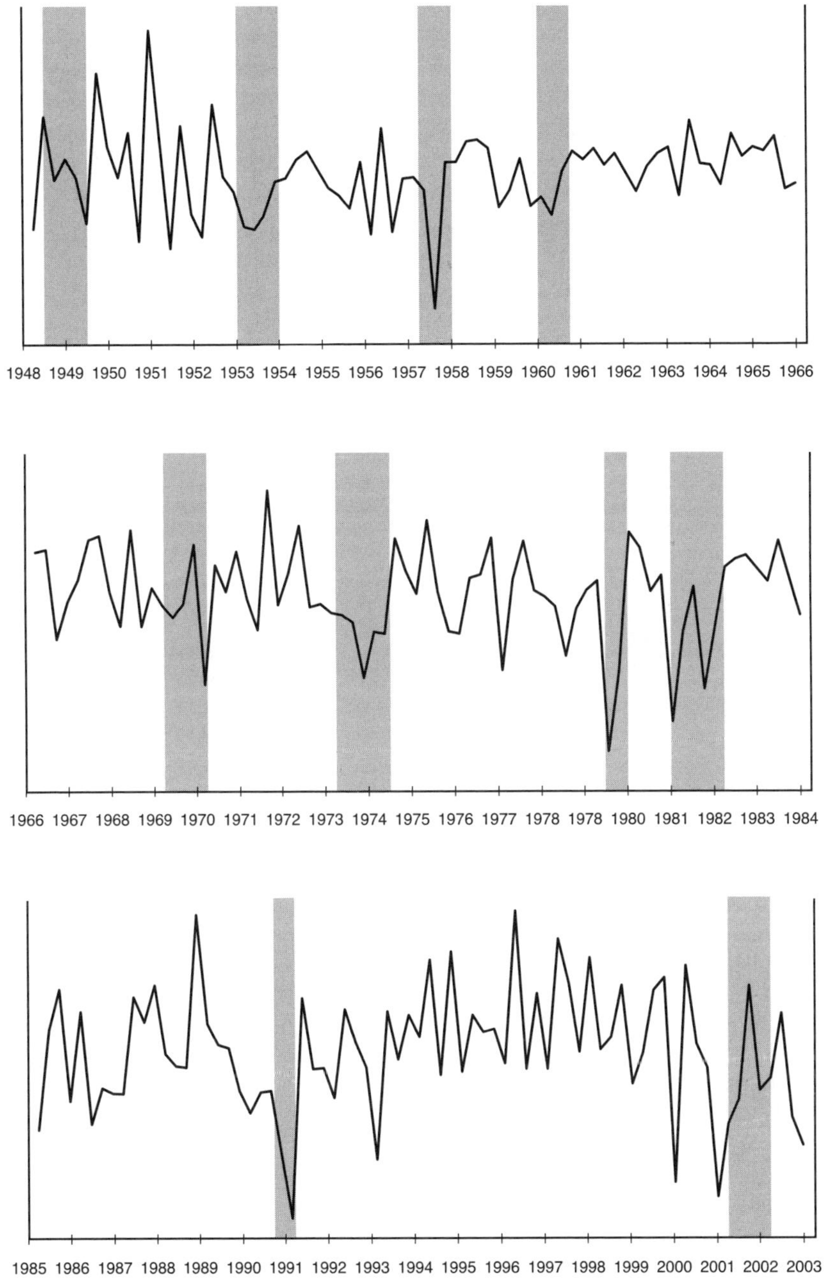

Figure 8.15 Smoothed innovations to the technology shock.

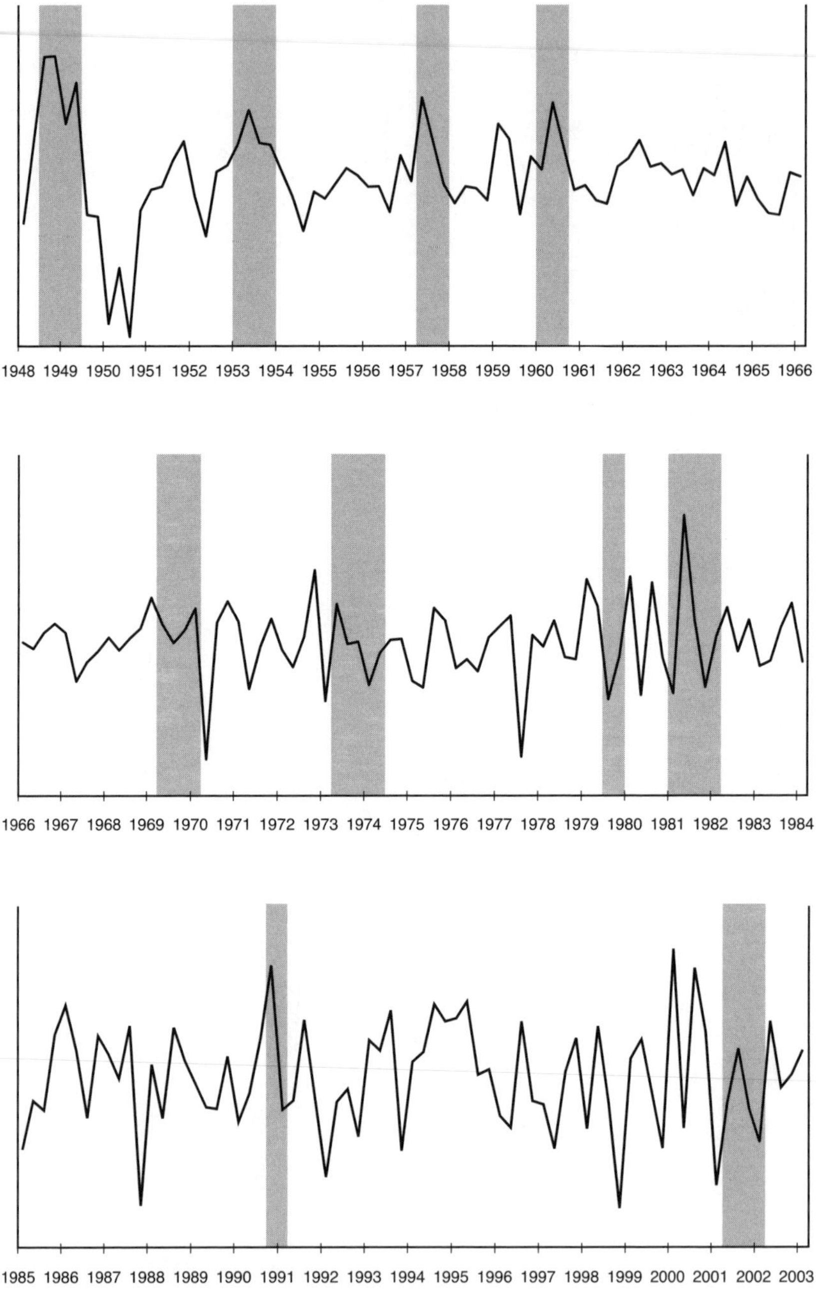

Figure 8.16 Smoothed policy shock.

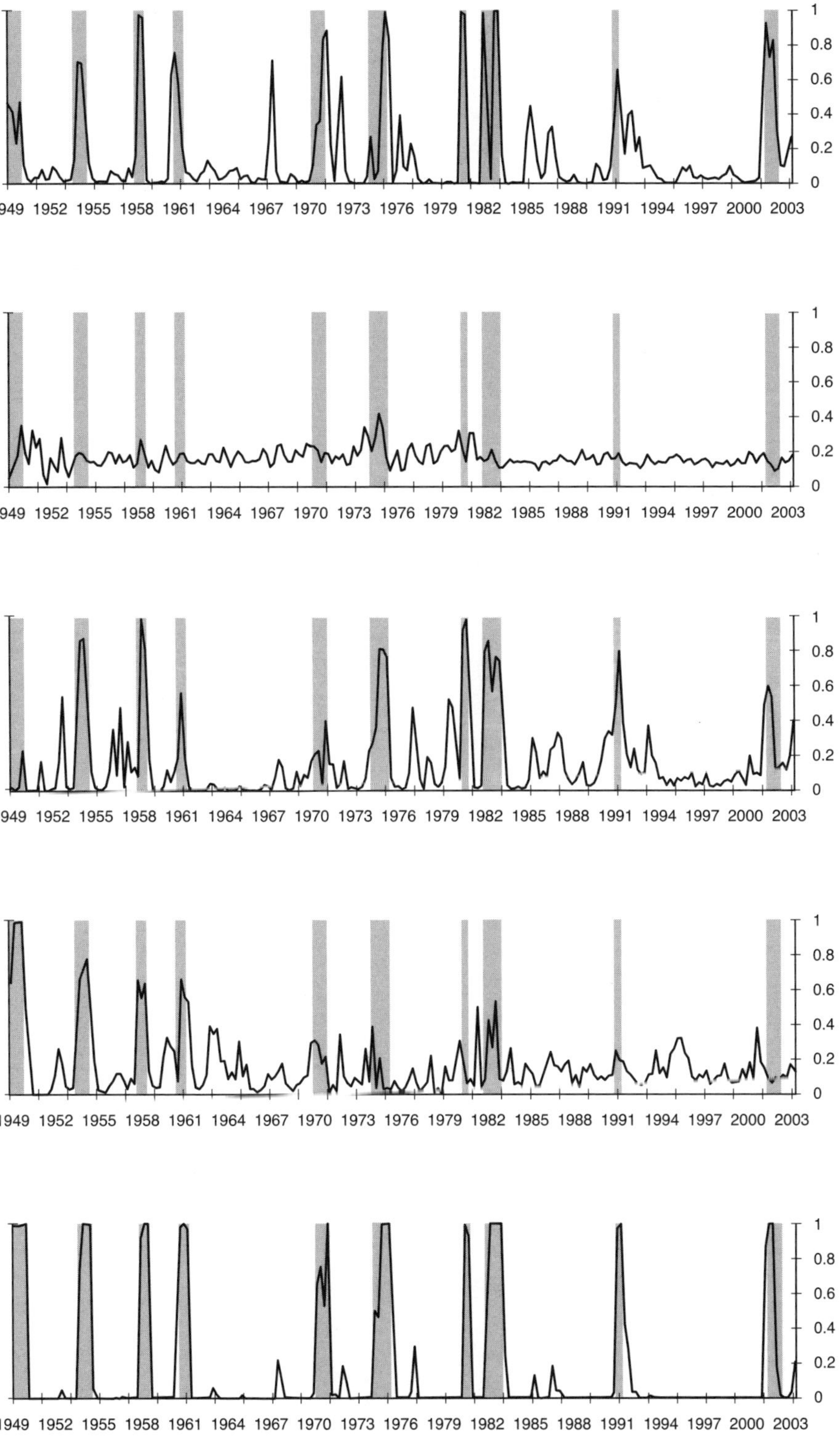

Figure 8.17 Fitted probabilities of NBER-dated recessions. Explanatory variables from top to bottom: demand-push, cost-push, technology, policy, and all shocks.

trigger probabilities for identifying the onset of a recession, we obtained successful predictions of all 10 recessions observed over the sample period, and obtained no false positive predictions. The demand and technology shocks are most important in contributing towards this performance. Using the former series in isolation, we obtained successful predictions for 7 of the 10 recessions with no false positives using the 0.75 trigger, and 9–10 successful predictions with 2 false positives using the 0.5 trigger. Comparable numbers for the latter series are (6, no false) and (8, two false). In contrast, only the first two recessions were successfully predicted using the policy-shock series and the 0.75 rule, whereas the first four recessions, along with the 1981 recession, were successfully predicted using the 0.5 trigger. This may indicate that policy responses became less distinct over the latter half of the sample. Finally, the cost-push shock never generated predicted probabilities in excess of 0.45.

Chapter 9

Bayesian Methods

9.1 Overview of Objectives

Chapter 8 demonstrated the use of the Kalman filter for evaluating the likelihood function associated with a given state-space representation. It then described the pursuit of empirical objectives using classical estimation methods. This chapter characterizes and demonstrates an alternative approach to this pursuit: the use of Bayesian methods.

A distinct advantage in using structural models to conduct empirical research is that a priori guidance concerning their parameterization is often much more readily available than is the case in working with reduced-form specifications. The adoption of a Bayesian statistical perspective in this context is therefore particularly attractive, because it facilitates the formal incorporation of prior information in a straightforward manner.

The reason is that from a Bayesian perspective, parameters are interpreted as random variables. In the estimation stage, the objective is to make conditional probabilistic statements regarding the parameterization of the model. Conditioning is made with respect to three factors: the structure of the model, the observed data, and a prior distribution specified for the parameters. The structure of the model and the observed data combine to form a likelihood function. Coupling the likelihood function with a prior distribution using Bayes' Rule yields an associated posterior distribution.

Note that under the Bayesian perspective, both the likelihood function and posterior distribution can be used to assess the relative plausibility of alternative parameterizations of the model. Use of the likelihood function for this purpose gives exclusive voice to the data; use of the posterior distribution gives voice to both the data and the researcher. The point of this observation is that the incorporation of prior information is not what distinguishes classical from Bayesian analysis; the distinguishing feature is the probabilistic interpretation assigned to parameters under the Bayesian perspective.

So, it is not necessary to specify prior distributions to gain distinction as a Bayesian. But as noted, in the context of working with structural models, the ability to do so is often advantageous. Indeed, one interpretation of a calibration exercise is of a Bayesian analysis involving the specification of a point-mass prior over model parameters. The incorporation of prior uncertainty into such an analysis through the specification of a diffuse prior gives voice to the data regarding model parameterization, and in so doing enables the formal pursuit of a wide range of empirical objectives.

Broadly defined, Bayesian procedures have been applied to the analysis of DSGEs in pursuit of three distinct empirical objectives; all three are discussed and demonstrated in this chapter. First, they have been used to implement DSGEs as a source of prior information regarding the parameterization of reduced-form models. An important goal in this sort of exercise is to help provide theoretical context for interpreting forecasts generated by popular reduced-form models, most notably vector autoregressions (VARs). Second, they have been used to facilitate the direct estimation of DSGEs, and to implement estimated models in pursuit of a variety of empirical objectives. A leading objective has been the indirect measurement of unobservable facets of macroeconomic activity (e.g., time-series observations of productivity shocks, time spent outside the labor force on home-production and skill-acquisition activities, etc.). Third, Bayesian procedures have been used to facilitate model comparisons. As an alternative to the classical hypothesis-testing methodology, in the Bayesian context model comparison is facilitated via posterior odds analysis. Posterior odds convey relative probabilities assigned to competing models, calculated conditionally given priors and data. They are straightforward to compute and interpret even in cases where all competing models are known to be false, and when alternatives are non-nested.

The analyses described in this chapter entail the use of computationally intensive numerical integration procedures, and many alternative procedures are available for facilitating their implementation. We have sought to keep this chapter relatively user-friendly; the numerical methods presented here were chosen with this objective in mind. Guidance for readers interested in exploring alternative procedures is provided throughout the chapter. Overviews of numerical methods are provided by Geweke (1999a, 2005) and Robert and Casella (1999). In addition, Koop (2003) provides a general overview of Bayesian statistical methods with an eye towards discussing computational issues. Finally, Bauwens, Lubrano, and Richard (1999) provide a computationally based overview of the application of Bayesian methods to the study of a broad range of dynamic reduced-form models. Beyond the treatment of computational issues, more general textbook overviews of Bayesian methods are provided by Zellner (1971), Leamer (1978), Poirier (1995), and Lancaster (2004).

9.2 Preliminaries

Likelihood functions provide the foundation for both classical and Bayesian approaches to statistical inference. To establish the notation used throughout this chapter, let us briefly reestablish their derivation. We begin with a given structural model A with parameters collected in the vector μ. Log-linearization of the model yields a state-space representation with parameters collected in the vector $\Lambda(\mu)$. Coupled with a distributional assumption regarding the disturbances included in the model, the state-space representation yields an associated likelihood function, which can be evaluated using the Kalman filter. Letting X denote the sample of observations on the observed variables in the system, the likelihood function is written as $L(X|\mu, A)$. Note that the mapping from μ to Λ is taken for granted under this notation; this is because μ typically serves as the primary focus of the analysis. When working with only a single model, the dependence of the likelihood function on A will also be taken for granted, and the function will be written as $L(X|\mu)$.

From a classical perspective, parameters are interpreted as fixed but unknown entities, and the likelihood function is interpreted as a sampling distribution for the data. The realization of X is thus interpreted as one of many possible realizations from $L(X|\mu)$ that could have been obtained. Inferences regarding the specification of μ center on statements regarding probabilities associated with the particular observation of X for given values of μ.

From a Bayesian perspective, the observation of X is taken as given, and inferences regarding the specification of μ center on statements regarding probabilities associated with alternative specifications of μ conditional on X. This probabilistic interpretation of μ gives rise to a potential avenue for the formal incorporation of a priori views regarding its specification. This is facilitated via the specification of a prior distribution for μ, denoted as $\pi(\mu)$.

To motivate the incorporation of $\pi(\mu)$ into the analysis, recall the definition of conditional probability, which holds that the joint probability of (X, μ) can be calculated as

$$p(X, \mu) = L(X|\mu)\pi(\mu), \tag{9.1}$$

or reversing the roles of μ and X,

$$p(X, \mu) = P(\mu|X)p(X). \tag{9.2}$$

In (9.1) the likelihood function is used to perform the conditional probability calculation, and conditioning is made with respect to μ; $\pi(\mu)$ in turn assigns probabilities to specific values of μ. In (9.2), $P(\mu|X)$ is used to perform the conditional probability calculation, and conditioning is made with respect to X; $p(X)$ in turn assigns probabilities to specific values of X. Eliminating $p(X, \mu)$ by equating (9.1) and (9.2) and solving for $P(\mu|X)$ yields Bayes' Rule:

$$P(\mu|X) = \frac{L(X|\mu)\pi(\mu)}{p(X)}$$
$$\propto L(X|\mu)\pi(\mu), \tag{9.3}$$

where $p(X)$ is a constant from the point of view of the distribution for μ.

In (9.3), $P(\mu|X)$ is the posterior distribution. Conditional on X and the prior $\pi(\mu)$, it assigns probabilities to alternative values of μ; this distribution is the central focus of Bayesian analyses.

The typical objective of a Bayesian analysis involves the calculation of the conditional expected value of a function of the parameters $g(\mu)$:

$$E[g(\mu)] = \frac{\int g(\mu)P(\mu|X)d\mu}{\int P(\mu|X)d\mu}. \tag{9.4}$$

(The denominator is included in (9.4) to cover the general case in which $p(X)$ in (9.3) is unknown, and thus $P(\mu|X)$ does not integrate to 1.) This objective covers a broad range of cases, depending upon the specification of $g(\mu)$. For example, if $g(\mu)$ is simply the identity function, then (9.4) delivers the posterior mean of μ. Alternatively, if $g(\mu)$ is an indicator over a small interval for μ^j, the jth element of μ (e.g., $g(\mu) = 1$ for $\mu^j \in [\underline{\mu}^j\ \overline{\mu}^j)$, and 0 otherwise), then assigning indicators over the support of each element of μ would enable the construction of marginal predictive density functions (p.d.f.s) for each structural parameter of the underlying model. (Referring to the p.d.f. of μ^j, the term *marginal* indicates that the p.d.f. is unconditional on the values of the additional elements of μ. Further elaboration for this important example is provided below in this section.) Marginal p.d.f.s for additional functions such as spectra, impulse response functions, predictive densities, and time-series observations of unobservable variables included in the structural model can be constructed analogously. Regardless of the specification of $g(\mu)$, (9.4) has a standard interpretation: $E[g(\mu)]$ is the weighted average of $g(\mu)$, with the weight assigned to a particular value of μ determined jointly by the data (through the likelihood function) and the prior.

As noted, numerical integration procedures feature prominently in Bayesian analyses. This is due to the fact that in general, it is not possible to calculate $E[g(\mu)]$ analytically. Instead, numerical methods are used to approximate the integrals that appear in (9.4).

In the simplest case, it is possible to simulate random drawings of μ directly using the posterior distribution $P(\mu|X)$. In this case, (9.4) can be approximated via direct Monte Carlo integration. (Rubinstein, 1981, describes algorithms for obtaining simulated realizations from a wide range of p.d.f.s. Monte Carlo methods were introduced in the economics literature by Kloek and van Dijk, 1978.) Let μ_i denote the ith of a sequence of N draws obtained from $P(\mu|X)$. Then by the law of large numbers (e.g., as in Geweke, 1989):

$$\overline{g}_N = \left(\frac{1}{N}\right)\sum_{i=1}^{N} g(\mu_i) \rightarrow E[\,g(\mu)], \tag{9.5}$$

where $\rightarrow$ indicates convergence in probability. The numerical standard error associated with $\overline{g}_N$ is $1/\sqrt{N}$ times the standard deviation of $g(\mu)$:

$$s.e.(\overline{g}_N) = \frac{\sigma(g(\mu))}{\sqrt{N}}. \tag{9.6}$$

Defining $\overline{\sigma}_N(g(\mu))$ as the sample standard deviation of $g(\mu)$,

$$\overline{\sigma}_N(\,g(\mu)) = \left[\left(\frac{1}{N}\right)\sum_{i=1}^{N} g(\mu_i)^2 - \overline{g}_N^2\right]^{1/2}, \tag{9.7}$$

$s.e.(\overline{g}_N)$ is estimated in practice using

$$s.e.(\,\overline{g}_N) = \frac{\overline{\sigma}_N(\,g(\mu))}{\sqrt{N}}. \tag{9.8}$$

A typical choice for N is 10,000, in which case $1/\sqrt{N} = 1\%$.

Consider the objective of approximating the marginal p.d.f. of a function $g(\mu)$ via direct Monte Carlo integration. This can be accomplished via the construction of a histogram using the following steps. First, partition the range of $g(\mu)$ into equally spaced intervals, and let p_k denote the probability assigned by the actual p.d.f. to a realization of $g(\mu)$ within the kth interval. Next, let $\iota_k(\,g(\mu))$ denote an indicator function that equals 1 when $g(\mu)$ falls within the kth interval and 0 otherwise. Then approximate p_k using

$$\overline{p_k} = \left(\frac{1}{N}\right)\sum_{i=1}^{N} \iota_k(\,g(\mu_i)). \tag{9.9}$$

The assignment of $\overline{p_k}$ as the height of the histogram over bin k yields the desired approximation.[1] Moreover, interpreting each drawing μ_i as a Bernoulli trial with success defined as $\iota_k(\,g(\mu_i)) = 1$, so that the probability

[1] Denoting the number of bins comprising the approximating histogram by K, and the range spanned by the histogram by R, it is necessary to adjust $\overline{p_k}$ by the factor K/R to insure that the histogram integrates to 1.

of success is given by p_k, Geweke (1989) notes that the standard error associated with $\overline{p_k}$ is given by

$$s.e.(\overline{p_k}) = \left(\frac{p_k(1-p_k)}{N} \right)^{1/2}, \tag{9.10}$$

thus the standard error of $\overline{p_k}$ given $N = 10,000$ is no greater than 0.005.

Exercise 9.1

Let μ consist of a single element, $P(\mu|X)$ be a $N(0,1)$ p.d.f., and $g(\mu) = \mu^2$. Using a histogram consisting of 11 equally spaced bins over the range $[0, 8]$, approximate the p.d.f. of $g(\mu)$ for $N = 100; 1{,}000; 10{,}000$. Compare your results with a $\chi^2(1)$ distribution: this is what you are approximating! Repeat this exercise using histograms consisting of 21, 51, and 101 bins. (Be sure to incorporate the normalizing factor K/R mentioned in footnote 1 to insure your approximations integrate to 1.) Note how the quality of the approximations varies as a function of N and the number of bins you use; why is this so?

With these preliminaries established, we turn in section 9.3 to a discussion of an important class of empirical applications under which integrals of interest can be approximated via direct Monte Carlo integration. Under this class of applications, structural models are used as sources of prior information to be combined with likelihood functions associated with reduced-form models, typically in pursuit of forecasting applications. Judicious choices of prior distributions in this case can yield posterior distributions from which sample realizations of μ can be simulated. However, in working with state-space representations directly, this is no longer the case. Thus section 9.4 returns to the problem of approximating $E[g(\mu)]$, and introduces more sophisticated numerical integration techniques.

9.3 Using Structural Models as Sources of Prior Information for Reduced-Form Analysis

When available, the choice of pursuing an empirical question using either a structural or reduced-form model typically involves a trade-off: reduced-form models are relatively easy to work with, but generate results relatively lacking in theoretical content. Here we discuss a methodology that strikes a compromise in this trade-off. The methodology involves the use of structural models as sources of prior distributions for reduced-form models. This section presents a general characterization of a popular implementation of this methodology, and section 9.6 presents a forecasting application based on an autoregressive model.

Let Θ denote the collection of parameters associated with the reduced-form model under investigation. The goal is to convert a prior distribution $\pi(\mu)$ specified over the parameters of a corresponding structural model into a prior distribution for Θ. If the mapping from μ to Θ was one-to-one and analytically tractable, the distribution over Θ induced by $\pi(\mu)$ could be constructed using a standard change-of-variables technique. But for cases of interest here, with μ representing the parameters of a nonlinear expectational difference equation, analytically tractable mappings will rarely be available. Instead, numerical mappings are used.

Numerical mappings are accomplished using simulation techniques. A simple general simulation algorithm is as follows. Given a parameterization μ, a corresponding parameterization $\Lambda(\mu)$ of the associated state-space representation is obtained using the model-solution methods introduced in chapter 2. Next, a simulated sequence of structural shocks $\{\upsilon_t\}$ is obtained from their corresponding distribution, and then fed through the parameterized state-space model to obtain a corresponding realization of model variables $\{x_t\}$. Next, $\{x_t\}$ is fed into the observer equation $X_t = H(\mu)'x_t$ to obtain a corresponding realization of observable variables $\{X_t\}$. Finally, the artificially obtained observables are used to estimate the reduced-form parameters Θ. Repeating this process for a large number of drawings of μ from $\pi(\mu)$ yields a corresponding prior distribution for Θ, $\pi(\Theta)$.

As an important leading example, outlined by Zellner (1971) in full detail, consider the case in which the reduced-form model under investigation is of the form

$$\Upsilon = XB + U, \tag{9.11}$$

where Υ is $T\times n$, X is $T\times k$, B is $k\times n$, U is $T\times n$, and the rows of U are $iidN(0,\Sigma)$. (Note the slight abuse of notation: in the remainder of this section, (Υ, X) will constitute the observable variables of the structural model.) The likelihood function for

$$\Theta \equiv (B, \Sigma)$$

is given by

$$L(\Upsilon, X|B,\Sigma) \propto |\Sigma|^{-T/2} \exp\left\{-\frac{1}{2} tr\left[(\Upsilon - XB)'(\Upsilon - XB)\Sigma^{-1}\right]\right\}, \tag{9.12}$$

where $tr[\cdot]$ denotes the trace operation. In this case, it is not only possible to induce a prior over Θ using $\pi(\mu)$, but it is possible to do so in such a way that the resulting posterior distribution $P(\Theta|\Upsilon, X)$ can be implemented directly as a sampling distribution in pursuit of calculations of $E[g(\Theta)]$, as discussed in section 9.2.

To explain how this is accomplished, it is useful to note before proceeding that the likelihood function in (9.12) can itself be interpreted as a posterior distribution for Θ. Specifically, combining (9.12) with a prior distribution that is proportional to $|\Sigma|^{-(n+1)/2}$, and thus uninformative over B (the so-called Jeffreys prior), the resulting posterior distribution for Θ can be partitioned as $P(B|\Sigma)P(\Sigma)$, where the dependency on (Υ, X) has been suppressed for ease of notation. The conditional distribution $P(B|\Sigma)$ is multivariate normal, and the marginal distribution $P(\Sigma)$ is inverted-Wishart. Specifically, letting $\widehat{B}$ denote the ordinary least squares (OLS) estimate of B,

$$\widehat{H} = (\Upsilon - X\widehat{B})'(\Upsilon - X\widehat{B}),$$

and defining

$$\widehat{\beta} = vec(\widehat{B}),$$

so that $\widehat{\beta}$ is $(kn \times 1)$, the distributions of $P(B|\Sigma)$ and $P(\Sigma)$ are given by

$$P(B|\Sigma) \sim N(\widehat{\beta}|\Sigma \otimes (X'X)^{-1}) \tag{9.13}$$

$$P(\Sigma) \sim IW(\widehat{H}, \tau, n), \tag{9.14}$$

where $IW(\widehat{H}, \tau, n)$ denotes an inverted-Wishart distribution with $n \times n$ parameter matrix $\widehat{H}$ and τ degrees of freedom, and $\otimes$ denotes the Kronecker product. In this case, $\tau = T - k + n + 1$.

Continuing with the example, the attainment of sample drawings of $\Theta \equiv (B, \Sigma)$ directly from the Normal-Inverted Wishart (N-IW) distribution given in (9.13) and (9.14) for the purpose of computing $E[g(\Theta)]$ via Monte Carlo integration can be accomplished using the following algorithm. First, calculate $\widehat{\beta}$ and

$$\begin{aligned}\widehat{S} &= \left(\frac{1}{T-k}\right)(\Upsilon - X\widehat{B})'(\Upsilon - X\widehat{B}) \\ &\equiv \left(\frac{1}{\tau - n - 1}\right)\widehat{H}\end{aligned}$$

via Ordinary Least Squares (OLS). Next, construct $\widehat{S}^{-1/2}$, the $n \times n$ lower triangular Cholesky decomposition of $\widehat{S}^{-1}$; that is,

$$\widehat{S}^{-1} = \left(\widehat{S}^{-1/2}\right)\left(\widehat{S}^{-1/2}\right)'.$$

Next, calculate the Cholesky decomposition of $(X'X)^{-1}$, denoted as $(X'X)^{-1/2}$. The triple

$$\left(\widehat{\beta}, \widehat{S}^{-1/2}, (X'X)^{-1/2}\right)$$

constitute inputs into the algorithm.

To obtain a sample drawing of Σ, Σ_i, draw ξ_i, an $n \times (T-k)$ matrix of independent $N(0,(T-k)^{-1})$ random variables, and construct Σ_i using

$$\Sigma_i = \left[\left(\widehat{S}^{-1/2}\xi_i\right)\left(\widehat{S}^{-1/2}\xi_i\right)'\right]^{-1}. \tag{9.15}$$

To obtain a sample drawing of β, β_i, calculate the Cholesky decomposition of the drawing Σ_i, denoted as $\Sigma_i^{1/2}$, and construct β_i using

$$\beta_i = \widehat{\beta} + \left(\Sigma_i^{1/2} \otimes (X'X)^{-1/2}\right) w_i, \tag{9.16}$$

where w_i is a sample drawing of $(nk) \times 1$ independent $N(0,1)$ random variables. The drawing

$$\beta_{i+1} = \widehat{\beta} - \left(\Sigma_i^{1/2} \otimes (X'X)^{-1/2}\right) w_i$$

is an antithetic replication of this process; (β_i, β_{i+1}) constitute an antithetic pair (see Geweke, 1988, for a discussion of the benefits associated with the use of antithetic pairs in this context).[2]

A similar distributional form for the posterior distribution will result from the combination of an informative N-IW prior specified over (B, Σ), coupled with $L(\Upsilon, X|B, \Sigma)$ in (9.12). In particular, letting the prior be given by

$$P(\beta|\Sigma) \sim N(\beta^*|\Sigma \otimes N^{*-1}) \tag{9.17}$$

$$P(\Sigma) \sim IW(H^*, \tau^*, n), \tag{9.18}$$

the corresponding posterior distribution is given by

$$P(\beta|\Sigma) \sim N(\beta^P|\Sigma \otimes (X'X + N^*)^{-1}) \tag{9.19}$$

$$P(\Sigma) \sim IW(H^P, \tau + \tau^*, n), \tag{9.20}$$

[2] The GAUSS procedure `niw.prc` is available for use in generating sample drawings from Normal/Inverted-Wishart distributions.

where

$$\beta^P = [\Sigma^{-1} \otimes (X'X + N^*)]^{-1} \left[(\Sigma^{-1} \otimes X'X)\widehat{\beta} + (\Sigma^{-1} \otimes N^*)\beta^* \right] \tag{9.21}$$

$$H^P = \tau^* H^* + \widehat{H} + (\widehat{B} - B^*)' N^* (X'X + N^*)^{-1} (X'X)(\widehat{B} - B^*). \tag{9.22}$$

Note that the conditional posterior mean β^P is a weighted average of the OLS estimate $\widehat{\beta}$ and the prior mean β^*. Application of the algorithm outlined above to (9.19) and (9.20) in place of (9.13) and (9.14) enables the calculation of $E[g(\Theta)]$ via direct Monte Carlo integration.

Return now to the use of $\pi(\mu)$ as the source of a prior distribution to be combined with $L(\Upsilon, X|B, \Sigma)$ in (9.12). A methodology that has been used frequently in pursuit of forecasting applications involves a restriction of the prior over (B, Σ) to be of the N-IW form, as in (9.17) and (9.18). (Examples include DeJong, Ingram, and Whiteman, 1993; Ingram and Whiteman, 1994; Sims and Zha, 1998; and Del Negro and Schorfheide, 2004.) Once again, this enables the straightforward calculation of $E[g(\Theta)]$ via direct Monte Carlo integration, using (9.19) and (9.20). The only complication in this case involves the mapping of implications of $\pi(\mu)$ for β^*, N^*, and H^*.

A simple algorithm for performing this mapping is inspired by the problem of pooling sample information obtained from two sources. In this case, the two sources are the likelihood function and the prior. The algorithm is as follows. As described above, begin by obtaining a drawing μ_i from $\pi(\mu)$, and simulate a realization of observable variables $\{\Upsilon_i, X_i\}$ from the structural model. Using these simulated variables, estimate the reduced-form model (9.11) using OLS, and use the estimated values of β_i and H_i for β^* and $\tau^* H^*$ in (9.17) and (9.18). Also, use the simulated value of $(X_i' X_i)$ in place of N^*, and denoting the sample size of the artificial sample as T^*, note that $\tau^* = T^* - k + n + 1$.[3] Using

$$(\beta_i, H_i, (X_i' X_i), T^* - k + n + 1)$$

in place of

$$(\beta^*, \tau^* H^*, N^*, \tau^*)$$

[3] For cases in which the dimensionality of X is such that the repeated calculation of $(X'X)^{-1}$ is impractical, shortcuts for this step are available. For example, DeJong, Ingram, and Whiteman (1993) use a fixed matrix C in place of $(X'X)^{-1}$, designed to assign harmonic decay to lagged values of coefficients in a VAR specification.

in (9.19)–(9.22), construct the corresponding posterior distribution, and obtain simulated drawings of Θ using the algorithm outlined above. Note that at this stage, the posterior distribution is conditional on μ_i. As a suggestion, obtain 10 drawings of Θ_i for each drawing of μ_i. Finally, repeating this process by drawing repeatedly from $\pi(\mu)$ enables the approximation of $E[g(\Theta)]$.

By varying the ratio of the artificial to actual sample sizes in simulating $\{\Upsilon_i, X_i\}$, the relative influence of the prior distribution can be adjusted. Equal sample sizes ($T = T^*$) assign equal weight to the prior and likelihood functions; increasing the relative number of artificial drawings assigns increasing weight to the prior. Note (in addition to the strong resemblance to sample pooling) the strong resemblance of this algorithm to the mixed-estimation procedure of Theil and Goldberger (1961). For a discussion of this point, see Leamer (1978).

9.4 Implementing Structural Models Directly

We return to the problem of calculating (9.4), focusing on the case in which the posterior distribution is unavailable as a direct source of sample drawings of μ. In the applications of interest here, this will be true in general due to the complexity of likelihood functions associated with state-space representations, and because likelihood functions are specified in terms of the parameters $\Lambda(\mu)$, whereas priors are specified in terms of the parameters μ. However, it remains the case that we can calculate the likelihood function and posterior distribution for a given value of μ, with aid from the Kalman filter; these calculations are critical components of any approximation procedure.

Given unavailability of the posterior as a sampling distribution, we are faced with the problem of choosing a stand-in density for obtaining sample drawings μ_i. Effective samplers have two characteristics, accuracy and efficiency; they deliver close approximations of $E[g(\mu)]$, and do so using a minimal number of draws. The benchmark for comparison is the posterior itself; when available, it represents the pinnacle of accuracy and efficiency.

9.4.1 Implementation via Importance Sampling

Closest in spirit to direct Monte Carlo integration is the importance-sampling approach to integration. The idea behind this approach is to generate sample drawings $\{\mu_i\}$ from a stand-in distribution for the posterior, and assign weights to each drawing so that they can be thought of as originating from the posterior distribution itself. The stand-in density is called the importance sampler, denoted as $I(\mu|\theta)$, where θ represents the parametrization of $I(\mu|\theta)$.

To motivate this approach, it is useful to introduce $I(\mu|\theta)$ into (9.4) as follows:

$$E[g(\mu)] = \frac{\int g(\mu)\frac{P(\mu|X)}{I(\mu|\theta)} I(\mu|\theta) d\mu}{\int \frac{P(\mu|X)}{I(\mu|\theta)} I(\mu|\theta) d\mu}, \tag{9.23}$$

or defining the weight function

$$w(\mu) = \frac{P(\mu|X)}{I(\mu|\theta)},$$

$$E[g(\mu)] = \frac{\int g(\mu) w(\mu) I(\mu|\theta) d\mu}{\int w(\mu) I(\mu|\theta) d\mu}. \tag{9.24}$$

Under (9.4), $E[g(\mu)]$ is the weighted average of $g(\mu)$, with weights determined directly by $P(\mu|X)$; under (9.24), $E[g(\mu)]$ is the weighted average of $g(\mu)w(\mu)$, with weights determined directly by $I(\mu|\theta)$. Note the role played by $w(\mu)$: it counters the direct influence of $I(\mu|\theta)$ in obtaining a given realization μ_i by transferring the assignment of "importance" from $I(\mu|\theta)$ to $P(\mu|X)$. In particular, $w(\mu)$ serves to downweight those μ_i that are overrepresented in the importance sampling distribution relative to the posterior distribution, and upweight those that are underrepresented.

Just as (9.5) can be used to approximate (9.4) via direct Monte Carlo integration, Geweke (1989) shows that so long as the support of $I(\mu|\theta)$ includes that of $P(\mu|\theta)$, and $E[g(\mu)]$ exists and is finite, the following sample average can be used to approximate (9.24) via Importance Sampling:

$$\overline{g}_N = \frac{\sum_{i=1}^N g(\mu_i) w(\mu_i)}{\sum_{i=1}^N w(\mu_i)} \rightarrow E[g(\mu)]. \tag{9.25}$$

The associated numerical standard error is

$$s.e.(\overline{g}_N)_I = \frac{\sum_{i=1}^N (g(\mu_i) - \overline{g}_N)^2 w(\mu_i)^2}{\left[\sum_{i=1}^N w(\mu_i)\right]^2}. \tag{9.26}$$

Note that in calculating (9.25) and (9.26), it is not necessary to use the proper densities associated with $I(\mu|\theta)$ and $P(\mu|X)$ in calculating $w(\theta)$; instead, it is sufficient to work with their kernels only. The impact of ignoring the integrating constants is eliminated by the inclusion of the accumulated weights in the denominator of these expressions. Note also that when $P(\mu|X)$ serves as the importance sampler, the weight assigned to each μ_i will be one; (9.25) and (9.5) will then be identical, as will (9.26) and (9.8). This is the benchmark for judging importance samplers.

In practice, off-the-rack samplers will rarely deliver anything close to optimal performance: a good sampler requires tailoring. The consequence of working with a poor sampler is slow convergence. The problem is that if the importance sampler is ill-fitted to the posterior, enormous weights will be assigned occasionally to particular drawings, and a large share of drawings will receive virtually no weight. Fortunately, it is easy to diagnose an ill-fitted sampler: rather than being approximately uniform, the weights it generates will be concentrated over a small fraction of drawings, a phenomenon easily detected via the use of a histogram plotted for the weights.

A formal diagnostic measure, proposed by Geweke (1989), is designed to assess the relative numerical efficiency (RNE) of the sampler. Let $\overline{\sigma}_N(g(\mu))$ once again denote the sample standard deviation estimated for $g(\mu)$, calculated using an importance sampler as

$$\overline{\sigma}_N(g(\mu)) = \left[\frac{\sum_{i=1}^{N} g(\mu)^2 w(\mu_i)}{\sum_{i=1}^{N} w(\mu_i)} - \overline{g}_N^2 \right]^{1/2}. \tag{9.27}$$

Then RNE is given by

$$RNE = \frac{[\overline{\sigma}_N(g(\mu))]^2}{N[s.e.(\overline{g}_N)_I]^2}. \tag{9.28}$$

Comparing (9.26) and (9.27), note that RNE will be one under the benchmark, but will be driven below one given the realization of unevenly distributed weights. For the intuition behind this measure, solve for $s.e.(\overline{g}_N)_I$ in (9.28):

$$s.e.(\overline{g}_N)_I = \frac{\overline{\sigma}_N(g(\mu))}{\sqrt{RNE \cdot N}}. \tag{9.29}$$

Now comparing $s.e.(\overline{g}_N)_I$ in (9.29) with $s.e.(\overline{g}_N)$ in (9.8), note that $\sqrt{RNE \cdot N}$ has replaced $\sqrt{N}$ as the denominator term. Thus RNE serves as an indication of the extent to which the realization of unequally distributed weights has served to reduce the effective number of drawings used to compute $\overline{g}_N$.

In tailoring an efficient sampler, two characteristics are key: it must have fat tails relative to the posterior, and its center and rotation must not be too unlike the posterior. In a variety of applications of Bayesian analyses to the class of state-space representations of interest here, multivariate-t densities have proven to be effective along these dimensions (e.g., see DeJong, Ingram, and Whiteman, 2000a,b; DeJong and Ingram, 2001; and DeJong and Ripoll, 2004). Thus, for the remainder of this section, we discuss the issue of tailoring with specific reference to multivariate-t densities.

The parameters of the multivariate-t are given by

$$\theta \equiv (\gamma, V, \nu).$$

For a k-variate specification, the kernel is given by

$$p(x|\gamma, V, \nu) \propto [\nu + (x - \gamma)' V (x - \gamma)]^{-(k+\nu)/2}; \tag{9.30}$$

its mean and second-order moments are γ and $\left(\frac{\nu}{\nu-2}\right) V^{-1}$.

Regarding the first key characteristic, tail behavior, posterior distributions in these settings are asymptotically normal under weak conditions (e.g., Heyde and Johnstone, 1979); and it is a simple matter to specify a multivariate-t density with fatter tails than a normal density. All that is needed is the assignment of small values to ν (e.g., 5). (An algorithm for obtaining drawings from a multivariate-t is provided below.)

Regarding center and rotation, these of course are manipulated via (γ, V). One means of tailoring (γ, V) to mimic the posterior is sequential. A simple algorithm is as follows. Beginning with an initial specification (γ_0, V_0), obtain an initial sequence of drawings and estimate the posterior mean and covariance matrix of μ. Use the resulting estimates to produce a new specification (γ_1, V_1), with γ_1 specified as the estimated mean of μ, and V_1 as the inverse of the estimated covariance matrix. Repeat this process until posterior estimates converge. Along the way, in addition to histograms plotted for the weights and the RNE measure (9.28), the quality of the importance sampler can be monitored using

$$\varpi = \max_j \left[\frac{w(\mu_j)}{\sum w(\mu_i)} \right], \tag{9.31}$$

that is, the largest weight relative to the sum of all weights. Weights in the neighborhood of 2% are indicative of approximate convergence.

An alternative means of tailoring (γ, V) follows an adaptation of the efficient importance sampling methodology of Richard and Zhang (1997, 2004). The idea is to construct (γ, V) using a weighted least squares regression procedure that yields parameter estimates that can be used to establish effective values of (γ, V). Implementation proceeds under the assumption that the kernel of the logged posterior is reasonably approximated by a quadratic specification:

$$\begin{aligned}\log P(\mu|X) &\equiv \log P(\mu|\varphi,\Sigma)\\ &= const. - \frac{1}{2}(\mu-\varphi)'\Sigma^{-1}(\mu-\varphi)\\ &= const. - \frac{1}{2}(\mu' H\mu - 2\mu' H\varphi + \varphi' H\varphi), \qquad (9.32)\end{aligned}$$

where k is the dimension of μ, and H^{jl} is the $(j,l)^{\text{th}}$ element of $H = \Sigma^{-1}$. Note that the parameters (φ, Σ) are functions of X. Beginning with an initial specification (γ_0, V_0), generate a sequence of drawings of $\{\mu_i\}$, and compute corresponding sequences $\{\log P(\mu_i|X)\}$ and $\{w(\mu_i)\}$. The observations $\{\log P(\mu_i|X)\}$ serve as the dependent variable in the regression specification. Explanatory variables are specified so that their associated parameters can be mapped into estimates of (φ, Σ). For a given drawing μ_i, they consist of a constant, μ_i and the lower-triangular elements of $\mu_i\mu_i'$ (beginning with the $(1,1)$ element, followed by the $(2,1)$ and $(2,2)$ elements, etc.).[4] Assigning these variables into the $1 \times K$ vector x_i, with

$$K = 1 + k + 0.5k(k+1),$$

the ith row of the regression specification is given by

$$\log P(\mu_i|X)w(\mu_i)^{1/2} = w(\mu_i)^{1/2}x_i'\beta + e_i. \qquad (9.33)$$

To map the estimates of β obtained from this regression into (φ, Σ), begin by mapping the $k+2$ through K elements of β into a symmetric matrix $\widetilde{H}$, with the jth diagonal element corresponding to the coefficient associated with the squared value of the jth element of μ, and the $(j,k)^{\text{th}}$ element corresponding to the coefficient associated with the product of the jth and k^{th} elements of μ.[5] Next, multiply all elements of $\widetilde{H}$ by -1, and then multiply the diagonal elements by 2. Inverting the resulting matrix yields the desired approximation of Σ. Finally, postmultiplying the approximation of Σ by the 2nd through $k+1$ coefficients of β yields the desired approximation of φ. Having obtained an approximation of (φ, Σ), construct (γ_1, V_1) and repeat until convergence.

Depending upon the quality of the initial specification (γ_0, V_0), it may be necessary to omit the weights $w(\mu_i)$ in estimating β in the first iteration, because the effective number of available observations may be limited.

[4] The GAUSS command vech accomplishes this latter step.

[5] The GAUSS command xpdn accomplishes this mapping.

Regarding initial specifications of (γ_0, V_0), an effective starting point under either tailoring algorithm can be obtained by maximizing $\log P(\mu|X)$ with respect to μ, and using the maximizing values along with their corresponding Hessian matrix to construct (γ_0, V_0).

Given (γ, V, ν), an algorithm for obtaining sample drawings of μ from the multivariate-t is as follows. Begin by drawing a random variable s_i from a $\chi^2(\nu)$ distribution (i.e., construct s_i as the sum of ν squared $N(0,1)$ random variables). Use this to construct

$$\sigma_i = (s_i/\nu)^{-1/2},$$

which serves as a scaling factor for the second-moment matrix. Finally, obtain a $k \times 1$ drawing of $N(0, 1)$ random variables w_i, and convert this into a drawing of μ_i as follows:

$$\mu_i = \gamma + \sigma_i V^{-1/2} w_i, \tag{9.34}$$

where $V^{-1/2}$ is the $k \times k$ lower triangular Cholesky decomposition of V^{-1}. As in drawing from a Normal-Inverted Wishart distribution, it is beneficial to complement μ_i with its antithetic counterpart[6]

$$\mu_i = \gamma - \sigma_i V^{-1/2} w_i.$$

9.4.2 *Implementation via MCMC*

As its name suggests, the approximation of (9.4) via a Markov Chain Monte Carlo (MCMC) method involves the construction of a Markov chain in μ whose distribution converges to the posterior of interest $P(\mu|X)$. (For an introduction to Markov chains, see Hamilton, 1994; or Ljungqvist and Sargent, 2004; and for a detailed probabilistic characterization, see Shiryaev, 1995.)

In short, a stochastic process $\{x_i\}$ has a Markov property if for all i,

$$\Pr(x_{i+1}|x_i, x_{i-1}, x_{i-2}, \ldots) = \Pr(x_{i+1}|x_i). \tag{9.35}$$

In a time-series context i corresponds to a time index; here i corresponds to an index of Monte Carlo replications. To characterize the stochastic behavior of x_i via a Markov chain, we suppose that x_i can take on one of n possible values which collectively define the state space over x. The movement of x_i over i is characterized via P, an $n \times n$ transition matrix. The $(q, r)^{\text{th}}$ element of P is denoted as p_{qr}, and indicates the probability that x_i

[6] The GAUSS procedure `multit.prc` is available for use in generating sample drawings from multivariate-t distributions.

will transition to state r in replication $i+1$ given its current state q. Thus, the qth row of P indicates the entire conditional probability distribution for x_{i+1} given the current state q in replication i.

The original algorithm used to accomplish numerical integration via Markov chain approximation was developed by Metropolis et al. (1953), and was subsequently refined by Hastings (1970). In these algorithms, sample drawings of μ represent links in the chain; corresponding calculations of $g(\mu)$ for each link serve as inputs in the approximation of (9.4). Many extensions of these algorithms have been developed in subsequent work. Here we discuss three leading approaches to simulating Markov chains: the Gibbs Sampler, and the independence and random walk variants of the Metropolis-Hastings Algorithm. Further details are provided, for example, by Geweke (1999a) and Robert and Casella (1999).

THE GIBBS SAMPLER

The Gibbs sampler provides an alternative approach to that outlined in section 9.2 for obtaining drawings of μ from the exact distribution $P(\mu|X)$. Although once again this will rarely be possible in applications of interest here, it is instructive to consider this case before moving on to more complicated scenarios.

Rather than obtaining drawings of μ from the full distribution $P(\mu|X)$, with a Gibbs sampler one partitions μ into $m \leq k$ blocks,

$$\mu = (\mu^1|\mu^2|\ldots|\mu^m),$$

and obtains drawings of the components of each block μ^j from the conditional distribution $P(\mu|X,\mu^{-j})$, $j = 1\ldots m$, where μ^{-j} denotes the removal of μ^j from μ. This is attractive in scenarios under which it is easier to work with $P(\mu|X,\mu^{-j})$ rather than $P(\mu|X)$. For example, a natural partition arises in working with the Normal-Inverted Wishart distribution given in (9.13) and (9.14). Note that when $m = 1$, we are back to the case in which μ is drawn directly from $P(\mu|X)$.

Proceeding under the case in which $m = 2$, the Gibbs sampler is initiated with a specification of initial parameter values

$$\mu_0 = (\mu_0^1|\mu_0^2).$$

Thereafter, subsequent drawings are obtained from the conditional posteriors

$$\mu_{i+1}^1 \sim P(\mu^1|X,\mu_i^2) \tag{9.36}$$

$$\mu_{i+1}^2 \sim P(\mu^2|X,\mu_i^1). \tag{9.37}$$

This process generates a Markov chain $\{\mu_i\}_{i=1}^N$ whose ergodic distribution is $P(\mu|X)$. To eliminate the potential influence of μ_0, it is typical to discard the first S draws from the simulated sample, a process known as "burn-in". Hereafter, N represents the number of post-burn-in draws; a common choice for S is 10% of N.

As with direct sampling, the approximation of $E[g(\mu)]$ using

$$\overline{g}_N = \left(\frac{1}{N}\right)\sum_{i=1}^{N} g(\mu_i)$$

yields convergence at the rate $1/\sqrt{N}$ (e.g., see Geweke, 1992). However, because the simulated drawings μ_i are not serially independent, associated numerical standard errors will be higher than under direct sampling (wherein serial independence holds). Following Bauwens et al. (1999), letting γ_0 denote the variance of $g(\mu)$, and γ_l the lth-order autocovariance of $g(\mu)$, the numerical standard error of $\overline{g}_N$ can be approximated using

$$s.e.(\overline{g}_N)_G = \left[\frac{1}{N}\left(\overline{\gamma_0} + 2\sum_{l=1}^{N-1}\overline{\gamma_l}\frac{N-l}{N}\right)\right]^{1/2}, \tag{9.38}$$

where $\overline{\gamma_l}$ denotes the numerical estimate of the lth-order autocovariance of $g(\mu)$ obtained from the simulated μ_i's.

Geweke (1992) suggests a convenient means of judging whether estimates obtained under this procedure have converged. Partition the simulated drawings of μ_i into three subsets, I, II, and III (e.g., into equal $1/3s$), and let $[\overline{g}_N]^J$ and $[s.e.(\overline{g}_N)_G]^J$ denote the sample average and associated numerical standard error calculated from subset J. Then under a central limit theorem,

$$CD = \frac{[\overline{g}_N]^I - [\overline{g}_N]^{III}}{[s.e.(\overline{g}_N)_G]^I + [s.e.(\overline{g}_N)_G]^{III}} \tag{9.39}$$

will be distributed as $N(0,1)$ given the attainment of convergence. A test of the "null hypothesis" of convergence can be conducted by comparing this statistic with critical values obtained from the standard normal distribution. The reason for separating the subsamples I and III is to help assure their independence.

An additional diagnostic statistic, suggested by Yu and Mykland (1994), is based on a CUSUM statistic. Let $\overline{g}_N$ and $\overline{\sigma}_N(g(\mu))$ denote the sample mean and standard deviation of $g(\mu)$ calculated from a chain of length N. Then continuing the chain over t additional draws, the CS_t statistic is

$$CS_t = \frac{\overline{g}_t - \overline{g}_N}{\overline{\sigma}_N(g(\mu))}. \tag{9.40}$$

Thus CS_t measures the deviation of $\overline{g}_t$ from $\overline{g}_N$ as a percentage of the estimated standard deviation of $g(\mu)$. Given convergence, CS_t should approach 0 as t increases; Bauwens and Lubrano (1998) suggest 5% as a criterion for judging convergence.

METROPOLIS-HASTINGS ALGORITHMS

We now turn to the case in which $P(\mu|X, \mu^{-j})$ is unavailable as a sampling distribution for μ^j. In this case, it is still possible to generate a Markov chain $\{\mu_i\}$ with ergodic distribution $P(\mu|X)$. There are many alternative possibilities for doing so; an overview is provided by Chib and Greenberg (1995). Here, we focus on two important variants of the Metropolis-Hastings Algorithm: the independence chain and random walk algorithms. (For examples of the use of Metropolis-Hastings Algorithms in estimating DSGE models, see Otrok, 2001; Fernandez-Villaverde and Rubio-Ramirez, 2004a; and Smets and Wouters, 2005.)

Beginning with a characterization of the general Metropolis-Hastings Algorithm, we take the first $i-1$ Monte Carlo drawings as given, and consider the attainment of μ_i. (Once again, the process is initialized with a starting specification μ_0, the influence of which is eliminated via a burn-in phase.) The attainment of μ_i is accomplished through the use of a stand-in density, denoted as $\iota(\mu|\mu_{i-1}, \theta)$. Note that the center and rotation of $\iota(\mu|\mu_{i-1}, \theta)$ are determined in general by (μ_{i-1}, θ). Just as in the case of importance sampling, $\iota(\mu|\mu_{i-1}, \theta)$ is ideally designed to have fat tails relative to the posterior; and center and rotation not unlike the posterior. Its implementation as a sampling distribution proceeds as follows.

Let μ_i^* denote a drawing obtained from $\iota(\mu|\mu_{i-1}, \theta)$ that serves as a candidate to become the next successful drawing μ_i. Under the Metropolis-Hastings Algorithm, this will be the case according to the probability

$$q(\mu_i^*|\mu_{i-1}) = \min\left[1, \frac{P(\mu_i^*|X)}{P(\mu_{i-1}|X)} \frac{\iota(\mu_{i-1}|\mu_{i-1}, \theta)}{\iota(\mu_i^*|\mu_{i-1}, \theta)}\right]. \tag{9.41}$$

In practice, the outcome of this random event can be determined by comparing $q(\mu_i^*|\mu_{i-1})$ with a sample drawing ς obtained from a uniform distribution over $[0,1]$: $\mu_i^* = \mu_i$ if $q(\mu_i^*|\mu_{i-1}) > \varsigma$, else μ_i^* is discarded and replaced with a new candidate drawing.

Note that for the case in which

$$\iota(\mu|\theta) \equiv P(\mu|X),$$

the probability

$$q(\mu_i^*|\mu_{i-1}) = 1 \qquad \forall \mu_i^*,$$

and we have reverted to the direct-sampling case.

Finally, letting $\{\mu_i\}$ denote the sequence of accepted drawings, $E[g(\mu)]$ is once again approximated via

$$\overline{g}_N = \frac{1}{N}\sum_{1}^{N} g(\mu_i),$$

with associated numerical standard error estimated as in (9.38).

Note the parallels between the role played by $q(\mu_i^*|\mu_{i-1})$ in this algorithm, and the weight function

$$w(\mu) = \frac{P(\mu|X)}{I(\mu|\theta)}$$

in the importance-sampling algorithm. Both serve to eliminate the influence of their respective proposal densities in estimating $E[g(\mu)]$, and reserve this role to the posterior distribution. In this case, $q(\mu_i^*|\mu_{i-1})$ will be relatively low when the probability assigned to μ_i^* by $\iota(\mu|\mu_{i-1},\theta)$ is relatively high; and $q(\mu_i^*|\mu_{i-1})$ will be relatively high when the probability assigned to μ_i^* by $P(\mu|X)$ is relatively high.

As with the Gibbs sampler, numerical standard errors, the CD statistic (9.39), and the CS_t statistic (9.40) can be used to check for the convergence of $\overline{g}_N$. In addition, a symptom of an ill-fitted specification of $\iota(\mu|\theta)$ in this case is a tendency to experience high rejection frequencies.

Turning to the independence chain variant of this algorithm, the stand-in density $\iota(\mu|\mu_{i-1},\theta)$ specializes to

$$\iota(\mu|\mu_{i-1},\theta) = \iota(\mu|\theta).$$

That is, the stand-in density is independent across Monte Carlo replications, precisely as with the case of the importance sampling counterpart $I(\mu|\theta)$.

Under the random walk variant, candidate drawings μ_i^* are obtained according to

$$\mu_i^* = \mu_{i-1} + \varepsilon_i, \tag{9.42}$$

where the density specified over ε is symmetric about 0, and its rotation is determined by θ. In this case, the stand-in density specializes to

$$\iota(\mu|\mu_{i-1},\theta) = \iota(\mu - \mu_{i-1}|\theta),$$

so that the center of $\iota(\mu|\mu_{i-1},\theta)$ evolves over Monte Carlo replications following a random walk.

The approaches to tailoring $I(\mu|\theta)$ described above can be adopted to tailoring $\iota(\mu|\mu_{i-1},\theta)$ under either variant of the algorithm. For example, under the independence chain algorithm, θ can be constructed to mimic posterior estimates of the mean and covariance of μ obtained given an initial specification θ_0, and updated sequentially. And a good initial specification can be fashioned after maximized values of the mean and covariance of μ obtained via the application of a hill-climbing procedure to $P(\mu|X)$. Likewise, under the random walk algorithm the rotation of $\iota(\mu - \mu_{i-1}|\theta)$ can be constructed to mimic estimates of the covariance of μ.

9.5 Model Comparison

Just as posterior distributions can be used to assess conditional probabilities of alternative values of μ for a given model, they can also be used to assess conditional probabilities associated with alternative model specifications. The assessment of conditional probabilities calculated over a set of models lies at the heart of the Bayesian approach to model comparison. (For examples of applications to DSGE models, see Geweke, 1999b; Schorfheide, 2000; Fernandez-Villaverde and Rubio-Ramirez, 2004; and DeJong and Ripoll, 2004.)

Relative conditional probabilities are calculated using a tool known as a posterior odds ratio. To derive this ratio for the comparison of two models A and B, we begin by rewriting the posterior distribution as represented in (9.3). We do so to make explicit that the probability assigned to a given value of μ is conditional not only on X, but also on the specified model. For model A, the posterior is given by

$$P(\mu_A|X, A) = \frac{L(X|\mu_A, A)\pi(\mu_A|A)}{p(X|A)}, \tag{9.43}$$

where we use μ_A to acknowledge the potential for μ to be specific to a particular model specification. Integrating both sides with respect to μ_A, and recognizing that the left-hand side integrates to 1, we have

$$p(X|A) = \int L(X|\mu_A, A)\pi(\mu_A|A)d\mu_A. \tag{9.44}$$

This is the marginal likelihood associated with model A: it is the means by which the quality of the model's characterization of the data is measured. The measure for model B is analogous.

Just as Bayes' Rule can be used to calculate the conditional probability associated with μ_A, it can also be used to calculate the conditional probability associated with model A:

$$p(A|X) = \frac{p(X|A)\pi(A)}{p(X)}, \tag{9.45}$$

where $\pi(A)$ indicates the prior probability assigned to model A. Substituting (9.44) into (9.45) yields

$$p(A|X) = \frac{\left[\int L(X|\mu_A, A)\pi(\mu_A|A)d\mu_A\right]\pi(A)}{p(X)}. \tag{9.46}$$

Finally, taking the ratio of (9.46) for models A and B (a step necessitated by the general inability to calculate $p(X)$) yields the posterior odds ratio

$$PO_{A,B} = \frac{\left[\int L(X|\mu_A, A)\pi(\mu_A|A)d\mu_A\right]\pi(A)}{\left[\int L(X|\mu_B, B)\pi(\mu_B|B)d\mu_B\right]\pi(B)}. \tag{9.47}$$

The ratio of marginal likelihoods is referred to as the Bayes factor, and the ratio of priors as the prior odds ratio. Extension to the analysis of a larger collection of models is straightforward.

Approaches to model comparison based on posterior-odds ratios have several attractive features. First, all competing models are treated symmetrically; there is no null model being compared to an alternative, just a collection of models for which relative conditional probabilities are computed. Relatedly, no difficulties in interpretation arise for the case in which all models are known to be approximations of reality (i.e., false). The question is simply: which among the collection of models has the highest conditional probability? Finally, the models need not be nested to facilitate implementation.

Regarding implementation, this can be achieved using importance-sampling or MCMC methods. The only complication relative to the calculation of $E[g(\mu)]$ is that in this case, proper densities must be used in calculating $w(\mu)$. Given proper densities,

$$\int L(X|\mu_A, A)\pi(\mu_A|A)d\mu_A \tag{9.48}$$

can be approximated via importance sampling using

$$\overline{w} = \sum_{i=1}^{N} w(\mu_i). \tag{9.49}$$

Using MCMC in the independence chain Metropolis-Hastings algorithm, with $\iota(\mu|\theta)$ serving as the proposal density, and μ_i^* representing the proposal drawn on the ith iteration, define

$$w(\mu_i^*) = \frac{L(X|\mu_i^*)\pi(\mu_i^*)}{\iota(\mu_i^*|\theta)}. \tag{9.50}$$

In this case, $\int L(X|\mu_A, A)\pi(\mu_A|A)d\mu_A$ can be approximated using

$$\overline{w} = \sum_{i=1}^{N} w(\mu_i, \mu_i^*). \tag{9.51}$$

Geweke (1999a) provides details for both approximations.

In addition to these traditional means of calculating marginal likelihoods, Geweke (1999b) proposes a posterior-odds measure similar in spirit to a methods-of-moments analysis. The construction of the measure begins with the specification of a reduced-form model for the observable variables under investigation. Using this specification and an uninformative prior, the corresponding posterior distribution over a collection of moments m is estimated. Finally, the overlap between this distribution and distributions associated with competing structural models is measured, and converted into a posterior-odds measure. The construction of all posteriors is straightforward, involving the calculation of $E[g(\mu)]$ as described above. Schorfheide (2000) proposes a related procedure under which a loss function is specified over m, enabling the researcher to adjust the relative weights assigned to specific elements of m in judging overlap.

Let $P_A(m)$ denote the posterior distribution of m associated with model A, and $V(m)$ the posterior distribution of m associated with the reduced-form model. The posterior odds in favor of model A relative to B are defined in this case as

$$PO_{A,B} = \frac{\left[\int P_A(m)V(m)dm\right]\pi(A)}{\left[\int P_B(m)V(m)dm\right]\pi(B)}; \tag{9.52}$$

thus $PO_{A,B}$ provides a characterization of the relative overlap between the reduced-form density over m and the posterior densities associated with models A and B. The greater the overlap exhibited by model A relative to model B, the greater will be $PO_{A,B}$.

Evaluation of the integrals required to calculate $PO_{A,B}$ can be facilitated by kernel density approximation. Let $m_A(i)$ denote the ith of M drawings of m obtained from $P_A(m)$ (or given the use of an importance-sampling approximation, a suitably weighted drawing from the importance density associated with $P_A(m)$), and $m_V(j)$ denote the jth of N drawings obtained from $V(m)$. Then the numerator of $PO_{A,B}$ can be approximated using

$$\frac{1}{MN}\sum_{i=1}^{M}\sum_{j=1}^{N} K(m_A(i), m_V(j)), \tag{9.53}$$

and likewise for the denominator. $K(m_A(i), m_V(j))$ denotes a density kernel used to judge the distance between $m_A(i)$ and $m_V(j)$. For details on kernel density approximation, see, for example, Silverman (1986).

Guidance for interpreting the "weight of evidence" conveyed by the data for model A against model B through a posterior odds calculation is provided by Jeffreys (1961). Odds ranging from 1:1–3:1 constitute "very slight evidence" in favor of A; odds ranging from 3:1–10:1 constitute "slight evidence" in favor of A; odds ranging from 10:1–100:1 constitute "strong to very strong evidence" in favor of A; and odds exceeding 100:1 constitute "decisive evidence" in favor of A.

9.6 Using an RBC Model as a Source of Prior Information for Forecasting

> The future ain't what it used to be.
> —Yogi Berra

To demonstrate the use of structural models as a source of prior information for reduced-form analysis, here we pursue a forecasting application. The goal is to forecast output using an autoregressive specification featuring a unit root with drift. Versions of this workhorse specification provide a common benchmark against which alternative forecasting models are often compared, thus it serves as a useful example for this demonstration (e.g., see Pesaran and Potter, 1997; and DeJong, Liesenfeld, and Richard, 2005b).

One motivation for introducing a structural model into such an analysis is that autoregressive models, along with their multivariate vector-autoregressive counterparts, tend to produce large forecast errors. Following Doan, Litterman, and Sims (1984), a leading response to this problem involves the use of a prior distribution as a gentle means of imposing parameter restrictions on the forecasting model. The restrictions serve to enhance forecasting precision. Working in the context of a VAR model, the so-called "Minnesota prior" used by Doan et al. is centered on a parameterization under which the data are modeled as independent unit-root processes. As noted in section 9.3, the extensions to this work pursued by DeJong, Ingram, and Whiteman (1993); Ingram and Whiteman (1994); Sims and Zha (1998); and Del Negro and Schorfheide (2004) have enabled the use of structural models as an alternative source of prior information that have also proven effective in enhancing forecasting precision. Here we use the RBC model introduced in chapter 5 as a source of prior information.

As a measure of output we consider the post-war quarterly series introduced in chapter 3. We use the data spanning 1947:I–1997:IV for estimation, and compare the remaining observations through 2004:IV with 1- through 28-step-ahead forecasts. Letting Δy_t denote the first difference of logged output, the model is given by

$$\Delta y_t = \underline{\rho}_0 + \underline{\rho}_1 \Delta y_{t-1} + \underline{\rho}_2 \Delta y_{t-2} + \varepsilon_t, \qquad \varepsilon_t \sim iidN(0, \sigma^2); \quad (9.54)$$

that is, Δy_t follows an AR(2) specification. We chose this particular specification following DeJong and Whiteman (1994a), who examined its forecasting performance in application to the 14 macroeconomic time series originally studied by Nelson and Plosser (1982), and extended by Schotman and van Dijk (1991). As DeJong and Whiteman illustrated, although point-forecasts (e.g., means of predictive densities) generated by this model tend to be accurate, they also tend to be imprecise (e.g., as indicated by coverage intervals of predictive densities, described below).

Three alternative representations of (9.54) will prove to be convenient for the purposes of estimation and forecasting. Adding y_{t-1} to both sides of (9.54), we obtain an expression for the level of y_t given by

$$\begin{aligned} y_t &= \underline{\rho}_0 + (1 + \underline{\rho}_1) y_{t-1} + (-\underline{\rho}_1 + \underline{\rho}_2) y_{t-2} - \underline{\rho}_2 y_{t-3} + \varepsilon_t \\ &\equiv \rho_0 + \rho_1 y_{t-1} + \rho_2 y_{t-2} + \rho_3 y_{t-3} + \varepsilon_t. \end{aligned} \quad (9.55)$$

Thus we see that the AR(2) specification for Δy_t implies a restricted AR(3) specification for y_t. The restrictions

$$\rho_1 = (1 + \underline{\rho}_1), \rho_2 = (-\underline{\rho}_1 + \underline{\rho}_2), \rho_3 = -\underline{\rho}_2 \quad (9.56)$$

imply that the polynomial

$$\rho(L) = (1 - \rho_1 L - \cdots - \rho_3 L)$$

in the lag operator L has a unit root, and thus ρ_0 captures the growth rate of y_t (see chapter 3 for a discussion).

For the purpose of forecasting it is convenient to express (9.55) in companion form:

$$\begin{bmatrix} y_t \\ y_{t-1} \\ y_{t-2} \\ 1 \end{bmatrix} = \begin{bmatrix} \rho_1 & \rho_2 & \rho_3 & \rho_0 \\ 1 & 0 & 0 & 0 \\ 0 & 1 & 0 & 0 \\ 0 & 0 & 0 & 1 \end{bmatrix} \begin{bmatrix} y_{t-1} \\ y_{t-2} \\ y_{t-3} \\ 1 \end{bmatrix} + \begin{bmatrix} \varepsilon_t \\ 0 \\ 0 \\ 0 \end{bmatrix}, \quad (9.57)$$

or more compactly,

$$z_t = A z_{t-1} + u_t,$$

where

$$z_t = [\, y_t \; y_{t-1} \; y_{t-2} \; 1]',$$

and

$$u_t = [\varepsilon_t \; 0 \; 0 \; 0].$$

Then letting e be a 5×1 row vector with a 1 in the first row and zeros elsewhere, so that $e' z_t = y_t$, y_{T+J} is given by

$$y_{T+J} = e' A^J z_T + e' \sum_{j=0}^{J-1} A^j u_{T+J-j}. \tag{9.58}$$

Finally, for the purpose of estimation, it is convenient to express the AR(2) model (9.54) for Δy_t in terms of standard regression notation:

$$y = X\underline{\beta} + \upsilon, \tag{9.59}$$

where

$$y = [\Delta y_2 \; \Delta y_3 \ldots \Delta y_T]',$$

$$\underline{\beta} = [\underline{\rho}_0 \; \underline{\rho}_1 \; \underline{\rho}_2],$$

and so on. This is a special case of the reduced-form specification (9.11) involving a single variable rather than a collection of n variables. As such, its associated posterior distribution is a slight modification of the Normal/inverted-Wishart distributions for $(B, \; \Sigma)$ associated with (9.11), which are given in (9.13) and (9.14). Specifically, the conditional posterior distribution for $\underline{\beta}$ is once again normal:

$$P(\underline{\beta}|\sigma^2) \sim N(\widehat{\underline{\beta}}, \sigma^2(X'X)^{-1}), \tag{9.60}$$

where $\widehat{\underline{\beta}}$ is the OLS estimate of $\underline{\beta}$. Then defining

$$\widehat{h} = (y - X\underline{\beta})'(y - X\underline{\beta}),$$

the distribution of σ^2 is now inverted-Gamma rather than inverted-Wishart:

$$P(\sigma^2) \sim IG(\widehat{h}, \tau), \tag{9.61}$$

where τ once again represents degrees of freedom: $\tau = T - k$.

The algorithm described in section 9.3 for obtaining artificial drawings of Σ from an inverted-Wishart distribution can also be used to obtain artificial drawings of σ^2 from an inverted-Gamma distribution. The lone difference is that in this case

$$\widehat{S} = \left(\frac{1}{T-k}\right)(y - X\underline{\beta})'(y - X\underline{\beta})$$

is a single value rather than a matrix. Thus given OLS estimates $\widehat{\underline{\beta}}$ and $\widehat{h}$, calculations of $E(g(\underline{\beta}))$ can be obtained via the direct-sampling method described in sections 9.2 and 9.3: obtain a drawing of σ_i^2 from $IG(\widehat{h}, \tau)$, obtain a drawing of $\underline{\beta}_i$ from $P(\underline{\beta}|\sigma^2)$, calculate $g(\underline{\beta}_i)$, and approximate $E(g(\underline{\beta}))$ by computing the sample average $\overline{g}_N$ over N replications.

The object of interest in this application is a predictive density. To ease notation, let

$$\Theta = [\underline{\beta}' \; \sigma^2]$$

collect the full set of parameters associated with (9.54), so that

$$P(\Theta) \propto P(\underline{\beta}|\sigma^2)P(\sigma^2). \tag{9.62}$$

Also, let

$$\widetilde{y} = [y_{T+1} \; y_{T+2} \ldots y_{T+J}]'$$

denote a J-vector of future observations of y_t. By Bayes' Rule, the joint posterior distribution of $\widetilde{y}$ and Θ is given by

$$P(\widetilde{y}, \Theta) = P(\widetilde{y}|\Theta)P(\Theta), \tag{9.63}$$

and the predictive density of $\widetilde{y}$ is obtained by integrating (9.63) with respect to Θ :

$$P(\widetilde{y}) = \int_{\theta} P(\widetilde{y}|\Theta)P(\Theta)d\Theta. \tag{9.64}$$

Note that by integrating over Θ, the resulting predictive density is unconditional on a given parameterization of the model; the only conditioning is with respect to the data.

In the present application, the algorithm for approximating (9.64) works as follows. First, (9.54) is estimated via OLS, yielding $\widehat{\underline{\beta}}$ and $\widehat{h}$. Along with $\tau = T - k$, these parameterize the Normal/inverted-Gamma distributions over σ^2 and $\underline{\beta}$ defined in (9.60) and (9.61), which are used to generate artificial drawings σ_i^2 and $\underline{\beta}_i$ as described above. For a given drawing, a sequence of disturbances $[u_{iT+1} \; u_{iT+2} \ldots u_{iT+J}]$ is obtained from a $N(0, \sigma_i^2)$ distribution, and $\underline{\beta}_i$ is mapped into $[\rho_{i0} \; \rho_{i1} \; \rho_{i2} \; \rho_{i3}]$ as indicated in (9.56). Finally, these are fed into (9.58) to obtain a sample drawing of $\widetilde{y}$. Histograms compiled over 10,000 replications of this process for each element of $\widetilde{y}$ approximate the predictive densities we seek. Below, means of these densities provide point forecasts, and associated measures of precision are provided by upper and lower boundaries of 95% coverage intervals.

Before presenting forecasts obtained in this manner, we describe the method employed for introducing prior information into the analysis, using the RBC model as a source. Recall briefly the structural parameters included in the model: capital's share of output α; the subjective discount factor $\beta = \frac{1}{1+\varrho}$, where ϱ is the subjective discount rate; the degree of relative risk aversion ϕ; consumption's share (relative to leisure) of instantaneous utility φ; the depreciation rate of physical capital δ; the AR parameter specified for the productivity shock ρ; and the standard deviation of innovations to the productivity shock σ.

Collecting these structural parameters into the vector μ, the methodology begins with the specification of a prior distribution $\pi(\mu)$. The objective of the methodology is to map the prior over μ into a prior over the parameters Θ of the reduced-from model. For a given drawing μ_i from $\pi(\mu)$, this is accomplished as follows. First the model is solved, yielding a parameterized specification for the model variables x_t:

$$x_t = F_i x_{t-1} + e_t, \qquad e_t \sim N(0, Q_i). \tag{9.65}$$

Next, a simulated realization $\{e_{it}\}_{t=1}^{T^*}$ is obtained from $N(0, Q_i)$, which along with $x_0 = 0$ is fed into (9.65) to produce a simulated realization of $\{x_{it}\}_{t=1}^{T^*}$. The simulated realization of output $\{y_{it}\}_{t=1}^{T^*}$we seek is obtained by applying an appropriately defined observation matrix H to the realized sequence of x_{it}: $y_{it} = H' x_{it}$.

Given $\{y_{it}\}_{t=1}^{T^*}$, the next step is to use these observations to estimate the AR(2) model (9.54) via OLS. Casting the model in the standard OLS form (9.59), as output from this step the following terms are collected:

$$\widehat{\underline{\beta}}_i, \qquad (X_i' X_i),$$

$$\widehat{h}_i = (y - X\underline{\beta})'(y - X\underline{\beta}).$$

Coupled with $\tau^* = T^* - k$, these terms serve to parameterize the Normal/inverted-Gamma prior distributions associated with μ_i:

$$P(\beta|\sigma^2) = N(\widehat{\underline{\beta}}_i|\sigma^2(X_i' X_i)^{-1}), \tag{9.66}$$

$$P(\sigma^2) \sim IG(\widehat{h}_i, \tau^*). \tag{9.67}$$

Combining these distributions with the Normal/inverted-Gamma distributions (9.60) and (9.61) associated with the actual data, we obtain the modified distributions

$$P(\beta|\sigma^2) \sim N(\beta^P|\sigma^2(X'X + X_i' X_i)^{-1}) \tag{9.68}$$

$$P(\sigma^2) \sim IG(h^P, \tau + \tau^*), \tag{9.69}$$

where

$$\beta^P = [\sigma^{-2}(X'X + X_i'X_i)]^{-1}\left[(\sigma^{-2}X'X)\widehat{\beta} + (\sigma^{-2}X_i'X_i)\widehat{\beta}_i\right] \quad (9.70)$$

$$H^P = \widehat{h}_i + \widehat{H} + (\widehat{\beta} - \widehat{\beta}_i)'(X_i'X_i)(X'X + X_i'X_i)^{-1}(X'X)(\widehat{\beta} - \widehat{\beta}_i). \quad (9.71)$$

Predictive densities can be constructed numerically using these modified distributions precisely as described above.

Recall that (9.68)–(9.71) are constructed from a single realization of structural parameters μ_i from the prior distribution $\pi(\mu)$. In the results presented below, for each of 10,000 realizations of μ_i we obtained, we generated 10 realizations of Θ_i from (9.68)–(9.71), each of which was used to construct a realization of $\widetilde{y}$.

Regarding the specification of $\pi(\mu)$, this was patterned closely after the calibration exercise conducted in chapter 6, section 6.4. Its foundation is a sequence of independent Normal distributions specified over β, δ, and ϕ; the respective means (standard deviations) used to produce the results reported below are 0.99 (0.005), 0.025 (0.01), 1.5 (1). The distribution over β was truncated from above at 0.995 and from below at 0.98, and the distributions over δ and ϕ were truncated from below at 0 (the imposition of truncation is described below).

Given a drawing of (β, δ, ϕ), the remaining parameters were constructed using the following sequence of steps. Using $\beta = 1/\varrho - 1$ and δ, α was constructed as described in chapter 6 as the value necessary for matching the steady state investment/output ratio with its empirical counterpart:

$$\alpha = \left(\frac{\delta + \varrho}{\delta}\right)\frac{\overline{i}}{\overline{y}}$$
$$= \left(\frac{\delta + \varrho}{\delta}\right)0.175. \quad (9.72)$$

In addition, α was restricted to lie between 0.15 and 0.4. Likewise, φ was constructed as the value necessary for matching the steady state consumption/output ratio with its empirical counterpart:

$$\varphi = \frac{1}{1 + \frac{2(1-\alpha)}{\overline{c}/\overline{y}}}$$
$$= \frac{1}{1 + \frac{2(1-\alpha)}{0.825}}. \quad (9.73)$$

Next, δ was used to construct a realization of the implied trajectory of the physical capital stock $\{k_t\}_{t=1}^{T}$ using the perpetual inventory method. Along with the realization of α, this in turn was used to generate a realization of the Solow residual $\{\log z_t\}_{t=1}^{T}$. The growth rate of $\log z_t$, the parameter g, was then calculated and used to construct the growth rate of the artificial realization of output: $g_y = g/(1-\alpha)$. To maintain consistency with the unit-root specification for output, the AR parameter ρ was fixed at 1. Finally, σ was constructed as the standard deviation of $\Delta \log z_t$.

To summarize, a drawing μ_i from $\pi(\mu)$ was obtained by drawing (β, δ, ϕ) from their respective Normal densities, and then constructing $(\alpha, \varphi, g_y, \sigma)$ as described above. The truncation restrictions noted above were imposed by discarding any μ_i that included an element that fell outside of its restricted range. Approximately 15% of the 100,000 total drawings of μ_i we obtained were discarded in this application.

Given a successful drawing of μ_i, $\{y_{it}\}_{t=1}^{T^*}$ was simulated from (9.65) as described above. Recall that this series is measured in terms of logged deviations of the level of output from steady state. Thus a final adjustment is necessary to convert y_{it} to a measure of the corresponding level of output. The steady state trajectory of output is given by

$$\overline{y}_t = \overline{y}_0(1+g_y)^t, \tag{9.74}$$

where $\overline{y}_0$ represents an arbitrary initial steady state value (subsequent first-differencing eliminates it from the analysis). Let the level of output corresponding with y_{it} be given by Υ_{it}. Then

$$y_{it} = \log\left(\frac{\Upsilon_{it}}{\overline{y}_0(1+g_y)^t}\right), \tag{9.75}$$

and thus the theoretical characterization of the level of output is given by

$$\Upsilon_{it} = \overline{y}_0(1+g_y)^t e^{y_{it}}. \tag{9.76}$$

It is the first difference of the log of Υ_{it} that is used to estimate (9.54) in the numerical integration algorithm described above.

The results of this exercise are presented in table 9.1 and figure 9.1. The table presents posterior means and standard deviations of Θ; the figure illustrates the actual data, point forecasts, and 95% coverage intervals. Five sets of estimates are presented: those obtained in the absence of theoretical restrictions imposed by $\pi(\mu)$, and four sets obtained using alternative specifications of τ^*/τ: 1, 2, 5, 10. (Point forecasts obtained given the restrictions imposed by $\pi(\mu)$ are virtually indistinguishable from those obtained in the absence of $\pi(\mu)$, thus only the latter are illustrated in the figure.) Recall that τ^*/τ measures the ratio of artificial to actual degrees of freedom used in the construction of $P(\beta|\sigma^2)$ and $P(\sigma^2)$ in (9.68) and (9.69). The greater is this ratio, the greater is the influence of $\pi(\mu)$ in the analysis. (Results

TABLE 9.1
Posterior Estimates of the AR(2) Model

τ^*/τ	$\underline{\rho}_0$	$\underline{\rho}_1$	$\underline{\rho}_2$	σ
Means				
0	0.0030	0.384	0.041	0.0096
1	0.0036	0.242	0.073	0.0095
2	0.0038	0.191	0.076	0.0081
5	0.0042	0.139	0.073	0.0072
10	0.0043	0.113	0.071	0.0069
Std. devs.				
0	0.0008	0.072	0.071	0.0005
1	0.0007	0.063	0.061	0.0006
2	0.0006	0.050	0.049	0.0005
5	0.0004	0.037	0.037	0.0005
10	0.0003	0.030	0.030	0.0006

obtained using $\tau^*/\tau = 100$ closely resemble those obtained using $\tau^*/\tau = 10$, thus this case appears to approximate a limiting scenario.)

Three aspects of the changes in parameter estimates obtained in moving from $\tau^*/\tau = 0$ to $\tau^*/\tau = 10$ are notable. First, posterior means of $\underline{\rho}_1$ are reduced by a factor of 3, implying that fluctuations in Δy_t become increasingly less persistent as the influence of the RBC model is increased. Second, the posterior standard deviations associated with $(\underline{\rho}_0\ \underline{\rho}_0\ \underline{\rho}_2)$ are reduced by a factor of 2. Third, posterior means of σ fall from 0.0096 to 0.0069, approaching the standard deviation of $\log z_t$ of 0.0067 obtained under the benchmark parameterization of the model in the calibration exercise conducted in chapter 6 (summarized in table 6.4). All three factors help account for the increased precision of forecasts that results from increases in τ^*/τ, as illustrated in figure 9.1.

To quantify this shrinkage, table 9.2 reports the percentage difference in the levels of output that define upper- and lower-95% coverage intervals at 1-, 4-, 8-, and 12-quarter forecast horizons for all five sets of forecasts. Shrinkage is noticeable even at the 1-quarter horizon, falling from 4% to 3% in moving from $\tau^*/\tau = 0$ to $\tau^*/\tau = 10$. Respective shrinkages at the 4-, 8-, and 12-quarter horizons are from 9.75% to 6%, 13% to 8.3%, and 15.75% to 10%.

Exercise 9.2

Explore the sensitivity of the results of this exercise to changes in $\pi(\mu)$. Are there particular elements of μ that are particularly influential? Why might this be so?

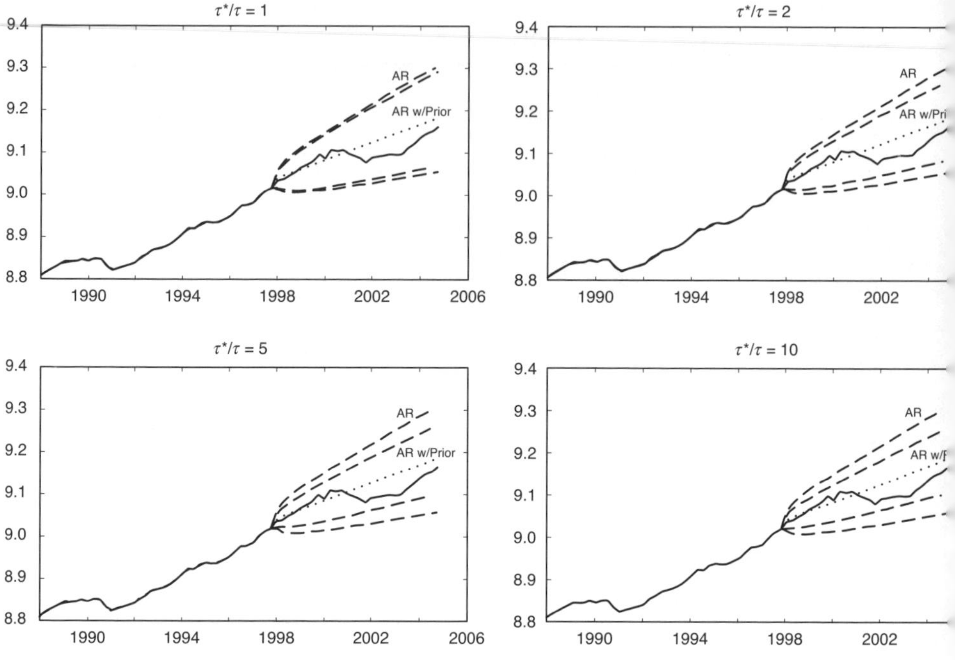

Figure 9.1 Predictive densities.

TABLE 9.2
Coverage-Interval Spreads (%)

Horizon:	*1*	*4*	*8*	*12*
τ^*/τ				
0	4.00	9.75	13.00	15.75
1	4.00	8.75	12.00	14.25
2	3.50	7.50	10.30	12.00
5	3.25	6.50	8.75	10.50
10	3.00	6.00	8.30	10.00

9.7 Estimating and Comparing Asset-Pricing Models

To demonstrate the use of Bayesian methods for model estimation and comparison, we conclude this chapter by analyzing two versions of Lucas' (1978) one-tree model of asset pricing behavior, introduced in chapter 5. Both versions feature a representative household and a single asset. The price of the asset reflects the future dividend stream it is expected to

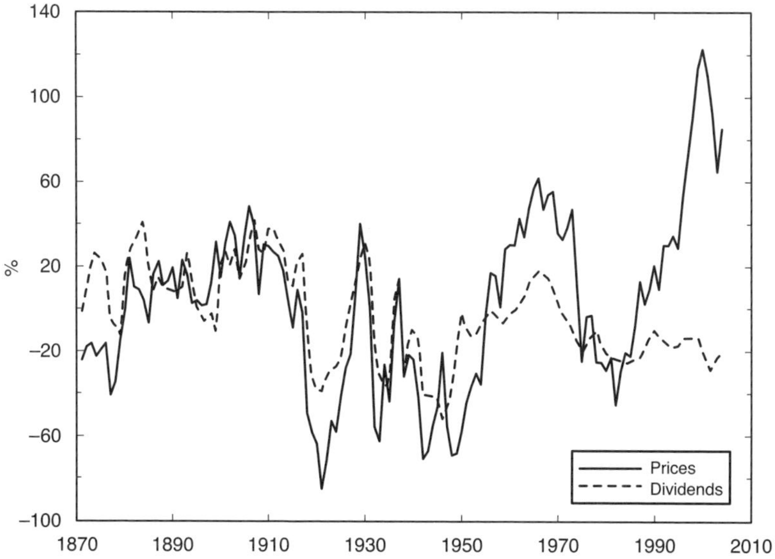

Figure 9.2 Stock prices and dividends (logged deviations from trend).

generate, weighted by the household's marginal rate of substitution. Consumption is financed by dividend payments and an exogenous endowment; innovations to these stochastic processes drive stock prices.

The analysis centers on a puzzle first noted by LeRoy and Porter (1981) and Shiller (1981). In aggregate data on stock prices and corresponding dividends, prices and dividends are closely correlated, but prices are far more volatile. The excess volatility of stock prices over dividends is difficult to reconcile with standard models of asset-pricing behavior, hence the puzzle.

The joint behavior of prices and dividends is illustrated in figure 9.2 for an extended version of the annual Standard and Poor's 500 data analyzed by Shiller. The data span 1871–2004, and are contained in the file `S&PData.txt`, available at the textbook Web site.

The data depicted in the figure are measured as logged deviations from a common trend (details regarding the trend are provided below). Prices are far more volatile than dividends: respective standard deviations are 40.97% and 22.17%. The correlation between the series is 0.409. As discussed below, absent this correlation virtually any preference specification can account for the observed pattern of volatility in Lucas' one-tree environment, if coupled with a sufficiently volatile endowment process. The problem is that endowment innovations weaken the link between price and dividend movements. Accounting for both the high volatility and correlation patterns observed in the data represents the crux of the empirical challenge facing the model.

The analysis presented here follows that of DeJong and Ripoll (2004), which is based on the data measured through 1999. The first version of the model features CRRA preferences; the second features preferences specified following Gul and Pesendorfer (2004), under which the household faces a temptation to deviate from its intertemporally optimal consumption plan by selling its entire holding of shares and maximizing current-period consumption. This temptation imposes a self-control cost that affects the household's demand for share holdings. DeJong and Ripoll's analysis centers on the relative ability of these models to account for the joint behavior of prices and dividends.

Each version of the model reduces to a system of three equations: a pricing kernel that dictates the behavior of p_t, laws of motion for dividends (d_t), and the household's endowment (q_t), which are taken as exogenous. Dropping time subscripts, so that p_t and p_{t+1} are represented as p and p', and so on, and letting MRS denote the marginal rate of substitution between periods t and $t+1$, the equations are given by

$$p = \beta E_t[MRS \cdot (d' + p')], \tag{9.77}$$

$$\log d' = (1 - \rho_d)\log(\overline{d}) + \rho_d \log(d) + \varepsilon_{dt} \tag{9.78}$$

$$\log q' = (1 - \rho_q)\log(\overline{q}) + \rho_q \log(q) + \varepsilon_{qt}, \tag{9.79}$$

with $|\rho_i| < 1$, $i = d, q$, and

$$\begin{bmatrix} \varepsilon_{dt} \\ \varepsilon_{qt} \end{bmatrix} \sim iidN(0, \Sigma). \tag{9.80}$$

Under CRRA preferences, (9.77) is parameterized as

$$p = \beta E_t \left\{ \frac{(d' + q')^{-\gamma}}{(d + q)^{-\gamma}} (d' + p') \right\}, \tag{9.81}$$

where $\gamma > 0$ measures the degree of relative risk aversion. Regarding the stock-price volatility puzzle, notice that a relatively large value of γ intensifies the household's desire for maintaining a smooth consumption profile, leading to an increase in the predicted volatility of price responses to exogenous shocks. Thus any amount of price volatility can be captured through the specification of a sufficiently large value of γ. However, increases in γ entail the empirical cost of decreasing the predicted correlation between p_t and d_t, because increases in γ heighten the role assigned to q_t in driving price fluctuations. This is the puzzle in a nutshell.

Under self-control preferences, the momentary and temptation utility functions are parameterized as

$$u(c) = \frac{c^{1-\gamma}}{1-\gamma}, \tag{9.82}$$

$$v(c) = \lambda \frac{c^{\phi}}{\phi}, \tag{9.83}$$

with $\gamma > 0$, $\lambda > 0$, and $1 > \phi > 0$. These imply the following specification for the pricing kernel:

$$p = \beta E \left[\frac{\frac{(d'+q')^{-\gamma}}{(d+q)^{-\gamma}} + \lambda(d+q)^{\gamma}[(d'+q')^{\phi-1} - (d'+q'+p')^{\phi-1}]}{1+\lambda(d+q)^{\phi-1+\gamma}} \right] \times [d'+p']. \tag{9.84}$$

Notice that when $\lambda = 0$, there is no temptation, and the pricing equation reduces to the CRRA case.

To consider the potential for temptation in helping to resolve the stock-price volatility puzzle, suppose $\lambda > 0$. Then given a positive shock to either d or q, the term

$$\lambda(d+q)^{\gamma}[(d'+q')^{\phi-1} - (d'+q'+p')^{\phi-1}],$$

which appears in the numerator of the pricing kernel, increases. However, if $\phi - 1 + \gamma > 0$, that is, if the risk-aversion parameter $\gamma > 1$, then the denominator of the kernel also increases. If the increase in the numerator dominates that in the denominator, then higher price volatility can be observed under temptation than in the CRRA case.

To understand this effect, note that the derivative of the utility cost of self-control with respect to wealth is positive given $\phi < 1$, so that $v(\cdot)$ is concave:

$$v'(d'+q') - v'(d'+q'+p') > 0.$$

That is, as the household gets wealthier, self-control costs become lower. A reduction in self-control costs serves to heighten the household's incentive to save, and thus its demand for asset holdings. Thus an exogenous shock to wealth increases share prices beyond any increase resulting from the household's incentives for maintaining a smooth consumption profile. This explains why it might be possible to get higher price volatility in this case. Whether this extension is capable of capturing the full extent of the volatility observed in stock prices, while also accounting for the close correlation observed between prices and dividends, is the empirical question to which we now turn.

The first empirical objective is to obtain parameter estimates for each model. This is accomplished using as observables $X_t = (p_t \; d_t)'$, which as noted are measured as logged deviations from a common trend. Regarding the trend, Shiller's (1981) analysis was based on the assumption that dividends and prices are trend stationary; DeJong (1992) and DeJong and Whiteman (1991, 1994b) provided subsequent empirical support for this assumption. Coupled with the restriction imposed by the asset-pricing kernel between the relative steady state levels of dividends and prices, this assumption implies a restricted trend-stationarity specification for prices.

Regarding steady states, since $\{d_t\}$ and $\{q_t\}$ are exogenous, their steady states $\overline{d}$ and $\overline{q}$ are simply parameters. Normalizing $\overline{d}$ to 1 and defining $\eta = \frac{\overline{q}}{\overline{d}}$, so that $\eta = \overline{q}$, the steady state value of prices implied by (9.81) for the CRRA specification is given by

$$\overline{p} = \frac{\beta}{1-\beta}\overline{d} = \frac{\beta}{1-\beta}. \tag{9.85}$$

Letting $\beta = 1/(1+r)$, where r denotes the household's discount rate, (9.85) implies $\overline{p}/\overline{d} = 1/r$. Thus as the household's discount rate increases, its asset demand decreases, driving down the steady state price level. Empirically, the average price/dividend ratio observed in the data serves to pin down β under this specification of preferences.

Under the temptation specification, the steady state specification for prices implied by (9.84) is given by

$$\overline{p} = \beta(1+\overline{p})\left[\frac{(1+\eta)^{-\gamma} + \lambda(1+\eta)^{\phi-1} - \lambda(1+\eta+\overline{p})^{\phi-1}}{(1+\eta)^{-\gamma} + \lambda(1+\eta)^{\phi-1}}\right]. \tag{9.86}$$

The left-hand side of this expression is a 45-degree line. The right-hand side is strictly concave in $\overline{p}$, has a positive intercept, and positive slope that is less than one at the intercept. Thus (9.86) yields a unique positive solution for $\overline{p}$ for any admissible parameterization of the model. An increase in λ causes the function of $\overline{p}$ on the right-hand side of (9.86) to shift down and flatten, thus $\overline{p}$ is decreasing in λ. The intuition for this is that an increase in λ represents an intensification of the household's temptation to liquidate its asset holdings. This drives down its demand for asset shares, and thus $\overline{p}$. Note the parallel between this effect and that generated by an increase in r, or a decrease in β, which operates analogously in both (9.85) and (9.86).

Returning to the problem of detrending, given the value of $\overline{p}/\overline{d}$ implied under either (9.85) or (9.86), the assumption of trend-stationarity for dividends, coupled with this steady state restriction yields:

$$\ln(\overline{d}_t) = \phi_0 + \phi_1 t$$
$$\ln(\overline{p}_t) = \left[\phi_0 + \ln\left(\frac{\overline{p}}{\overline{d}}\right)\right] + \phi_1 t. \qquad (9.87)$$

Thus detrending is achieved by computing logged deviations of prices and dividends from the restricted trajectories given in (9.87). Because the restrictions are a function of the collection of deep parameters μ, the raw data must be retransformed for every re-parameterization of the model. Specifically, given a particular specification of μ, which implies a particular value for $\overline{p}/\overline{d}$, logged prices and dividends are regressed on a constant and linear time trend, given the imposition of the parameter restrictions indicated in (9.87). Deviations of the logged variables from their respective trend specifications constitute the values of X_t that correspond with the specific parameterization of μ.[7]

Under the CRRA specification, the collection of parameters to be estimated are the discount factor β; the risk-aversion parameter γ; the AR parameters ρ_d and ρ_q; the standard deviations of innovations to d and q, denoted as $\sigma_{\varepsilon d}$ and $\sigma_{\varepsilon q}$; the correlation between these innovations $corr(\varepsilon_d, \varepsilon_q)$, and the steady state ratio $\eta = \frac{\overline{q}}{\overline{d}}$. Under the temptation specification, the curvature parameter ϕ and the temptation parameter λ are added to this list.

In specifying prior distributions, DeJong and Ripoll placed an emphasis on standard ranges of parameter values, while assigning sufficient prior uncertainty to allow the data to have a nontrivial influence on their estimates. The priors they used for this purpose are summarized in table 9.3. In all cases, prior correlations across parameters are zero, and each of the informative priors we specify is normally distributed (but truncated when appropriate).

Consider first the parameters common across both models. The prior mean (standard deviation) of the discount factor β is 0.96 (0.02), implying an annual discount rate of 4%. (This compares with an average dividend/price ratio of 4.6% in the data.) The prior for the risk aversion parameter γ is centered at 2 with a standard deviation of 1. A noninformative prior is specified over the covariance matrix of the shocks Σ, proportional to $det(\Sigma)^{-(m+1)/2}$ (where m is the dimension of Σ, or 2 in this case), and the priors over the persistence parameters (ρ_d, ρ_q) are

[7] The GAUSS procedure `ct.prc` is available for use in removing a common trend from a collection of variables.

TABLE 9.3
Parameter estimates

	β	γ	λ	ϕ	ρ_d	ρ_q	$\sigma_{\varepsilon d}$	$\sigma_{\varepsilon q}$	$\chi_{\varepsilon_d,\varepsilon_q}$	$\frac{\overline{q}}{\overline{d}}$
Means:										
Prior	0.960	2.000	0.0000	0.4	0.900	0.900	UN	UN	UN	10.0[illegible]
CRRA	0.957	2.884	NA	NA	0.876	0.913	0.114	0.097	0.313	10.6[illegible]
Self-con.	0.966	1.973	0.00286	0.30	0.880	0.911	0.115	0.154	0.290	5.9[illegible]
Std. dev.:										
Prior	0.020	1.000	0.01	0.2	0.050	0.050	UN	UN	UN	5.0[illegible]
CRRA	0.004	0.814	NA	NA	0.033	0.026	0.007	0.035	0.124	4.3[illegible]
Self-con.	0.007	0.422	0.00182	0.14	0.027	0.023	0.007	0.034	0.108	3.2[illegible]

Posterior Correlations

	$\gamma, \sigma_{\varepsilon q}$	$\gamma, \chi_{\varepsilon_d,\varepsilon_q}$	$\sigma_{\varepsilon q}, \chi_{\varepsilon_d,\varepsilon_q}$	$\chi_{\varepsilon_d,\varepsilon_q}, \frac{\overline{q}}{\overline{d}}$
CRRA	−0.836	−0.302	0.165	0.520
Self-con.	−0.718	−0.343	0.047	0.553

Notes: UN denotes "uninformative prior"; NA denotes "not applicable"; and $\chi_{x,y}$ denotes correlatio between x and y.

centered at 0.9, with standard deviations of 0.05. The prior over $\eta = \overline{q}/\overline{d}$ is more problematic, because neither the literature nor a priori guidance is available to aid in its specification. DeJong and Ripoll considered two alternative specifications of prior means (standard deviations) for η: 5 (3) and 10 (5). In so doing, they found that the data are relatively uninformative regarding the location of η, so that the prior dominates the posterior along this dimension. They also found that the prior over η turned out have little influence both on the fit of the competing models and on estimates of the additional parameters. Here we report results obtained using the (10, 5) specification. Finally, the priors over (β, ρ_d, ρ_q) are truncated from below at zero and from above at 1, and the prior over η is truncated from below at zero.

Priors for the self-control parameters λ and ϕ were specified by focusing on the implications they carry for the steady state relationship between prices and dividends, as indicated in (9.86). Note that along with λ and ϕ, the parameters β, γ, and η also influence this relationship. When $\lambda = 0$, the model reverts to the CRRA case, under which the prior over β is centered on 0.96, implying an annual rate of return of 4%, or a steady state price/dividend ratio of 24. As noted, the average rate of return in the data is 4.6%, implying an average price/dividend ratio of approximately 22. Thus parameterizations of λ and ϕ were chosen with this ratio as an approximate target. Fixing β, γ, and η at their prior means, (λ, ϕ) combinations in the respective ranges ([0, 0.001], [0, 0.75]) deliver this behavior. Increasing β by one prior standard deviation, up to 0.98, moves these ranges to ([0, 0.006], [0, 0.8]); recentering β at 0.96 and decreasing γ by one standard deviation to 1 moves these ranges to ([0, 0.014], [0, 0.8]); and recentering γ and decreasing η by one standard deviation to 5 moves these ranges to ([0, 0.004], [0, 0.7]). Thus notice that small changes in λ can have large impacts on steady state price/dividend values, whereas changes in ϕ have relatively small impacts. Recall the intuition behind the impact of λ: as the household's temptation to consume increases, its demand for asset holdings decreases, thus driving down $\overline{p}$. In light of these calculations, DeJong and Ripoll specified a normal distribution for λ centered and truncated from below at 0, with a standard deviation of 0.01; and a normal distribution for ϕ centered at 0.4 with a standard deviation of 0.2, truncated from below at 0 and from above at 1.

The models were estimated using the sequential importance sampling procedure described in section 9.4. A multivariate-t distribution was specified for $I(\mu|\theta)$, centered initially on prior means specified for the individual elements of μ. The initial covariance matrix specified for $I(\mu|\theta)$ was diagonal, with standard deviations specified as two times larger than the standard deviations specified under the prior. A second specification of $I(\mu|\theta)$ was then constructed using the estimated posterior mean and covariance matrix obtained for μ based on drawings from the initial sampler. After several rounds, moment calculations converged (subject to numerical sampling error) to those reported below.

Due to the method used to detrend the data, the algorithm used to facilitate integration works as follows. Obtain a drawing of μ from $I(\mu|\theta)$. Calculate $\overline{p}/\overline{d}$ based on this drawing, and detrend the raw data using (9.87). Solve the model, and evaluate the likelihood function associated with the corresponding state-space representation. Calculate the weight $w(\mu)$ associated with the drawing, along with functions of interest $g(\mu)$. Finally, compute weighted averages $\overline{g}_N$ as in (9.25) given N replications of this process.

9.7.1 Estimates

Posterior means and standard deviations obtained in this manner for both model specifications are presented in table 9.3. For the CRRA specification, marginal posterior distributions of parameters are graphed in figure 9.3; for the temptation specification, these distributions are graphed in figure 9.4.

For the CRRA specification, the posterior distribution of β is centered very close to the prior (with respective means of 0.957 and 0.96), but

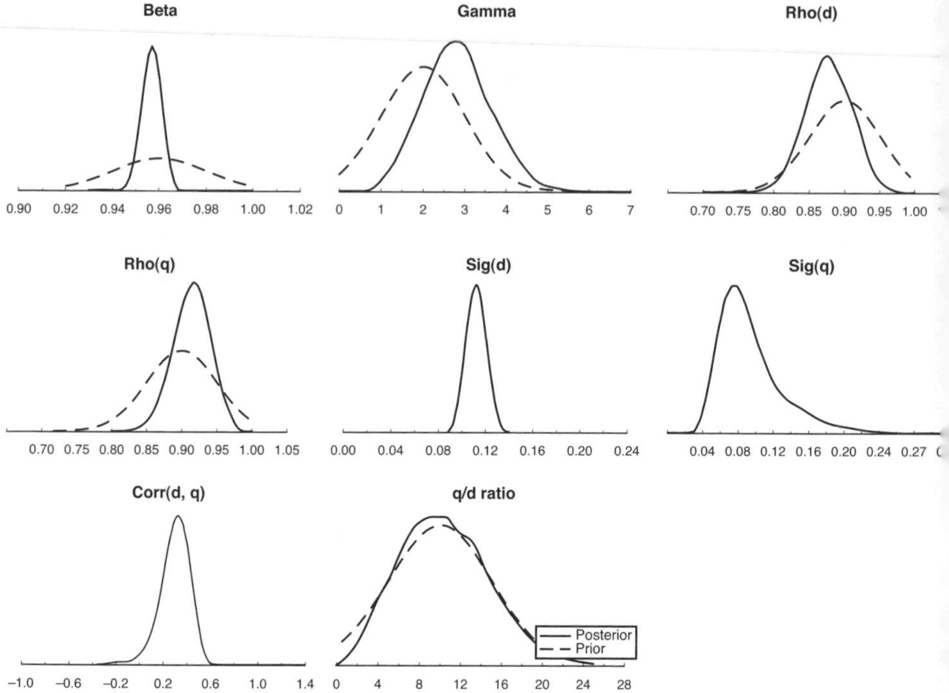

Figure 9.3 Parameter estimates, CRRA preferences.

is much more tightly distributed (its standard deviation of 0.004 is five times less than the prior's). In contrast, the posterior and prior dispersions of γ are similar (respective standard deviations are 0.814 and 1), whereas the posterior distribution is moderately right-shifted relative to the prior (respective means are 2.884 and 2). Thus the data indicate a somewhat higher degree of risk aversion than was embodied in the prior, but not by a dramatic amount: the means differ by less than one prior standard deviation. Regarding the shocks, the persistence of the endowment shock is greater than that of the dividend shock (posterior means of ρ_d and ρ_q are 0.876 and 0.913, with standard deviations of 0.033 and 0.026), and the shocks are positively correlated (the posterior mean of $corr(\varepsilon_d, \varepsilon_q)$ is 0.313, with posterior standard deviation of 0.124). Regarding the size of the shocks, the posterior distributions of $\sigma_{\varepsilon d}$ and $\sigma_{\varepsilon q}$ have similar means (0.114 and 0.097, respectively), but the standard deviation of $\sigma_{\varepsilon q}$ is five times that of $\sigma_{\varepsilon d}$, and is skewed substantially to the right. Finally, as noted above, the prior and posterior distributions of $\eta = \overline{q}/\overline{d}$ are virtually indiscernible, indicating that the data are uninformative regarding the location of this ratio.

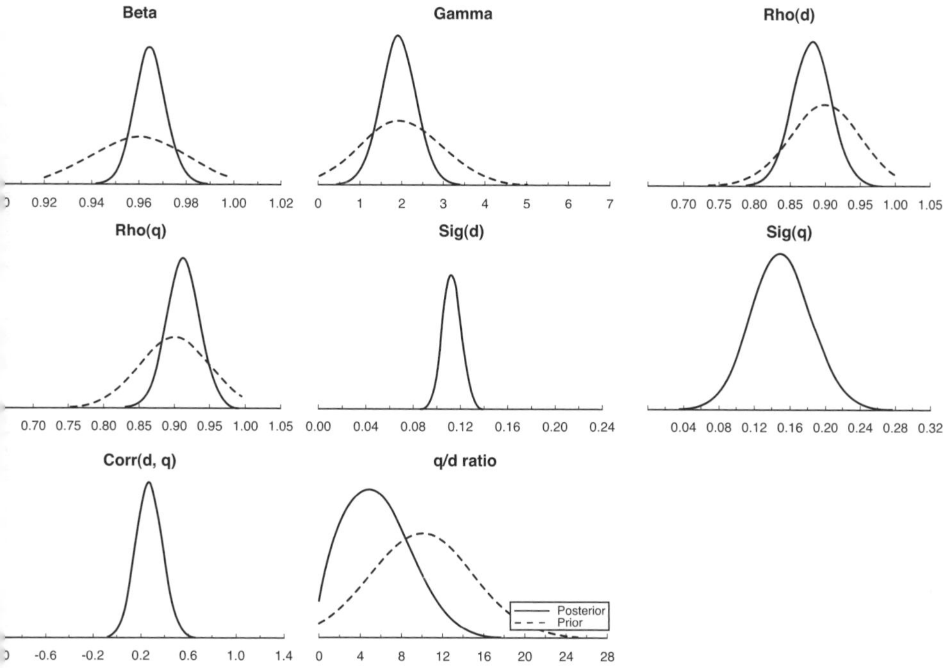

Figure 9.4 Parameter estimates, self-control preferences.

To gain intuition for these results, it is important to keep in mind that the empirical problem confronting the model is largely two-dimensional: simultaneously account for the relatively high volatility of stock prices, and the close correlation observed between prices and dividends. Four parameters play a critical role in confronting this problem. First, large values of $\sigma_{\varepsilon q}$ and η are useful in helping the model along the former dimension: by respectively increasing the volatility and importance of the household's endowment in the budget constraint, these parameters serve to increase the volatility of stock prices without requiring an increase in the volatility of dividends. But these effects are harmful along the latter dimension: they serve to weaken the correlation between movements in prices and dividends. However, this harm can be offset given a large corresponding value of $corr(\varepsilon_d, \varepsilon_q)$, because this boosts the correlation between dividends and the endowment process, and thus between dividends and prices. Finally, large values of γ provide help along the former dimension by boosting the volatility of the household's marginal rate of substitution for a given volatility of consumption. But this again serves to weaken the correlation between prices and dividends, because dividend fluctuations do not constitute the exclusive source of fluctuations in consumption.

These considerations are helpful in understanding, for example, why the posterior distribution of γ is only moderately right-shifted relative to the prior, and why the data clearly favor a positive value for $corr(\varepsilon_d, \varepsilon_q)$. They are also helpful in interpreting the posterior correlations estimated between the parameters of the model. Among the eight parameters featured in this version of the model, there are four nontrivial posterior correlations (reported in table 9.3): between γ and $\sigma_{\varepsilon q}(-0.836)$, γ and $corr(\varepsilon_d, \varepsilon_q)$ (-0.302), $\sigma_{\varepsilon q}$ and $corr(\varepsilon_d, \varepsilon_q)$ (0.165), and $corr(\varepsilon_d, \varepsilon_q)$ and η (0.520). So for example, given a relatively large value of $\sigma_{\varepsilon q}$, $corr(\varepsilon_d, \varepsilon_q)$ is also relatively large, and γ is relatively small: adjustments in these latter parameters help combat the decreased dividend/price correlation associated with the large value of $\sigma_{\varepsilon q}$.

Turning to results obtained using the temptation specification, the estimates obtained for the parameters common to both the self-control and CRRA specifications are relatively distinct. Most notably, the posterior mean of β increases by approximately one standard deviation under the self-control specification; the means of γ and η decrease by approximately one standard deviation; and the mean of $\sigma_{\varepsilon q}$ increases by more than 1.5 standard deviations. Anticipating the discussion of fit to follow, the decreases in γ and η will serve to increase the correlation between prices and dividends in the model, while dampening the volatility of prices; the increase in $\sigma_{\varepsilon q}$ will have the opposite effect. This raises the question of why these offsetting factors arise. The key lies in reconsidering the relationship between steady state prices and dividends given in (9.86). Movements away from zero by the self-control parameters λ and ϕ cause sharp declines in the steady state price/dividend ratio; decreases in γ and η, and increases in β, can serve to offset these effects. Thus it appears that the altered estimates of γ, η, and β arise from an empirical preference for non-zero values of λ and ϕ; the posterior estimates of these self-control parameters confirm this observation.

The posterior mean of ϕ is 0.3, roughly one posterior standard deviation below its prior mean, but still significantly higher than zero. And the posterior mean of λ is 0.00286, which coincides closely with its mode, and lies approximately 1.5 posterior standard deviations above the prior mode of zero. To appreciate the quantitative significance of this estimate, consider two alternative calculations. First, returning to (9.86), if γ, η, β, and ϕ are fixed at their posterior means, an increase of λ from zero to 0.00286 implies a decrease in the steady state price/dividend ratio from approximately 28 to 20.46, implying an increase in annual average returns from 3.57% to 4.89%. In other words, a household endowed with the self-control preferences associated with these parameter estimates would demand an annual "return premium" over a household endowed with CRRA preferences of 1.32%, representing a 36% difference. Second, consider the quantity of

TABLE 9.4
Summary statistics

	σ_p	σ_d	$\frac{\sigma_d}{\sigma_p}$	$\chi_{p,d}$
Means:				
VAR	0.620	0.268	0.448	0.672
CRRA	0.434	0.244	0.571	0.536
Self-control	0.418	0.248	0.608	0.564
Std. dev.:				
VAR	0.183	0.065	0.095	0.178
CRRA	0.067	0.041	0.101	0.079
Self-control	0.069	0.035	0.125	0.101

Notes: VAR statistics summarize flat-prior posterior distributions associated with a six-lag vector autoregression; σ_x denotes the standard deviation of the logged deviation of x from its steady state value; and $\chi_{x,y}$ denotes the correlation between logged deviations from steady state values of x and y.

steady state consumption a household endowed with the temptation specification we estimate would be willing to sacrifice in order to be rid of this temptation. This is the value x such that

$$u(\bar{c} - x) = u(\bar{c}) + v(\bar{c}) - v(\tilde{c}),$$

where here $\tilde{c}$ denotes the steady state value of temptation consumption. Using posterior means of parameter estimates, the implied value of x amounts to 5.25% of $\bar{c}$. Thus these results support the presence of a quantitatively significant temptation effect in the data.

9.7.2 Model Comparison

To assess the relative ability of the competing models to account for the behavior of dividends and prices, DeJong and Ripoll conducted a moment-based posterior-odds comparison following Geweke (1999b), as described in section 9.5. Four moments were chosen for comparison: the standard deviations of prices and dividends σ_p and σ_d, the ratio of standard deviations σ_d/σ_p, and the correlation between prices and dividends $corr(p, d)$. In order to characterize implications for these moments conveyed by the data, posterior distributions were constructed using a six-lag VAR specified for the data. Posterior means and standard deviations obtained using the data and both versions of the model are reported in table 9.4. Corresponding posterior-odds calculations were obtained by approximating the integrals in (9.52) using the kernel density approximation given by (9.53), with a

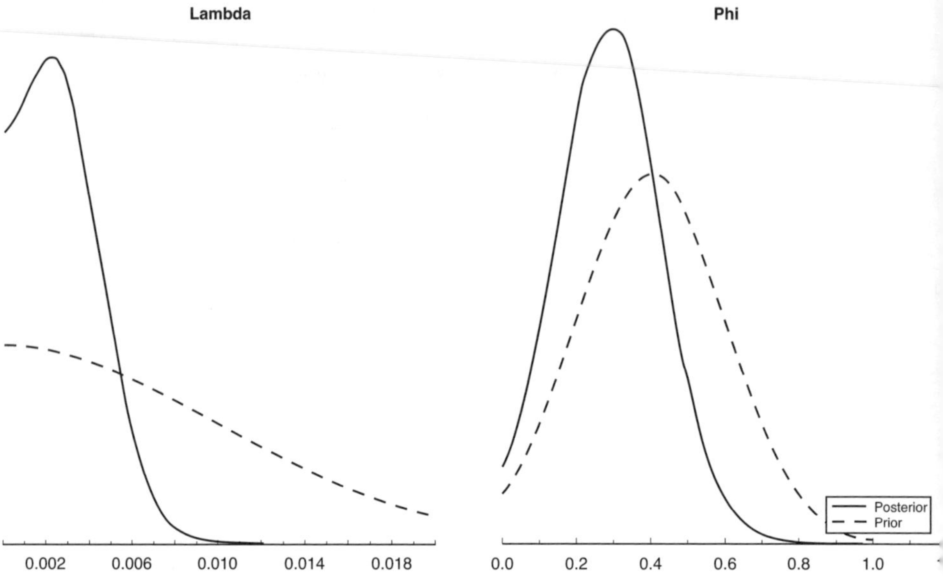

Figure 9.5 Parameter estimates, self-control preferences, continued.

density kernel provided by the Normal distribution. These are also reported in table 9.4. Finally, marginal posterior distributions over these statistics obtained under the CRRA and self-control specifications are depicted in figures 9.5 and 9.6. For comparison, corresponding distributions obtained using the VAR specification are also depicted in both figures.

Regarding the distributions obtained using the VAR specification, note that the distributions over σ_p and $corr(p, d)$ exhibit considerable skewness. As a result, for example, the posterior mean of σ_p (0.62) lies considerably above its sample average of 0.406 (computed using the data measured through 1999).

The relative performance of the competing models in matching the data along these dimensions is very similar. Along the σ_p dimension, respective posterior means (standard deviations) are 0.62 (0.183) in the data, 0.434 (0.067) under the CRRA specification, and 0.418 (0.069) under the self-control specification. Along the $corr(p, d)$ dimension, respective means (standard deviations) are 0.672 (0.178), 0.536 (0.079), and 0.564 (0.101). These differences translate into a posterior-odds ratio of 2.4:1 in favor of the self-control specification, which constitutes "very slight evidence" in favor of the self-control specification according to Jeffreys' (1961) guidelines.

In conclusion, although the parameter estimates reported above support the presence of a nontrivial self-control affect, the affect fails to translate

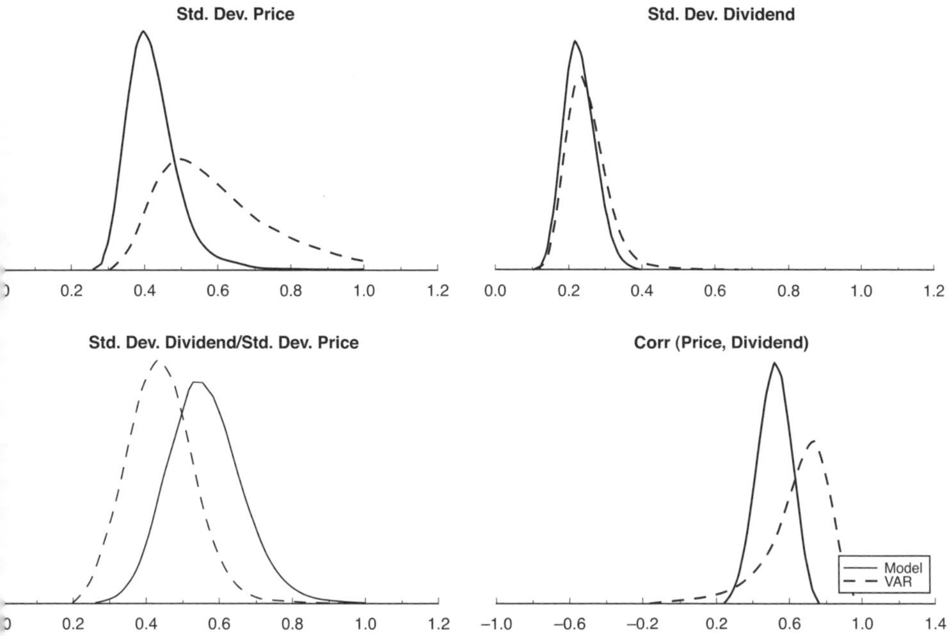

Figure 9.6 Summary statistics, CRRA preferences.

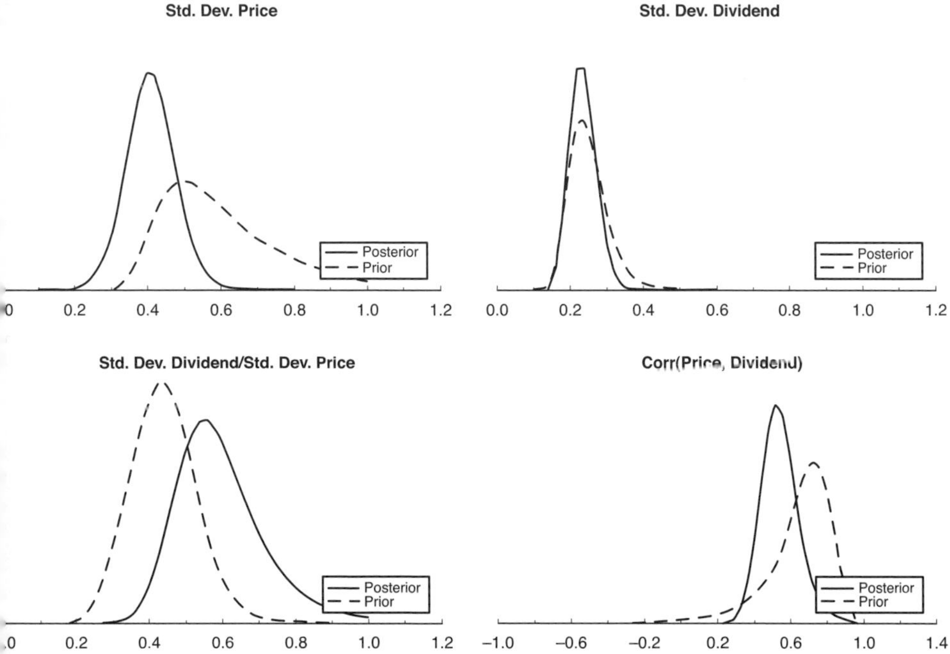

Figure 9.7 Summary statistics, self-control preferences.

into a significant improvement over the account of the stock-price volatility puzzle provided by CRRA preferences. Moreover, in an extension of this analysis to the two-asset environment introduced in chapter 5, section 5.3.2., DeJong and Ripoll (2006) obtained a similar result given the joint investigation of the volatility, risk-free rate, and equity premium puzzles.

Part III

Beyond Linearization

Close only counts in horseshoes and handgrenades.
—Anonymous

Chapter 10

Nonlinear Approximation Methods

IN PRESENTING THE METHODOLOGIES we have described for implementing structural models empirically, we have taken as a point of departure a linearized representation of the underlying model. This final section describes how nonlinear model representations can be used in place of linearized representations in pursuing the empirical objectives we have described. This chapter presents three leading methodologies for obtaining nonlinear model representations: projection methods, value-function iterations, and policy-function iterations. For additional textbook discussions of these and other solution methods, see Judd (1998), Adda and Cooper (2003), Ljungqvist and Sargent (2004), Heer and Maussner (2005), and Canova (2006).[1]

Having characterized nonlinear approximation methods, we go on to show in chapter 11 how the empirical methodologies presented in part II of this book can be applied to nonlinear model representations. Chapter 11 also presents a small simulation exercise under which we compare sets of maximum likelihood estimates obtained using linear and nonlinear approximations of the optimal growth model. The data we analyze were simulated from the model using a known parameterization. The goal is to evaluate how closely the two sets of estimates come to matching the actual model parameterization.

10.1 Notation

To begin, it is useful to specialize the notation we have used throughout the text. Let s_t denote the vector of state variables of the model, with law of motion determined by

[1] GAUSS code for implementing approximation methods that accompanies the text of Heer and Maussner (2005) is available at http://www.wiwi.uni-augsburg.de/vwl/maussner/dgebook/download.html

Fortran code for implementing projection methods that accompanies the text of Judd (1998) is available at http://bucky.stanford.edu/MWRJET/Judd.txt

Similar GAUSS, Matlab, and Fortran code developed by Wouter denHaan and Christian Haefke is available at

http://weber.ucsd.edu/~wdenhaan/peanew.html

The GAUSS code we have developed is described below.

$$s_t = f(s_{t-1}, \upsilon_t), \tag{10.1}$$

where υ_t continues to represent the collection of structural shocks incorporated in the model. Further, let c_t denote the vector of control variables of the model. Unless indicated otherwise, variables in this case are represented in terms of levels, and are taken to be stationary.

The solution to the model we seek is of the form

$$c_t = c(s_t), \tag{10.2}$$

which we refer to hereafter as the policy function of the model's decision makers. The policy function is derived as the solution to

$$F(c(s)) = 0, \tag{10.3}$$

where $F(\cdot)$ is an operator defined over function spaces. Finally, for empirical implementation, (10.1) and (10.2) are mapped into observables by the observation equation

$$\begin{aligned} X_t &= \widetilde{g}(s_t, c_t, \upsilon_t, u_t) \\ &\equiv g(s_t, u_t), \end{aligned} \tag{10.4}$$

where u_t continues to represent measurement error.

To fix ideas, we will work with a simple version of the optimal growth model, which is a modification of the RBC model introduced in chapter 5, section 5.1, under which labor supply is fixed exogenously (and normalized to unity). Briefly, the model is given by

$$y = ak^{\alpha} \tag{10.5}$$

$$y = c + i \tag{10.6}$$

$$k' = i + (1 - \delta)k \tag{10.7}$$

$$\ln(a') = \rho \ln(a) + \varepsilon', \tag{10.8}$$

where (y, k, c, i, a) denote time-t values of output, capital, consumption, investment, and total factor productivity (TFP), and k' denotes the time-$(t+1)$ value of k, and so on. Taking (k_0, a_0) as given, and with $\{\varepsilon_t\}$ following a known stochastic process, the representative household in this model seeks to maximize the expected value of its discounted stream of lifetime utility:

$$U = \max_{\{c_t\}} \quad E_0 \sum_{t=0}^{\infty} \beta^t \frac{c_t^{1-\phi}}{1-\phi}. \tag{10.9}$$

The collection of parameters $\mu = (\alpha, \delta, \rho, \beta, \phi, \sigma_\varepsilon)$ represent capital's share of output, depreciation, the persistence of innovations to $\ln(a)$, the household's subjective discount factor, the coefficient of relative risk aversion, and the standard deviation of innovations to $\ln(a)$.

The model can be collapsed into laws of motion for $s = (a\ k)'$ and a first-order condition for choosing c:

$$k' = ak^\alpha + (1-\delta)k - c \tag{10.10}$$

$$\ln(a') = \rho \ln(a) + \varepsilon' \tag{10.11}$$

$$c^{-\phi} = \max \left\{ \begin{array}{c} \beta E_t \left[(c'^{-\phi})(\alpha a' k'^{\alpha-1} + 1 - \delta) \right] \\ (ak^\alpha)^{-\phi} \end{array} \right\} \tag{10.12}$$

In terms of the general notation introduced above, (10.10) and (10.11) combine to comprise (10.1); ε comprises υ; and (10.12) represents the functional equation to be solved in deriving $c(s)$. The max{} operator is included in (10.12) to account for the possibility of a corner solution under which the household consumes all of its available time-t output: $c = y = ak^\alpha$.

10.2 Projection Methods

10.2.1 Overview

As is true for the example presented in section 10.1, it is not possible in general to derive $c(s)$ analytically, thus we rely instead upon numerical approximation methods, which yield as output $\widehat{c}(s)$. Projection methods are a collection of approximation techniques differentiated along two dimensions: the functional form over s chosen as the basis upon which $\widehat{c}(s)$ is constructed, and the criterion used to judge whether the approximation to (10.3)

$$F(\widehat{c}(s)) = 0 \tag{10.13}$$

is satisfactory. Our presentation of these methods begins with the case in which s is one-dimensional; we then extend the discussion to the multidimensional case.

Regarding the construction of $\widehat{c}(s)$, the point of departure is the Weierstrass theorem, which states that any continuous function $c(\cdot)$ can be approximated uniformly well over the range $s \in [\underline{s}, \overline{s}]$ by a sequence of r polynomials $p_r(s)$ (for details, e.g., see Judd, 1998). That is,

$$\lim_{r \to \infty} \max_{s \in [\underline{s}, \overline{s}]} |c(s) - p_r(s)| = 0. \tag{10.14}$$

A simple example of $p_r(s)$ for the case in which s is one-dimensional is a linear combination of monomials in s,

$$\{s^0, s^1, \ldots, s^r\}:$$

$$p_r(s) = \sum_{i=0}^{r} \chi_i s^i. \tag{10.15}$$

Let $\chi = [\chi_0 \; \chi_1 \ldots \chi_r]'$. In using $p_r(s)$ to construct $\widehat{c}(s, \chi)$, the goal is to choose the parameters collected in the vector χ to provide an optimal characterization of $c(s)$. But although this example is illustrative, it turns out that approximations constructed using (10.15) as a functional form are not particularly effective in practice, due in part to collinearity between elements of the resulting polynomial.

Two leading alternatives to the use of powers of s as a basis for constructing $\widehat{c}(s)$ involve the use of finite element methods and orthogonal polynomials. Details regarding the former are available, for example, from McGrattan (1996, 1999) and Aruoba, Fernandez-Villaverde, and Rubio-Ramirez, (2003); details regarding the latter are available, for example, from Judd (1992).

10.2.2 Finite Element Methods

Finite element methods begin by establishing a grid over the sample space. In the one-dimensional case, the grid is in the form of nonoverlapping line segments. Denoting grid points as $\{s^i\}_{i=1}^r$, the ith component of $p_r(s)$, $p_r^i(s)$, is specified over a single element of s as

$$p_r^i(s) = \left\{ \begin{array}{ll} \frac{s - s^{i-1}}{s^i - s^{i-1}}, & s \in [s^{i-1}, s^i] \\ \frac{s^{i+1} - s}{s^{i+1} - s^i}, & s \in [s^i, s^{i+1}] \\ 0, & \text{otherwise.} \end{array} \right\} \tag{10.16}$$

This forms a sequence of overlapping tent functions over the grid. Centered at the ith grid point, $p_r^i(s)$ increases linearly from zero to 1 as s ranges from

s^{i-1} to s^i, and then decreases linearly towards zero as s ranges from s^i to s^{i+1}. The approximation $\widehat{c}(s,\chi)$ is then constructed using

$$\widehat{c}(s,\chi) = \sum_{i=0}^{r} \chi_i p_r^i(s). \tag{10.17}$$

10.2.3 Orthogonal Polynomials

The definition of an orthogonal polynomial is based on the inner product between two functions f_1 and f_2, given the weighting function w:

$$\langle f_1, f_2 \rangle = \int_{\underline{s}}^{\overline{s}} f_1(s) f_2(s) w(s) ds. \tag{10.18}$$

The family of polynomials $\{\varphi_r\}$ is defined to be mutually orthogonal with respect to $w(s)$ if and only if $\langle \varphi_r, \varphi_q \rangle = 0$ for $r \neq q$. One such family is the Chebyshev family, which is defined over $s \in [-1,1]$ and the weighting function $w(s) = (1-s^2)^{-1/2}$. Given the use of an rth-order Chebyshev polynomial for constructing $\widehat{c}(s,\chi)$, the resulting approximation takes the form

$$\widehat{c}(s,\chi) = \sum_{i=0}^{r} \chi_i T_i(s), \tag{10.19}$$

where

$$\begin{aligned} T_i(s) &= \cos(i \cos^{-1}(s)) \\ &= \cos(i\theta), \qquad s = \cos(\theta). \end{aligned} \tag{10.20}$$

For a given value of s, the corresponding value of $\widehat{c}(s,\chi)$ can be calculated using the following algorithm due to Judd (1998). First, set

$$T_0(s) = 1, \qquad T_1(s) = s. \tag{10.21}$$

Next, perform the recursion

$$T_{i+1}(s) = 2sT_i(s) - T_{i-1}(s), \qquad i = 1, \ldots, r. \tag{10.22}$$

Finally, collecting the $T_i(s)$ terms in the $r+1 \times 1$ vector $T(s)$, calculate

$$\widehat{c}(s,\chi) = T(s)'\chi. \tag{10.23}$$

Although s must be constrained between $[-1,1]$ in working with Chebyshev polynomials, note that a simple transformation can be used to map a state variable defined over a general range $[\underline{s},\overline{s}]$ into a variable defined over the range $[-1, 1]$. For example, for an element of s ranging $\pm\omega$ units above and below the steady state value s^*, the transformation

$$\widetilde{s} = \frac{s - s^*}{\omega} \qquad (10.24)$$

yields the desired range. Hereafter, we take this transformation as granted in working with Chebyshev polynomials.

10.2.4 Implementation

Given the use of either a finite-element method or orthogonal polynomials for constructing $\widehat{c}(s, \chi)$, the approximation of $c(s)$ boils down to the task of choosing χ to "nearly" satisfy

$$F(\widehat{c}(s, \chi)) = 0. \qquad (10.25)$$

In the case of the optimal growth model (with $a \equiv 1$ in the one-dimensional case), $F(\widehat{c}(s, \chi))$ is given by

$$F(\widehat{c}(k, \chi)) = \widehat{c}(k)^{-\phi} - \max\left\{ \begin{array}{c} \beta E_t \left[\begin{array}{c} (\widehat{c}(ak^{\alpha} + (1-\delta)k - \widehat{c}(k))^{-\phi}) \\ (\alpha a'(ak^{\alpha} + (1-\delta)k - \widehat{c}(k))^{\alpha-1} + 1 - \delta \end{array} \right] \\ (ak^{\alpha})^{-\phi} \end{array} \right\}, \qquad (10.26)$$

which emerges from the replacement of k' with $ak^{\alpha} + (1-\delta)k - \widehat{c}(k)$ in (10.12).

Alternative choices of the criterion upon which judgements regarding the quality of approximation are based establish the second dimension along which projection methods are differentiated. Returning to the use of inner products, in general terms the approximation we seek is defined by the parameter vector χ that minimizes

$$\langle F(\widehat{c}(s, \chi)), f(s) \rangle = \int_{\underline{s}}^{\overline{s}} F(\widehat{c}(s, \chi)) f(s) w(s) ds. \qquad (10.27)$$

Alternative specifications for $f(s)$ and $w(s)$ differentiate projection methods along this dimension.

The choice of $F(\widehat{c}(s, \chi)$ for $f(s)$ casts (10.27) in the form of a weighted-least-squares problem. Choosing N distinct values for s ranging over $[\underline{s}, \overline{s}]$, (10.27) can be approximated using

$$\sum_{i=1}^{N} F(\widehat{c}(s_i, \chi))^2 w(s_i), \qquad (10.28)$$

which is a single-valued objective function that can be optimized using, for example, the derivative-based methods discussed in chapter 8. Regarding the specification of $w(s)$, a tent function specified over the range $[\underline{s}, \overline{s}]$, and peaking at the steady state, s^* could be used to assign relatively heavy weights to values of s in the neighborhood of the model's steady state. An alternative specification that serves this purpose is given by

$$w(s) = 1 - \left(\left| \frac{s - s^*}{s^*} \right| \right)^{\kappa}. \tag{10.29}$$

Under the finite element method, a common choice for $f(s)$ (along with $w(s) = 1$) is the sequence of basis functions $p_r^i(s)$, $i = 1, \ldots r$, as defined in (10.16). In this case, known as the Galerkin method, a single-valued objective function is replaced by a system of r equations, which are to be solved by the choice of the r-dimensional vector of coefficients χ:

$$\langle F(\widehat{c}(s,\chi)), p_r^i(s) \rangle = \int_{\underline{s}}^{\overline{s}} F(\widehat{c}(s,\chi)) p_r^i(s) ds = 0, \qquad i = 1, \ldots r. \tag{10.30}$$

The integrals in (10.30) can again be approximated using a sum over a range of distinct values chosen for s. Also, derivative-based methods akin to those available for solving single-valued objective functions are available for solving nonlinear systems of the form (10.30).[2]

Finally, an additional choice for $f(s)$ (once again, coupled with $w(s) = 1$) is the indicator function $\delta(s - s_i)$, $i = 1, \ldots r$, with

$$\delta(s - s_i) = \begin{Bmatrix} 1, & s = s_i \\ 0, & s \neq s_i \end{Bmatrix}. \tag{10.31}$$

Under $\delta(s - s_i)$, the functional equation $F(\cdot) = 0$ is restricted to hold exactly at r fixed points. Approximations based on $\delta(s - s_i)$ are referenced as having been obtained using the collocation method. Once again, the resulting system can be solved using derivative-based methods.

As Judd (1998) notes, the collocation method is particularly attractive in using Chebyshev polynomials for constructing $\widehat{c}(s,\chi)$. This is due to the Chebyshev interpolation theorem, which provides a means of optimizing the r choices of s used to construct $\delta(s - s_i)$. Specifically, let $\{\widetilde{s}_i\}_{i=1}^r$ denote the roots of the rth-order component $T_r(s)$. Then if $F(\widehat{c}(\widetilde{s}_i,\chi)) = 0$ for $i = 1, \ldots, r$ and $F(\widehat{c}(s,\chi))$ is continuous, $F(\widehat{c}(s,\chi))$ will be be close to 0 over the entire range $[-1, 1]$.

[2] GAUSS's `nlsys` package is available for this purpose.

Regarding the roots of $T_r(s)$, recall that

$$\cos(\widehat{\theta}_j) = 0, \qquad \widehat{\theta}_j = (2j-1)\frac{\pi}{2}, \qquad j = 1, 2, \ldots, r \tag{10.32}$$

(i.e., $\cos(\widehat{\theta}) = 0$ for all odd multiples of $\frac{\pi}{2}$). Thus with s defined as $s = \cos(\theta)$ in (10.20), the r roots of $T_r(s)$ are given by

$$\widehat{s}_j = \frac{(2j-1)}{r}\frac{\pi}{2}, \qquad j = 1, 2, \ldots, r. \tag{10.33}$$

A simple means of assessing the quality of a given approximation $\widehat{c}(s, \chi)$ is to assess the resulting residual function $F(\widehat{c}(s, \chi))$ over a range of values chosen for s. Plots of the residual function, sums of squared residual errors, and so on, are effective diagnostic tools. In using collocation methods, choices for s other than those used to construct $\widehat{c}(s, \chi)$ are advisable.

We conclude this general discussion with a note regarding starting values. Depending upon the particular problem and approximation method, the construction of accurate approximations to $c(s)$ can depend critically upon good choices of starting values for the vector of parameters χ. The identification of good starting values is particularly important in using these solution methods as a basis for conducting empirical work, because empirical analyses of the model in question typically require that the model be solved repeatedly for alternative specifications of the structural parameters μ. The ability to obtain accurate approximations quickly and reliably is therefore critical in this context.

Unfortunately, the identification of effective starting values is highly problem-specific. However, a good general approach is to select starting values that mimic the behavior of $c(s)$ estimated using a linearized approximation of the model in the neighborhood of the steady state. For example, the first two elements of an rth-order Chebyshev polynomial are $[1, s]$; thus a good candidate choice of starting values can be obtained by setting initial values of χ_0 and χ_1 in a way that captures the estimated linear relationship between c and s in the neighborhood of c^* and s^*, and setting all other initial values of χ_i to zero. Further elaboration on this example is provided in section 10.2.6.

10.2.5 Extension to the ℓ-dimensional Case

The extension of projection methods to the ℓ-dimensional case is accomplished through the construction of multi-dimensional functions specified over $s = (s_1\ s_2 \ldots s_\ell)'$. One approach to this construction involves the use of tensor products of univariate functions specified over the individual elements of s. Let $p_{r_j}(s_j)$ denote an r_j^{th}-order sequence of polynomials specified for the jth element of s. Then the ℓ-dimensional tensor product of $p_{r_j}(s_j)$, $j = 1, \ldots, \ell$, is given by

$$P = \prod_{j=1}^{\ell} p_{r_j}(s_j). \tag{10.34}$$

For example, with $\ell = 2$, $r_1 = 2$, $r_2 = 3$, and $p_{r_j}(s_j)$ representing Chebyshev polynomials, we have

$$P = (1 + s_1 + T_2(s_1))\,(1 + s_2 + T_2(s_2) + T_3(s_2)), \tag{10.35}$$

where $T_i(s_j)$ is the ith-order term corresponding with the jth element of s, and is defined as in (10.22).

Using a given tensor product, the approximation $\widehat{c}(s,\chi)$ is constructed using

$$\widehat{c}(s,\chi) = \sum_{i_1=1}^{r_1}\sum_{i_2=1}^{r_2}\cdots\sum_{i_\ell=1}^{r_\ell} \chi_{i_1 i_2 \ldots i_\ell} P_{i_1 i_2 \ldots i_\ell}(s_1, s_2, \ldots, s_\ell), \tag{10.36}$$

where

$$P_{i_1 i_2 \ldots i_\ell}(s_1, s_2, \ldots, s_\ell) = p_{i_1}(s_1) p_{i_2}(s_2) \ldots p_{i_\ell}(s_\ell). \tag{10.37}$$

In the example of (10.35), the elements $P_{i_1 i_2 \ldots i_\ell}(s_1, s_2, \ldots, s_\ell)$ can be constructed by forming the vectors

$$T^1 = (1 \;\, s_1 \;\, T_2(s_1))',$$
$$T^2 = (1 \;\, s_2 \;\, T_2(s_2) \;\, T_3(s_2))',$$

and retrieving the elements of the 3×4 matrix $T = T^1 T^{2\prime}$.

Regarding the estimation of $\chi_{i_1 i_2 \ldots i_\ell}$, the procedures described above for the univariate case extend naturally. For example, the collocation method remains an attractive means of implementing Chebyshev polynomials for constructing $\widehat{c}(s,\chi)$, because the Chebyshev interpolation theorem continues to apply. Specifically, letting $\{\widetilde{s}_{j,i}\}_{i=1}^{r_j}$ denote the roots of the r_j^{th}-order component $T_{r_j}(s_j)$, if $F(\widehat{c}(\widetilde{s}_{j,i},\chi)) = 0$ for $i = 1, \ldots, r_j$, $j = 1, \ldots, \ell$, and $F(\widehat{c}(s,\chi))$ is continuous, $F(\widehat{c}(s,\chi))$ will be close to 0 over the entire ℓ-dimensional hypercube ranging over $[-1, 1]$ in each dimension.

Although conceptually straightforward, extensions to the ℓ-dimensional case involving tensor products can be complicated by a computational challenge when ℓ is large: as ℓ increases, the number of elements $\chi_{i_1 i_2 \ldots i_\ell}$ that must be estimated to construct the approximation $\widehat{c}(s,\chi)$ increases exponentially. This phenomenon is a manifestation of the curse of dimensionality. One means of combating it in this context is to keep the polynomial orders $r_1, r_2, \ldots, r_\ell$ relatively modest. An alternative means is to replace tensor products with complete polynomials.

The complete set of polynomials of degree k is given by the collection of terms that appear in the kth-order Taylor Series approximation of $c(s)$ about an arbitrary value s^0. Recall that this approximation is given by

$$c(s) \approx c(s^0) + \sum_{i=1}^{\ell} \frac{\partial c(s)}{\partial s_i}(s^0)(s_i - s_i^0)$$

$$+ \frac{1}{2!} \sum_{i_1=1}^{\ell} \sum_{i_2=1}^{\ell} \frac{\partial^2 c(s)}{\partial s_{i_1} \partial s_{i_2}}(s^0)(s_{i_1} - s_{i_1}^0)(s_{i_2} - s_{i_2}^0)$$

$$\ldots$$

$$+ \frac{1}{k!} \sum_{i_1=1}^{\ell} \cdots \sum_{i_k=1}^{\ell} \frac{\partial^k c(s)}{\partial s_{i_1} \ldots \partial s_{i_k}}(s^0)(s_{i_1} - s_{i_1}^0) \ldots (s_{i_k} - s_{i_k}^0).$$

Thus for $k = 1$, the complete set of polynomials for the ℓ-dimensional case is given by

$$P_1^\ell = \{1, s_1, s_2, \ldots, s_\ell\}.$$

For $k = 2$ the set expands to

$$P_2^\ell = P_1^\ell \cup \{s_1^2, s_2^2, \ldots, s_\ell^2, s_1 s_2, s_1 s_3, \ldots, s_1 s_\ell, s_2 s_3, \ldots, s_{\ell-1} s_\ell\},$$

and so on. So in the two-dimensional case, whereas the tensor product of third-order polynomials involves 16 terms, the complete set of third-degree polynomials involves only 10 terms.

An approximation of $\widehat{c}(s, \chi)$ based on the complete set of k-degree polynomials can be obtained, for example, using a weighted-least-squares procedure, as in (10.28).

10.2.6 Application to the Optimal Growth Model

We now demonstrate the application of these methods, working in the context of the optimal growth model. This is done for three alternative assumptions regarding the behavior of a. We begin by working with a nonstochastic specification under which a is fixed at unity. Next, we specify a as following a two-state Markov process (defined below). Finally, we specify $\ln(a)$ as following an AR(1) process, as in (10.8). Under the first two specifications the remaining parameters are fixed at $(\alpha, \beta, \delta, \phi) = (0.33, 0.96, 0.1, 2)$; under the latter specification the parameters are given by $(\alpha, \beta, \delta, \phi) = (0.33, 0.96, 1, 1)$. We chose the latter specification because it admits an exact solution to the policy function. Specifically, the policy function in this case is given by

$$c = (1 - \alpha\beta)ak^{\alpha}, \tag{10.38}$$

a result we invite the reader to verify. Thus under this parameterization, we have an exact benchmark available for judging the accuracy of our approximation algorithm.[3]

Beginning with the nonstochastic specification, approximation was achieved using as an objective function the weighted-least-squares function (10.28), with $w(k)$ specified as indicated in (10.29), with $\kappa = 0.1$. We used an 11th-order Chebyshev polynomial as a basis function for constructing $\widehat{c}(k, \chi)$. Recall that since Chebyshev polynomials are defined over $[-1, 1]$, we worked with the normalization

$$\widetilde{k} = \frac{k - k^*}{\omega_k}. \tag{10.39}$$

Finally, we used the derivative-based optimization algorithm of Broyden, Fletcher, Goldfarb, and Shanno (BFGS) to minimize (10.28) with respect to χ (implemented using the Gauss package `optmum`). We used trial-and-error to specify starting values for χ in this case, and we encourage the reader to investigate the delicate sensitivity of the estimated policy function we obtained to alternative specifications, along with the accuracy of the corresponding estimates (using `determa.prg`). The policy function we derived in this manner is illustrated in figure 10.1. The range over which the policy function is plotted is $[k^* - \omega_k, k^* + \omega_k]$, which is partitioned into 101 equally spaced intervals using $\omega_k = 0.25 * k^*$, (i.e., the range is 25% above and below k^*).

The top panel of the figure depicts the policy function itself; the bottom panel depicts its slope. The slope declines from 0.156 to 0.128 over the range of k, a decrease of nearly 22%. In a $\pm 5\%$ range around the steady state, the percentage change in the slope is roughly 6%. These slope calculations are of interest for comparison with a linear approximation of the policy function, under which the slope is constant over the range of k.

Turning to the stochastic specification of the model, two critical differences arise: the functional equation (10.26) now requires the calculation of a conditional expectation, and the state vector s is now two-dimensional.

[3] The GAUSS programs `determa.prg`, `markova.prg`, and `ara.prg` were used to perform the calculations described here. In addition, the collection of procedures in `stogro.src` and `stogrowm_nonlin_exact.src` served as inputs to these programs. The former solves the model under an arbitrary parameterization of the model; the latter is specialized to the case in which $\delta = 1, \phi = 1$.

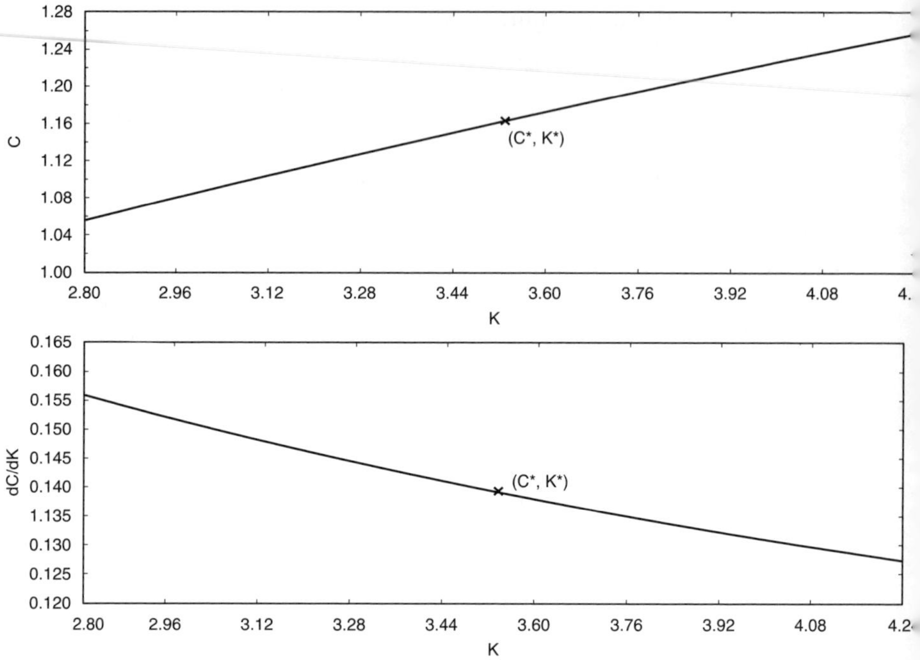

Figure 10.1 Policy function for the nonstochastic optimal growth model.

To describe how the first issue was addressed, we pause to characterize the two-state Markov process specified for a. This was constructed by discretizing the state space over a into one of two outcomes: $a = aL = 0.95$ in state L (low productivity) and $a = aH = 1.05$ in state H (high productivity). Given this discretization, the stochastic behavior of a, which is manifested by movements between low and high states, was modeled by specifying that movements across states are dictated by the following matrix of transition probabilities:

$$P = \begin{bmatrix} p_{LL} & 1 - p_{HH} \\ 1 - p_{LL} & p_{HH} \end{bmatrix}. \tag{10.40}$$

Here, p_{LL} denotes the probability of a remaining in the low state given that it began in the low state, and so on. For a general n-state process, the transition matrix P is $n \times n$, with entries contained in the ith column indicating transition probabilities given that the process is initially in state i; that is, the (row-j, column-i) element of P indicates the probability of ending up in state j given that the current state is i.

Following Hamilton (1994), we note that there is a close relationship between a two-state Markov process and an AR(1) specification. To see this, let ξ_t be a 2×1 vector with a 1 in the first row and a zero in the second row given that $a_t = aL$, and a 0 in the first row and a 1 in the second row given that $a_t = aH$. Then the conditional expectation of ξ_{t+1} given ξ_t is given by

$$E_t \xi_{t+1} = P\xi_t, \tag{10.41}$$

and thus

$$\xi_{t+1} = P\xi_t + \varsigma_{t+1}, \tag{10.42}$$

where $\varsigma_{t+1} = \xi_{t+1} - E_t \xi_t$ is a mean-zero unforecastable stochastic process.

Note that (10.42) is in the form of a first-order VAR specified for ξ_{t+1}. Further, noting that the second element of ξ_t, denoted as ξ_{2t}, can be written as $\xi_{2t} = 1 - \xi_{1t}$, (10.42) can be rewritten as

$$\begin{bmatrix} \xi_{1t+1} \\ \xi_{2t+1} \end{bmatrix} = \begin{bmatrix} p_{LL} & 1 - p_{HH} \\ 1 - p_{LL} & p_{HH} \end{bmatrix} \begin{bmatrix} \xi_{1t} \\ \xi_{2t} \end{bmatrix} + \begin{bmatrix} \varsigma_{1t+1} \\ \varsigma_{2t+1} \end{bmatrix}. \tag{10.43}$$

Rearranging the first row of (10.43), we obtain

$$\xi_{1t+1} = (1 - p_{22}) + (-1 + p_{11} + p_{22})\xi_{1t} + \varsigma_{1t+1}, \tag{10.44}$$

which is in the form of an AR(1) representation for ξ_{1t+1}. With $p_{11} = p_{22}$, the selection of $\rho = 0.8$ translates into probability of transition between states of 0.1. The results presented below were obtained using this specification.

Returning to the first issue then, under the Markov specification the conditional expectation $E_t a'$ is the weighted average of aL and aH, with relative weights given by $[0.1, 0.9]$ given the initial value of a in the low state, and $[0.9, 0.1]$ given the initial value of a in the high state.

Under the AR(1) specification for $\ln(a')$, the situation is slightly more complicated, because the conditional expectation in (10.12) cannot be calculated analytically. Calculation in this case is accomplished via numerical approximation, using what are known as quadrature methods. To describe how this is done, we begin by defining $z' = \ln(a')$, and the normalized counterpart $\widetilde{z}' = \frac{z'}{\omega_z} = \rho\widetilde{z} + \widetilde{\varepsilon}$, $\widetilde{\varepsilon} = \frac{\varepsilon}{\omega_z}$, which is restricted to the range $[-1, 1]$. With the policy function for c defined over $(\widetilde{z}, \widetilde{k})$, and in this case with $\phi = \delta = 1$, the expectation we must approximate is given by

$$
\begin{aligned}
I &= \beta E_t\left[\left(\frac{1}{\widehat{c}(\widetilde{z}', \widetilde{k}')}\right)\alpha k'^{\alpha-1}e^{\rho z+\varepsilon'}\right] \\
&= \frac{1}{\sigma_\varepsilon\sqrt{2\pi}}\int_{-\infty}^{\infty} f(\varepsilon'|z,k)e^{-\frac{\varepsilon'^2}{2\sigma_\varepsilon^2}}d\varepsilon' \\
&= \frac{\omega_z}{\sigma_\varepsilon\sqrt{2\pi}}\int_{-\infty}^{\infty} f(\widetilde{\varepsilon}'|z,k)e^{-\frac{(\omega_z\widetilde{\varepsilon}')^2}{2\sigma_\varepsilon^2}}d\widetilde{\varepsilon}'. \qquad (10.45)
\end{aligned}
$$

The second equality is obtained by defining

$$
f(\varepsilon'|z,k) = \beta\left(\frac{1}{\widehat{c}(\widetilde{z}', \widetilde{k}')}\right)\alpha k'^{\alpha-1}e^{\rho z+\varepsilon'}
$$

and replacing E_t with the integral over the $N(0,\sigma_\varepsilon^2)$ density for ε' it entails. The third equality is obtained by implementing a change in variables from ε to $\widetilde{\varepsilon}$. To see why, recall that for some general transformation $\varepsilon' = g(\widetilde{\varepsilon}')$, the change-of-variables formula is given by

$$
\int_a^b f(\varepsilon')d\varepsilon = \int_{g^{-1}(a)}^{g^{-1}(b)} f(g(\widetilde{\varepsilon}'))g'(\widetilde{\varepsilon}')d\widetilde{\varepsilon}'. \qquad (10.46)
$$

Having set notation, note that the integral in (10.45) is a specific example of a generic integral of the form

$$
\int_a^b f(x)dx.
$$

Quadrature methods comprise a wide class of numerical tools available for approximating many alternative specific examples of such an integral (for an overview, e.g., see Judd, 1998). Gaussian quadrature methods comprise a specific subclass of methods that use the orthogonal approach to functional approximation to evaluate such integrals. Gaussian quadrature approximations take the form

$$
\int_a^b f(x)dx \approx \sum_{i=1}^{n} w_i f(x_i), \qquad (10.47)
$$

where the nodes x_i and corresponding weights w_i are chosen to provide accurate and efficient approximations. Specifically, the nodes and weights are chosen so that if $f(\cdot)$ were in fact a polynomial of degree $2n-1$, then the approximation (10.47) will be exact given the use of n nodes and weights.

Gauss-Hermite nodes and weights are tailored specifically for cases in which integrals are of the form

$$\int_{-\infty}^{\infty} f(x)e^{-x^2}\,dx,$$

which arises naturally in working with normal random variables, as is the case in this application. In particular, defining

$$\widetilde{\varepsilon}' = \frac{\sigma_{\varepsilon}\sqrt{2}}{\omega_z}x,$$

use of the change-of-variables formula (10.46) enables the approximation of the conditional expectation (10.45) via

$$\begin{aligned} I &= \frac{\omega_z}{\sigma_{\varepsilon}\sqrt{2\pi}}\int_{-\infty}^{\infty} f(\widetilde{\varepsilon}'|z,k)e^{-\frac{(\omega_z\widetilde{\varepsilon}')^2}{2\sigma_{\varepsilon}^2}}\,d\,\widetilde{\varepsilon}' \\ &\approx \frac{1}{\sqrt{\pi}}\sum_{i=1}^{n} w_i(f(\sigma_{\varepsilon}\sqrt{2})x_i) \qquad (10.48) \end{aligned}$$

using Gauss-Hermite weights and nodes.[4]

Turning now to the latter issue, with the state vector being two-dimensional, we approximated the policy function using an orthogonal collocation scheme applied to a tensor product of Chebyshev polynomials. Because under the Markov specification a can take on only one of two values, we specified a second-order polynomial along the a dimension, and a fifth-order polynomial along the k dimension. Under the AR(1) specification we specified a fourth-order polynomial along the $\ln(a) = z$ dimension, but higher-order specifications are feasible in this case.

Regarding the range chosen for z in the approximation, care must be taken to insure that in the Gauss-Hermite approximation (10.48), the set of nodes x_i are chosen subject to the restriction that the corresponding values of $\widetilde{z}_i'$ remain bounded between $[-1,1]$, because we are using Chebyshev polynomials to construct $\widehat{c}(\widetilde{z}',\widetilde{k}')$. To achieve this here we follow Judd (1992) by constructing the upper and lower bounds for z as

$$(\underline{z},\overline{z}) \pm \frac{1}{1-\rho}3\sigma_{\varepsilon};$$

that is, the bounds are set as the values of z that would be attained if every single realized ε innovation were either three times larger or smaller than

[4] A table of Gauss-Hermite weights and nodes is available at the textbook Web Site.

the expected value of 0. With $\rho = 0.8$, this range is $\pm 15\sigma_\varepsilon$, enabling the specification of a large number of Gauss-Hermite nodes that lie within the required bounds. We used seven nodes to obtain the results reported below.

Given these choices for ranges and nodes, the corresponding parameterization χ was obtained as the solution to the system of equations

$$F(\widehat{c}(\widetilde{s}_{j,i}, \chi)) = 0, \qquad i = 1, \ldots, r_j, \; j = z, k. \tag{10.49}$$

Under the AR(1) specification, $\{\widetilde{s}_{j,i}\}_{i=1}^{r_j}$ denotes the roots of the r_j^{th}-order component $T_{r_j}(s_j)$, $j = z, k$. Under the Markov specification, $\widetilde{s}_{j,i}$ was constructed using the roots of the r_j^{th}-order component $T_{r_j}(s_j)$ along the k dimension, and using aL and aH along the a dimension. (In this case, we used Gauss's `nlsys` routine to solve the corresponding systems of equations.)

As with the deterministic specification, the ability to obtain accurate approximations again hinges critically upon the identification of reliable starting values for χ. But encouragingly, the use of starting values fashioned from the log-linear approximation of the model around its steady state turned out to provide reliable values that quickly and consistently led to accurate approximations for a wide range of alternative parameterizations of the model.

To describe the construction of starting values, let σ_a and σ_k denote the elasticity of c with respect to a and k, respectively, calculated using the log-linear approximation of the model. (Here we are supposing that the policy function is defined over a and k; the case for which the policy function is instead defined over z and k proceeds analogously.) In terms of levels of variables, in the neighborhood of the steady state an approximation of c can be constructed using σ_a and σ_k as

$$c \approx c^* + \frac{\partial c}{\partial a}(a^*, k^*)(a - a^*) + \frac{\partial c}{\partial k}(a^*, k^*)(k - k^*)$$
$$+ \frac{1}{2}\frac{\partial^2 c}{\partial a \partial k}(a^*, k^*)(a - a^*)(k - k^*) \tag{10.50}$$

$$= c^* + \frac{c^*}{a^*}\sigma_a(a - a^*) + \frac{c^*}{k^*}\sigma_k(k - k^*)$$
$$+ \frac{1}{2}\left(\frac{c^*}{a^*}\sigma_a\right)\left(\frac{c^*}{k^*}\sigma_k\right)(a - a^*)(k - k^*). \tag{10.51}$$

Of course, additional terms could also be incorporated in this approximation. Given the use of a tensor product representation, the corresponding approximation of $\widehat{c}(a, k, \chi)$ we seek is of the form

$$\widehat{c}(a,k,\chi) \approx \chi_{11} + \chi_{12}\left(\frac{a-a^*}{\omega_a}\right) + \chi_{21}\left(\frac{k-k^*}{\omega_k}\right) + \chi_{22}\left(\frac{a-a^*}{\omega_a}\right)\left(\frac{k-k^*}{\omega_k}\right) + \ldots . \tag{10.52}$$

Matching terms across representations yields the suggested starting values

$$\chi_{11} = c^*, \quad \chi_{12} = \sigma_a\omega_a\frac{a^*}{c^*}, \quad \chi_{21} = \sigma_k\omega_k\frac{k^*}{c^*},$$
$$\chi_{22} = \frac{1}{2}\left(\sigma_a\omega_a\frac{a^*}{c^*}\right)\left(\sigma_k\omega_k\frac{k^*}{c^*}\right). \tag{10.53}$$

The remaining values of χ were initiated at 0. As noted, use of these starting values turned out to yield an effective means of approximating the policy function for both the Markov and AR specifications for $\ln(a)$. Indeed, `nlsys` typically generated a model solution using only two or three quasi-Newton iterations for a wide range of alternative parameterizations of the model. We invite the reader to verify this performance (working with `markova.prg` and `ara.prg`).

The policy functions obtained using the Markov specification for a are depicted in figure 10.2. The upper (lower) curve depicts the policy function given an initial value of a in the high (low) state. Note that the functions closely parallel each other, and shift roughly symmetrically above and below the policy function obtained under the non-stochastic specification. As with figure 10.1, the range for k over which the policy function is plotted is $[k^* - \omega_k, k^* + \omega_k]$, which is partitioned into 101 equally spaced intervals using $\omega_k = 0.25k^*$.

The policy function obtained using the AR(1) specification follows the pattern depicted in figure 10.2 closely, and thus is not illustrated here. Instead, we conclude this application section with a note regarding the accuracy of the approximation we obtained in this case. Recall that under the AR(1) specification, we are able to compare our approximation with the exact solution, which is given by (10.38). Over a set of values ranging over $k \in [k^* - \omega_k, k^* + \omega_k]$, $\omega_k = 0.25$ and $z \in [-\omega_z, \omega_z]$, $\omega_z = \frac{1}{1-\rho}3\sigma_\varepsilon$, the maximum approximation error we obtained amounts to a difference in consumption values of only 0.0003% of the steady state value of consumption. As we shall see in chapter 11, section 11.3, this high degree of accuracy turns out to be critical in conducting likelihood-based empirical analyses.

Exercise 10.1

Using a projection method, construct policy functions for the choice of both consumption and leisure for the RBC model introduced in chapter 5.

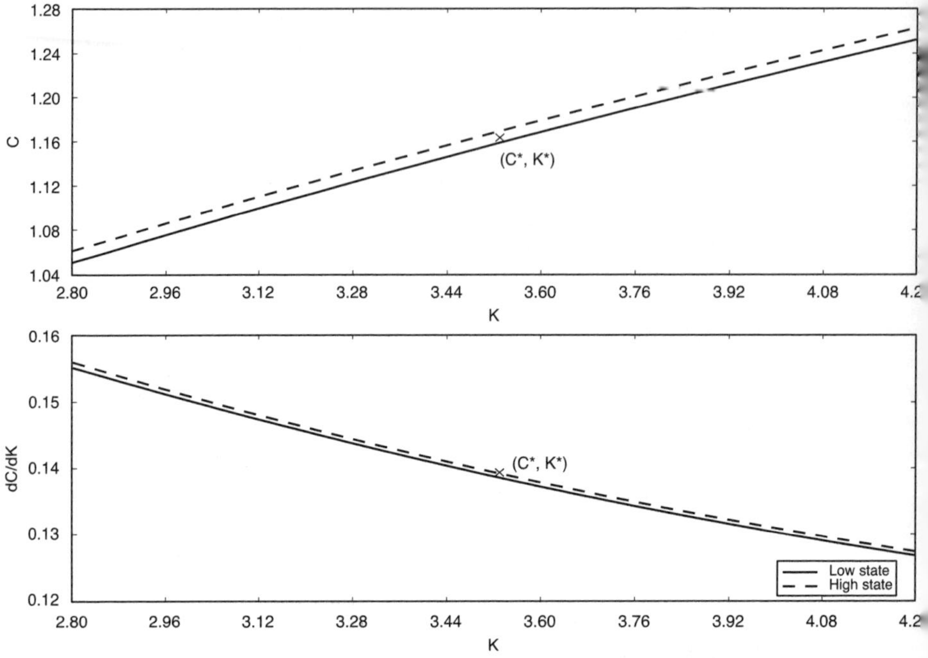

Figure 10.2 Policy function for the stochastic optimal growth model.

Parameterize the model as specified in table 6.4 of chapter 6. Use the Gauss programs available at the textbook Web site for guidance. [Hint: Note from the intratemporal optimality condition which determines the labor/leisure trade-off that the policy function for determining c implicitly serves to determine the policy function over labor supply. Exploit this fact in deriving policy functions.]

10.3 Value-Function and Policy-Function Iterations

10.3.1 Dynamic Programming

Value-function and policy-function iterations are alternative methods for constructing $\widehat{c}(s)$ that are closely linked to the dynamic programming approach to solving sequential optimization problems. We begin here by providing a brief overview of this approach. Far more detailed textbook treatments are provided, for example, by Sargent (1987b) and Stokey and Lucas (1989). In addition, Judd (1998), Adda and Cooper (2003), Ljungqvist and Sargent (2004), and Heer and Maussner (2005) describe links between dynamic programming and the iterative methods for approximating $\widehat{c}(s)$ described here.

To begin, we establish explicitly the optimization problem that gives rise to the policy function $c(s)$. We seek to choose an infinite sequence $\{c_t\}$ that maximizes

$$E_0 \sum_{t=0}^{\infty} \beta^t u(c_t, s_t),$$

subject to the law of motion for the state

$$s_{t+1} = g(s_t, c_t, \upsilon_{t+1}), \tag{10.54}$$

taking s_0 as given. The parameter $0 < \beta < 1$ is the usual subjective discount factor, and E_0 is the expectations operator conditional on information available at time 0 (i.e., s_0). Moreover, in order for the problem to be well-defined, $u(c_t, s_t)$ must be concave, and the set

$$\{(s_{t+1}, s_t) : s_{t+1} \leqslant g(s_t, c_t, \upsilon_t)\}$$

must be convex and compact.

The policy function is a contingency plan for choosing the optimal value of c_t given the realization of the state s_t: $c_t = c(s_t)$. Using this rule to substitute for c_t in (10.54) yields the alternative characterization of the law of motion for the state we have used throughout the text: $s_t = f(s_{t-1}, \upsilon_t)$.

Let $V(s_0)$ denote the value of behaving optimally over the lifetime of the problem given the initial endowment of the state s_0. This as-yet-unknown function is linked with the policy function $c(s_0)$ via Bellman's equation:

$$V(s_0) = \max_{c_0}\{u(c_0, s_0) + \beta E_0 V(s_1)\}, \tag{10.55}$$

subject to (10.54). In words, Bellman's equation states that the value of behaving optimally over the lifetime of the problem is equal to the value of behaving optimally in the initial period, plus the expected discounted value of behaving optimally thereafter.

Substituting for s_1 in (10.55) using (10.54), we obtain

$$V(s_0) = \max_{c_0}\{u(c_0, s_0) + \beta E_0 V(g(s_0, c_0, \upsilon_1))\}. \tag{10.56}$$

Also, substituting for c_0 using the as-yet-unknown policy function $c_t = c(s_t)$, the max operator is eliminated from (10.56), yielding

$$V(s_0) = u(c(s_0), s_0) + \beta E_0 V(g(s_0, c(s_0), \upsilon_1)). \tag{10.57}$$

Having made these substitutions, we have transformed Bellman's equation into a functional equation involving $V(s)$ and $c(s)$. Given the concavity of $u(c_t, s_t)$ and the convexity and compactness of

$$\{(s_{t+1}, s_t) : s_{t+1} \leqslant g(s_t, c_t, \upsilon_t)\},$$

the $V(s)$ satisfying (10.57) will be strictly concave, and will be approached in the limit via iterations on

$$V^{j+1}(s) = \max_c \{u(c, s) + \beta EV^j(g(s, c, \upsilon'))\}. \quad (10.58)$$

Moreover, the $c(s)$ that maximizes the right-handside of (10.56) will be unique and time-invariant. For details see Stokey and Lucas (1989).

The fact that iterations on (10.58) are convergent implies that (10.56) is a contraction mapping. This property is critical in establishing value-function iterations and policy-function iterations as viable techniques for constructing $\widehat{c}(s)$.

10.3.2 Value-Function Iterations

As its name implies, the value-function-iteration approach uses iterations on (10.58) to generate an approximation of $\widehat{c}(s)$. To operationalize (10.58), we begin by constructing a discretization of the state space. That is, we divide the state space in such a way that s can take on only one of n possible values:

$$s \in \{s_1, \ldots, s_n\}.$$

Also, we restrict c to take on only one of m possible values:

$$c \in \{c_1, \ldots, c_m\}.$$

The finer the grid specified over $\{s, c\}$, the more accurate will be the resulting approximation; the importance of approximation accuracy in the context of empirical applications is discussed in chapter 11. Note that as the dimensionality of the state space increases, for a given number of grid points specified along each dimension, n will increase exponentially. This phenomenon is another manifestation of the curse of dimensionality.

Given this discretization, the next step is to calculate a corresponding set of transition probabilities. This entails the use of (10.54), coupled with the distributional assumption made for υ_t. For each possible value s_i in the state-space grid, (10.54) and the distributional assumption made for υ_t imply that a given choice of c induces a probability associated with the transition to the state-space value s_j, $j = 1, \ldots, n$ in the following period. Let this probability be given by $\pi_{ij}(c)$. In practice, $\pi_{ij}(c)$ can be constructed using Markov-transition matrices or quadrature-approximation methods, both of which were introduced in section 10.2.

The collection of probabilities $\pi_{ij}(c)$ calculated for a given c comprise a Markov transition matrix $\Pi(c)$. Given the present state s_i, the ith row of

$\Pi(c)$ indicates the probability distribution induced over the state space in the next period given the specific choice of c.

Having constructed transition probabilities, the iteration process can be implemented. Let V denote the $n \times 1$ vector of values associated with the initial endowment of the n possible values of s in the discretized state space. That is, the ith element of V, denoted as V_i, is given by

$$\begin{aligned} V_i &= \max_{c \in \{c_1,\ldots,c_m\}} \left\{ u(c, s_i) + \beta \sum_{j=1}^{n} \pi_{ij}(c) V_j \right\} \\ &= \max_{c \in \{c_1,\ldots,c_m\}} \{ u(c, s_i) + \beta \Pi_i(c) V \}, \end{aligned} \tag{10.59}$$

where $\Pi_i(c)$ is the ith row of $\Pi(c)$. Our goal is to obtain the solution to (10.59), which takes the form of two vectors: the vector of optimized values V^*, and the associated $n \times 1$ vector of controls C^*. Specifically, the ith element of C^* is given by

$$C_i^* = \arg \max_{c \in \{c_1,\ldots,c_m\}} \{ u(c, s_i) + \beta \Pi_i(c) V \}. \tag{10.60}$$

Note that C_i^* emerges as the best of the m possible choices for c available in the set $\{c_1, \ldots, c_m\}$.

To explain the solution strategy it is useful at this point to simplify notation. Let S be an $n \times 1$ vector containing the n possible values of the state space. Replacing s_i with S in (10.59), and replacing $\Pi_i(c)$ with $\Pi(c)$, (10.59) can be rewritten as

$$\begin{aligned} V &= \max_{c \in \{c_1,\ldots,c_m\}} \{ u(c, S) + \beta \Pi(c) V' \} \\ &\equiv TV', \end{aligned} \tag{10.61}$$

where V' is next period's value function. This defines T as a mapping from next period's value function into today's. Likewise, (10.60) can be rewritten as

$$\begin{aligned} C^* &= \arg \max_{c \in \{c_1,\ldots,c_m\}} \{ u(c, S) + \beta \Pi(c) V' \} \\ &\equiv \Gamma V'. \end{aligned} \tag{10.62}$$

Now, the iteration process is initiated with a guess for V, V^0. Using this guess, we generate the sequence

$$V^{j+1} = TV^j, \qquad j = 1, \ldots. \tag{10.63}$$

Because (10.56) is a contraction mapping, this sequence is guaranteed to converge. Using a convergence criterion of the form $\| V^{j+1} - V^j \| < \varepsilon$, we obtain a stopping rule. Once a stopping point has been realized, an approximation to V^* has been obtained; the associated policy function is then obtained as $C^* = \Gamma V^*$. The $n \times 1$ elements of C^* map directly into the elements of S; this mapping yields the approximation $\widehat{c}(s)$ we set out to obtain.

Exercise 10.2

Reconduct exercise 10.1 using a value-function iteration method in place of a projection method. Experiment with alternative grid densities specified over the state space, and compare the resulting approximations with your previous findings.

10.3.3 Policy-Function Iterations

Iterations on (10.63) can often be slow to converge in practice, a point emphasized, for example, by Ljungqvist and Sargent (2004). Convergence can often be enhanced significantly using policy-function iterations, sometimes referenced as the Howard improvement algorithm.

In order to describe this algorithm, we require some additional notation. Let the $n \times 1$ vector C^1 be the candidate guess for C^* associated with the guess chosen for V; that is, $C^1 = \Gamma V^0$. Next, let U^1 denote an $n \times 1$ vector containing values of the current-period objective function evaluated at the n values that comprise S and C^1:

$$U^1 = u(C^1, S). \tag{10.64}$$

Finally, let Π^1 denote the Markov transition matrix induced by coupling the corresponding elements of S and C^1; that is, given the state s_i in the current period, the ith element of C^1 is chosen as the control, inducing the ith row of probabilities contained in Π^1.

Now, note from the Bellman equation expressed in (10.59) that if C^1 was in fact the optimal specification C^*, then replacing the individual elements c and s_i with the vectors C^* and S, the max operator would be eliminated, yielding

$$V^* = U^* + \beta \Pi^* V^*. \tag{10.65}$$

Solving for V^*, we obtain

$$V^* = (I - \beta \Pi^*)^{-1} U^*. \tag{10.66}$$

If C^1 is not optimal, (10.66) instead serves as an updating equation in the Howard improvement algorithm.

Specifically, the algorithm works as follows. Beginning with a guess V^0, construct the corresponding guess $C^1 = \Gamma V^0$. Next, construct U^1 using

(10.64), and the associated transition matrix Π^1. Inserting (U^1, Π^1) into (10.66), obtain an updated vector V^2. By the jth iteration, the updating equation becomes

$$V^{j+1} = (I - \beta \Pi^j)^{-1} U^j. \tag{10.67}$$

Once again, because (10.56) is a contraction mapping, the resulting sequence $\{V^j\}$ is guaranteed to converge. Using a convergence criterion of the form $\| V^{j+1} - V^j \| < \varepsilon$, obtain a stopping rule. Once a stopping point has been realized, an approximation to V^* has been obtained; the associated policy function is again given by $C^* = \Gamma V^*$.

Exercise 10.3

Reconduct exercise 10.1 using a policy-function iteration method in place of a projection method. For alternative grid densities specified over the state space, compare the convergence speeds you obtain using this algorithm with those obtained using the value-function iterations used in exercise 10.2.

Chapter 11

Implementing Nonlinear Approximations Empirically

THE PREVIOUS CHAPTER PRESENTED methodologies for obtaining nonlinear model approximations. In this chapter, we illustrate how the full range of empirical methodologies presented in part II of the text can be used to analyze the model under investigation once a nonlinear approximation has been obtained. Applications of calibration and moment-matching exercises can be based on model simulations, and classical and Bayesian full-information analyses can be pursued by substituting a particle filter for the Kalman filter as a means of evaluating the likelihood function.

To briefly reestablish notation, recall that s_t denotes the vector of state variables of the model. Its law of motion is given by

$$s_t = f(s_{t-1}, \upsilon_t), \tag{11.1}$$

where υ_t represents the collection of structural shocks incorporated in the model. Further, c_t denotes the vector of control variables of the model. The policy function for c_t is given by

$$c_t = c(s_t); \tag{11.2}$$

its approximated counterpart is given by

$$c_t = \widehat{c}(s_t). \tag{11.3}$$

The full collection of model variables are contained in the vector $x_t = (s_t', c_t')'$. Finally, for empirical implementation, (11.1) and (11.3) are mapped into observables by the observation equation

$$\begin{aligned} X_t &= \widetilde{g}(s_t, c_t, \upsilon_t, u_t) \\ &\equiv g(s_t, u_t), \end{aligned} \tag{11.4}$$

where u_t represents measurement error.

11.1 Model Simulation

The recursive nature of DSGE models renders the task of model simulation straightforward (for details regarding the accuracy of simulations involving

DSGE models, see Santos and Peralta-Alva, 2005). The list of inputs to the simulation process includes a specification of the initial state vector s_0, which can be taken either as known or as a realization obtained from an underlying distribution. The stationary nature of the model (typically induced by an appropriate transformation of variables) renders this distinction as unimportant in simulations designed to characterize the asymptotic properties of the model. Additional inputs include the law of motion (11.1) for s_t, the approximated policy function $\widehat{c}(s_t)$, the mapping (11.4) from model variables x_t to observables X_t, and a random number generator used to obtain artificial drawings of stochastic shocks (and if appropriate, measurement errors) from their underlying distributions. The parameterization of these inputs is determined by a specific specification chosen for the structural parameters of the underlying model, denoted by μ.

Given these inputs, model simulation proceeds exactly as in the linear case. From (11.1), s_0 and $\{\upsilon_t\}_{t=1}^T$ yield $\{s_t\}_{t=1}^T$ directly. Using this series as an input to the policy function yields $\{c_t\}_{t=1}^T$. Then $\{s_t\}_{t=1}^T$ and $\{c_t\}_{t=1}^T$ combine to form $\{x_t\}_{t=1}^T$ ($x_t \equiv (s_t', c_t')$), which combined with $\{u_t\}_{t=1}^T$ maps into X_t as in (11.4). Functions of interest can then be computed using the simulated realizations of $\{X_t\}_{t=1}^T$. To eliminate the influence of the starting value chosen for s_0, a burn-in phase can be implemented. This merely involves discarding the first, say 1,000 artificial realizations obtained for $\{s_t\}_{t=1}^T$. Finally, numerical standard errors can be virtually eliminated using a sufficiently large number of artificial realizations (see chapter 9 for details regarding numerical standard errors).

A novelty in this case arises when using a Markov process to represent the evolution of a stochastic process. For example, recall from the specification of the optimal growth model used in chapter 10 that a Markov process was used to represent the behavior of total factor productivity (TFP) $\{a_t\}_{t=1}^T$. A simple algorithm for generating artificial realizations of $\{a_t\}_{t=1}^T$ for the two-state case is as follows (extension to the n-state case is straightforward). Begin with a particular specification of ξ_0, the 2×1 vector with a 1 in the first row and a zero in the second row given state one (e.g., the low state for a_t), and a 0 in the first row and a 1 in the second row given state two (e.g., the high state). Set a_0 accordingly (e.g., either $a_0 = aL$ or $a_0 = aH$). With P again denoting the state-transition matrix, the probabilities of realizing states one and two next period are given by $P\xi_0 = [p_1, p_2]'$. To determine the outcome of this random event, draw a random variable u distributed uniformly over the $[0, 1]$ interval (e.g., using the GAUSS command `rndu`), and infer the realization of state one if $p_1 > u$ and state two otherwise. Update ξ_1 accordingly and repeat until T realizations of a_t are obtained.

To calibrate the Markov process to match an AR(1) specification

$$a_t = (1-\rho)\overline{a} + \rho a_{t-1} + \varepsilon_t, \qquad s.e.(\varepsilon) = \sigma_\varepsilon, \tag{11.5}$$

TABLE 11.1
Model Simulations

	Linear Approximation				*Nonlinear Approximation*			
j	σ_j	$\frac{\sigma_j}{\sigma_y}$	$\varphi(1)$	$\varphi_{j,y}(0)$	σ_j	$\frac{\sigma_j}{\sigma_y}$	$\varphi(1)$	$\varphi_{j,y}(0)$
y	0.0199	1.00	0.94	1.00	0.0151	1.00	0.89	1.00
c	0.0156	0.78	0.96	0.99	0.0109	0.72	0.96	0.95
i	0.0350	1.76	0.90	0.99	0.0330	2.19	0.79	0.94
k	0.0348	1.75	0.98	0.95	0.0184	1.22	0.99	0.76
a	0.0112	0.56	0.80	0.88	0.0112	0.74	0.80	0.94

Note: $\varphi(1)$ denotes first-order serial correlation; $\varphi_{j,y}(0)$ denotes contemporaneous correlation between variables j and y. Model moments based on the parameterization

$$\mu = [\alpha\ \beta\ \delta\ \phi\ \rho\ \sigma]' = [0.33\ 0.96\ 0.1\ 2.0\ 0.8\ 0.0067]'.$$

set the diagonal elements of P as

$$p_{11} = p_{22} = \frac{\rho + 1}{2}, \tag{11.6}$$

and the values for a_t in states one and two as

$$a_1 = \overline{a} - \sigma_a, \qquad a_2 = \overline{a} + \sigma_a, \tag{11.7}$$

$$\sigma_a = \sigma_e \sqrt{\left(\frac{1}{1-\rho^2}\right)}. \tag{11.8}$$

Under this specification, a_t bounces one standard deviation above and below its mean value $\overline{a}$.

11.1.1 Simulating the Optimal Growth Model

To demonstrate differences in model inferences that can arise in working with nonlinear rather than linear model approximations, table 11.1 presents a collection of moments calculated using linear and nonlinear approximations of the stochastic growth model presented in chapter 10. Both sets of simulations are based on the use of steady state values for s_0, 1,000 burn-in drawings, and 10,000 retained drawings. Simulations of the linear approximation were based on the use of an AR(1) specification for a_t, under the assumption of normality for its innovations υ_t. Simulations of the nonlinear approximation were based on the use of a two-state Markov process, as described above. In both cases, moments were calculated for logged deviations of the model variables from steady state values.

Although many of the moment calculations are similar across solution methods, there are some notable differences. Most obviously, k is much less volatile relative to y under the nonlinear approximation, and is also less-strongly correlated with y. The opposite pattern is true of the relationship between a and y. This seems to have more to do with the linear approximation of the production function rather than the policy function, because differences in the relationship between c, i, and y across solution methods are less distinct. One difference across simulation methodologies that does not account for these differences in moment calculations is the alternate AR and Markov specifications employed for a_t used under the linear and non-linear approximations, as the following exercise demonstrates.

Exercise 11.1

As an alternative to the two-state Markov process specified for a_t under the nonlinear approximation, reconstruct table 11.1 using an AR(1) specification, parameterized as indicated in table 11.1, along with the associated policy function approximation constructed using `ara.prg`. Under this exercise, you should be able to match closely the calculations reported in the table.

11.2 Full-Information Analysis Using the Particle Filter

We now describe how full-information analyses can be conducted using nonlinear model approximations by substituting a particle filter for the Kalman filter as a means of evaluating the likelihood function. The application of particle filters to the analysis of DSGE models has been advanced by Fernandez-Villaverde and Rubio-Ramirez (2004b, 2005), and a textbook reference on particle filters is available from Doucet, deFreita, and Gordon (2001). Just as the case with nonlinear solution methods, many alternative specific algorithms can be used to implement particle filters. Pitt and Shephard (1999) provide an overview of alternative algorithms, and demonstrate applications to ARCH and stochastic-volatility models. Here we follow Fernandez-Villaverde and Rubio-Ramirez in focusing on a specific algorithm with close ties to the Monte Carlo integration technique of importance sampling, described in detail in chapter 9.

11.2.1 Overview

As we have seen in chapters 8 and 9, full-information analyses entail calculations of the probability or likelihood associated with the realization of an observed sample $X \equiv \{X_t\}_{t=1}^{T}$. In chapter 4, section 4.3, we characterized the Kalman filter as an algorithm designed to execute this calculation recursively, following the recursive nature of its associated structural model. Although the specific implementation of the Kalman filter is specialized to the case in which the underlying state-space representation is linear and structural innovations and measurement errors are normally distributed, the underlying algorithm can be applied more generally. Indeed, the particle filter retains this algorithm; only the details regarding implementation differ.

Recall that the idea behind the algorithm is to produce assessments of the conditional probability associated with the time-t observation X_t, given the history of past realizations $X^{t-1} \equiv \{X_j\}_{j=1}^{t-1}$. Denote this probability as $L(X_t|X^{t-1})$, with $L(X_1|X^0)$ denoting the unconditional likelihood associated with X_1. The sequence of conditional likelihoods $\{L(X_t|X^{t-1})\}_{t=1}^{T}$ are independent across time, thus the likelihood associated with X is given by the product of the individual conditional likelihoods:

$$L(X) = \prod_{t=1}^{T} L(X_t|X^{t-1}).$$

Regarding the structure of $L(X_t|X^{t-1})$, this is most simply described for the case in which each of the elements of x_t, including s_t, is observable. Conditional on $\{s_j\}_{j=1}^{t-1}$, from (11.1) we observe that the optimal forecast of s_t is given by

$$\widehat{s_t} = f(s_{t-1}, 0).$$

Moreover, the inferred realization of υ_t is that which reconciles the difference between the forecasted and observed value of s_t; that is, $\widehat{\upsilon}_t$ is constructed to satisfy

$$\widehat{s_t} - f(s_{t-1}, \widehat{\upsilon}_t) = 0.$$

The conditional likelihood associated with the observation of X_t can thus be assessed as the likelihood assigned to $\widehat{\upsilon}_t$ by its assumed probability distribution (say, p_υ):

$$L(X_t|X^{t-1}) = p_\upsilon(\widehat{\upsilon}_t).$$

As with the Kalman filter, the details behind the particle filter are slightly more complicated when certain elements of x_t are unobservable, but the basic idea is the same: conditional likelihoods represent probabilities associated with the realization of observables at time t, given the sequence of variables that were observed previously.

11.2.2 Case 1: No Measurement Error

We begin with the case in which no measurement error is associated with the observation of X_t. In this case the model can be expressed as

$$s_t = f(s_{t-1}, \upsilon_t) \tag{11.9}$$

$$X_t = g(s_t), \tag{11.10}$$

where the policy function $c(s_t)$ is subsumed in (11.9) and/or (11.10). The specification of the model is closed with a distributional assumption for the structural shocks υ_t, the dimension of which matches the dimension of X_t to avoid a structural singularity problem. Let this distribution be given by $p(\upsilon_t)$. Once again, the parameterizations of $f(s_{t-1}, \upsilon_t)$, $g(s_t)$, and $p(\upsilon_t)$ are determined by the specification of the parameters μ.

LIKELIHOOD CONSTRUCTION

Full-information analysis regarding the specification of μ is accomplished through the analysis of the likelihood function $L(X^T|\mu)$, where $X^T = \{X_j\}_{j=1}^T$. An overview of the construction of $L(X^T|\mu)$ is as follows. First, (11.9) and (11.10) are used to obtain an expression for υ_t as a function of $X^t = \{X_j\}_{j=1}^t$, s_0, and μ. This expression enables inference regarding the behavior of the unobservable structural shocks, conditional on the parameterized model, the observed data, and s_0. The probability assigned to this behavior by $p(\upsilon_t)$ provides the basis upon which the probability associated with the corresponding specification of μ is assessed.

To derive the desired expression for υ_t, begin by solving for s_t in (11.10):

$$s_t = g^{-1}(X_t). \tag{11.11}$$

Next, substitute for s_t in (11.9) to obtain

$$g^{-1}(X_t) = f(s_{t-1}, \upsilon_t). \tag{11.12}$$

Finally, solve for υ_t to obtain

$$\upsilon_t = \upsilon(X_t, s_{t-1}). \tag{11.13}$$

At this point, (11.13) can be combined with the updating equation (11.9) to establish a recursion for constructing the sequences $s^T = \{s_t\}_{t=1}^T$ and $\upsilon^T = \{\upsilon_t\}_{t=1}^T$ as functions of X^T and s_0. This proceeds as follows. Along with a given s_0, insert X_1 into (11.13) to obtain

$$\upsilon_1 = \upsilon(X_1, s_0). \tag{11.14}$$

Next, insert the inferred value of υ_1 into (11.9) to calculate the transition it implies from s_0 to s_1:

$$s_1 = f(s_0, \upsilon(X_1, s_0)). \tag{11.15}$$

For the subsequent steps $t = 2, \ldots, T$, υ_t is constructed using X_t and s_{t-1} as inputs in (11.13), and s_t is updated using s_{t-1} and υ_t as inputs in (11.9). Hereafter, we will denote the resulting sequences as $s^T(X^T, s_0)$ and $\upsilon^T(X^T, s_0)$, with t^{th} elements denoted as $s_t(X^t, s_0)$ and $\upsilon_t(X^t, s_0)$.

Because υ_t is serially uncorrelated by assumption, the likelihood function for X^T, which at this point is conditional upon s_0, is constructed as the product of the individual likelihoods $p(\upsilon_t(X^t, s_0))$:

$$L(X^T|s_0, \mu) = \prod_{t=1}^{T} p(\upsilon_t(X^t, s_0)). \tag{11.16}$$

To eliminate conditionality on s_0, $L(X^T|s_0, \mu)$ is integrated over the distribution for s_0 implied by the specification of the model and the observed data. Denoting this distribution as $p(s_0|X^t)$, the unconditional likelihood function is given by

$$L(X^T|\mu) = \prod_{t=1}^{T} \int p(\upsilon_t(X^t, s_0))p(s_0|X^t)ds_0. \tag{11.17}$$

Consider the construction of the likelihood function associated with the optimal growth model. Recall that in this case the state is $s_t = [a_t \; k_t]'$, and the single structural shock is $\upsilon_t = \varepsilon_t$, where ε_t is the innovation to TFP appearing in (10.8). The distribution of this innovation is given by $p(\varepsilon_t)$. Let output y_t serve as the single observable variable in this example, and take the availability of the policy function for consumption, denoted as

$$c_t = c(a_t, k_t), \tag{11.18}$$

as having been determined via an approximation scheme. In this case, (11.9) is given by the transition equations

$$\ln(a_t) = \rho \ln(a_{t-1}) + \varepsilon_t, \tag{11.19}$$

$$k_t = a_{t-1}k_{t-1}^{\alpha} - c(a_{t-1}, k_{t-1}) + (1 - \delta)k_{t-1}. \tag{11.20}$$

Also, the observation equation (11.10) is given by

$$y_t = a_t k_t^{\alpha}. \tag{11.21}$$

Substituting for a_t and k_t in (11.21) using (11.19) and (11.20), respectively, and then solving for ε_t, we obtain

$$\varepsilon_t = \ln\left[\frac{y_t}{e^{(\rho a_{t-1})}(a_{t-1}k_{t-1}^{\alpha} - c(a_{t-1}, k_{t-1}) + (1-\delta)k_{t-1})^{\alpha}}\right]$$

$$\equiv \varepsilon(y_t, a_{t-1}, k_{t-1}). \tag{11.22}$$

Given $s_0 = [a_0\ k_0]'$ and y_1, the implied value of ε_1 can be obtained using (11.22). Next, the implied values of $s_1 = [a_1\ k_1]'$ can be obtained by inserting $(a_0\ k_0\ \varepsilon_1)$ into the transition equations (11.19) and (11.20). Repeating this process for $t = 2, \ldots, T$ yields $\{\varepsilon_t\}_{t=1}^{T}$, and thus the sequence $\{p(\varepsilon_t)\}_{t=1}^{T}$.

LIKELIHOOD EVALUATION

Returning to the general model representation, inferences made conditionally upon s_0 do not require the calculation of an integral in the likelihood evaluation step. All that is required in this case is the construction of $\upsilon^T(X^T, s_0)$ as described above, which immediately enables the evaluation of $L(X^T|s_0, \mu)$ in (11.16). However, if the value of s_0 is unknown, the integral in (11.17) must be calculated, and the particle filter comes into play.

Before describing the particle filter, we pause to discuss the conditionality of the distribution $p(s_0|X^t)$ on X^t. This conditionality is important: introduction of the particle filter is unnecessary in its absence (for reasons we will explain shortly). The intuition behind conditionality is perhaps best seen by reverting to the example of the optimal growth model, and considering (11.22). Suppose y_1 is large relative to its steady state value. Then clearly, alternative candidate values of $[a_0\ k_0]'$ are not equally likely. In particular, the specification of relatively small values for $[a_0\ k_0]'$ imply the realization of very large TFP innovations ε_1, which are assigned relatively little weight from their corresponding distribution $p(\varepsilon_t)$. Moreover, because the model in question will typically embody a nontrivial degree of persistence, the influence of $[a_0\ k_0]'$ on inferences regarding ε_t will extend beyond the first period. Thus the plausibility of a particular specification of $[a_0\ k_0]'$ will tend to hinge not only upon y_1, but in general on y^t.

Returning again to the general model representation, suppose for illustrative purposes that $p(s_0|X^t)$ is not conditional upon X^t. In this case, a simple numerical integration algorithm can be used to approximate the integral appearing in (11.17). A single step in the algorithm involves obtaining a drawing s_0 from its unconditional distribution $p(s_0)$, coupling this drawing with X^T to construct $\upsilon^T(X^T, s_0)$, and then calculating the likelihood value

$$L(X^T|s_0,\mu) = \prod_{t=1}^{T} p(\upsilon_t(X^t, s_0)).$$

Let the likelihood value associated with the ith of N such drawings be given by $L(X^T|s_0^i,\mu)$. Then the approximation to (11.17) we seek is given by the sample average

$$\overline{L(X^T,\mu)}_N = \frac{1}{N}\sum_{i=1}^{N} L(X^T|s_0^i,\mu). \tag{11.23}$$

This algorithm is directly related to that used to approximate the posterior mean of some function $g(\mu)$ for the case in which it is possible to obtain drawings of μ directly from its associated posterior distribution $P(\mu|X^T)$. See chapter 9, section 9.2, for details regarding this algorithm.

As discussed in chapter 9, one means of overcoming the inability to obtain drawings of μ directly from $P(\mu|X^T)$ is the use of an importance sampling algorithm. Briefly, this involves obtaining drawings of μ from a stand-in distribution $I(\mu)$, and approximating $Eg(\mu)$ using the weighted average

$$\overline{g(\mu)}_N = \frac{\sum_{i=1}^{N} g(\mu^i)w(\mu^i)}{\sum_{i=1}^{N} w(\mu^i)}, \tag{11.24}$$

where the weighting function is given by

$$w(\mu) = \frac{P(\mu|X^T)}{I(\mu)}. \tag{11.25}$$

The purpose of the weights is to offset the influence of $I(\mu)$ on the resulting inferences; given their use, the sample drawings $\{\mu^i\}_{i=1}^{N}$ can be thought of as having been obtained from the posterior distribution itself. See chapter 9, section 9.4.1, for details.

THE PARTICLE FILTER

Recall that our objective is to evaluate the likelihood function $L(X^T|\mu)$ in (11.17), which requires approximations of the sequence of integrals

$$\int p(\upsilon_t(X^t, s_0))p(s_0|X^t)ds_0, \quad t = 1, \ldots, T.$$

The particle filter we now describe can be thought of as a particular type of importance sampling algorithm designed to approximate these integrals.

Its use in place of (11.23) becomes necessary given the conditionality of $p(s_0|X^t)$ on X^t, which generally eliminates the ability to obtain drawings of s_0 directly from $p(s_0|X^t)$.

To describe the particle filter, we require additional notation. Let $s_0^{t,i}$ denote the ith of N drawings of s_0 obtained from the conditional distribution $p(s_0|X^t)$. A single drawing $s_0^{t,i}$ is referred to as a particle, and the sequence $\{s_0^{t,i}\}_{i=1}^N$ is referred to as a swarm of particles. Also, let $\{s_0^{0,i}\}_{i=1}^N$ be a particle swarm obtained from the unconditional distribution of s_0, denoted as $p(s_0|X^0)$, with X^0 indicating an absence of observations on X. We note that if $p(s_0|X^0)$ is unknown, it may be approximated, for example, using a uniform distribution centered on the steady state value s^*.

Consider first the integral for $t = 1$. Using the unconditional density $p(s_0|X^0)$, begin by generating a particle swarm $\{s_0^{0,i}\}_{i=1}^N$. Combining each particle $s_0^{0,i}$ with $X_1 \equiv X^1$ in (11.14), obtain the associated sequence

$$\{\upsilon_1(X^1, s_0^{0,i})\}_{i=1}^N.$$

Note that the likelihood value associated with $s_0^{0,i}$ is given by $p(\upsilon_1(X^1, s_0^{0,i}))$. The average value of these associated likelihood values yields the approximation we seek for $t = 1$:

$$\int p(\upsilon_1(X^1, s_0))p(s_0|X^1)ds_0 \approx \frac{1}{N}\sum_{i=1}^{N} p(\upsilon_1(X^1, s_0^{0,i})). \tag{11.26}$$

Although we have now approximated the integral we seek for $t = 1$, an additional step is required before moving to $t = 2$. This involves the construction of an approximation of the conditional density $p(s_0|X^1)$. To construct this density, let q_1^i denote the *relative* likelihood value associated with $s_0^{0,i}$, where relativity is with respect to its counterparts in the swarm:

$$q_1^i = \frac{p(\upsilon_1(X^1, s_0^{0,i}))}{\sum_{j=1}^N p(\upsilon_1(X^1, s_0^{0,j}))}. \tag{11.27}$$

In the particle filter, the role of q_1^i is analogous to that of the weighting function in an importance sampling algorithm.

Now, let $\{s_0^{1,i}\}_{i=1}^N$ denote a second sequence of drawings from the original swarm $\{s_0^{0,i}\}_{i=1}^N$. This second swarm is obtained by drawing with replacement from the original swarm, with the probability of obtaining a drawing of $s_0^{0,i}$ determined by q_1^i. Under mild regularity conditions (e.g., as described by Fernandez-Villaverde and Rubio-Ramirez, 2004b), this second swarm of particles represents a drawing from the conditional distribution $p(s_0|X^1)$.

For each particle in this second swarm, along with its associated structural shock $\upsilon_1(X^1, s_0^{1,i})$, obtain the corresponding value of $s_1^{1,i}$ using the updating equation (11.9). Combine this with $s_0^{1,i}$ to establish the sequence

$$s^1(X^1, s_0^{1,i}) = [s_1^{1,i}\ s_0^{1,i}]'.$$

This will ultimately contain $T+1$ components, representing the time series of state variables implied by X^T and s_0. The swarm $\{s^1(X^1, s_0^{1,i})\}_{i=1}^N$ is then carried to the $t=2$ stage.

For $t = 2, \ldots, T$, the algorithm generalizes as follows. First, combine $\{s_{t-1}^{t-1,i}\}_{i=1}^N$ with X_t in (11.13) to obtain the associated swarm $\{\upsilon_t(X^t, s_0^{t-1,i})\}_{i=1}^N$. Note that $s_{t-1}^{t-1,i}$ is the most recently obtained component of the sequence $s^{t-1}(X^{t-1}, s_0^{t-1,i})$. Using this swarm, approximate the integral for period t as

$$\int p(\upsilon_t(X^t, s_0))p(s_0|X^t)ds_0 \approx \frac{1}{N}\sum_{i=1}^{N} p(\upsilon_t(X^t, s_0^{t-1,i})). \tag{11.28}$$

Next, compute the weight assigned to $s_{t-1}^{t-1,i}$ as

$$q_t^i = \frac{p(\upsilon_t(X^t, s_0^{t-1,i}))}{\sum_{j=1}^N p(\upsilon_t(X^t, s_0^{t-1,j}))}. \tag{11.29}$$

Then draw from $\{s^{t-1}(X^{t-1}, s_0^{t-1,i})\}_{i=1}^N$ with replacement, using q_t^i as the probability assigned to the attainment of $s^{t-1}(X^{t-1}, s_0^{t-1,i})$. Denote the resulting swarm as $\{s^{t-1}(X^{t-1}, s_0^{t,i})\}_{i=1}^N$; this represents a set of drawings obtained from $p(s_0|X^t)$. Denote the most recently obtained component of $s^{t-1}(X^{t-1}, s_0^{t,i})$ as $s_{t-1}^{t,i}$. Combine this second swarm with X_t in (11.13) to obtain the associated swarm $\{\upsilon_t(X^t, s_0^{t,i})\}_{i=1}^N$. For each particle $s_{t-1}^{t,i}$ and its associated shock $\upsilon_t(X^t, s_0^{t,i})$, obtain the corresponding value of $s_t^{t,i}$ using the updating equation (11.9). Augment $s^{t-1}(X^{t-1}, s_0^{t,i})$ with $s_t^{t,i}$ to establish

$$s^t(X^t, s_0^{t,i}) = [s_t^{t,i}\ s_{t-1}^{t,i} \ldots s_1^{t,i}\ s_0^{t,i}]'.$$

Repeat these steps until $t = T$.

Having completed all T steps, the approximation to the integral we seek is given by

$$L(X^T|\mu) \approx \prod_{t=1}^{T} \left[\frac{1}{N} \sum_{i=1}^{N} p(\upsilon_t(X^t, s_0^{t-1,i})) \right]. \tag{11.30}$$

In turn, the $(T+1) \times 1$ sequence

$$\overline{s^T(X^T, s_0^T)}_N = \frac{1}{N} \sum_{i=1}^{N} s^T(X^T, s_0^{T,i}) \tag{11.31}$$

represents "smoothed" values of the state variable implied by X^T, conditional on the model. Finally,

$$\overline{\upsilon^T(X^T, s_0^T)}_N = \frac{1}{N} \sum_{i=1}^{N} \upsilon^T(X^T, s_0^{T,i}) \tag{11.32}$$

represents smoothed values of the structural shocks.

Exercise 11.2

Construct a procedure for evaluating $L(X^T|\mu)$ for the optimal growth model. Assume the TFP innovations ε_t are *iidN* random variables with standard deviation σ_ε, which is a parameter to be estimated. For a given candidate μ, use a projection scheme to construct the policy function $c_t = c(z_t, k_t)$ in (11.18). As a suggestion, use the orthogonal collocation scheme implemented using `ara.prg` for this purpose. Organize the procedure as follows:

- Linearize the model, and use the elasticities σ_a and σ_k to construct starting values for $(\chi_{11}, \chi_{12}, \chi_{21}, \chi_{22})$ as described in chapter 10, section 10.2.6, equation (10.53).
- Construct the approximated policy function.
- Initiate the $t = 1$ step of the particle filter by obtaining 10,000 drawings of $s_0 = [z_0\ k_0]'$ from a uniform distribution ranging ± 10 standard deviations above and below the steady state values z^* and k^*.
- Approximate $L(X^T|\mu)$ using (11.26), (11.28), and (11.30).
- Obtain the smoothed series $\overline{a^T}_N$ and $\overline{k^T}_N$ using (11.31), and $\overline{\varepsilon^T}_N$ using (11.32).

11.2.3 Case 2: Measurement Error

Turning to the case involving the presence of measurement error, the model is given by

$$s_t = f(s_{t-1}, \upsilon_t) \tag{11.33}$$

$$X_t = g(s_t, u_t), \tag{11.34}$$

where the policy function $c(s_t)$ has once again been subsumed in (11.33) and/or (11.34). The distributions of υ_t and u_t are given by $p(\upsilon_t)$ and $p(u_t)$; also, υ_t and u_t are taken as *iid*, and independent from each other. As usual, the parameterizations of $f(s_{t-1}, \upsilon_t)$, $g(s_t)$, $p(\upsilon_t)$, and $p(u_t)$ are determined by the specification of μ.

As an example, consider the following representation of the optimal growth model. The transition equations are as given above:

$$\ln(a_t) = \rho \ln(a_{t-1}) + \varepsilon_t, \tag{11.35}$$

$$k_t = a_{t-1}k_{t-1}^{\alpha} - c(a_{t-1}, k_{t-1}) + (1-\delta)k_{t-1}. \tag{11.36}$$

But in this case, suppose output and investment are available as observable variables, each of which is measured with error. Then the observation equations are given by

$$y_t = a_t k_t^{\alpha} + u_{yt} \tag{11.37}$$

$$i_t = a_t k_t^{\alpha} - c(a_t, k_t) + u_{it}. \tag{11.38}$$

LIKELIHOOD CONSTRUCTION

To construct the likelihood function $L(X^T|\mu)$ in this case, (11.33) and (11.34) are used to obtain an expression for u_t as a function of X^t, υ^t, s_0, and μ. The probability assigned to this behavior by $p(u_t)$ provides the basis upon which the probability associated with the corresponding specification of μ is assessed. Conditionality on υ^t and s_0 is eliminated by integrating over the distribution $p(\upsilon^t, s_0|X^t)$; integration is once again facilitated via use of a particle filter.

To begin, solve for u_t using (11.33) and (11.34) to obtain an expression of the form

$$u_t = u(X_t, \upsilon_t, s_{t-1}). \tag{11.39}$$

Coupled with the transition equation (11.33), a recursive scheme for constructing $u_t(X^t, \upsilon^t, s_0)$ and $s_t(X^t, \upsilon^t, s_0)$, $t = 1, \ldots, T$, is as follows. For $t = 1$, combine a given s_0 and υ_1 with X_1 in (11.39) to obtain the implied u_1. Then combine s_0 and υ_1 in (11.33) to obtain s_1. For $t = 2, \ldots, T$, the value of s_{t-1} obtained in the previous step is combined with υ_t and

X_t in (11.39) to obtain the implied u_t, and with υ_t in (11.33) to obtain the implied s_t. The result is the pair of sequences $u^T(X^T, \upsilon^T, s_0) \equiv \{u_t(X^t, \upsilon^t, s_0)\}_{t=1}^T$ and $s^T(X^T, \upsilon^T, s_0) \equiv \{s_t(X^t, \upsilon^t, s_0)\}_{t=0}^T$.

Because u_t is taken as *iid*, the likelihood function for X^T, which at this point is conditional upon υ^T and s_0, is given by the product of individual likelihoods

$$L(X^T|\upsilon^T, s_0, \mu) = \prod_{t=1}^T p(u_t(X^t, \upsilon^t, s_0)). \tag{11.40}$$

To eliminate conditionality upon υ^T and s_0, $L(X^T|\upsilon^T, s_0, \mu)$ is integrated over the sequence of conditional distributions $p(\upsilon^t, s_0|X^t)$, $t = 1, \ldots, T$:

$$L(X^T|\mu) = \prod_{t=1}^T \int\int p(u_t(X^t, \upsilon^t, s_0))p(\upsilon^t, s_0|X^t)d\upsilon_t ds_0. \tag{11.41}$$

Exercise 11.3

Derive the expression $u_t = u(X_t, \upsilon_t, s_{t-1})$ in (11.39) for the optimal growth model, and use this expression to sketch the construction of $u^T(X^T, \varepsilon^T, s_0)$, $a^T(X^T, \varepsilon^T, s_0)$, and $k^T(X^T, \varepsilon^T, s_0)$.

LIKELIHOOD EVALUATION VIA THE PARTICLE FILTER

As with the case of no measurement error, inferences made conditionally upon s_0 (and additionally, υ^T) do not require the calculation of an integral in the likelihood evaluation step. All that is required is the construction of $u^T(X^T, \upsilon^T, s_0)$, which immediately enables the evaluation of $L(X^T|\upsilon^T, s_0, \mu)$ in (11.40). However, if s_0 and υ^T are unknown, we must approximate the sequence of integrals

$$\int\int p(u_t(X^t, \upsilon^t, s_0))p(\upsilon^t, s_0|X^t)d\upsilon_t ds_0,$$

bringing the particle filter into play.

Regarding notation, let $s_0^{t,i}$ continue to denote the ith of N drawings of s_0 obtained from the conditional distribution $p(\upsilon^t, s_0|X^t)$, and $s_0^{0,i}$ the ith of N drawings obtained from the unconditional distribution $p(s_0)$. In addition, let $\upsilon_t^{l,i}$ denote the ith of N drawings of υ_t obtained from the conditional distribution $p(\upsilon^t, s_0|X^l)$, and $\upsilon_t^{0,i}$ from the unconditional distribution $p(\upsilon_t)$. For $t = 1, \ldots, T$, we will approximate the required integrals numerically by obtaining conditional drawings of $s_0^{t,i}$ and $\upsilon_t^{t,i}$ from $p(\upsilon^t, s_0|X^t)$. Once again, it is not possible to obtain these drawings directly from

$p(v^t, s_0|X^t)$; instead, the particle filter will be implemented to circumvent this problem.

The filter for $t = 1$ is initiated by obtaining a swarm of drawings $\{s_0^{0,i}\}_{i=1}^N$ from the unconditional distribution $p(s_0)$. This is augmented with an additional swarm of drawings $\{v_1^{0,i}\}_{i=1}^N$ obtained from the unconditional distribution $p(v_t)$. (Recall that the parameterization of $p(v_t)$ is determined by the specification of μ.) Combining particle pairs $(s_0^{0,i}, v_1^{0,i})$ with $X_1 \equiv X^1$ in (11.39) yields the associated sequence $\{u_1(X^1, v_1^{0,i}, s_0^{0,i})\}_{i=1}^N$. Note that the likelihood value associated with $(s_0^{0,i}, v_1^{0,i})$ is given by $p(u_1(X^1, v_1^{0,i}, s_0^{0,i}))$. Therefore, the integral for $t = 1$ can be approximated using

$$\int\int p(u_1(X^1, v^1, s_0))p(v^1, s_0|X^1)dv_1\, ds_0 \approx \frac{1}{N}\sum_{i=1}^{N} p(u_1(X^1, v_1^{0,i}, s_0^{0,i})).$$

Next, let q_1^i denote the relative likelihood value associated with $(s_0^{0,i}, v_1^{0,i})$, where relativity is with respect to its counterparts in the swarm:

$$q_1^i = \frac{p(u_1(X^1, v_1^{0,i}, s_0^{0,i}))}{\sum_{j=1}^{N} p(u_1(X^1, v_1^{0,j}, s_0^{0,j}))}. \tag{11.42}$$

Also, let $\{s_0^{1,i}, v_1^{1,i}\}_{i=1}^N$ denote a second sequence of drawings obtained by drawing with replacement from the original swarm, with the probability of obtaining the ith particle pair determined by q_1^i. As in the case of no measurement error, this second swarm of particles once again represents a drawing from the conditional distribution $p(v^1, s_0|X^1)$.

To advance to the $t = 2$ stage, use each particle pair $(s_0^{1,i}, v_1^{1,i})$ to obtain the corresponding value of $s_1^{1,i}$ using the updating equation (11.33). Combine this with $s_0^{1,i}$ to establish the sequence

$$s^1(X^1, v_1^{1,i}, s_0^{1,i}) = [s_1^{1,i}\; s_0^{1,i}]'.$$

Also, use $v_1^{1,i}$ to establish the sequence

$$v^1(X^1, v_1^{1,i}, s_0^{1,i}) = [v_1^{1,i}].$$

These sequences will ultimately contain $T + 1$ and T components, respectively, representing the time series of state variables and structural shocks implied by X^T, conditional on the model. The swarm of sequences

$$\{s^1(X^1, v_1^{1,i}, s_0^{1,i}),\; v^1(X^1, v_1^{1,i}, s_0^{1,i})\}_{i=1}^N$$

is then carried to the $t = 2$ stage.

For $t = 2, \ldots, T$, the algorithm generalizes as follows. First, combine $\{s_{t-1}^{t-1,i}\}_{i=1}^{N}$ with X_t and an additional swarm of drawings $\{\upsilon_t^{t-1,i}\}_{i=1}^{N}$ obtained from the unconditional distribution $p(\upsilon_t)$ in (11.39) to obtain the associated swarm

$$\{u_t(X^t, \upsilon_t^{t-1,i}, s_0^{t-1,i})\}_{i=1}^{N}.$$

Note that $s_{t-1}^{t-1,i}$ is the most recently obtained component of the sequence $s^{t-1}(X^{t-1}, \upsilon_{t-1}^{t-1,i}, s_0^{t-1,i})$. Augment the sequence $\upsilon^{t-1}(X^{t-1}, \upsilon_{t-1}^{t-1,i}, s_0^{t-1,i})$ with $\upsilon_t^{t-1,i}$ to construct the new sequence

$$\upsilon^t(X^{t-1}, \upsilon_t^{t-1,i}, s_0^{t-1,i}) = [\upsilon_t^{t-1,i} \; \upsilon_{t-1}^{t-1,i} \ldots \upsilon_1^{t-1,i}]'.$$

The likelihood value associated with $(s_0^{t-1,i}, \upsilon_t^{t-1,i})$ is given by $p(u_t(X^t, \upsilon_t^{t-1,i}, s_0^{t-1,i}))$, thus the integral for period t is approximated as

$$\int\int p(u_t(X^t, \upsilon^t, s_0))p(\upsilon^t, s_0|X^t)d\upsilon_t ds_0 \approx \frac{1}{N}\sum_{i=1}^{N} p(u_t(X^t, \upsilon_t^{t-1,i}, s_0^{t-1,i})).$$

Next, compute the weight assigned to $(s_{t-1}^{t-1,i}, \upsilon_t^{t-1,i})$ as

$$q_t^i = \frac{p(u_t(X^t, \upsilon_t^{t-1,i}, s_0^{t-1,i}))}{\sum_{j=1}^{N} p(u_t(X^t, \upsilon_t^{t-1,j} s_0^{t-1,j}))}. \tag{11.43}$$

Then draw from

$$\{s^{t-1}(X^{t-1}, \upsilon_{t-1}^{t-1,i}, s_0^{t-1,i}),\; \upsilon^t(X^{t-1}, \upsilon_t^{t-1,i}, s_0^{t-1,i})\}_{i=1}^{N}$$

with replacement, using q_t^i as the probability assigned to the attainment of the ith particle pair. Denote the resulting swarm of sequences as

$$\{s^{t-1}(X^{t-1}, \upsilon_{t-1}^{t,i}, s_0^{t,i}),\; \upsilon^t(X^{t-1}, \upsilon_t^{t,i}, s_0^{t,i})\}_{i=1}^{N};$$

this represents a set of drawings obtained from the conditional distribution $p(\upsilon^t, s_0|X^t)$. Finally, for each particle pair $(s_{t-1}^{t,i}, \upsilon_t^{t,i})$ and its associated error $u_t(X^t, \upsilon_t^{t,i}, s_0^{t,i})$, obtain the corresponding value of $s_t^{t,i}$ using the updating equation (11.33). Augment $s^{t-1}(X^{t-1}, \upsilon_{t-1}^{t,i}, s_0^{t,i})$ with $s_t^{t,i}$ to establish

$$s^t(X^t, \upsilon_t^{t,i}, s_0^{t,i}) = [s_t^{t,i} \; s_{t-1}^{t,i} \ldots s_1^{t,i} \; s_0^{t,i}]'.$$

The swarm of sequences

$$\{s^t(X^t, \upsilon_t^{t,i}, s_0^{t,i}),\ \upsilon^t(X^t, \upsilon_t^{t,i}, s_0^{t,i})\}_{i=1}^N$$

is then carried to the next stage. Repeat these steps until $t = T$.

Having completed all T steps, the approximation to the integral we seek is given by

$$L(X^T|\mu) \approx \prod_{t=1}^{T}\left[\frac{1}{N}\sum_{i=1}^{N} p(u_t(X^t, \upsilon_t^{t-1,i}, s_0^{t-1,i}))\right]. \tag{11.44}$$

In turn, the $(T+1)\times 1$ sequence

$$\overline{s^T(X^T, \upsilon^T, s_0^T)}_N = \frac{1}{N}\sum_{i=1}^{N} s^T(X^T, \upsilon^{T,i}, s_0^{T,i}) \tag{11.45}$$

represents "smoothed" values of the state variable implied by X^T, conditional on the model. Also,

$$\overline{\upsilon^T(X^T, \upsilon^T, s_0^T)}_N = \frac{1}{N}\sum_{i=1}^{N} \upsilon^T(X^T, \upsilon^{T,i}, s_0^{T,i}) \tag{11.46}$$

represents smoothed values of the structural shocks. Finally,

$$\overline{u^T(X^T, \upsilon^T, s_0^T)}_N = \frac{1}{N}\sum_{i=1}^{N} u^T(X^T, \upsilon^{T,i}, s_0^{T,i}) \tag{11.47}$$

represents smoothed values of the measurement errors.

Exercise 11.4

Repeat exercise 11.3 for the version of the optimal growth model featuring measurement error.

11.2.4 Approximating the Unconditional Distribution of s_0

As we have described, the particle filter is initiated by obtaining a swarm of drawings $\{s_0^{0,i}\}_{i=1}^N$ from the unconditional distribution $p(s_0)$. Here we briefly describe how an approximation of this distribution can be obtained using the log-linear approximation of the underlying model.

Recall that log-linear model approximations are of the form

$$\begin{aligned} x_t &= Fx_{t-1} + Gv_t \\ &= Fx_{t-1} + e_t, \end{aligned} \tag{11.48}$$

where the model variables x_t are represented as logged deviations from steady state values (e.g., $\widetilde{a}_t = \ln(\frac{a_t}{a^*})$, and thus $a_t = a^* e^{\widetilde{a}_t}$). With $Ee_t e_t' = Q$, the variance-covariance matrix of x_t, denoted as $\Gamma(0)$, is given by

$$vec[\Gamma(0)] = [I - F \otimes F]^{-1}\, vec[Q],$$

where $\otimes$ denotes the Kronecker product (see chapter 4 for details).

Unconditionally then, according to the log-linearized model, the distribution of the state variables included in x_t have an expected value of 0 and variance-covariance matrix $\Gamma_s(0)$, which denotes the sub-matrix of $\Gamma(0)$ that corresponds with the state variables of the model. For example, in the case of the optimal growth model $\Gamma_s(0)$ is the 2×2 submatrix of $\Gamma(0)$ corresponding with $(\widetilde{a}_t, \widetilde{k}_t)$. Moreover, $(\widetilde{a}_t, \widetilde{k}_t)$ will be Normally distributed, following the distributional assumption made for TFP innovations. In sum,

$$p(\widetilde{a}_t, \widetilde{k}_t) \sim N(0, \Gamma_s(0)).$$

Drawings obtained from this distribution can be transformed into drawings of (a_t, k_t) via $a_t = a^* e^{\widetilde{a}_t}$ and $k_t = k^* e^{\widetilde{k}_t}$.

Exercise 11.5

Repeat exercises 11.3 and 11.4 by replacing the uniform distribution specified for $p(s_0)$ with the specification obtained using the log-linear approximation.

11.2.5 Data Alignment

As is the case in working with log-linear model approximations, it is important to align the actual data with their theoretical counterparts in working with nonlinear model approximations. We conclude this subsection with a brief discussion of this issue.

Recall that in working with log-linear approximations, the theoretical data are measured in terms of logged deviations from steady state values. Therefore, interpreting trend trajectories observed in the actual data as representing steady state behavior, the actual data are typically logged and detrended prior to empirical analysis.

In contrast, in working with nonlinear model approximations, it is typically the case that the theoretical variables are represented in terms of levels of variables that exhibit stationary fluctuations around steady state values. In such cases, the actual data should be transformed accordingly. For example, return to the specific case of the optimal growth model, which is to be estimated using output, consumption, and investment as observable variables. This model carries two implications regarding trend behavior. First, the variables follow a common trend. Second, long-run ratios of the variables (i.e., the relative heights of trend lines) should align with steady state ratios predicted by the model. Therefore, by detrending the data while preserving their relative means, the data can not only be aligned with the model, but their relative means can be used to help identify the model's structural parameters.

One means of implementing this approach to alignment is as follows. Begin by eliminating the trend components of logged values of each series. This may be accomplished, for example, by applying the Hodrick-Prescott filter or by subtracting a linear trend estimated via OLS. (If it is desired that a common growth rate be imposed in this step, the GAUSS procedure `ct.prc` can be used for this purpose.) Let the logged, detrended variables be denoted as $\widehat{y}_t$, and so on. Next, construct new series $(\widetilde{y}_y, \widetilde{c}_t, \widetilde{i}_t)$ as

$$\widetilde{y}_t = e^{\widehat{y}_t}, \quad \widetilde{c}_t = \frac{\overline{c}}{\overline{y}} e^{\widehat{c}_t}, \quad \widetilde{i}_t = \frac{\overline{i}}{\overline{y}} e^{\widehat{i}_t}, \tag{11.49}$$

where $\overline{y}$ is the sample mean of y_t, and so on. The resulting series will be detrended, and ratios of their sample means will approximate their untransformed counterparts (and the level of $\widetilde{y}_t$, which serves as a numeraire, will approximately equal 1).

These transformed series are carried into the likelihood-evaluation stage of the analysis. However, for each candidate parameterization of the structural model μ, a final adjustment is necessary. This involves scaling the series so that the sample average of one of the variables matches the steady state value of its theoretical counterpart. For example, let $y_{ss}(\mu)$ represent the steady state value of y for a given parameterization μ. Then by scaling $\widetilde{y}_t$ by $y_{ss}(\mu)$, creating $\widetilde{\widetilde{y}}_t = y_{ss}(\mu)\widetilde{y}_t$, the sample average of the scaled series will approximate its steady state counterpart. The additional series $\widetilde{c}_t$ and $\widetilde{i}_t$ are also scaled by $y_{ss}(\mu)$, so that the relative sample averages of $(\widetilde{\widetilde{y}}_t, \widetilde{\widetilde{c}}_t, \widetilde{\widetilde{i}}_t)$ will continue to match their unadjusted counterparts. Then if the particular parameterization μ implies counterfactual ratios between y, c, and i, the sample means of $(\widetilde{\widetilde{c}}_t, \widetilde{\widetilde{i}}_t)$ will fail to align with their corresponding steady state values $c_{ss}(\mu)$ and $i_{ss}(\mu)$, and thus the value of the likelihood function associated with μ will reflect the failure of μ to account for this particular aspect of the data.

11.3 Linear Versus Nonlinear Model Approximation

As we have seen, linear and nonlinear model approximations serve as alternative points of departure for implementing structural models empirically. The choice between these two general alternatives involves a trade-off. One one hand, linear approximations are both easy to program and computationally inexpensive relative to their nonlinear counterparts. Moreover, the Kalman filter is both easy to program and computationally inexpensive relative to the particle filter. On the other hand, approximation errors associated with the use of nonlinear methods are in general less severe than those associated with the use of linear methods. In short, the trade-off involves a choice between simplicity and speed versus accuracy.

Methodological and computational advances have already served to help mitigate concerns regarding costs associated with the use of nonlinear model approximations. Undoubtedly, such concerns will continue to erode over time, although as we shall see below, costs at this point remain nontrivial. However, an outstanding question involves the relative benefits associated with their use. Specifically, the question is whether the superior accuracy associated with nonlinear model approximations is significant empirically: do nonlinear approximations yield substantive differences regarding the empirical question at hand? Unfortunately, the answer to this question is likely to be somewhat specific, both to the particular model under investigation and to the empirical question the model is being used to address. However, general guidance may emerge through experiments designed to address this question in specific contexts.

An example of such an experiment is provided by Fernandez-Villaverde and Rubio-Ramirez (2005), who conducted a likelihood-based analysis of an RBC model closely related to that introduced in chapter 5. In their experiment, they generated two artificial data sets using two alternative parameterizations of the model. For each data set, they obtained flat-prior posterior estimates of the model parameters using log-linear and nonlinear approximation methods, and compared the estimates they obtained to the actual parameters. They found that although point estimates associated with each approximation method were comparable, and provided close matches with their corresponding actual values, distributions obtained using the nonlinear model approximation they used were more tightly concentrated around these actual values.

To convey the flavor of their results, here we report on a similar exercise patterned after an extension of the Fernandez-Villaverde/Rubio-Rameriz experiment conducted by Fernandez-Villaverde, Rubio-Ramirez, and Santos (2006). The exercise focuses on maximum likelihood (ML) estimates obtained using an artificial data set generated using the optimal growth model, parameterized so that an exact analytical solution of the policy function is available.

Specifically, the model specification is given by (11.35)–(11.38), with

$$(\alpha, \beta, \delta, \phi) = (0.33, 0.96, 1, 1),$$

so that the policy function is given by (10.38). The AR(1) representation for $\ln(a_t)$ was parameterized as

$$(\rho, \sigma_\varepsilon) = (0.8, 0.0067),$$

with the TFP innovations ε_t specified as being Normally distributed. Output and investment were treated as observable variables subject to measurement error. The errors associated with the observation of both variables were also specified as being Normally distributed, with standard deviations set to 0.5% of their corresponding steady state values. We worked with a sample size of 100, using data simulated as described in exercise 11.2.

ML estimates were obtained subject to the restriction that the steady state investment-output ratio corresponds with the sample mean of its empirical counterpart. With the steady state ratio given by

$$\frac{i^*}{y^*} = \alpha\beta,$$

this restriction was imposed using

$$\beta = \frac{1}{\alpha}\overline{\left(\frac{i}{y}\right)},$$

with $\overline{\left(\frac{i}{y}\right)}$ denoting the sample mean of $\left(\frac{i_t}{y_y}\right)$. This restriction was imposed primarily as a practical matter, because deviations from the restriction are assigned very little weight by the likelihood function under any representation of the model. (This illustrates the strong source of parameter identification that can arise from the preservation of relative means in the actual data.)

Our initial implementation of this exercise was programmed in GAUSS. However, here we confronted a computational hurdle: the evaluation of the likelihood function for a single candidate parameterization turned out to require approximately 24 seconds of CPU time on a 3 GHz Pentium 4 desktop computer using a 20,000-element particle swarm. In contrast, likelihood evaluation was accomplished at the rate of 15 per second in working with the log-linear approximation. This large computational cost prompted us to explore the payoff of switching from GAUSS to Fortran in executing this application. (This also follows Fernandez-Villaverde

TABLE 11.2
Maximum Likelihood Estimates

Parameter	*Actual Value*	*Log-Lin. Appx.*	*Nonlin. Appx.*	*Exact Policy Fcn.*
α	0.33	0.330 $(3.14e-05)$	0.327 $(1.11e-05)$	0.327 $(3.77e-05)$
β	0.96	0.962 $(9.16e-05)$	0.968 $(1.04e-04)$	0.968 $(3.52e-05)$
ρ	0.80	0.784 $(2.29e-02)$	0.794 $(5.10e-05)$	0.809 $(2.80e-05)$
σ_{ε}	0.0067	0.0063 $(5.21e-04)$	0.0061 $(1.01e-06)$	0.0061 $(1.08e-06)$
$\sigma_{u,y}$	0.00284	0.00539 $(4.96e-04)$	0.00309 $(2.77e-07)$	0.00316 $(6.90e-07)$
$\sigma_{u,i}$	0.0090	0.00484 $(5.12e-04)$	0.00086 $(7.81e-09)$	0.00087 $(6.76e-09)$
$\log L$:		782.75	917.74	917.78

Notes: Standard deviations are in parentheses.

and Rubio-Ramirez, 2005, who implemented their investigation using Fortran.)

Due to a considerable advantage in dealing with large particle swarms, the payoff turned out to be substantial: the cost of likelihood evaluation was reduced to approximately 4 seconds of CPU time using Fortran. (Roughly 87% of the CPU time required by GAUSS to achieve likelihood evaluation is devoted to implementation of the particle filter. In contrast, roughly 3 seconds is devoted to approximating the policy function.) In order to provide guidance for achieving the conversion from GAUSS to Fortran, code used to facilitate likelihood evaluation in this application is available in both programming languages at the textbook Web site.[1]

Table 11.2 presents three sets of parameter estimates. The first set was obtained by combining the log-linear model approximation with the Kalman filter; the second by combining a nonlinear model approximation with the particle filter; and the third by combining the exact policy function with the particle filter. The nonlinear model approximation was constructed using the orthogonal collocation scheme described in chapter 10, section 10.2 (for the case in which $\ln(a)$ follows (10.8)).

[1]GAUSS procedures used to accomplish likelihood evaluation are provided in `nonling.src`; corresponding Fortran procedures are provided in `nonlinf.src`. We are deeply indebted to Hariharan Dharmarajan for executing the transition to Fortran in this application.

Notice that the three sets of estimates obtained for $(\alpha, \beta, \rho, \sigma_\varepsilon)$ are quite similar, and correspond closely to their associated "true" values. However, the same is not true of the estimates obtained for $(\sigma_{u,y}, \sigma_{u,i})$ (denoting standard deviations of the measurement errors associated with the observation of y and i). Although the estimates obtained for $\sigma_{u,y}$ using the exact and nonlinear model approximations differ from their corresponding true value by approximately 10% (and by approximately 4% for $\sigma_{u,i}$), estimates obtained using the log-linear approximation differ roughly by factors of 2 for $\sigma_{u,y}$ and 5 for $\sigma_{u,y}$. In turn, whereas the difference in log-likelihood values observed in moving from the exact policy function to the nonlinear approximation is a mere 0.04, the difference in moving to the log-linear approximation is 135. The pattern of these results closely matches the findings of Fernandez-Villaverde and Rubio-Ramirez (2005) and Fernandez-Villaverde, Rubio-Ramirez, and Santos (2006).

Seeking to account for this Monte Carlo evidence, Fernandez-Villaverde, Rubio-Ramirez, and Santos (2006) have discovered that the source of likelihood differences arising from alternative approaches to model approximation can be traced to errors associated with policy function approximations. Specifically, they have shown that approximation errors in representing the policy function translate into errors in associated approximations of the likelihood function. Moreover, the mapping of errors from policy to likelihood functions is compounded by sample size: period by period, errors in approximating the policy function accumulate as the size of the sample expands. Thus second-order approximation errors in the policy function translate into first-order approximation errors in the likelihood function, and so on.

In working with nonlinear approximations of the policy function, this problem can be combated by working with approximations of the policy function that increase in quality with the sample size (e.g., by increasing the order of Chebyshev polynomials used in implementing orthogonal collocation approximations, or refining the grid over which the state space is divided in working with value-function and policy-function approximations). However, no such remedy is available in working with log-linear approximations: in this case, the quality of approximation is determined strictly by the proximity of the actual model representation to linearity.

It is too early to fully discern the implications this "compounding" problem carries for the future use of log-linear approximations as foundations for conducting likelihood-based empirical analyses. For example, suppose that in a given application the problem merely affected measurements of the absolute height of the likelihood function, but left measurements of its relative height at alternative candidate parameterizations intact. Then calculations of posterior means and ML point estimates would not be prone to the compounding problem, whereas cross-model likelihood comparisons (e.g., posterior odds calculations or likelihood ratio tests) would. The mixed pattern of discrepancies between actual and estimated parameters that have been reported to date have left this question largely unresolved, and further research on this issue is clearly warranted.

But even if the compounding problem proves to be problematic in general, there remains an important role for log-linear approximations in conducting likelihood analyses. This is the case along at least two dimensions. First, recall from chapter 10, section 10.2, the important role played by the log-linear approximation of the optimal growth model in providing starting values for implementing the orthogonal collocation approximation of the policy function. In empirical applications that involve repeated approximations of the policy function for each candidate parameterization of the model, the ability to obtain fast, accurate, and reliable approximations is critical. By providing an automated means of constructing effective starting values for this purpose, log-linear approximations serve as an instrumental input in the estimation process. Second, recall from section 11.2 that log-linear approximations can also be used to construct an approximation of the unconditional distribution $p(s_0)$ that is used to initiate the particle filter. This too is critical, because an inappropriate specification of this distribution can introduce an additional source of error in working with likelihood approximations obtained using the particle filter.

In sum, recent research suggests that the relatively large approximation errors associated with log-linear model representations may limit the usefulness of these representations as foundations upon which full information empirical analyses involving DSGE models are conducted. However, more research on this subject is needed before general conclusions can be drawn. But as we have illustrated, log-linear approximations can serve to provide important inputs into the process of implementing nonlinear model representations empirically. Thus even as the state-of-the art advances towards a more widespread use of nonlinear model approximations, we envision a lasting complementary role for log-linear approximations in conducting structurally based empirical research.

Bibliography

Adda, J., and R. Cooper, 2003. *Dynamic Economics.* Cambridge, MA: MIT Press.

Akaike, H., 1974. "A New Look at the Statistical Model Identification," *IEEE Transactions on Automatic Control*, AC 19, 716–23.

Altug, S., 1989. "Time-to-Build and Aggregate Fluctuations: Some New Evidence," *International Economic Review*, 30, 889–920.

Amemiya, T., 1985. *Advanced Econometrics*, Cambridge, MA: Harvard University Press.

Andrews, D.W.K., 1993. "Tests for Parameter Instability and Structural Change with Unknown Change Point," *Econometrica*, 61, 821–56.

Andrews, D.W.K., and R. C. Fair, 1988. "Inference in Nonlinear Econometric Models with Structural Change," *Review of Economic Studies* 55, 615–40.

Aruoba, S. B., J. Fernandez-Villaverde, and J. Rubio-Ramirez, 2003. "Comparing Solution Methods for Dynamic Equilibrium Economies," *Federal Reserve Bank of Atlanta Working Paper*, 27.

Azariadis, C., 1993. *Intertemporal Macroeconomics*, Oxford: Blackwell Publishing.

Bank of Sweden, 1989. Press Release: "The Sveriges Riksbank (Bank of Sweden) Prize in Economic Sciences in Memory of Alfred Nobel for 1989," http://nobelprize.org/economics/laureates/1989/press.html.

———, 2004. Press Release: "The Sveriges Riksbank (Bank of Sweden) Prize in Economic Sciences in Memory of Alfred Nobel for 2004," http://nobelprize.org/economics/laureates/2004/press.html.

Barro, R. J., 1989. *Modern Business Cycle Theory*, Cambridge, MA: Harvard University Press.

Barro, R. J., and X. Sala-i-Martin, 2004. *Economic Growth*, 2nd Ed., Cambridge, MA: MIT Press.

Bauwens, L., and M. Lubrano, 1998. "Bayesian Inference on GARCH Models using the Gibbs Sampler," *The Econometrics Journal*, 1, C23–C46.

Bauwens, L., M. Lubrano, and J.-F. Richard, 1999. *Bayesian Inference in Dynamic Econometric Models*, Oxford: Oxford University Press.

Baxter, M., and R. G. King, 1999. "Measuring Business Cycles: Approximate Band-Pass Filters for Economic Time Series," *Review of Economics and Statistics*, 81, 575–93.

Bell, W. R., and B. C. Monsell, 1992. "X-11 Symmetric Linear Filters and their Transfer Functions," *Bureau of the Census Statistical Research Division Report Series*, RR–92/15.

Benassy, J., 2002. *The Macroeconomics of Imperfect Competition and Nonclearing Markets*, Cambridge, MA: MIT Press.

Benhabib, J., R. Rogerson, and R. Wright, 1991. "Homework in Macroeconomics: Household Production and Aggregate Fluctuations," *Journal of Political Economy*, 99, 1,166–87.

Berger, J. O., and R. L. Wolpert, 1988. *The Likelihood Principle*, 2nd Ed., Hayward, CA: Institute of Mathematical Statistics.

Blanchard, O. J., and S. Fischer, 1998. *Lectures on Macroeconomics*, Cambridge, MA: MIT Press.

Blanchard, O. J., and C. M. Kahn, 1980. "The Solution of Linear Difference Models Under Rational Expectations," *Econometrica*, 48, 1,305–11.

Boldrin, M., L. J. Christiano, and J. Fisher, 2001. "Asset Pricing Lessons for Modeling Business Cycles," *American Economic Review*, 91, 149–66.

Brown, J. W., and R. V. Churchill, 2003. *Complex Variables and Applications*, 7th Ed., Boston: McGraw-Hill.

Burnside, C., and M. Eichenbaum, 1997. "Factor-Hoarding and the Propagation of Business-Cycle Shocks," *American Economic Review*, 86, 1,154–74.

Burnside, C., M. Eichenbaum, and S. Rebelo, 1993. "Labor Hoarding and the Business Cycle," *Journal of Political Economy*, 101, 245–73.

Campbell, J. Y., A. W. Lo, and A. C. MacKinlay, 1997. *The Econometrics of Financial Markets*, Princeton: Princeton University Press.

Canova, F., 1995. "Sensitivity Analysis and Model Evaluation in Simulated Dynamic General Equilibrium Models," *International Economic Review*, 36, 477–501.

———, 2006. *Methods for Applied Macroeconomic Research*, forthcoming, Princeton: Princeton University Press.

Chan, K., J. C. Hayya, and K. Ord, 1977. "A Note on Trend Removal Methods: The Case of Polynomial Versus Variate Differencing," *Econometrica*, 45, 737–44.

Chari, V. V., P. J. Kehoe, and E. R. McGrattan, 2004. "Business Cycle Accounting," Working Paper 10351, *National Bureau of Economic Research*, Cambridge, MA.

———, 2005. "A Critique of Structural VARs Using Business Cycle Theory," Research Department Staff Report 364, Federal Reserve Bank of Minneapolis.

Chib, S., and E. Greenberg, 1995. "Understanding the Metropolis-Hastings Algorithm," *The American Statistician*, 49, 327–35.

Christiano, L. J., 2002. "Solving Dynamic Equilibrium Models by a Method of Undetermined Coefficients," *Computational Economics*, 20, 21–55.

Christiano, L. and M. Eichenbaum, 1992. "Current Real-Business-Cycle Theories and Aggregate Labor Market Fluctuations," *American Economic Review*, 82, 430–50.

Christiano, L., M. Eichenbaum, and C. L. Evans, 2005. "Nominal Rigidities and the Dynamic Effects of a Shock to Monetary Policy," *Journal of Political Economy*, 113, 1–45.

Christiano, L. J., M. Eichenbaum, and R. Vigfusson, 2003. "What Happens After a Technology Shock?" *International Finance Discussion Paper Number 768*, Board of Governors of the Federal Reserve System.

Christiano, L. J., and T. J. Fitzgerald, 1999. "The Band Pass Filter," *Federal Reserve Bank of Cleveland Working Paper*.

Christiano, L. J., and R. M. Todd, 1996. "Time to Plan and Aggregate Fluctuations," *Federal Reserve Bank of Minneapolis Quarterly Review*, Winter, 14–27.

Clarida, R., J. Gali, and M. Gertler, 2000. "Monetary Policy Rules and Macroeconomic Stability: Evidence and Some Theory," *Quarterly Journal of Economics*, 115, 147–80.

Cochrane, J. H., 2001. *Asset Pricing*, Princeton: Princeton University Press.

Cogley, T. and J. M. Nason, 1995. "Effects of the Hodrick-Prescott Filter on Trend and Difference Stationary Time Series: Implications for Business Cycle Research," *Journal of Economic Dynamics and Control*, 19, 253–78.

Cooley, T. F., 1995. *Frontiers of Business Cycle Research*, Princeton: Princeton University Press.

Cooley, T. F., and E. C. Prescott, 1995. "Economic Growth and Business Cycles," in *Frontiers of Business Cycle Research*, T. F. Cooley, Ed. 1–38. Princeton: Princeton University Press.

DeJong, D. N., 1992. "Co-Integration and Trend-Stationarity in Macroeconomic Time Series," *Journal of Econometrics*, 52, 347–70.

DeJong, D. N., and B. F. Ingram, 2001. "The Cyclical Behavior of Skill Acquisition," *Review of Economic Dynamics*, 4, 536–61.

DeJong, D. N., B. F. Ingram, and C. H. Whiteman, 1993. "Evaluating VARs with Monetary Business Cycle Priors," *Proceedings of the American Statistical Association, Bayesian Statistical Science Section*, 1993. 160–69.

———, 1996. "A Bayesian Approach to Calibration," *Journal of Business and Economic Statistics*, 14, 1–9.

———, 2000a. "Keynesian Impulses Versus Solow Residuals: Identifying Sources of Business Cycle Fluctuations," *Journal of Applied Econometrics*, 15, 311–29.

———, 2000b. "A Bayesian Approach to Dynamic Macroeconomics," *Journal of Econometrics*, 98, 203–23.

DeJong, D. N., R. Liesenfeld, and J.-F. Richard, 2005a. "Timing Structural Change: A Conditional Likelihood Approach," *Journal of Applied Econometrics*, forthcoming.

———, 2005b. "A Nonlinear Forecasting Model of GDP Growth," *Review of Economics and Statistics*, 87, 697–708.

DeJong, D. N., and M. Ripoll, 2004. "Self-control Preferences and the Volatility of Stock Prices," working paper, University of Pittsburgh.

———, 2006. "Do Self-control Preferences Help Explain the Puzzling Behavior of Asset Prices?" *Journal of Monetary Economics*, forthcoming.

DeJong, D. N., and C. H. Whiteman, 1991a. "The Temporal Stability of Dividends and Prices: Evidence from the Likelihood Function," *American Economic Review*, 81, 600–617.

———, 1991b. "Trends and Random Walks in Macroeconomic Time Series: A Reconsideration Based on the Likelihood Principle," *Journal of Monetary Economics*, 28, 221–54.

———, 1993. "Unit Roots in U.S. Macroeconomic Time Series: A Survey of Classical and Bayesian Methods," in D. Brillinger et al., Eds. *New Directions in Time Series Analysis, Part II*, Berlin: Springer-Verlag.

———, 1994a. "The Forecasting Attributes of Trend- and Difference-Stationary Representations for Macroeconomic Time Series," *Journal of Forecasting*, 13, 279–97.

———, 1994b. "Modeling Stock Prices Without Pretending to Know How to Induce Stationarity," *Econometric Theory*, 10, 701–19.

Del Negro, M., and F. Schorfheide, 2004. "Priors from General Equilibrium Models for VARs," *International Economic Review*, 45, 643–73.

Diebold, F. X., L. E. Ohanian, and J. Berkowitz, 1998. "Dynamic Equilibrium Economies: A Framework for Comparing Model and Data," *Review of Economic Studies*, 65, 433–51.

Doan, T., R. Litterman, and C. Sims, 1984. "Forecasting and Conditional Projection Using Realistic Prior Distributions," *Econometric Reviews*, 3, 1–100.

Doucet, A., N. de Freitas, and N. Gordon, 2001. *Sequential Monte Carlo Methods in Practice*, Berlin: Springer-Verlag.

Duffie, D., and K. Singleton, 1993. "Simulated Moment Estimation of Markov Models of Asset Prices," *Econometrica*, 61, 929–52.

Eichenbaum, M. S., 1983. "A Rational Expectations Equilibrium Model of Inventories of Finished Goods and Employment," *Journal of Monetary Economics*, 12, 71–96.

Einarsson, T., and M. H. Marquis, 1997. "Home Production with Endogenous Growth," *Journal of Monetary Economics*, 39, 551–69.

Fernandez-Villaverde, J., and J. Rubio-Ramirez, 2004a. "Comparing Dynamic Equilibrium Models to Data: A Bayesian Approach," *Journal of Econometrics*, 123, 153–87.

———, 2004b. "Estimating Macroeconomic Models: A Likelihood Approach," working paper, University of Pennsylvania.

———, 2005. "Estimating Dynamic Equilibrium Economies: Linear versus Nonlinear Likelihood," *Journal of Applied Econometrics*, forthcoming.

Fernandez-Villaverde, J., J. Rubio-Ramirez, and M. S. Santos, 2006. "Convergence Properties of the Likelihood of Computed Dynamic Models," *Econometrica*, 74, 93–119.

Fernandez-Villaverde, J., J. Rubio-Ramirez, and T. J. Sargent, 2005. "A, B, C's (and D)'s for Understanding VARs," working paper, Federal Reserve Bank of Atlanta.

Ferson, W. E., and G. M. Constantinides, 1991. "Habit Formation and Durability in Aggregate Consumption: Empirical Tests," *Journal of Financial Economics*, 29, 199–240.

Francis, N., and V. A. Ramey, 2003. "Is the Technology-Driven Real Business Cycle Hypothesis Dead? Shocks and Aggregate Fluctuations Revisited," working paper, University of California at San Diego.

Frisch, R., 1933a. "Editorial," *Econometrica*, 1, 1–5.

———, 1933b. "Propagation Problems and Impulse Problems in Dynamic Economics," in *Economic Essays in Honor of Gustav Cassel*, London.

———, 1970. "Econometrics in the World Today," in *Induction, Growth and Trade: Essays in Honor of Sir Roy Harrod*, W. A. Eltis, M.F.G. Scott, and J. N. Wolf, Eds., 152–66. Oxford: Clarendon Press.

Gali, J., 1999. "Technology, Employment, and the Business Cycle: Do Technology Shocks Explain Aggregate Fluctuations?," *American Economic Review*, 89, 249–71.

Geweke, J., 1988. "Antithetic Acceleration of Monte Carlo Integration in Bayesian Inference," *Journal of Econometrics*, 38, 73–89.

———, 1989. "Bayesian Inference in Econometric Models using Monte Carlo Integration," *Econometrica*, 57, 1,317–39.

———, 1992. "Evaluating the Accuracy of Sampling-Based Approaches to the Calculation of Posterior Moments," in Bernardo, et al., Eds., *Bayesian Statistics*, 4, Oxford: Clarendon Press.

———, 1999a. "Using Simulation Methods for Bayesian Econometric Models: Inference, Development, and Communication," *Econometric Reviews*, 18, 1–126.

———, 1999b. "Computational Experiments and Reality," working paper, University of Iowa.

———, 2005. *Contemporary Bayesian Econometrics and Statistics*, Hoboken, NJ: Wiley.

Ghez, G. R., and G. S. Becker, 1975. *The Allocation of Time and Goods over the Life Cycle*, New York: Columbia University Press.

Gourieroux, C., and A. Monfort, 1996. *Simulation-Based Econometric Methods*, Oxford: Oxford University Press.

Gourieroux, C., A. Monfort, and E. Renault, 1993. "Indirect Inference," *Journal of Applied Econometrics*, 8, S85–S118.

Greene, W. H., 2003. *Econometric Analysis*, 5th Ed., Upper Saddle River, NJ: Prentice Hall.

Greenwood, J., and Z. Hercowitz, 1991. "The Allocation of Capital and Time over the Business Cycle," *Journal of Political Economy*, 99, 1,188–1,214.

Gul, F., and W. Pesendorfer, 2004. "Self-control, Revealed Preference, and Consumption Choice," *Review of Economic Dynamics*, 7, 243–64.

Haavelmo, T., 1944. "The Probability Approach in Econometrics," *Econometrica*, 12 (supplement), iii–vi and 1–115.

Hamilton, J. D., 1994. *Time Series Analysis*, Princeton: Princeton University Press.

Hannan, E. J., 1970. *Multiple Time Series*, New York: Wiley.

Hansen, B. E., 1997. "Approximate Asymptotic p-values for Structural Change Tests," *Journal of Business and Economic Statistics*, 15, 60–67.

Hansen, G. D., 1985. "Indivisible Labor and the Business Cycle," *Journal of Monetary Economics*, 16, 309–27.

Hansen, L. P., 1982. "Large Sample Properties of Generalized Method of Moments Estimators," *Econometrica*, 50, 1029–54.

Hansen, L. P., and J. J. Heckman, 1996. "The Empirical Foundations of Calibration," *Journal of Economic Perspectives*, 10, 87–104.

Hansen, L. P., and T. J. Sargent, 1980. "Formulating and Estimating Dynamic Linear Rational Expectations Models," *Journal of Economic Dynamics and Control*, 2, 7–46.

———, 1981. "Exact Linear Rational Expectations Models: Specification and Estimation," *Federal Reserve Bank of Minneapolis Staff Report*, 71.

———, 2005. *Recursive Models of Dynamic Linear Economies*, manuscript, New York University.

Hansen, L. P., and K. J. Singleton, 1982. "Generalized Instumental Variables Estimation of Nonlinear Rational Expectations Models," *Econometrica*, 50, 1,269–86.

———, 1983. "Stochastic Consumption, Risk Aversion, and the Temporal Behavior of Asset Prices," *Journal of Political Economy*, 91, 249–65.

Hansen, B., and K. West, 2002. "Generalized Method of Moments and Macroeconomics," *Journal of Business & Economic Statistics*, 20, 460–69.

Harvey, A. C., 1993. *Time Series Models*, Cambridge, MA: MIT Press.

———, 1999. *The Econometric Analysis of Time Series*, Cambridge, MA: MIT Press.

Harvey, A. C., and A. Jaeger, 1993. "Detrending, Stylized Facts and the Business Cycle," *Journal of Econometrics*, 8, 231–47.

Hastings, W. K., 1970. "Monte Carlo Sampling Methods Using Markov Chains and Their Application," *Biometrika*, 57, 97–109.

Heaton, J., 1985. "An Empirical Investigation of Asset Pricing with Temporally Dependent Preference Specifications," *Econometrica*, 63, 681–717.

Heer, B., and A. Maussner, 2005. *Dynamic General Equilibrium Modelling, Computational Methods and Applications*, Berlin, Springer.

Heyde, C. C., and I. M. Johnstone, 1979. "On Asymptotic Posterior Normality for Stochastic Processes," *Journal of the Royal Statistical Society*, Series B 41, 184–89.

Houthakker, H., 1956. "The Pareto Distribution and the Cobb-Douglas Production Function," *Review of Economic Studies*, 23, 27–31.

Ingram, B. F., N. R. Kocherlakota, and N. E. Savin, 1994. "Explaining Business Cycles: A Multiple-Shock Approach," *Journal of Monetary Economics*, 34, 415–28.

Ingram, B. F., and C. H. Whiteman, 1994. "Supplanting the 'Minnesota' Prior: Forecasting Macroeconomic Time Series Using Real Business Cycle Model Priors," *Journal of Monetary Economics*, 34, 497–510.

Ireland, P., 2004a. "Technology Shocks in the New Keynesian Model," *Review of Economics and Statistics*, 86, 923–36.

———, 2004b. "A Method for Taking Models to Data," *Journal of Economic Dynamics and Control*, 28, 1,205–26.

Jeffreys, H., 1961. *Theory of Probability*, 3rd Ed., Oxford: Clarendon Press.

Judd, K., 1992. "Projection Methods for Solving Aggregate Growth Models," *Journal of Economic Theory*, 58, 410–52.

Judd, K. L., 1998. *Numerical Methods in Economics*, Cambridge, MA: MIT Press.

Judge, G. G., W. E. Griffiths, R. Carter Hill, H. Lutkepohl, and T.-C. Lee, 1985. *The Theory and Practice of Econometrics*, New York: Wiley.

Kaiser, R., and A. Maravall, 2001. *Measuring Business Cycles in Economic Time Series*, Berlin: Springer-Verlag.

King, R. G., C. I. Plosser, and S. T. Rebelo, 1988. "Production, Growth and Business Cycles. I. The Basic Neoclassical Model," *Journal of Monetary Economics*, 21, 195–232.

King, R. G., and M. W. Watson, 2002. "System Reduction and Solution Algorithms for Solving Linear Difference Systems under Rational Expectations," *Computational Economics*, 20, 57–86.

Klein, P., 2000. "Using the Generalized Schur Form to Solve a Multivariate Linear Rational Expectations Model," *Journal of Economic Dynamics and Control*, 24, 1,405–23.

Kloek, T., and H. K. van Dijk, 1978. "Bayesian Estimates of Equation System Parameters: An Application of Integration by Monte Carlo," *Econometrica*, 46, 1–19.

Kocherlakota, N. R., 1990. "On Tests of Representative Consumer Asset Pricing Models," *Journal of Monetary Economics*, 26, 285–304.

———, 1996. "The Equity Premium: It's Still a Puzzle," *Journal of Economic Literature*, 34, 42–71.

Koop, G., 2003. *Bayesian Econometrics*, New York: Wiley.

Koopmans, T. C., 1949. "The Econometric Approach to Business Fluctuations," *American Economic Review*, 39, 64–72.

Krusell, P., and A. A. Smith Jr., 1999. "On the Welfare Effects of Eliminating Business Cycles," *Review of Economic Dynamics*, 2, 245–72.

Kydland, F. E. and E. C. Prescott, 1982. "Time to Build and Aggregate Fluctuations," *Econometrica*, 50, 1,345–70.

———, 1991a. "The Econometrics of the General Equilibrium Approach to Business Cycles," *Scandinavian Journal of Economics*, 93, 161–78.

———, 1991b. "Hours and Employment Variation in Business Cycle Theory," *Economic Theory*, 1, 63–81.

———, 1996. "The Computational Experiment: An Econometric Tool," *Journal of Economic Perspectives*, 10, 69–85.

Lagarias, J. C., J. A. Reeds, M. H. Wright, and P. E. Wright, 1998. "Convergence Properties of the Nelder-Mead Simplex Method in Low Dimensions," *SIAM Journal of Optimization*, 9, 112–47.

Lancaster, T., 2004. *An Introduction to Modern Bayesian Econometrics*, Oxford: Blackwell.

Lay, D., 2002. *Linear Algebra and Its Applications*, Reading, MA: Addison Wesley.

Leamer, E. E., 1978. *Specification Searches*, New York: Wiley.

Lee, B. S., and B. F. Ingram, 1991. "Simulation Estimation of Time-Series Models," *Journal of Econometrics*, 47, 197–205.

LeRoy, S. F., and R. D. Porter, 1981. "Stock Price Volatility: Tests Based on Implied Variance Bounds," *Econometrica*, 49, 97–113.

Ljungqvist, L., and T. Sargent, 2004. *Recursive Macroeconomic Theory*, Cambridge, MA: MIT Press.

Lucas, R. E., 1976. "Econometric Policy Evaluation: A Critique," *The Phillips Curve and Labor Markets* K. Brunner and A. Meltzer, Eds. Carnegie-Rochester Conference Series on Public Policy, Vol. 1. Amsterdam: North-Holland.

———, 1978. "Asset Prices in an Exchange Economy," *Econometrica*, 46, 1,429–45.

———, 1980. "Methods and Problems in Business Cycle Theory," *Journal of Money, Credit and Banking*, 12, 696–715.

———, 1987. *Models of Business Cycles*, Oxford: Blackwell.

———, 2003. "Macroeconomic Priorities," *American Economic Review*, 93, 1–14.

Lucas, R. E., and T. J. Sargent, 1979. "After Keynesian Macroeconomics," *Federal Reserve Bank of Minneapolis Quarterly Review*, vol. 3, no. 2.

Lundberg, E., 1969. Nobel Prize in Economics Presentation Speech, http://nobelprize.org/economics/laureates/1969/press.html

Mankiw, N. G., and D. Romer, 1991. *New Keynesian Economics*, Cambridge, MA: MIT Press.

McFadden, D., 1989. "A Method of Simulated Moments for Estimation of Discrete Response Models Without Numerical Integration," *Econometrica*, 57, 995–1026.

McGrattan, E. R., 1994. "The Macroeconomic Effects of Distortionary Taxation," *Journal of Monetary Economics*, 94, 573–601.

———, 1996. "Solving the Stochastic Growth Model with a Finite Element Method," *Journal of Economic Dynamics and Control*, 20, 19–42.

———, 1999. "Application of Weighted Residuals Methods to Dynamic Economic Models," in R. Marimon and A. Scott, Eds., *Computational Methods for the Study of Dynamic Economies*, Oxford: Oxford University Press.

McGratten, E. R., R. Rogerson, and R. Wright, 1997. "An Equilibrium Model of the Business Cycle with Household Production and Fiscal Policy," *International Economic Review*, 38, 267–90.

Mehra, R., and E. C. Prescott, 1985. "The Equity Premium: A Puzzle," *Journal of Monetary Economics*, 15, 145–61.

———, 2003. "The Equity Premium in Retrospect," in *Handbook of the Economics of Finance*, G. M. Constantinides, M. Harris and R. Stulz, Eds., 889–936, Amsterdam: Elsevier.

Metropolis, N., A. W. Rosenbluth, M. N. Rosenbluth, A. H. Teller, and E. Teller, 1953. "Equations of State Calculations by Fast Computing Machines," *The Journal of Chemical Physics*, 21, 1,087–92.

Murray, C. J., 2003. "Cyclical Properties of Baxter-King Filtered Time Series," *Review of Economics and Statistics*, 85, 472–76.

Nelder, J. A., and R. Mead, 1965. "A Simplex Method for Function Minimization," *Computer Journal*, 7, 308–13.

Nelson, C., and H. Kang, 1981. "Spurious Periodicity in Inappropriately Detrended Time Series," *Econometrica*, 49, 741–51.

Nelson, C., and C. I. Plosser, 1982. "Trends and Random Walks in Macroeconomic Time Series," *Journal of Monetary Economics*, 10, 139–62.

Nelson, C., and R. Startz, 1990a. "Some Further Results on the Exact Small Sample Properties of the Instrumental Variables Estimator," *Econometrica*, 58, 967–76.

———, 1990b. "The Distribution of the Instrumental Variables Estimator and Its t-ratio when the Instrument is a Poor One," *Journal of Business*, 63, 5,125–40.

Newey, W., and K. West, 1987a. "A Simple Positive Semi-Definite, Heteroscedasticity and Autororrelation Consistent Covariance Matrix," *Econometrica*, 55, 703–8.

———, 1987b. "Hypothesis Testing with Efficient Method of Moments Estimation," *International Economic Review*, 28, 777–87.

Nordhaus, W., 2004. "Retrospective on the 1970s Productivity Slowdown," *NBER Working Paper*, No. 10950, Cambridge, MA: NBER.

Otrok, C., 2001. "On Measuring the Welfare Cost of Business Cycles," *Journal of Monetary Economics*, 47, 61–92.

Pakes, A., and D. Pollard, 1989. "Simulation and the Asymptotics of Optimization Estimators," *Econometrica*, 57, 1,027–57.

Palka, B., 1991. *An Introduction to Complex Function Theory*, Berlin: Springer.

Pearson, K., 1894. "Contribution to the Mathematical Theory of Evolution," *Philosophical Transactions of the Royal Society of London*, Series A 185, 71–110.

Perli, R., and P. Sakellaris, 1998. "Human Capital Formation and Business Cycle Persistence," *Journal of Monetary Economics*, 42, 67–92.

Perron, P., 1989. "The Great Crash, the Oil Shock, and the Unit Root Hypothesis," *Econometrica*, 57, 1,361–1,401.

Pesaran, M. H., and S. M. Potter, 1997. "A Floor and Ceiling Model of US Output," *Journal of Economic Dynamics and Control*, 21, 661–95.

Phillips, P.C.B., 1991. "To Criticize the Critics: An Objective Bayesian Analysis of Stochastic Trends," *Journal of Applied Econometrics*, 6, 333–64.

Pitt, M. K., and N. Shephard, 1999. "Filtering via Simulation: Auxiliary Particle Filters," *Journal of the American Statistical Association*, 94, 590–99.

Poirier, D. J., 1995. *Intermediate Statistics and Econometrics: A Comparative Approach*, Cambridge, MA: MIT Press.

Prescott, E. C., 1986. "Theory Ahead of Business Cycle Measurement," *Federal Reserve Bank of Minneapolis Quarterly Review*, 10, 9–22.

Prescott, E. C., 2006. "Nobel Lecture: The Transformation of Macroeconomic Policy and Research," *Journal of Political Economy*, 114, 203–35.

Ramsey, F. K., 1928. "A Mathematical Theory of Saving," *Economic Journal*, 38, 543–59.

Richard, J.-F., and W. Zhang, 1997. "Accelerated Monte Carlo Integration: An Application to Dynamic Latent Variable Models," in R. Mariano, M. Weeks, and T. Schuermann, Eds., *Simulation Based Inference in Econometrics: Methods and Applications*, Cambridge: Cambridge University Press.

———, 2004. "Efficient High-Dimensional Monte Carlo Importance Sampling," working paper, *University of Pittsburgh*.

Robert, C. P., and G. Casella, 1999. *Monte Carlo Statistical Methods*, New York: Springer-Verlag.

Rogerson, R., 1988. "Indivisible Labor, Lotteries and Equilibrium," *Journal of Monetary Economics*, 21, 3–16.

Roman, S., 2005. *Graduate Texts in Mathematics #135: Advanced Linear Algebra*, Berlin: Springer.

Romer, D., 2006. *Advanced Macroeconomics*, 3rd Ed., Boston: McGraw-Hill/Irwin.

Rowenhorst, G., 1991. "Time to Build and Aggregate Fluctuations: A Reconsideration," *Journal of Monetary Economics*, 27, 241–54.

Rubinstein, R. Y., 1981. *Simulation and the Monte Carlo Method*, New York: Wiley.

Ruge-Murcia, F. J., 2003. "Methods to Estimate Dynamic Stochastic General Equilibrium Models," manuscript, University of Montreal.

Santos, M. S., and A. Peralta-Alva, 2005. "Accuracy of Simulations for Stochastic Dynamic Models," *Econometrica*, 73, 1939–76.

Sargent, T. J., 1987a. *Macroeconomic Theory*, 2nd Ed., London: Academic Press.

———, 1987. *Dynamic Macroeconomic Theory*, Cambridge: Harvard University Press.

———, 1989. "Two Models of Measurements and the Investment Accelerator," *Journal of Political Economy*, 97, 251–87.

Scarf, H., and T. Hansen, 1973. *The Computation of Economic Equilibria*, New Haven: Yale University Press.

Schmitt-Grohe S., and M. Uribe, 2002. "Solving Dynamic General Equilibrium Models Using a Second-Order Approximation of the Policy Function," *NBER Technical Working Paper* No. 0282, Cambridge: NBER.

Schorfheide, F., 2000. "Loss Function-Based Evaluation of DSGE Models," *Journal of Applied Econometrics*, 15, 645–70.

Schotman, P. C., and H. K. van Dijk, 1991. "On Bayesian Routes to Unit Roots," *Journal of Applied Econometrics*, 6, 387–401.

Schwarz, G., 1978. "Estimating the Dimension of a Model," *The Annals of Statistics*, 6, 461–64.

Sedaghat, H., 2003. *Nonlinear Difference Equations: Theory with Applications to Social Science Models*, Berlin: Springer.

Shiller, R. J., 1981. "Do Stock Prices Move too Much to be Justified by Subsequent Changes in Dividends?," *American Economic Review*, 71, 421–36.

———, 1989. *Market Volatility*, Cambridge, MA: MIT Press.

Shiryaev, A. N., 1995. *Probability*, Berlin: Springer Graduate Texts in Mathematics.

Shoven, J. B., and J. Whalley, 1972. "A General Equilibrium Calculation of the Effects of Differential Taxation of Income from Capital in the U.S.," *Journal of Public Economics*, 1, 281–322.

Silverman, B. W., 1986. *Density Estimation*, London: Chapman and Hall.

Sims, C. A., 1972. "Money, Income, and Causality," *American Economic Review*, 62, 540–52.

———, 1980. "Macroeconomics and Reality," *Econometrica*, 48, 1–48.

———, 1996. "Macroeconomics and Methodology," *Journal of Economic Perspectives*, 10, 105–20.

———, 2001. "Solving Linear Rational Expectations Models," *Computational Economics*, 20, 1–20.

Sims, C. A., and T. Zha, 1998. "Bayesian Methods for Dynamic Multivariate Models," *International Economic Review*, 39, 949–68.

———, 2005. "Vintage Article: Does Monetary Policy Generate Recessions?" *Macroeconomic Dynamics*, forthcoming.

Smith, A., 1993. "Estimating Nonlinear Time-Series Models using Simulated Vector Autoregressions," *Journal of Applied Econometrics*, 8, S63–84.

Solow, R. M., 1965. "A Contribution to the Theory of Economic Growth," *Quarterly Journal of Economics*, 70, 65–94.

Stock, J. H., 2004. "Unit Roots, Structural Breaks, and Trends," in R. F. Engle and D. L. McFadden, Eds. *Handbook of Econometrics, Vol. 4*, Amsterdam: North Holland.

Stock, J. H., J. H. Wright, and M. Yogo, 2002. "A Survey of Weak Instruments and Weak Identification in Generalized Method of Moments," *Journal of Business and Economic Statistics*, 20, 518–29.

Stokey, N. L., and R. E. Lucas, 1989. *Recursive Methods in Economic Dynamics*, Cambridge, MA: Harvard University Press.

Summers L., 1986. "Some Skeptical Observations on Real Business Cycle Theory," *Federal Reserve Bank of Minneapolis Quarterly Review*, 10, 23–28.

Sustek, R., 2005. "Essays on Aggregate Fluctuations," Doctoral Dissertation, *Carnegie-Mellon University.*

Tauchen, G., 1986. "Statistical Properties of Generalized Method-of-Moments Estimators of Structural Parameters Obtained from Financial Market Data," *Journal of Business and Economic Statistics*, 4, 397–416.

Theil, H., 1971. *Principles of Econometrics*, New York: Wiley.

Theil, H., and A. S. Goldberger, 1961. "On Pure and Mixed Statistical Estimation in Economics," *International Economic Review*, 2, 65–78.

Uhlig, H., 1999. "A Toolkit for Analyzing Non-linear Dynamic Stochastic Models Easily," in Ramon Marimon and Andrew Scott Eds., *Computational Methods for the Study of Dynamic Economies*, Oxford University Press, New York, 30–61.

Watson, M., 1993. "Measures of Fit for Calibrated Models," *Journal of Political Economy*, 101, 1,011–41.

———, 1994. "Vector Autoregressions and Cointegration," *Handbook of Econometrics, Vol. 4*, R. F. Engle and D. L. McFadden, Eds., Amsterdam: Elsevier.

Weil, P., 1989. "The Equity Premium Puzzle and the Risk-Free Rate Puzzle," *Journal of Monetary Economics*, 24, 401–21.

Wen, Y., 1998. "Can A Real Business Cycle Model Pass the Watson Test?" *Journal of Monetary Economics*, 42, 185–203.

———, 2002. "The Business Cycle Effects of Christmas," *Journal of Monetary Economics*, 49, 1,289–1,314.

Woitek, U., 1998. "A Note on the Baxter-King Filter," working paper, *University of Glasgow*.

Woodford, M., 2003. *Interest and Prices: Foundations of a Theory of Monetary Policy*, Princeton: Princeton University Press.

Wouters, R., and F. Smets, 2005. "Comparing Shocks and Frictions in US and Euro Area Business Cycles: a Bayesian DSGE Approach," *Journal of Applied Econometrics*, 20, 161–83.

Yu, B., and P. Mykland, 1994. "Looking at Markov Samplers through CUSUM Path Plots: A Simple Diagnostic Idea," Technical Report 413, Department of Statistics, University of California at Berkeley.

Zellner, A., 1971. *An Introduction to Bayesian Inference in Econometrics*, New York: Wiley.

Index